COM101: HUMAN COMMUNICATION

Department of Communication Studies
Ashland University

Third Edition

Kendall Hunt
publishing company

www.kendallhunt.com
Send all inquiries to:
4050 Westmark Drive
Dubuque, IA 52004-1840

TABLE OF CONTENTS

COM 101:
HUMAN COMMUNICATION
ASHLAND UNIVERSITY

Welcome to COM 101: Human Communication at Ashland University. Communicating is something that most people believe they do well. After all, we have been communicating all our lives with many different people and in many different situations. However, how much do we really think about communicating? How many people simply engage in the same old scripts with the same people over and over?

When we think of communication, we should be thinking of it as a tool to be developed and used in ways that can best serve us, our communities, and our world. It should be a mindful activity as opposed to one that is simply left to familiar ways of speaking to others devoid of planning or consideration. Consider your choice of college major. Perhaps it is biology, theater, sports management, business, nursing, or something else. How much of the career that you are planning for involves communication? The answer to this question, regardless of your major, is a considerable amount.

It is estimated that 75 percent of a person's day is spent speaking and listening. In fact, in a recent poll of 330 industry leaders, 96 percent of executives rated communication and interpersonal skills as the most valuable employee traits (Cline, 2005). These data are only a sample of a common belief that is shared universally.

Communication matters and it is hard work to be an effective and appropriate communicator. It is our goal to make you a better communicator at many levels, including public speaking, group and team communication, and interpersonal communication. Perhaps the value of communication skills is best summed up by *The New York Times* award-winning columnist Thomas Friedman and author of the best-selling book, *The World Is Flat* (2006) when speaking about the skills and competencies that will be required of college graduates in the 21st century:

> *You need to like people. You need to be good at managing or interacting with other people. Although having good people skills has always been an asset in the working world, it will be even more so in a flat world [advances in technology and communication putting diverse people in touch as never before]. That said, I am not sure how you teach that as part of a classroom curriculum, but someone had better figure it out. (p. 106)*

DIFFERENT TYPES OF COMMUNICATION

The following is but a short list provided by the National Communication Association (2011) of how communication is studied, as well as where it is studied. By no stretch is this list exhaustive; it is provided to give you a sampling of the many ways people use communication:

- *Applied Communication:* The study of processes used to analyze communication needs of organizations and social interaction, including the design of training to improve communication between supervisors and employees.
- *Communication and Aging:* The study of the impact of aging on all aspects of communication, intergenerational relationships and communication, age stereotypes and communication, health issues of aging and communication, and lifespan and communication.
- *Communication Education:* The study of communication in the classroom and other pedagogical contexts.
- *Communication Theory:* The study of principles that account for the impact of communication in human social interaction.
- *Environmental Communication:* The study of the production, reception, contexts, or processes of human communication regarding environmental issues.
- *Family Communication:* The study of communication unique to family systems.
- *Gender Communication:* The study of gender and sex differences and similarities in communication and the unique characteristics of male-female communication.
- *Health Communication:* The study of communication as it relates to health professionals and health education, including the study of provider-client interaction, as well as the diffusion of health information through public health campaigns.
- *Interpersonal Communication:* The study of communication behaviors in dyads (pairs) and their impact on personal relationships.
- *Mediation and Dispute Resolution:* The study of understanding, management, and conflict resolution within intrapersonal, interpersonal, and intergroup situations.
- *Organizational Communication:* The study of processes used to analyze communication needs of organizations and social interaction, including the design of training to improve communication between supervisors and employees.
- *Performance Studies:* The study of components, such as performer(s), text, audience, and context, within the communication discipline.
- *Political Communication:* The study of the role communication plays in political systems.
- *Public Relations:* The study of the management of communication between an organization and its audiences.
- *Rhetorical Criticism:* The study of principles that account for the impact of human communication between speaker and audience.
- *Risk and Crisis Communication:* The study of how government agencies and organizations assess and manage risk and crisis situations, and how they communicate the nature of a crisis to stakeholders and members of the public.

- *Small Group Communication:* The study of communication systems among three or more individuals who interact around a common purpose and who influence one another.
- *Spiritual Communication:* The study of spirituality expressed through myriad experiences, practices, and belief systems in all communicative contexts.
- *Sport Communication:* The role of sports in our society and the relationships among sports content, relationships (e.g., player-coach, player-fan), and various audiences.

This list is but a microcosm of the larger field of communication studies. We hope that you will approach this course with eyes and mouth wide open as the opportunities for you, regardless of your plans for your future, will be made greater as a result of developing your speaking and listening skills.

The Department of Communication Studies at Ashland University offers three undergraduate major concentrations consisting of Health and Risk Communication, Sport Communication, and Public Relations & Strategic Communication. We also offer a 100% online Master of Arts degree program in Health and Risk Communication. The number of students has grown dramatically in the last several years. We in the Department of Communication Studies hope that your experiences in COM 101 are positive and productive.

REFERENCES

Cline, S. (2005, April). Soft skills make the difference in the workplace. *The Colorado Springs Business Journal.*

Friedman, T. L. (2006). *The world is flat: A brief history of the twenty-first century.* New York: Farrar, Straus, and Giroux.

National Communication Association. (2011). *Pathways to communication careers in the 21st century* (8th ed.). Washington, DC: National Communication Association.

WHAT IS COMMUNICATION?

LEARNING OBJECTIVES

After reading this chapter, you should understand the following concepts:

- The goal of communication is to build theory used to guide communicators in the formulation of strategies to achieve communication goals.
- There are many definitions of communication, but they share common characteristics: Communication is a process, messages are sent and received, participants interact in social contexts, and meaning is created and shared through symbols and behavior.
- The action model was the necessary first step in the evolution of communication models, but it has a weakness in that it lacks interaction.
- The interaction model includes the important aspect of feedback.
- The transactional model recognizes that communication is a process, it is irreversible, it means shared responsibility, and it occurs in context and culture.

KEYWORDS

theory
empirical
Aristotle
Claude Shannon
Warren Weaver
source
message
code
encoded
transmitted
channel
receiver
decodes
destination
noise
action model
interaction model
Wilbur Schramm
David Berlo
feedback
transactional model
process
participant
carrier
environmental noise
psychological noise
physical context
social context
culture

INTRODUCTION

"Oh, that's just a theory. It doesn't mean anything!"

Have you heard this before? There is a common misconception that a **theory** is the same thing as a "guess." A theory is a "shot from the hip," or it's a "Monday morning quarterback's" explanation of why his team won or lost on Sunday. Sometimes you hear people express doubt about "relativity" or "evolution" because they are "only theories," and not fact. Not true! A theory is not idle speculation unsupported by evidence that is spontaneously created or made up.

Theories are not guesses! Littlejohn states, "Any attempt to explain or represent an experience is a theory; an idea of how something happens."[1] Kerlinger says that a theory is "a set of interrelated constructs (concepts), definitions, and propositions that present a systematic view of phenomena by specifying relations among variables, with the purpose of explaining and predicting the phenomena."[2]

WHAT IS THE NATURE OF COMMUNICATION THEORY?

Our definition is that a theory is *an attempt to describe, predict, and / or explain an experience or phenomenon*. The purpose of generating a theory is the attempt to *understand* something:

- Theory is a collection of statements or conceptual assumptions.
- It specifies the relationships among concepts or variables and provides a basis for predicting behavior of a phenomenon.
- It explains a phenomenon.

Here's an illustration from the distant past:

Og the cave dweller comes out of his cave in the morning and sees the sun shining in the east. When Og visits the village well later in the day, he and his friends are able to *describe* what happened: "When I came out of my cave, I saw the bright light in the sky!" They can all try to agree on the description, and they will all know what happened.

Og the cave dweller systematically observes the environment.
© 2008, JupiterImages Corporation.

Over the next several months, Og and his pals emerge from their caves every morning, and every morning they see the sun in the eastern sky. They also notice that the sun has moved to the western sky when they return to their caves in the evening. After several conversations at the village well, they discover or recognize that a *pattern* seems to exist in the behavior of the sun. In the morning, the bright light is over there. But in the evening, the bright light is on the other side. They set up an observational plan to see if their pattern holds up. In the mornings, when Og comes from his cave (which faces south), he looks to his left and he *expects* to see the sun. There it is! Eureka! The observations support the hypothesis (or informed assumption) that the sun will rise in the east! Og and his associates can now *predict* the behavior of the sun!

Og is attempting to build a theory. He is able to describe and predict, but he still comes up short because he does not understand *why* the sun behaves as it does. Og still has much uncertainty about the sun's behavior, and that makes him and all the rest of us humans uncomfortable. So we continue to study it. Now, please "fast forward" from this point several thousand years when, after gathering lots and lots of information, we were finally able to *explain* why the sun appears to rise in the east and set in the west.

Og and his buddies made some observations of phenomena and were able to describe it, then they noticed patterns in the phenomena and were able to predict its behavior. They might have even tried to explain the activity they observed, but they did not have enough knowledge to make a good explanation. The explanation came much later and is beyond the scope of this book. But you can go look it up!

What they *did* do was create a partial theory, and that theory was based on empirical observation. Not bad for cave dwellers! **Empirical** means that knowledge claims are based on observations of reality (i.e., the real world) and are not merely subjective speculation based on the observer's perspective. The conclusions are based on *observed* evidence, which helps the observer

Observation ⟶ Pattern Recognition ⟶ Theory ⟶ Hypotheses ⟶ Observation

remain more objective.[3] The cycle of study is repeated over and over: Observation is made, which leads to recognizing a pattern; attempts to predict and explain are made, which become basic theories; the theories help the observer create new hypotheses (predictions) about the behavior of the phenomenon; observation is made and the information analyzed in search of patterns; and those recognized patterns add to the basic theory.[4] As this cycle repeats itself, the body of theory becomes larger and more sophisticated, and the field of study matures.

The goal of any field of study, including communication, is to *build theory*. The body of communication theory is subsequently used to guide communicators in the formulation of strategies for achieving communication goals and to help communicators understand what skills are necessary for carrying out the strategies.

The purpose of this chapter is to help you understand the basic theory supporting human communication behavior. The skills and strategies necessary to accomplish your communication goals are derived from this theory. This chapter includes the following:

- A definition of communication
- An evolution of conceptions of communication
- A transactional model of communication
- A discussion of essential terms

HOW IS COMMUNICATION DEFINED?

Defining communication is not quite as easy as it sounds because almost all people, even scholars, think they know what it is. We all communicate every day, so we all have an opinion. The problem is that nearly nobody agrees! Clevenger says that the term *communication* is one of the most "overworked terms in the English language."[5]

To try to make sense of the literally hundreds of different definitions, we will examine some significant attempts to define communication, and then we will draw out the commonalities in the attempt to build our own point of view. Here are some influential examples:

- An individual transmits stimuli to modify the behavior of other individuals.[6]
- Social interaction occurs through symbols and message systems.[7]
- A source transmits a message to receiver(s) with conscious intent to affect the latter's behavior.[8]
- "Senders and receivers of messages interact in given social contexts."[9]
- "Shared meaning through symbolic processes" is created.[10]
- There is mutual creation of shared meaning through the simultaneous interpretation and response to verbal and nonverbal behaviors in a specific context."[11]
- "Communication occurs when one person sends and receives messages that are distorted by noise, occur within a context, have some effect, and provide some opportunity for feedback."[12]

☆ – communication

The perspective of this book is that *communication is a process in which participants create meaning by using symbols and behavior to send and receive messages within a social and cultural context*. This perspective will be expanded and explained in the remainder of this chapter.

HOW HAVE THE CONCEPTIONS OF COMMUNICATION EVOLVED?

Now that we have a working definition of communication, let's examine where it came from. This section looks at classic models of communication spanning about 2,500 years. The goal of this section is to illustrate the evolution of the communication perspective taken by this book; to show you how we arrived at the point of view that influences every strategy and skill that we teach. We believe that if you understand why we teach it, you will be more motivated to learn and to use this point of view to plan and execute your own communication strategies!

WHAT ARE THE MODELS OF COMMUNICATION?

You have seen and used a map many times. If you are looking for a particular street in your town, you pick up a map to find where the street is and to learn how to get there from where you are. A map is not your town, however, but a *representation* of your town. It's a picture or drawing that helps you understand the way your town is arranged. A *model* is the very same thing. But instead of representing a physical space, like a town, the model represents a process, or the way something happens.

The models discussed here represent three views of communication that have enjoyed popularity over the years. Those three views are action (or linear), interaction, and transaction. These models help illustrate and explain the current view of communication, the transactional perspective. Each will be discussed in the following pages.

As a map represents a place, a model represents a process.
© Stephen VanHorn, 2008, Shutterstock.

The Action Model

Although many perspectives of communication contributed to what we are calling the action model, Aristotle and the Shannon and Weaver models had the most impact.

We'll start with **Aristotle,** a philosopher, scientist, and teacher who lived in ancient Greece. Educated by Plato and the son of a physician, he was trained as a biologist.[13] He was skilled at observing and describing, and at categorizing his observations.[14] Aristotle found himself interested in nearly all things that occupied the attention of the citizens of Athens, including the study of speaking.

Ancient Athens was a democracy, and all citizens had the right and opportunity to influence public affairs and public policy. The more articulate citizens were able to affect events by persuading or influencing other citizens and law makers in public meetings. Because individual citizens had a voice, teachers of public speaking and persuasion were always in demand.

Aristotle's *Rhetoric* is a published collection of his teachings,[15] and it has been suggested that it is the "most important single work on persuasion ever written."[16] The focus of the *Rhetoric* is primarily on the speaker and the message. Some, but little, attention is paid to the audience. The philosophy is that a well-crafted message delivered by a credible speaker will have the desired effect with the audience. If Aristotle had a model of persuasion, the simple version would probably look something like this:

Aristotle used his observation skills to study communication in ancient Greece.
© 2008 JupiterImages Corporation.

> WELL-CRAFTED MESSAGE + CREDIBLE SOURCE = DESIRED EFFECT

Aristotle's contribution to communication would not have been this model. His contributions came in the form of instructions for how to use logic and emotions (*logos* and *pathos*) to craft a message, and how to establish and build credibility as a speaker or source of a message *(ethos)*.

For the second time in this chapter, please fast forward in time, but this time only about two thousand years. Stop when you get to the 1940s, and we'll take a look at **Claude Shannon** and **Warren Weaver.** Claude Shannon was a mathematician who worked at Bell Labs, and he was interested in ways to make more efficient use of telephone lines for the transmission of voices. He was not concerned about human communication, but he was very focused on electronic communication. Shannon teamed with Warren Weaver, a scientist and mathematician, to publish the *Mathematical Theory of Communication.* Shannon's focus was on the engineering aspects of the theory, while Weaver was more interested in the human and other implications. Communication scholars found this model to be very useful in helping them to explain *human* communication.[17]

The Shannon–Weaver model is consistent with Aristotle's point of view, and it extends it to include a transmitter, a channel, and a receiver. It also introduces the concept of *noise* to the explanation. The process is illustrated in Figure 2.1. The **source** (a person) initiates a **message** that is turned into a **code** (language), and the **encoded** message is sent **(transmitted)** through a **channel** (sound waves created by the voice, or some mediated signal). The **receiver decodes** the signal (turning it again into a message), which is sent to the **destination** (the other person). **Noise** is anything that can interfere with the signal. See Figure 2.1.

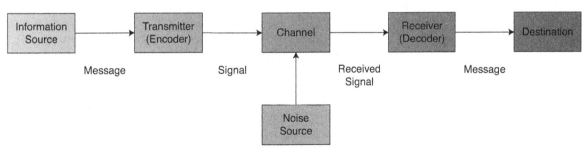

Figure 2.1
The Shannon–Weaver Mathematical Model

A message in a bottle lacks the interaction we have in everyday conversations.
© R. Gino Santa Maria, 2008, Shutterstock.

This model helps to understand human communication, but it has a significant shortcoming: it doesn't adequately capture the reality or the complexity of the process. It assumes that the participants in the process take on discrete speaker or listener roles, and that while one person speaks, the other person quietly listens with no response, until the speaker is finished. Then the roles are reversed. Then the roles are reversed again, and again and again, until the conversation is complete. *Human communication is arguably not that linear!* It is equivalent to placing a message in a bottle, throwing it into the sea, and waiting for it to reach the proper destination. The person (receiver) removes the message from the bottle, reads the message, writes a new message, places it back in the bottle, and throws it back into the sea. The model works, but it doesn't represent the way that we communicate in everyday conversations. It lacks *interaction!*

As you consider the two models just discussed, you can see that they are primarily concerned with the source of the message and the content of the message itself. The focus is on the source and how he or she constructs and delivers the message. So a source that creates well-designed messages has done everything possible to ensure effective communication. Say the right thing and you will be successful! If something goes wrong, or if the source is not clearly understood by the potential receiver, the **action model** states that the fault is with the source. However, when everything goes well and the message is clearly understood, it is because the source crafted and sent a good-quality message. See Figure 2.2 for a depiction of the action model. The action model was the necessary first step in the evolution of the contemporary communication model.

SOURCE ——————— Message ———————→ RECEIVER
                         Channel

Figure 2.2
Action Model

The Interaction Model

The **interaction model** remains linear, like the action model, but it begins to view the source and receiver as a team in the communication process.

Wilbur Schramm introduced a model of communication that includes a notion of *interaction*.[18] The Schramm model does not consider the context or environment in which the communication takes place, and it does not explicitly treat codes (language) or noise. Although it is still very linear, it describes the dual roles played by the participants instead of viewing one as a source (speaker) and the other as a receiver (listener), and it makes a strong case for *interaction* among the participants. The flow of information can be seen as more ongoing or continuous, rather than a linear, back-and-forth type of flow. The conception of communication is emerging as a *process*. See Figure 2.3.

David Berlo, in *The Process of Communication*, began to discuss process and the complexity of communication.[19] This model fully includes the receiver, and it places importance on the *relationship* between the source and receiver. It also illustrates that the source and receiver are not just reacting to the environment or each other, but that each possesses individual differences

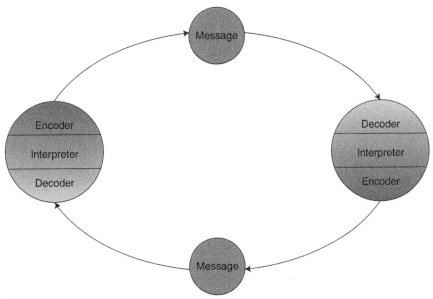

Figure 2.3
Schramm's Model of Communication

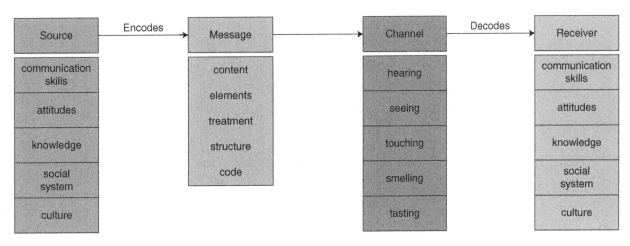

Figure 2.4
Berlo's Model of Communication

based on knowledge and attitudes, and that each operates within a cultural and social system that influences meaning. Because we all have different knowledge and attitudes, we interpret or give meaning to messages in different ways. This makes human communication very complex!

Although it was not explicitly mentioned in the model (see Figure 2.4), Berlo discussed the notion of **feedback** in his book. Feedback is information that is routed to the source, or fed back, from the receiver. Berlo said, "Feedback provides the source with information concerning his success in accomplishing his objective. In doing this, it exerts control over future messages which the source encodes."[20]

Figure 2.5
Interaction Model

Berlo completed the loop left unfinished by the Shannon–Weaver model. The source encodes a message, sent through a channel to a receiver, who decodes it and assigns meaning. The receiver then sends a message back to the source (feedback) indicating, among other things, that the message was understood. Even though this is still a linear model, we are getting closer to a model that begins to capture the nature of human communication. But it's not quite there yet!

These two models, and models like them, can be *summarized* in what we call the *interaction model* (see Figure 2.5). A source sends a message through a noise-filled channel to a receiver. The receiver responds to the source through feedback, which is a message sent by the receiver to the source through a noise-filled channel. The core of the interaction model is that the source is the originator and that the receiver creates feedback to that message. Like the action model, the interaction model implies that the process is linear; that is, communicators take turns being first a source then a receiver, and so on. The interaction model was the second step in the evolution of the contemporary communication model.

The Transactional Model

More contemporary conceptions view communication as an ongoing process in which all participants send and receive messages simultaneously. All participants are both speakers *and* listeners.[21] "A person is giving feedback, talking, responding, acting, and reacting through a communication event."[22] The **transactional model** incorporates this point of view along with the notion that the creation of the meaning of a message is not the sole responsibility of the source or the receiver, but a responsibility that is shared among all participants in a communication situation or event.

Properties of Transactional Communication. To get a clear view of the transactional model of communication, it is necessary to understand the important properties of communication. Properties include process, irreversibility, shared responsibility, context, and culture. These five properties are discussed in this section.

Communication Is a Process. Many conceptualizations of communication describe it as a **process**. The notion of process is not unique to communication; it comes to us from the literature of *theoretical physics*. A little closer to home, the notion of process and its relationship to human behavior can be found in *general systems theory*.[23] Although we use this term all the time, it's important to understand what the term *process* implies.

Process implies that communication is *continuous* and ongoing. It is *dynamic:* It never stops. Barnlund[24] says that a process has no beginning and no end. It constantly changes and evolves, new information and experience is added, and it becomes even more complex.[25] There is ongoing and constant mutual influence of the participants.[26] Participants are *constantly* sending and receiving verbal and nonverbal messages. You can try to take a "snapshot" of a single episode, and you can observe the date and time of its beginning and ending, but you can't say that this is where the communication began and ended. Heisenberg stated that to observe a process requires bringing it to a halt.[27] This gives us a fuzzy look at what is really happening, because stopping a process alters the process. So we have to do the best we can to observe, understand, and participate in communication events.

Consider, for example, a father asking his son to practice his saxophone. The father says, "Pete, please go to your room and practice your saxophone for 20 minutes." Pete (clearly annoyed) responds, "Come on, Dad! I'm right in the middle of this video game. Can't I do it later?" The father immediately gets angry and sends Pete to his room "to think about what he has done," followed by 20 minutes of saxophone practice.

The episode seems to be over, but we wonder why the young man was so annoyed at being asked to practice and why the father got angry so quickly. Could it be that this was only *one* installment in a series of episodes in which the father tries to get Pete to practice? Or could it be that Pete was having some difficulty with the saxophone that made him not want to practice? Or is there something else going on that we can't see in only this one episode? Will this episode affect future episodes?

The answer to the last question is yes! Communication is influenced by events that come before it, and it influences events that follow it.

Communication Is Irreversible. Messages are sent and received, and all participants give meaning to those messages as they happen. Once the behavior has occurred, it becomes part of history and can't be reversed. Have you ever said something that you wish you could take back? It doesn't matter if you meant it or not; once it's out there, you have to deal with it.

As mentioned in a previous section, the prior experience or history of the participants influences the meaning created in the current interaction. Even if you try to take something back or pretend it didn't happen, it still has influence in the current and future interactions. Occasionally, in a court case, an attorney or a witness will say something that the judge decides is inappropriate to the case, and he or she will instruct the jury to "disregard" the statement. Do you think the members of the jury are able to remove the statement from their memories? Have you ever heard that as a member of a jury? What did you do?

A friend of ours was asked the question that no married person wants to hear. While clothes shopping, the spouse asked, "Do these pants make me look fat?" Instead of pretending not to hear the question or saying an emphatic no, our friend said, "The pants are very nice, honey. It's your backside that makes you look fat!" For almost a whole minute, it seemed pretty funny. Multiple attempts to take back the comment failed. That communication episode affected the meaning of nearly every conversation they had for several months. *Communication is irreversible.* And you thought this book would have no practical advice!

> "You are the master of the *unspoken* word. Once the word is spoken, you are its slave."
>
> —Anonymous

Communication Means Shared Responsibility. Poor communication is not the fault of *one* participant in a conversation. If communication breaks down, you can't blame it on the "other guy." It is the fault of *all* the participants. The transactional perspective implies that it is the responsibility of all participants to cooperate to create a shared meaning. Even if a few of the participants are deficient in some communication skills, it is the responsibility of each person to adapt to the situation and ensure that everyone understands. Even the

less capable have responsibilities: If they do not understand, they have the responsibility to ask the other participants to help them understand. *All participants cooperate to create meaning.*

Communication Occurs in a Context. The participants in the communication event affect or influence each other, and they are also affected and influenced by the context or environment in which the communication event occurs.

Communication Occurs within Cultures. Much like context, the participants are affected or influenced by the culture of which they are members and by the culture in which the communication event takes place.

How does your culture affect communication?
© 2008 JupiterImages Corporation.

Specifics of the Transaction Model. The evolution of communication theory through the action and interaction models has brought us to the current perspective, the transaction model. This book is based on the transaction model, and all of the communication strategies we suggest are based on the model and its properties.

Wallace and others view the transactional perspective as *the joint creation of shared meaning through the simultaneous perception of verbal and nonverbal behaviors within a specific context.*[28] Although you are speaking or sending messages, you constantly receive and give meaning to information from the environment and from other participants. Similarly, while you are listening to another participant, you are sending nonverbal messages through eye contact, facial expressions, posture, and body movements. So we don't really take turns being the source and receiver as illustrated by the action and interaction models. Instead, we are constantly sending *and* receiving messages!

For example, a husband asks a wife if she minds if he plays golf on a Saturday afternoon. All the time he is asking the question, he is constantly scanning for every nonverbal clue to find out how she really feels. It might be her posture, or the way she looks at (or away from) him, or a particular facial expression, or some combination of everything that provides her response long before she speaks. Lots of information is being exchanged in this situation, which helps this couple create and share meaning.

Think about the first time you met your girlfriend's or boyfriend's parents. Think about your first date with somebody you were really interested in. Or consider meeting a potential client for a business deal. Doing business is important to both participants, so you both are very careful to gather all the available information to reduce uncertainty, become more comfortable, and formulate and confirm strategies for accomplishing communication goals. You use the information to create and share meaning!

How do you prepare for a meeting with a new business associate?
© Kiselev Andrey Valerevich, 2008, Shutterstock.

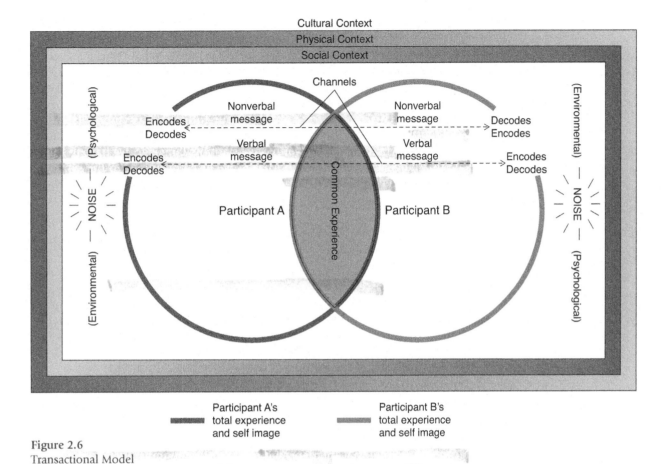

Figure 2.6
Transactional Model

In the transaction model, *participants create shared meaning* by simultaneously sending and receiving verbal and nonverbal messages within a specific context. Please see Figure 2.6 for a depiction of the model. The transaction model is reflected and applied in every chapter of this book.

WHAT DO THE TERMS MEAN?

We know that you're tired of all the theory talk, but we have to define some terms so that we are all on the same page. All of these terms have been used in this chapter, but some have been used in different ways in the various models. This section will establish the way each term will be used throughout the book.

Communicators/Participants

Although the action and interaction models use the terms *source* and *receiver* or *speaker* and *listener*, we will simply use the term **participant**. Because there is no exchange of speaker and listener roles, and because all persons in communication events are simultaneously sending and receiving verbal and nonverbal messages, the terms used in earlier models are no longer descriptive.

The message contains the content of the thought we wish to share with other participants.

Encoding/Decoding

Communication is symbolic. That is, we use symbols to convey our thoughts to each other in the effort to create meaning. When we have a thought or idea that we want to share with others, we must first translate that thought into a set of symbols, or a language, that the other participants will be able to understand. This process of converting our thoughts to symbols is called encoding.

In turn, when we listen to or receive symbols/language, we have to translate that language into thoughts. That is, we give "meaning" to the symbols. This process is called decoding. Symbols are used to represent objects or ideas.

Channel

The means by which a message is conducted or transmitted is the channel. Berlo says that a channel (or medium) is a **carrier** of messages.[29] As such, a channel can be sound waves that travel from a participant's mouth to another participant's ear. It can also be a form of sound amplification to reach a crowd of people in a large room. A channel can also be a radio or television signal, or a book or a newspaper that carries messages to millions of people. More recently, the Internet is a very popular channel for carrying messages to individuals or large groups of people.

Noise

Noise is anything that interferes with or distorts the transmission of the signal. **Environmental noise** is interference with the signal as it moves from the source to the destination. This could take the form of sounds in the room that prevent the receiver from hearing the message; it could be static on a telephone line, or even a dropped call on a cellular phone. **Psychological noise** takes place inside the sender or receiver, such as misunderstanding or failing to remember what was heard.

Context

How does an event's context affect communication?
© 2008 JupiterImages Corporation.

Context can be viewed as physical or social. The **physical context** is made up of the space surrounding the communication event, or the place in which the communication event occurs. The context could be a classroom, a meeting room at work, a church, a physician's office, your house, your favorite "night spot," or about any other place you can imagine. The place in which the event takes place influences communication behaviors and the meanings attributed to them. How would your behavior change if you moved from your favorite night spot to a classroom? Would you behave the same way?

The **social context** considers the nature of the event taking place in a physical context. The social expectations tied to particular events influence meaning attributed to communication. Even though you were still in a classroom, you would behave differently during an exam than during a group work session. You would behave differently in church during a funeral than celebrating a festive holiday, and you would certainly behave differently while playing bingo in the church basement!

Culture

The **culture** in which the communication occurs and the native cultures of the participants can influence meaning. People belong to a variety of nations, traditions, groups, and organizations, each of which has its own point of view, values, and norms.[30] A culture is made up of the collective beliefs or principles on which a community or part of a community of people is based. These beliefs are often passed from generation to generation and provide a perspective through which the community makes sense of its experiences. The culture, then, provides a very powerful context or backdrop for communication events and has a profound influence on the meaning that participants create and share.

SUMMARY

That's enough of the theory, at least for the moment. Let's get to the application! Keep in mind, however, that a solid understanding of the basics of the transactional model will provide a lot of help to you as you attempt to plan strategies and practice your skills to help you achieve your communication goals.

ENDNOTES

1. S. Littlejohn, *Theories of Human Communication* (Belmont, CA: Wadsworth, 1999), 2.

2. F. Kerlinger, *Foundations of Behavioral Research* (New York: Holt, Rinehart, and Winston, 1973), 9.

3. M. Polanyi, *Personal Knowledge* (Chicago: University of Chicago Press, 1958).

4. W. Wallace, *The Logic of Science in Sociology* (Chicago: Aldine, 1971).

5. T. Clevenger, "Can One Not Communicate? A Conflict of Models," *Communication Studies* 42 (1991), 351.

6. C. Hovland, I. Janis, and H. Kelley, *Communication and Persuasion* (New Haven, CT: Yale University Press, 1953).

7. G. Gerbner, "On Defining Communication: Still Another View," *Journal of Communication* 16 (1966), 99–103.

8. G. Miller, "On Defining Communication: Another Stab," *Journal of Communication* 16 (1966), 92.

9. K. Sereno and C. D. Mortensen, *Foundations of Communication Theory* (New York: Harper & Row, 1970), 5.

10. J. Makay, *Public Speaking: Theory into Practice* (Dubuque, IA: Kendall/Hunt, 2000), 9.

11. L. Hugenberg, S. Wallace, and D. Yoder, *Creating Competent Communication* (Dubuque, IA: Kendall/Hunt, 2003), 4.

12. J. DeVito, *Human Communication: The Basic Course* (Boston, Allyn & Bacon, 2006), 2.

13. J. Golden, G. Berquist, W. Coleman, and J. Sproule, *The Rhetoric of Western Thought, 8th ed.* (Dubuque, IA: Kendall/Hunt, 2003).

14. D. Stanton, and G. Berquist, "Aristotle's Rhetoric: Empiricism or Conjecture?" *Southern Speech Communication Journal* 41 (1975), 69–81.

15. L. Cooper, *The Rhetoric of Aristotle* (New York: Appleton-Century-Crofts, 1932).

16. Golden et al., 65.

17. C. Shannon, and W. Weaver, *The Mathematical Theory of Communication* (Urbana: University of Illinois Press, 1949). Also W. Weaver, "The Mathematics of Communication," in C. D. Mortensen (ed.), *Basic Readings in Communication Theory* (New York: Harper & Row, 1979).

18. W. Schramm, "How Communication Works," in W. Schramm, (ed.), *The Process and Effects of Communication* (Urbana: University of Illinois Press, 1954).

19. D. Berlo, *The Process of Communication* (New York: Holt, Rinehart, and Winston, 1960).

20. Ibid pp. 111–112.

21. Barnlund, D. (1970). "A Transactional Model of Communication," in *Foundations of Communication Theory*, Sereno, K. and Mortensen, C. D. (eds.). New York: Harper & Row, 1970. Also P. Watzlawick, *How Real Is Real? Confusion, Disinformation, Communication: An Anecdotal Introduction to Communications Theory* (New York: Vintage, 1977).

22. M. Burgoon and M. Ruffner, *Human Communication.* (New York: Holt, Rinehart, & Winston, 1978), 9.

23. E. Lazlo, *The Systems View of the World: A Holistic Vision for Our Time* (New York: Hampton Press, 1996). Also L. von Bertalanffy, *General System Theory: Foundations, Development, Applications* (New York: Braziller, 1976).

24. Barnlund.

25. F. Dance, "Toward a Theory of Human Communication," In F. Dance (ed.), *Human Communication Theory: Original Essays* (New York: Holt, 1967).

26. K. Miller, *Communication Theories: Perspectives, Processes, and Contexts* (New York: McGraw-Hill, 2005).

27. W. Heisenberg, *The Physical Principles of Quantum Theory* (Chicago: University of Chicago Press, 1930).

28. S. Wallace, D. Yoder, L. Hugenberg, and C. Horvath, *Creating Competent Communication,* 5th ed. (Dubuque, IA: Kendall/Hunt, 2006).

29. Berlo.

30. Yoder, Hugenberg, and Wallace. *Creating Competent Communication.* (Dubuque, IA: Kendall/Hunt, 1993).

REFERENCES

T. Newcomb, "An Approach to the Study of Communicative Acts," *Psychological review* 60 (1953), 393–404.

P. Watzlawick, J. Beavin, and D. Jackson, *Pragmatics of Human Communication* (New York: Norton, 1967).

DEFINITIONS AND MODELS

Do you have all that? Communication is a process, messages are sent and received, meaning is created and shared, and all this happens in a social context. Okay, let's move on. No! Wait a minute! The point of this chapter is to show you how remarkably complicated the act of communication is. Most of us have been doing it for so long that we take it for granted. We say something, and people either get it or they don't. We blame them for the misunderstanding and we move on. Unfortunately, we may be at fault. (Don't you hate when that happens?) We have all been the victims of a misunderstanding or miscommunication. A friend tweets you a funny message but you take it the wrong way. You use a term that is perfectly clear to you but your instructor has no idea what you mean. An international student tries to translate an idea from her culture to make sense to an Ashland University student.

Communication is difficult to do well. That is why you are in this class.

Lesson #1 in Communication Studies

There Is No *Perfect* in the Art of Communication.

Every person is different. We each see the world differently. So when we try to talk to someone, we have to overcome the differences between us. Communication really is an art. Do you think there is a perfect painting or a perfect song? No, great paintings and songs speak to us and show us great beauty but humans are imperfect beings/artists. Paintings and music represent what we see or how we feel, but a portrait is not the person and a love song cannot say everything about the emotion of love. As a result, our art and our messages are also imperfect. The purpose of this course is to help us think about our communication in the hope that we can do it better. Better communicators are better friends, parents, employees, and people. Do you see how important this class is now?

The second problem we encounter as students of communication is this: If everyone is different, how are we going to talk about communication? Think about it. You speak differently with your friends than you do with your parents. You might speak differently with a boyfriend/girlfriend than you do with your buddies. In fact, you probably speak a little differently with each of your friends. This means that every communication interaction is unique. Bob speaking with Mary is different than Jane speaking with Kahmal. And so on and so on.

To analyze and talk about communication we create **models** and **theories**. A **model** allows us to look at the **process** of communication. In this way, we can talk about all the things that must be present in an effective message. **Theories** have been given a bad name in recent years. Any idiot can create a theory. I believe that chicken soup causes cancer. You see, I knew a person who ate chicken soup and was diagnosed with cancer. Is it a theory: Yes. Is it a good theory: **No!** A scientific theory rises to a higher order of proof. Observation, testing, restatement, more testing, refinement; suddenly, the chicken soup statement is recognized as foolish.

Theories and models of communication will ground you in a better understanding of the research that has been conducted in the field of communication. The hope is that you will not only learn more about the communication process but you might become interested in the study of communication as well. There is some really interesting stuff here! Wait until you read about Verbal and Nonverbal Communication.

WHAT IS THE POWER OF VERBAL AND NONVERBAL COMMUNICATION?

LEARNING OBJECTIVES

After reading this chapter, you should understand the following concepts:

- Language is a shared system of symbols and structures in organized patterns to express thoughts and feelings.
- Language is arbitrary, it changes over time, it consists of denotative and connotative meaning, and it is structured by rules.
- The semantic triangle, Sapir–Whorf hypothesis, and muted group theory are three models that help explain how meaning is created.
- Strategies for using language effectively involve using accurate and appropriate language, using unbiased language, and avoiding verbal distractions.
- We constantly send nonverbal messages that present an image of ourselves to others, so it important to be aware of what those messages are saying.
- Nonverbal communication is often ambiguous, continuous, unconscious, sometimes learned and intentional—and usually, more believed than verbal communication.
- Nonverbal messages perform six functions to create meaning: complementing, substituting, repeating, contradicting, regulating, and deceiving.
- Types of nonverbal communication include body movement, use of space, dress and appearance, and eye contact.

INTRODUCTION

Using words to describe magic is like using a screwdriver to cut roast beef.
—Tom Robbins, twentieth century American author

Better wise language than well-combed hair.
—Icelandic Proverb

KEYWORDS

language
symbols
grammar
intersubjective meaning
denotative meanings
connotative meanings
phonological rules
syntactical rules
semantic rules
regulative rules
constitutive rules
semantic triangle
referent
reference
dual perspective
regionalisms
jargon
slang
clichés
trite words
loaded words
empty words
derogatory language
equivocal words
kinesics
emblem
illustrator
regulator
affect display
adaptors
personal space
primary territory
secondary territory
public territory
intrusion of territory
eye contact
expectancy violations theory

All credibility, all good conscience, all evidence of truth come only from the senses.
—Friedrich Wilhelm Nietzsche, nineteenth century German philosopher

Eloquence is the power to translate a truth into language perfectly intelligible to the person to whom you speak.
—Ralph Waldo Emerson, nineteenth century U.S. poet, essayist

Get in touch with the way the other person feels. Feelings are 55 percent body language, 38 percent tone and 7 percent words.
—author unknown

The limits of my language means the limits of my world.
—Ludwig Wittgenstein, twentieth century philosopher

The eyes are the windows to the soul.
—Yousuf Karsh, twentieth century Canadian photographer

The difference between the right word and the almost right word is the difference between lightning and a lightning bug.
—Mark Twain, nineteenth century American author

Dialogue should simply be a sound among other sounds, just something that comes out of the mouths of people whose eyes tell the story in visual terms.
—Alfred Hitchcock, twentieth century film director

Through these quotations, you've just been exposed to the *power of verbal and nonverbal communication* to define our beliefs, expose our values, and share our experiences. The words that you use and the nonverbal behaviors that accompany them are critically important as you communicate, because they have the ability to clarify your ideas to others or to confuse them. In this chapter, you'll learn about verbal language and nonverbal communication, to discover how they are used to create shared meaning.

Verbal language and nonverbal communication are used to create shared meaning.
© 2008, JupiterImages.

WHAT IS LANGUAGE?

So what do we know about language? Linguists estimate that there are about 5,000 to 6,000 different languages spoken in the world today; about 200 languages have a million or more native speakers. Mandarin Chinese is the most common, followed by Hindi, English, Spanish, and Bengali.[1] However, as technology continues to shrink the communication world, English is becoming more dominant in mediated communication. According to Internet World Stats, which charts usage and population statistics, the top ten languages used in the Web are English (31% of all Internet users), Chinese (15.7%), Spanish (8.7%), Japanese (7.4%), and French and German (5% each).[2] English is one of the official languages of the United Nation, the International Olympic Committee, in academics and in the sciences.[3] English is also the language spoken by air traffic controllers worldwide. Yet the English that we speak in the United States is really a hybrid, using vocabulary taken from many sources, influenced by media, technology, and globalization. Let's consider what all of this means for you as you try to share meaning with others.

Language is a shared system of symbols structured in organized patterns to express thoughts and feelings. **Symbols** are arbitrary labels that we give to some idea or phenomenon. For example, the word *run* represents an action that we do, while *bottle* signifies a container for a liquid. Words are symbols, but not all symbols are words. Music, photographs, and logos are also symbols that stand for something else, as do nonverbal actions such as "OK," and "I don't know." However, in this section, we're going to focus on words as symbols. Note that the definition of language says that it's structured and shared. Languages have a **grammar** (syntax, a patterned set of rules that aid in meaning). You've learned grammar as you've been taught how to write, and it's become an unconscious part of your daily communication. Take, for example, this sentence:

The glokkish Vriks mounged oupily on the brangest Ildas.

Now, we can answer these questions:

Who did something? The Vriks mounged.

What kind of Vriks are they? Glokkish

How did they mounge? Oupily

On what did they mounge? The Ildas

What kind of Ildas are they? Brangest

You might have difficulty identifying noun, verb, adverb, and adjective, but because you know the grammar of the English language, you're still able to decipher what this sentence is telling you because of the pattern, even if the symbols themselves lack meaning for now. That leads to the next part of the definition: *symbols must be shared in order to be understood.* George Herbert Mead's Symbolic Interaction Theory asserts that meaning is **intersubjective**; that means that **meaning** *can exist only when people share common interpretations of the symbols they exchange.*[4] So if you were given a picture of Vriks and were told that these were ancient hill people of a particular region of the country, you'd have a start at meaning!

In order to get a grasp on language, this section will uncover basic principles about language, introduce to you a few theoretical perspectives, and then will suggest language strategies to enhance your communication.

English is the language spoken by airline pilots and air traffic controllers all over the world.
© 2008, JupiterImages.

WHAT ARE THE BASIC PRINCIPLES OF LANGUAGE?

There are some basic principles of language. It is arbitrary, it changes over time, it consists of denotative and connotative meanings, and it is structured by rules. Let's look at these more closely.

Arbitrary

"Language is arbitrary" means that *symbols do not have a one-to-one connection with what they represent*. What is the computer form that you use if you take a test? Is it a bubble sheet? A scantron? An opscan? Each of these names has no natural connection to that piece of paper, and it's likely that at different universities, it's called different names. Because language is arbitrary, people in groups agree on labels to use, creating private codes. That's why your organization might have specialized terms, why the military uses codes, and why your family uses nicknames that only they understand. The language that you create within that group creates group meaning and culture. The arbitrary element of language also adds to its ambiguity; meanings just aren't stable. To me, a test is the same as an exam; to you, a test might be less than an exam. If you say to me, "I'll call you later," how do I define the term *later?* We often fall into the trap of thinking that everyone understands us, but the reality is, it's an amazing thing that we share meaning at all!

Changes over Time

Language *changes over time* in vocabulary, as well as syntax. New vocabulary is required for the latest inventions, for entertainment and leisure pursuits, for political use. In 2007, the top television buzzwords included *surge* and *D'oh*, while in 2006, they were *truthiness* and *wikiality*.[5] How many of those words play a role in your culture today? Words like *cell phones* and *Internet* didn't exist fifty years ago, for example. In addition, no two people use a language in exactly the same way. Teens and young adults often use different words and phrases than their parents. The vocabulary and phrases people use may depend on where they live, their age, education level, social status, and other factors. Through our interactions, we pick up new words and phases, and then we integrate them into our communication.

How is your language different from your parents' and grandparents'?
© 2008, JupiterImages.

Consists of Denotative and Connotative Meanings

Denotative meanings, the literal, dictionary definitions, are precise and objective. **Connotative meanings** reflect your personal, subjective definitions. They add layers of experience and emotions to meaning. Elizabeth J. Natalle examined this dichotomy in a case study of urban music, examining how our language has evolved over the years to include more negative connotation regarding talk about women as compared to talk about men. Think about *chick, sweetie, sugar pie* and *old maid*, versus *stud, hunk, playboy*, and *bachelor*. Do you get a different image? Using a study of rap music, she attempted to clarify how urban music names a particular world, creates male community, and has implications for power and gendered relationships.[6]

A simpler way to consider denotative and connotative meanings is to examine the terms President Bush used to describe the terrorists who crashed the planes on Sept. 11, 2001. Bush's labels on that day in various locations began with "those folks who committed this act" (remarks by the president

when he first heard that two planes crashed into World Trade Center)[7] to "those responsible for these cowardly acts" (remarks by the president upon arrival at Barksdale Air Force Base)[8] to "those who are behind these evil acts" and "the terrorists who committed these acts" (statement by the president in his address to the nation).[9] Consider how the connotative meaning shaped the image of the perpetrators.

David K. Berlo[10] provided several assumptions about meaning:

- Meanings are in people.
- Communication does not consist of the transmission of meanings, but of the transmission of messages.
- Meanings are not in the message; they are in the message users.
- Words do not mean at all; only people mean.
- People can have similar meanings only to the extent that they have had, or can anticipate having, similar experiences.
- Meanings are never fixed; as experience changes, so meanings change.
- No two people can have exactly the same meaning for anything.

These ideas echo the idea that when you use words, you need to be aware of the extent to which meaning is shared. For example, when an adoptive parent sees those "adopt a highway" locator signs, it's probable that that person sees something different than others might. "Adopt a" programs might be seen as confusing and misleading others about the term *adoption*. An adoptive parent might say that you don't adopt a road, a zoo animal, or a Cabbage Patch doll. Adoption is a means of family building, and it has a very subjective, emotional meaning.[11] To the town official who erected the sign, it's a representation of the good work being done by some group to keep the highway clean.

What does this sign's language mean to you?
© Robert J. Beyers II, 2008, Shutterstock.

Structured by Rules

As we understand and use the rules of language, we begin to share meaning. Think of rules as a shared understanding of what language means, as well as an understanding of what kind of language is appropriate in various contexts. Many of the rules you use weren't consciously learned; you gathered them from interactions with other people. Some, however, were learned aspects of your culture.

Phonological rules *regulate how words sound when you pronounce them.* They help us organize language. For instance, the word *lead* could be used to suggest a behavior that you do (you *lead* the group to show them the way) or a kind of toxic metallic element (*lead* paint in windows is harmful to children). Do you enjoy getting a *present*, or did you *present* one to someone else? Another example of phonological rules is demonstrated by your understanding of how letters sound when they're grouped in a particular way. Take for instance the letters *omb*. Now put a t in front of them, and you have *tomb*. Put a c in front, and it becomes *comb*. Put a b in front, and you have *bomb*. See how the sounds shift?

The way we make singular nouns plural is also phonological. It's not as simple as adding the letter s to the end of a word. The sound changes too: dog/dogs (sounds like a *z* at the end); cook/cooks (sounds like an *ess*); bus/buses (sounds like *ess-ez*). English has many inconsistent phonological rules like these, which makes making errors quite typical, especially for non-native English speakers.

Syntactical rules *present the arrangement of a language, how the symbols are organized.* You saw that earlier in the "glokkish Vriks" example; you're usually unaware of the syntactical rules until they're violated. In English, we put adjectives prior to most nouns: I live in a red house. In French, you live in a house red (the adjective follows the noun).

Semantic rules *govern the meaning of specific symbols.* Because words are abstractions, we need rules to tell us what they mean in particular situations. Take, for example, the headline, "School Needs to Be Aired." What does that mean? Is the school so smelly that it needs to be refreshed? Or are the needs of the school going to be broadcast or spoken in a public forum? Words can be interpreted in more than one way, and we need semantic rules to lead us to shared meaning. Although these three kinds of rules help us to pattern language, there are also rules that help us guide the entire communication event.[12]

Regulative rules *tell us when, how, where, and with whom we can talk about certain things.* You know when it's OK to interrupt someone; you know when turn-taking is expected. You may be enrolled in classes where you are expected to express your opinion; in other classes, you know to hold your tongue. How do you feel about public displays of affection? When is it OK to correct your boss? These regulative rules help us to maintain respect, reveal information about ourselves, and interact with others.

Constitutive rules *tell us how to "count" different kinds of communication.* These rules reveal what you feel is appropriate. You know that when someone waves or blows kisses, that person is showing affection or friendliness. You know what topics you can discuss with your parents, friends, teachers, co-workers, and strangers. You have rules that reveal your expectations for communication with different people; you expect your doctor to be informative and firm with advice, and you anticipate that your friend will compli-

You can count on a close friend for comfort when you have a problem.
© 2008, JupiterImages.

ment you and empathize. As we interact with others, we begin to grasp and use the rules. For instance, when you start a new job, you take in the rules on whom to talk with, how to talk with supervisors and co-workers, and what topics are appropriate, along with the mechanics of how to talk and the meaning of job-specific words. Interestingly enough, you might not even be aware of the rules until they're broken!

HOW DO THEORISTS DESCRIBE LANGUAGE AND MEANING?

Can you picture a book, a pen, a laptop, and a horse? Your ability to conjure up these images means that you've been exposed to the symbols that represent them in the English language. How about the picture shown on the right? What do you see? If you said "keys," then that shows how you have acquired language; you've been taught that these things are associated with the symbol "keys." How are you able to do those connections? There are a great number of perspectives related to language, meaning, and symbols. In this section, you'll be exposed to three models that present varying perspectives on the way that meaning is created.

© Costin Cojocaru, 2008, Shutterstock.

Semantic Triangle

One of the models that demonstrate how words come to have meaning is the **semantic triangle.**[13] Ogden and Richards suggest that a major problem with communication is that we tend to treat *words* as if they were the *thing*. As a result, we confuse the symbol for the thing or object.

At the bottom right hand of the triangle is the **referent,** the thing that we want to communicate about that exists in reality. As we travel up the right side, we find the **reference(s),** which consist of thoughts, experiences, and feelings about the referent. This is a causal connection; seeing the object

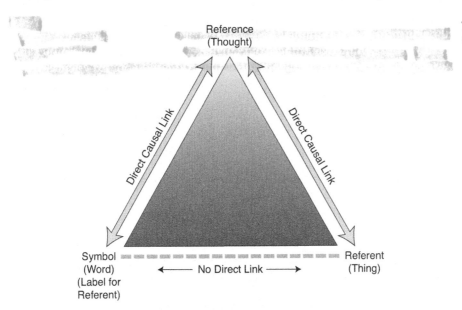

The Semantic Triangle— Ogden & Richards, 1923.

results in those thoughts. Another causal connection exists as you travel down the left side of the triangle, to the *symbol*, or *word*. That's the label we apply to that referent.

The problem is that there is not a direct connection between a symbol and referent; it's an indirect connection, shown by the dotted line. According to this model, it's that indirect link between *referent* and *symbol* that creates the greatest potential for communication misunderstandings. We assume that others share our references, and we think that they must use the same label or symbol because of that shared state of being. A simple example should help.

A mom is teaching her son words by reading simple children's books—books about tools, farms, trucks, zoos, and dinosaurs. Usually, this reading activity happens on the front porch. One day, the mom sees the neighbor's cat sneaking up on her birdfeeders, and under her breath, she mutters something about the "stupid cat." The next day, the toddler goes off to day care, and when mom comes to pick him up, she's met by the teacher. She laughingly tells how she was reading a book about animals that day, and when she got to the page with cute kittens on it, the little boy yelled out, "Stupid cat." The embarrassed mother just learned a lesson about the semantic triangle. For her, the referent (cat) evokes images of bird-murdering, allergy-causing felines (references). She creates the label "stupid cat." (symbol). When the boy sees a picture of one, he naturally thinks that is what those things are called. Unfortunately, that's not the universal name!

You can experience the same thing: If you tell others that you own a dog, what referent do you think they apply the label to? The semantic triangle is a practical tool that helps us to understand the relationship of referent, references, and symbol, or thing, thoughts, and word. It reminds us that one word doesn't necessarily evoke the same meaning in any two people.

Sapir–Whorf Hypothesis

Another theoretical approach to language is the *Sapir–Whorf hypothesis*[14] (also known as the theory of linguistic relativity). According to this approach, your perception of reality is determined by your thought processes, and your thought processes are limited by your language. Therefore, language shapes reality. Your culture determines your language, which, in turn, determines the way that you categorize thoughts about the world and your experiences in it. If you don't have the words to describe or explain something, then you can't really know it or talk about it.

For example, researchers Linda Perry and Deborah Ballard-Reisch suggest that existing language does not represent the reality that biological sex comes in more forms than female and male, gender identities are not neatly ascribed to one's biological sex, and sexual orientation does not fit snugly into, "I like men, I like women, I like both, I like neither," choices. They also assert that evolving new language such as the word *gendex* (representing the dynamic interplay of a person's sexual identity, sex preference, sexual orientation, and gender identity) can work against biases and discrimination.[15] Another example is the concept of *bipolar disorder*. It used to be called *manic depressive*, and it refers to a mood disorder characterized by unusual shifts in a person's mood, energy, and ability to function.[16] But if you don't know what that illness is, you might just agree with a family member who says, "You're just going through a phase." The lack of language restricts our ability to perceive the world. Reality is embedded in your language.

Muted Group Theory

As these perspectives suggest, the *words* that you use are powerful. They have the ability to express attitudes and to represent values. Communication scholar Cheris Kramarae developed the *muted group theory* to suggest that power and status are connected, and because muted groups lack the power of appropriate language, they have no voice and receive little attention.[17] Kramarae noted, "The language of a particular culture does not serve all its speakers, for not all speakers contribute in an equal fashion to its formulation. Women (and members of other subordinate groups) are not as free or as able as men are to say what they wish, when and where they wish, because the words and the norms for their use have been formulated by the dominant group, men."[18] She asserts that language serves men better than women (and perhaps European Americans better than African Americans or other groups) because the European American men's experiences are named clearly in language, and the experiences of other groups (women, people with disabilities, and ethnic minorities) are not. Due to this problem with language, muted groups appear less articulate than men in public settings.

The muted group theory suggests that language serves men better than women.
© 2008, JupiterImages.

The task of muted groups is to conceptualize a thought and then scan the vocabulary that is suited to men's thinking for the best way to encode the idea. The term *sexual harassment* is an example. Although the act of harassment has existed for centuries, it wasn't until sex discrimination was prohibited by Title VII of the 1964 Civil Rights Act. It also took the Clarence Hill–Anita Thomas hearing in 1991 to make the term *gender discrimination* part of the popular dialogue, as the media focused attention on the workplace issue.

Because they are rendered inarticulate, muted groups are silenced in a variety of ways. Ridicule happens when the group's language is trivialized (men talk, women gab). Ritual creates dominance (the woman changes her name at the wedding ceremony but the man doesn't). Control happens as the media present some points of view and ignore others (we don't hear from the elderly or homeless). Harassment results from the control that men exert over public spaces (women get verbal threats couched as compliments when they walk down the streets). This theory affirms that as muted groups create more language to express their experiences and as all people come to have similar experiences, inequalities of language (and the power that comes with it) should change.

Each of these perspectives demonstrates how language impacts meaning. They show how we believe meaning comes into being, how we are limited by the language we possess, and how language wields power. By now, you should be sensitive to the many ways that you can miscommunicate, or at least communicate ineffectively through language choices. How can you become more sensitive to strategic language choices?

HOW CAN I USE LANGUAGE EFFECTIVELY?

Communication scholar Julia T. Wood says that the single most important guideline is to engage in a **dual perspective**, recognizing another person's point of view and taking that into account as you communicate. Wood suggests that you should understand both your own and another's point of view and acknowledge each when you communicate.[19] You'll see that concept played out throughout this text; you need to consider your audience's beliefs, attitudes, and values as you create your message. Here are some strategic tips for effective language use to maintain that dual perspective.

Use Accurate Language

Make sure you are using the term correctly, and if you're unsure if the audience will understand your meaning, define it. You'll learn about defining in the chapter on informative speaking. Remember, what makes perfect sense to you may be gobbledygook to me. When the doctor tells you that you have a rather large contusion, do you know what that is?

Use Appropriate Language

It's important to use appropriate language for the occasion.
© 2008, JupiterImages.

Appropriate means that the language you use is suitable for the context, for the audience, for the topic, and for you. Some occasions call for more formal language (proposals to a client), while others will let slang pass (texting a friend). Some audiences expect technical language, while others need simple terms. Off-color humor might work in certain instances and with specific groups, but you probably shouldn't choose to use it at a church gathering. You need to consider if your audience utilizes **regionalisms** (words or phrases that are specific to one part of the country) or **jargon** (specialized professional language) as you speak with them.

Your topic also can determine suitable language. Some topics call for lots of vivid language and imagery, while others are better suited to simplicity. If you are honoring your boss upon his retirement, then the topic probably calls for words that evoke appreciation and emotion. But if you're telling someone how to put together a computer table, then simple explanatory words are expected. Finally, you need to use words that are appropriate to you. You have developed your own style of language over the years; do you use the same words as your parents? Don't try to use words that just don't flow easily from your mind; it's not going to sound like you.

Use Unbiased Language

Biased language includes any language that defames a subgroup (women; people from specific ethnic, religious, or racial groups; people with disabilities) or eliminates them from consideration. Even if you would never think about using language that defames anyone else, you can fall into using language that more subtly discriminates. Sexist language is replete with this: We use the masculine pronoun (he, him) when we don't have a referent. So if you personify "the judge," "the executive," "the director," as male by using the pronoun *he*, you eliminate one whole subgroup from consideration.

The same holds true when you use the word *man* in occupational terms, when the job holders could be either male or female. Examples are fireman, policeman, garbage man, chairman; they're easily made nonsexist by saying firefighter, police officer, garbage collector, and chair or presiding officer. Finally, while the generic use of *man* (like in mankind) originally was used to denote both men and women, its meaning has become more specific to adult males. It's simple to change the word to be more inclusive: mankind becomes people or human beings; man-made becomes manufactured; the common man becomes the average person.

The *Associated Press Stylebook* has a lengthy entry on "disabled, handicapped, impaired" terminology, including when to use (and not to use) terms such as *blind, deaf, mute, wheelchair-user,* and so on. A separate entry on *retarded* says "mentally retarded" is the preferred term. The World Bank advises using *persons with disabilities* and *disabled people,* not handicapped.

Use appropriate labels when referring to sexual orientation. The terms *lesbians, gay men,* and *bisexuals* or *bisexual women and men* are preferred to the term *homosexuals* (because the emphasis on the latter is on sex, while the former all refer to the whole person, not just the sex partner he or she chooses). In general, try to find out what the people's preferences are, and be specific when applicable. For instance, if all the subjects are either Navajo or Cree, stating this is more accurate than calling them Native Americans.

Avoid Verbal Distractions

If you divert the audience from your intended meaning by using confusing words, your credibility will be lowered and your audience may become lost. The following are distractions:

- **Slang** *consists of words that are short-lived, arbitrarily changed, and often vulgar ideas.* Slang excludes people from a group. Internet slang was usually created to save keystrokes and consists of "u" for *you*, "r" for *are*, and "4" for *for.* Poker slang includes *dead man's hand* (two pair, aces, and eights); to *act* (make a play); and *going all in* (betting all of your chips on the hand). *Daggy* means out of fashion or uncool; *fives* means to reserve a seat.[20]
- **Cliches** *or* **trite words** *have been overused and lose power or impact.* The Unicorn Hunters of Lake Superior University keeps a list of banished words that is regularly updated. In 2007, it listed words such as combined celebrity names (*Brangelina* and *Tomcat*), *awesome* (because it no longer means majestic), and *undocumented alien* (just use the word *illegal*).[21]
- **Loaded words** *sound like they're describing, but they're actually revealing your attitude.* When speaking of abortion, consider the different image created by the terms *unborn child* or *fetus.* Are you *thrifty* but your friend is *cheap*? How about your brother; is he one of those *health-nuts* who is dedicated to the cult of marathoning? Colorful language is entertaining, but if it distorts the meaning or distracts the audience, then don't use it.
- **Empty words** *are overworked exaggerations.* They lose their strength because their meaning is exaggerated. How many products are advertised as *new and improved* or *supersized*? What exactly does that mean?
- **Derogatory language** *consists of words that are degrading or tasteless.* If you use degrading terms to refer to ethnic groups (*Polack* for a person of Polish descent; *Chink* for someone from China; *Spic* for an Italian) then you are guilty of verbal bigotry.
- **Equivocal words** *have more than one correct denotative meaning.* A famous example is of a nurse telling a patient that he "wouldn't be needing" the books he asked to be brought from home. Although she meant that he was going home that day and could read there, the patient took that to mean that he was near death and wouldn't have time to read. One time while evaluating a debate, an instructor encountered students arguing the issue of the legalization of marijuana. The side arguing for the legalization used the Bible, citing chapter and verse and asserting that God

created the grass and said, "The grass is good." This sent the other side into a tailspin as they tried to refute the biblical passage. This simple equivocal use of the term *grass* lost the debate for the opposition!

WHAT SHOULD YOU TAKE FROM THIS SECTION ON LANGUAGE?

Because our language is arbitrary and evolving, it's easy to be misunderstood. You can attempt to enhance shared meaning by remembering that language is a shared system of symbols; through language, you share ideas, articulate values, transmit information, reveal experiences, and maintain relationships. Language is essential to your ability to think and to operate within the many cultures (community of meaning) that you travel through. You should be sensitive to the words you choose as you attempt to connect with others. Now let's turn our attention to the other means by which you create meaning: your nonverbal communication behaviors.

WHAT IS NONVERBAL COMMUNICATION?

Pretend you are hoarse and the doctor has told you not to speak at all for the next three days. Nor can you IM or text or do any other computer-related communication. How would you do the following?

- Let your friend know that you can't hear her. Or tell her that she's talking too loudly.
- Tell your lab partner that you want him to come where you are.
- Show the teacher that you don't know the answer to the question she just asked you.
- Let a child know that he needs to settle down; his play is getting too rough.
- Tell your significant other that you're not angry, and everything is OK.
- Express disappointment over a loss by your team, which always seems to lose the lead in the last two minutes.
- Signify that you're running late and have to leave.

How hard would it be to make yourself understood? What you've just attempted to do without verbal language is present a message nonverbally. We all constantly send nonverbal messages, giving our receivers all types of cues about ourselves. An awareness of nonverbal communication is important: your nonverbal behaviors present an image of yourself to those around you. They tell others how you want to relate to them, and they may reveal emotions or feelings that you either are trying to hide or simply can't express.

In the remainder of this chapter, you will be introduced to some of the elements of the study of nonverbal communication in the hopes of creating a greater awareness of these elements of the message. You will examine *definitions* of nonverbal communication, its *functions*, and *types* of nonverbal communication. Along the way, we will provide examples and illustrations to help you understand the applications of various nonverbal behaviors and how they can be used to help you interpret the messages of other people. You should also gain some insight into how to use nonverbal behaviors to enhance your own communication.

WHAT IS THE NATURE OF NONVERBAL COMMUNICATION?

Although nonverbal communication is a complex system of behaviors and meanings, its basic definition *can be* fairly straightforward. Here are four definitions for comparison:

1. All types of communication that do not rely on words or other linguistic systems[22]
2. Any message other than written or spoken words that conveys meaning[23]
3. Anything in a message besides the words themselves[24]
4. Messages expressed by nonlinguistic means[25]

Taking these definitions and the body of related research into consideration, we propose a very simple definition: nonverbal communication is *all nonlinguistic aspects of communication*. That definition covers quite a lot of territory. Except for the actual words that we speak, *everything* else is classified as nonverbal communication. The way you move, the tone of your voice, the way you use your eyes, the way you occupy and use space, the way you dress, the shape of your body, your facial expressions, the way you smell, your hand gestures, and the way you pronounce (or mispronounce) words are all considered nonverbal communication. Some of these behaviors have meaning independent of language or other behaviors; others have meaning only when considered with what is said, the context and culture in which a communication event takes place, and the relationship between the communicators.

Maybe you're getting a hint of the richness of nonverbal expression. Without any formal training, you already are able to interpret messages that others send nonverbally. Your skill level, however, may not be as strong as you think, so keep in mind the goal of increasing strategic communication as you continue. Researchers have also been fascinated with the extent to which nonverbal communication impacts meaning, and their findings provide glimpses into the impact of nonverbals on shared meanings and culture. If nothing else, by the end of this section, you will discover that the study of nonverbal communication has come a long way since it was referred to only as *body language!*

What can you say about her nonverbal communication?
© mehmet alci, 2008, Shutterstock.

WHAT ARE THE CHARACTERISTICS OF NONVERBAL COMMUNICATION?

Ambiguous

Most nonverbal behaviors have no generally accepted meaning. Instead, the connection between the behavior and its meaning is vague or *ambiguous*, leaving understanding open to various interpretations. The meaning we apply to words is fairly specific, but the meaning we give to nonverbal communication is nonspecific. The meanings you attribute to nonverbal behaviors are heavily dependent on the relationship between you and the others you're interacting with, the nature of the communication event, the content of the words that accompanies it, and the culture in which the event takes place. For example,

In the United States, a thumbs-up is appropriate for celebrating.
© Jason Stitt, 2008, Shutterstock.

consider the ubiquitous "thumbs up" hand gesture. In the United States it means, "OK" or "very good." In some eastern cultures, however, it is considered an insult and an obscene hand gesture. In Great Britain, Australia, and New Zealand, it could be a signal used by hitchhikers who are thumbing a lift; it could be an OK signal; it also could be an insult signal meaning "up yours" or "sit on this" when the thumb is jerked sharply upward. In Indonesia, the thumb gesture means "good job" in response to someone who has completed an excellent job, or "delicious" when great food is tasted. In another context, if you smile at a joke, that's understood in an entirely different way than if you do it after someone misses a chair and falls to the ground. A smile could also show affection, embarrassment, or even be used to hide pain or anger. As you can see, it is possible to find several meanings for the same nonverbal behavior, and it is possible to find several nonverbal behaviors that mean the same thing.[26]

Continuous

With verbal communication, if you stop speaking, listeners can't attribute any more meaning to your words. Nonverbal communication, by contrast, is so pervasive and complex that others can continue to gather meaning, even if you are doing absolutely nothing! The mere act of doing nothing can send a message; you might blush, stutter, wring your hands, or sweat unintentionally, causing others to react to you. You might not mean to send a message, but your lack of intention to communicate doesn't prevent other people from assigning meaning to your behavior. In addition, your appearance, the expression on your face, your posture, where (or if) you are seated, and how you use the space around you all provide information that is subject to interpretation by others.

Sometimes Unplanned and Unconscious

What can you tell by this woman's expression?
© Steve Luker, 2008, Shutterstock.

Nonverbal communication can be either unconscious or intentional, but most of our nonverbal behaviors are exhibited without much or any conscious thought. You rarely plan or think carefully about your nonverbal behaviors. When you are angry, it is naturally expressed on your face as well as elsewhere in your body. The same is true for how your voice changes when you're nervous, how your arms cross when you're feeling defensive, or how you scratch your head when you're unsure of something. These expressions and behaviors are rarely planned or structured; they just happen suddenly and without conscious thought.

Sometimes Learned and Intentional

Saying that some nonverbal behaviors are natural or occur without conscious thought doesn't mean that people are born with a *complete inventory* of instinctive nonverbal behaviors. Much of your nonverbal behavior is *learned* rather than instinctive or innate. You learn the "proper" way to sit or approach, how close to stand next to someone, how to look at others, how to use touch, all from your experiences and your culture. You have been taught their meaning through your experience in interactions with other people. As a result, you can structure some nonverbal behaviors to send intentional messages, such as disapproval when you shake your head from side to side or give a "high five" to show excitement. However, unlike the formal training you received in reading, writing, and speaking, you learned (and continue to learn) nonverbal communication in a much less formal and unceremonious way, and you use it in a much less precise way than spoken language. But *because* many of these behaviors are learned, you can actively work to improve your nonverbal skills. There is a debate as to whether unintentional nonverbal behaviors really count as communication. Since others incorporate their understanding of our nonverbals as part of shared meaning, we're going to say that intentional and unintentional nonverbals both are worth recognizing here.[27] Our position is that it's nearly impossible not to communicate nonverbally.

More Believable than Verbal

Communication textbooks have been saying for years that, when verbal and nonverbal messages contradict each other, people typically believe the nonverbal message. Because nonverbal is more spontaneous and less conscious, we don't or can't manipulate it as easily as we can control verbal communication. When you were younger and your parents thought that you might be lying to them, they would say, "Look me in the eye and say that again." Your face was more believable to them than what you were saying verbally. Your nonverbal messages would tell them the truth. How could this be so?

Research suggests that between 65 percent and 93 percent of the meaning people attribute to messages comes from the nonverbal channel.[28] There is a small fudge factor in those percentages, however, because the Mehrabian and Ferris study assumed up to 93 percent of meaning came from nonverbal messages in situations *where no other background information* was available.[29] The reality is that many factors affect the meaning given to messages, including how familiar the communicators are with the language being spoken, cultural knowledge, and even individual differences in personality characteristics.[30]

Regardless of the exact percentage of meaning that comes from the verbal or nonverbal channels, we still appear to get more meaning from the nonverbal channel. Unless you are very good at controlling all your nonverbal behaviors, your parents can probably still know when you are not telling the truth.

WHAT ARE THE FUNCTIONS OF NONVERBAL COMMUNICATION?

Types of nonverbal communication will be described a little later in the chapter, but you first need to understand what part nonverbals play in the communication process. Nonverbal communication performs six general functions that add information and insight to nonverbal messages to help us create meaning. Those functions are complementing, substituting, repeating, contradicting, regulating, and deceiving.

Complementing Verbal Messages

If someone shakes your hand while saying "Congratulations" at your college graduation, the handshake gives added meaning to the verbal message. Gestures, tone of voice, facial expressions, and other nonverbal behaviors can clarify, reinforce, accent, or add to the meaning of verbal messages. For instance, if you are angry with a friend and are telling him off, pounding your hand into your fist would add depth to your meaning. These nonverbal behaviors are usually not consciously planned, but they are spontaneous reactions to the context and the verbal message.

Substituting for Verbal Messages

You can use a nonverbal message *in the place of* a verbal message. A substituting behavior can be a clear "stop" hand gesture; it can be nodding the head up and down to say yes; or it can be a shoulder shrug to indicate "I don't know." When you use this kind of gesture, you don't have to supply any verbal message for the meaning to be clear to others. However, keep in mind that your nonverbals may be interpreted differently, given what you have learned from your context and culture. As an example, someone in Japan might act in a controlled fashion, while someone from the Mideast might seem more emotional, even when both are feeling the same intensity of emotion. Your interpretation of those postures, without accompanying verbals, might lead you to the wrong conclusions.

Repeating Verbal Messages

If a stranger on your college campus asks you for directions to the administration building, you might reply, "Carty Hall is two blocks south of here." While you are delivering the verbal message, you also *repeat* the message by pointing to the south. The gesture reinforces the meaning of the verbal message and provides a clear orientation to listeners who are unfamiliar with the campus.

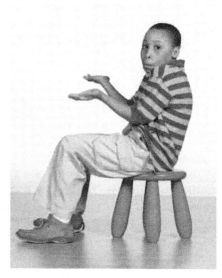

Nonverbal messages can substitute for verbal messages. What specific messages are being sent by the people in these photos?
© 2008, JupiterImages.

Contradicting Verbal Messages

Nonverbal messages sometimes *contradict* the verbal message. It can be done by accident, such as when you say "turn right" but you point to the left. Or it could be done without thinking (unconsciously), such as when you have a sour expression on your face as you tell your former girlfriend how much you "really like" her new boyfriend. Finally, you could use planned nonverbal behaviors, such as a wink of the eye and a sarcastic tone of voice, to contradict the verbal message, "Nice hat!" A famous example of this contradiction happened in September 1960, when 70 million U.S. viewers tuned in to watch Senator John Kennedy of Massachusetts and Vice President Richard Nixon in the first-ever televised presidential debate. The so-called Great Debates were television's first attempt to offer voters a chance to see the presidential candidates "in person" and head to head. Nixon was more well known, since he had been on the political scene as senator and two-term vice president. He had made a career out of fighting communism right in the midst of the Cold War. Kennedy was a relative newcomer, having served only a brief and undistinguished time as senator; he had no foreign affairs experience. Expectations were low for Kennedy; there seemed to be a huge reputation disparity between them.

"The street you are looking for is about one mile to the east." Nonverbal messages repeat verbal messages.
© 2008, JupiterImages.

During the debate, their points were fairly even. But it was the visual contrast between the two men that was astounding. Nixon had seriously injured his knee, had lost weight, and had recently suffered from the flu. When the first debate came, he was underweight and pasty looking, with a murky 5:00 shadow darkening his lower face. He wore a white, poorly fitting shirt and a gray suit that nearly blended into the background set, and he refused to wear make-up, even though he was advised to do so. Kennedy supplemented his tan with make-up, wore a dark suit, and had been coached on how to sit and where to look when he wasn't speaking. Kennedy's smooth delivery made him credible, because he came off as confident, vibrant, and poised. Nixon looked tired, pasty, and uncomfortable (he sweated heavily).

Polls taken after the first debate showed that most people who listened to it on the radio felt that Nixon had won, while most who watched it on television declared Kennedy the victor. Those television viewers focused on what they saw, not what they heard.[31]

Contradictory messages can be difficult for others to interpret, so it's important to monitor your nonverbal behaviors. People have a tendency to prefer the meaning of the nonverbal message when it conflicts with the verbal, so when you say turn right, you should try to point to the right. Or if you don't want your former girlfriend to know how jealous you are of her new boyfriend, try to guard against making that sour face. Most adults, however, will interpret the "Nice hat" comment as sarcasm and clearly understand the message.

Is there sarcasm detected in the "nice hat" comment?
© 2008, JupiterImages.

Regulating the Flow of Communication

Nonverbal behaviors help us to control the verbal messages we're presenting. To prevent chaos when two are more people are engaged in conversation, we use a system of signals to indicate whose turn it is speak. Think about that. How do you know when it is appropriate for you to begin speaking in a group or in a classroom? When you're talking, no one is there saying, "Now, it's your turn." You might use tone of voice to indicate that you want to speak and silence to show that you're ready to yield the floor. If you don't want to be interrupted, you might not make eye contact with the potential interruptor. If you expect an answer, you might directly look at the other person.[32] You probably also use nonverbals to let others know that you're trying to control their talk. Have you ever started to put your computer or lecture materials away before the professor is done speaking? You use nonverbal behavior to indicate that you want to speak, that you are finished speaking, that you want to continue speaking, or that you do not want to speak at all. The nonverbal signals include tone of voice, posture, gestures, eye contact, and other behaviors.

Deceiving Listeners

Sometimes, your nonverbal behaviors are attempts to mislead somebody or hide the truth. This deception doesn't have to be malicious or mean. If you're a poker player, you might wear sunglasses in order to shield your eyes; pupils dilate when you're excited, and you want to keep that excitement close to your vest. Sometimes, you deceive to protect yourself or the other person, like when you pat someone on the back and say, "Everything will be all right," even when you know it won't.

There are many movies based on the premise that you can learn to nonverbally behave like someone you're not in order to deceive others. In *Tootsie* (1982), Dustin Hoffman becomes the female star of a television soap opera. Robin Williams stars as *Mrs. Doubtfire* (1993), dressing as a woman so he can see his children. In *The Birdcage* (1996), Robin Williams attempts to teach Nathan Lane how to do an exaggerated John Wayne walk to disguise his effeminate stroll. *Mulan* (1998) is a young woman wanting to fight the Huns in the place of her father, so she poses as a male to join the army. *Big Momma's House* (2000) stars Martin Lawrence, who plays an FBI agent who goes undercover and dresses as a heavy-set woman. In *White Chicks* (2004) Shawn Wayans and Marlon Wayans are sibling FBI agents who must protect two cruise line heiresses from a kidnapping plot. Finally, in *The Lord of the Rings: The Return of the King* (2004), Éowyn dresses as a soldier to be allowed to fight with the men.

A great deal of research on deception has practical implications. For instance, some occupations, such as lawyers and actors, require you to act differently than you might feel. Research has found that they are more successful at deception than the rest of the general population.[33] People who monitor themselves have been found to be more effective in hiding deception cues than are people who are not as self-aware.[34] Just think about the last time you told someone a "white lie." Were you a little nervous? How did you show that? Did the words come easily? Did you stammer or have to search for words? When you fib, you have to weigh the consequences of being caught versus the need to fib (telling a child that Santa or the Easter Bunny exists). You have to look and act sincere and believable, even though you're churning inside. If you can look composed and natural, then you are more likely to be a successful liar.[35] In fact, research tells us that people with a greater social skills repertoire and more communication competence will generally be more proficient, alert, confident, and expressive, and less fidgety, nervous and rigid, making them more skilled at deception than others.[36]

Now that you see the many roles that nonverbals can play in communication, let's turn from the functions to the categories of nonverbal communication.

WHAT ARE THE TYPES OF NONVERBAL COMMUNICATION?

Although many types of behaviors can communicate, available space and the focus of this book limit our discussion of nonverbal communication to body movement (kinesics), the use of space (proxemics), dress and appearance, and eye contact (occulesics). Vocalics, or paralanguage (the use of the voice), is covered in the chapter on delivery.

Body Movement/Kinesics

R. Birdwhistell first identified **kinesics,** or the study of our use of the body to communicate. It includes gestures, posture, facial expressions, and other body movements.[37] Five research themes have emerged in kinesics: the use of emblems, illustrators, regulators, affect displays, and adaptors. A brief look at all five themes will provide a good orientation to the complex ways that we can use our bodies to send messages.

Emblems. An **emblem** is a nonverbal behavior that has a distinct verbal referent or even a denotative definition, and it is often used to send a specific message to others. The verbal referent is typically one or two words of a short phrase. For example, the "thumbs-up" hand gesture is listed in many dictionaries and is defined as a *gesture of approval*. There is a high level of agreement about the meaning of an emblem within cultures, but not usually across cultures.[38]

Most emblems are created with the hands, but we can create them in other ways. For example, a shoulder shrug suggests "I don't know," or a wrinkled nose indicates that "something stinks." But the emblems we are most familiar with are usually hand gestures. Try to make the gesture that goes with each of the following meanings:

- "Sit down beside me."
- "Follow me."
- "I can't hear you."
- "Be quiet!"
- "Shame on you!"

- "OK."
- "I promise."
- "What time is it?"
- "Good bye!"

In addition to everyday conversation, emblems are used by divers while under water, by police officers directing traffic, by construction workers, and by catchers, pitchers, and managers during baseball games. Don't forget the very familiar and more or less universal signal some people use to indicate displeasure with other drivers! Keep in mind, though, that the emblems you know are not always shared. The hand gesture we use for "come here," with the hand palm up with the index finger extending in and out three or four times, has a very different meaning in Latin America. It means that you are romantically interested in the person, and is considered a solicitation. Emblems can replace the verbal or reinforce it.

Police officers use emblems when directing traffic.
© Andrew Barker, 2008, Shutterstock.

Illustrators. An **illustrator** is a gesture that is used *with* language to emphasize, stress, or repeat what is being said. It can be used to give directions, show the size or shape of something, and give clarification. Can you imagine trying to explain to a new parent how to "burp" a baby without using illustrators? Can you give directions to the campus library with your hands in your pockets? Sure you could, but the illustrators add much meaning and clarification to your directions or instructions; they help with that function of clarifying. In a study done several years ago, speakers were found to be more persuasive when they used illustrators than when they did not.[39] More recent research has even extended the importance of illustrators. Robert Krauss found that gestures do more than amplify or accent verbal communication. They also help people retrieve ideas and words, such as when you try to define a term with a spatial meaning such as underneath, next to, and above, which Krauss calls *lexical retrieval*. If not done to excess, "talking with your hands" can be a very good thing!

Regulators. A **regulator** is a turn-taking signal that helps control the flow, the pace, and turn-taking in conversations, and you learned about their coordinating role earlier. If a group of people are talking and trying to share meaning, they must take turns speaking, and taking turns requires cooperation among the communicators. To accomplish this cooperation, along with the content of the conversation, participants must also communicate about who will speak next and when that turn will begin. Regulators help us with this task.[40]

Weimann and Knapp and Argyle identified four categories of turn related signals in a typical conversation:[41]

A common communication regulator is a turn-requesting signal.
© 2008, JupiterImages.

1. *Turn requesting* signals: These are used by a nonspeaker to take the floor. Nonverbal regulators used to request a turn include rapid head nods, forward leaning posture, and increased eye contact with the speaker.
2. *Turn yielding* signals: The speaker uses these to give up the floor. Nonverbal regulators used to yield a turn include increased eye contact with a nonspeaker, leaning back from a forward posture, or a sudden end to gesturing used while speaking.
3. *Turn maintenance* signals: These are used by the speaker to keep the floor (i.e., continue speaking). Nonverbal signals used to keep the turn include speaking louder or faster (increasing volume or rate of speech), continuing to gesture, or avoiding eye contact with the person requesting the turn.
4. *Back channel* signals: Nonspeaker refuses a turn that has been offered by the speaker. Nonverbal signals used to refuse a turn include nodding the head and avoiding eye contact with the person exhibiting a turn-yielding signal.

Affect Displays. An **affect display** is a form of nonverbal behavior that expresses emotions. Although this behavior is most often associated with facial expressions, affect can also be expressed through posture and gestures. These behaviors cannot only express the type of emotion being experienced, but can also express the intensity of the emotion. A smile suggests that you are happy. A slumped-over posture and a scowl on your face can suggest that you are unhappy, while your clinched fists and tense muscles can communicate just *how* unhappy you might be.

Can you make judgments about the nature and intensity of the emotions expressed on these faces?
© 2008, JupiterImages.

The emotions communicated by your face and body can affect the way you are perceived by other people. People who smile spontaneously are often considered by others to be more likable and more approachable than people who do not smile or people who just pretend to smile.[42]

Adaptors. Adaptors are behaviors that can indicate our internal conditions or feelings to other people. We tend to use these behaviors when we become excited or anxious. Think about the kind of things that you do in communication situations when you feel nervous or excited. Do you scratch your head? Bite your nails? Play with your glasses? Rub your nose? You might not know, because most people are not aware of displaying these behaviors.

Adaptors are generally considered the least desirable type of nonverbal communication. Self-touching in this way could be a distraction to the audience, and it is often perceived as a sign of anxiety. One study found that deceivers bob their heads more often than people who tell the truth.[43] Cultural guidelines may prohibit these behaviors, too. Wriggling your nose or having a disgusted facial look to show that you're repulsed seems to have a universal meaning.[44]

What do these adaptors tell you about the internal feelings of the people in the photos?
© 2008, JupiterImages.

However, in some cultures, people are socialized to mask emotional cues, and in others they're taught to emphasize them. Latin Americans will usually greet friends and relatives more personally than do Americans. Everyone hugs, including the men. Men usually also greet woman with *besitos*, meaning they touch cheeks while making a kissing noise with their lips. Women also greet other women with *besitos*. These little kisses are purely friendly and have no romantic meaning. Maslow and colleagues[45] suggested that the anxiety displayed by adaptors can be interpreted by other communicators as a sign of deception; you are anxious because you are not being honest with the others and you fear being discovered!

Use of Space/Proxemics

The study of proxemics is typically divided into two applications: The use of personal space and how people claim and mark territory as their own. Most of us don't even think about the impact of space on our relationships, but research has shown that your use of space can influence shared meaning and impact your relationship. Knapp and Hall[46] found that our use of space can seriously affect our ability to achieve desired goals. Both applications can be used and managed by people to communicate fairly specific messages, and they can provide evidence to help us make judgments about the person using the space.

Personal Space. When you consider the idea of personal space, think of a small amount of portable space that you carry around with you all the time. You control who is and who is not permitted inside of that space. Permission to enter that space is granted based on the relationship you have with that person, the context of the encounter, the culture in which you live, and your own personal preferences and tolerances. For example, you would be likely to allow business and professional colleagues to be reasonably close to you; you would allow good friends to be very close to you; and you would allow romantic partners to be closer still, even to the point of touching. In addition, you might allow people that you don't know to be very close to you in the appropriate context, like a crowded elevator or a busy airport.

When someone enters your space without permission, you can interpret it as a lack of courtesy, or even as a threat. You will feel uncomfortable, so you can either wait for the trespasser to move out of your space, or you can move away until you feel comfortable again.

The range of personal space varies across cultures. The box describes spaces typical to the culture in the United States. If you visit the United Kingdom, you will notice that these spaces are slightly expanded; that is, the British prefer just a bit more distance between people. By contrast, many Eastern cultures, including Asia and the Middle East, prefer a smaller distance. When these cultures meet, people from the United States often feel "crowded" by people from Asian cultures, while people from Japan might think that Americans are "cold" or "stand-offish" because of the increased interpersonal distances. As you can see, there is no shortage of opportunities for misunderstanding! Burgoon suggests that we want to stay near others, but we also want to maintain some distance—think about the dilemma this causes![47] Try to be sensitive to cultural norms when you assign meaning to the use of personal space.

Personal Distances

Hall recognized characteristic distances maintained between people in the U.S. culture, depending on their perceived relationships.[48] The distance categories are *intimate, personal, social,* and *public.*

Type	Distance	Who Is Permitted/Context
Intimate Distance  © Andrejs Pidjass, 2008, Shutterstock.	touching to 18 inches	**Who:** Spouses and family members, boyfriends and girlfriends, and very close friends. **Context:** A date with your spouse.
Personal Distance  © 2008, JupiterImages.	18 inches to 4 feet	**Who:** Good friends and people you know well. **Context:** Having lunch with a good friend or co-worker.
Social Distance  © 2008, JupiterImages.	4 feet to 12 feet	**Who:** Business associates, teachers, and people you know but with whom you have a professional but less social relationship. **Context:** A business meeting, small group discussion, or an employment interview.
Public Distance  © 2008, JupiterImages.	12 feet and beyond	**Who:** A person you don't know; a stranger on the street. **Context:** Giving a presentation to a large group; walking downtown on a public sidewalk.

Relationships affect the way we use space. Based on the use of space, describe the relationships in these photos. Be specific about the nonverbal clues that indicate the relationship.
(Photo credits: *left, center,* © 2008, JupiterImages, *right,* © Factoria singular fotografia, 2008, Shutterstock.)

Convo example

Sometimes we allow our personal space to be violated.
© Racheal Grazias, 2008, Shutterstock.

Territoriality. We also have a tendency to claim space as our own. We have just looked at personal space, which is portable space that you carry around with you. Territory, by contrast, is not mobile; it stays in one place. You can think of territory as a kind of extension of you that is projected on to space or objects. Space that you occupy or control, and objects that belong to you or that you use regularly, are all important to you. If any person not authorized by you occupies that space or touches those objects, you feel violated and threatened. To help describe this kind of attachment to places and things, we turn to Altman, who classified territory into three categories: primary, secondary, and public.[49]

Primary territory is space or those items that you personally control. This includes personal items that only you would use, like your clothes and your toothbrush. It also includes the private spaces in your house like your bathroom and bedroom. Many people treat still other places as primary territory such as their car, their office at work, and even their refrigerator!

People mark their territory in many ways.
© 2008, JupiterImages.

Secondary territory is not your private property. That is, it is not owned by you, but it is typically associated with you. Examples of secondary territory include the desk you always use in class, the seat you always sit in at the office conference table, your favorite fishing spot at the lake, or your usual table at the library.

Public territory is available to anyone, so any space that you try to claim is only temporary. You might define your space on the beach by using markers such as blankets, beach chairs, or umbrellas. Or you might spread out your books and notes at the library to claim space on a work table. Our use of the territory lasts as long as we are using it, or as long as other people respect our markers.[50]

Most of us pay little attention to these claims of space, and we probably don't even realize that we do it. However, these claims come clearly to our attention when they are violated. It seems like there is almost nothing worse than walking into the classroom on the day of the big exam to find someone else in your seat! Sure, any seat will work just as well, but that is *your* seat where you feel most comfortable and confident. We tend to feel violated whenever any unauthorized person uses our space or touches our stuff!

Lyman and Scott identified three levels of **intrusion of territory**: violation, invasion, and contamination.[51] A *violation* happens when your space or your stuff is used without your permission, like when a neighbor borrows one of your tools without asking first. An *invasion* occurs when an unauthorized person enters the territory that you have claimed with markers. They might move your books and notes at the library (while you were looking for a book) and take over your space at the table, or they could cut in front of you in a check-out line at the grocery store. Finally, a *contamination* occurs when space that you claim is used without your authorization, but your evidence of the use is not the presence of the user but objects left behind. For example, you arrive at your office in the morning to find cups and fast food wrappers on your desk. There is nobody in your office, but you know somebody *was* there, and he or she was eating at your desk. Territory that you claim as your own should not be used by anyone without your permission. How you respond to territory depends very much on who invaded the territory and why it was invaded, which you'll see explained in expectancy violations theory, which follows later in this chapter.

Dress/Appearance

Your appearance, along with the way you dress, influences the way other people respond to you. In some situations, your appearance can be the *primary* factor that determines the response of others.[52] *Physical attractiveness*, as well as personal grooming and hygiene, weigh heavily on judgments that are made about you every day. If that's not enough pressure, along with protecting you from the environment and fulfilling cultural requirements for modesty, *clothing* is also a potent source of nonverbal information about you. Morris tells us that clothing sends continuous signals about us and who we think we are.[53] For example, watch the scene in the 1990 movie *Pretty Woman* when the character played by Julia Roberts first enters a "high-class" clothing store and is treated poorly by the staff. What about her appearance led to that treatment?

No one likes to have their territory violated.
© 2008, JupiterImages.

Among other qualities, clothing can suggest social and economic status, education, level of success, or trustworthiness and character. Morris suggests that clothing can be a cultural display and one that communicates something special about the wearer.[54] People have a tendency to express certain values central to their belief systems that indicate the kind of people they perceive themselves to be. Katz tells us that we hold and express particular attitudes to satisfy this need and that those attitudes reflect a positive view of ourselves.[55] Clothing and appearance are consistent with this concept. For example, if you consider yourself to be the "artistic" type, or a successful business person, or a talented athlete, your clothing choices will likely reflect that self image.

Gordon et al., suggests that clothing fulfills a number of symbolic functions:[56]

- Traditional and religious ceremonies often involve specific clothing.
- Self-beautification (real or imagined) is often reflected in clothing.
- Clothing expresses cultural values regarding sexual identity and practice.
- Clothes differentiate roles and levels of authority.
- Clothing is used in the acquisition and display of status.

Think about the way you dress and why you make those clothing choices. What are you trying to say? Are you trying to fit in? Are you trying to identify yourself with a particular group? Are you trying to show respect for an occasion or person?

Clothing is not the only aspect of appearance to consider. Think of the other personal choices people make with tattoos, body art, and personal grooming. What are the impacts of blue hair, black nail colors, Mohawks or dreadlocks, multiple piercing and colorful tattoos? You have the right to communicate about yourself in any way you want, but remember that if you go against cultural norms, you may be creating perceptual barriers that impede communication. Your appearance is a prime source of information that others use to make judgments about you. Try to use some care when making choices about how you should look in particular situations. You can always maintain your individuality, but you should also dress to show respect for the occasion and the people that you will be coming into contact with. If you have to give a presentation for a business group, for example, you can show your respect for the group by dressing in more formal attire. Wearing jeans with ripped out knees may say a lot about who you think you are, but wearing the suit for the business group also communicates who you think you are. You are someone who combines your own needs with a respect for the needs of other people!

How could her tattoos impact others' perceptions?
© Ronald Sumners, 2008, Shutterstock.

Eye Movement/Occulesics

In many Western cultures, including the United States, making **eye contact** with another person is considered a sign of sincerity, caring, honesty, and sometimes power or status.[57] Pearson found that men sometimes use eye contact to challenge others and to assert themselves.[58] Women tend to hold eye contact more than men, regardless of the sex of the person that they're interacting with.[59] Some Eastern cultures view eye contact with others as an impolite invasion of privacy and they especially disapprove of eye contact with a person of higher status. In another study, it was found that inner-city

African-American persuaders look continually at the listener, and African-American listeners tend to look away from the persuader most of the time. The opposite is true of middle-class Whites; as persuaders, they look only occasionally at the listener, and White listeners look continuously at the persuader. This could explain why the two groups could have incorrect inferences about the amount of interest the other has when they communicate.[60]

We consider the use of eye contact to be an essential tool for achieving communication goals. In U.S. culture, how does it make you feel when someone will not make eye contact with you? Do you trust this person? Do you suspect his or her motives?

Eye contact helps us communicate in at least four ways: It can open a channel of communication, demonstrate concern, gather feedback, and moderate anxiety.[61]

Open a Communication Channel. You can let others know that you would like to communicate with them by simply looking at them. A brief moment of eye contact can open a channel of communication and make other messages possible.

Demonstrate Concern. Engaging other people in eye contact during conversations shows a concern for them, as well as your commitment that they understand your message. In addition, eye contact can be used to communicate liking and attraction.

Gather Feedback. If you would like information about what other people are thinking, take a look at their eyes. You won't be able to read thoughts, but you can certainly find clues to indicate that they are listening, that they understand the message, and perhaps that they care about what you are saying. The old adage that speakers should look at the back wall of the room when giving a public speech is pretty bad advice; you will miss out on critical information about the frame of mind of audience members, as well as other feedback essential to achieving your goals.

Moderate Anxiety. When speakers get nervous or anxious during a public presentation, they have a tendency to avoid eye contact with the listeners by either looking at the floor, the back wall of the room, or at their notes. As they continue to stare at the floor, anxiety (fear of unknown outcomes) continues to build. Occasionally, but rarely, anxiety can build to the point at which it completely takes over, and the speaker freezes. You can avoid this scenario through *careful preparation* for the event, and by allowing the listeners to provide you with support. By *establishing eye contact* with members of your audience, you will see listeners smiling at you or expressing support with their posture, head nods, or other behaviors. Not looking at the audience or conversational partners removes your opportunity to get or give supportive feedback. When others notice your anxiety, they usually want to help you. Look at the audience, feel the support and try to relax, and then refocus on your communication goals.

By making eye contact with others, you can find clues about their level of understanding and interest. © Dmitriy Shironosov, 2008, Shutterstock.

HOW DOES THEORY DESCRIBE NONVERBAL BEHAVIOR'S IMPACT ON RELATIONSHIPS?

Have you ever played elevator games with strangers? You know, you enter an empty elevator and take the "power position" by the buttons. At the next floor, someone enters and either asks you to push the button for a floor or reaches in front of you to select a floor and then retreats to the opposite corner away from you. There's no further talk or eye contact. The next person who enters does the same thing, finding a corner. Everyone faces the doors, anticipates its opening, watching the numbers change as if by magic. If others enter, their volume drops to a hush, or they stop talking until they leave. Now, have you ever tried *this?* Get on an elevator and keep walking until you face the back wall. After all, that's how you entered, right? Go stand right next to the power person, real close. Keep talking real loud. Sit down on your backpack or luggage. What do you think will happen? How will others react to you?

One theory that attempts to explain the influence of nonverbal communication on meaning and relationships is **expectancy violations theory**. Judee Burgoon said that "nonverbal cues are an inherent and essential part of message creation (production) and interpretation (processing)."[62] Expectancy violations theory (EVT) suggests that we hold expectations about the nonverbal behavior of others. It asserts that when communicative norms are violated, the violation may be perceived either favorably or unfavorably, depending on the perception that the receiver has of the violator. Burgoon's early writing on EVT integrated Hall's ideas on personal space (which you read about earlier) as a core aspect of the theory.[63] EVT says that our *expectancies* are the thoughts and behaviors anticipated when we interact with another.

We have expectations of how others ought to think and behave. Levine says that these expectancies are a result of social norms, stereotypes, and your own personal idiosyncrasies, and these expectancies cause us to interact with others.[64] We have both preinteractional and interactional expectations. *Preinteractional* expectations are made up of the skills and knowledge you bring to an interaction; *interactional expectations* are your skills and knowledge that let you carry out the interaction.

Another basic idea of EVT is that we learn our expectations from our cultures: You've learned what kind of touching is appropriate with whom, how to greet a stranger, and where to stand in relationship with another, for example.

Finally, EVT says that we make predictions about others based on their nonverbal behavior. So how does this work? Let's say you're standing in line at the grocery store, and the person in front of you looks at what you're about to buy and then makes eye contact with you. At first, you might be uncomfortable, thinking that the person is judging you by the way she is eyeing your groceries. If she then gives you a warm smile and points to her big pile containing the same things, you might feel a bit more comfortable. You've made predictions based on nonverbal behavior: The person is not threatening or judging you negatively.

But EVT is about *violations* of our expectations. Burgoon says that when people deviate from expectations, that deviation is judged based on the other's ability to reward us. A reward could be something as simple as a smile, friendliness, or acknowledgment of competence. This potential to reward is called *communicator reward valence*, which is the interactants' ability to reward or punish and the positive and negative characteristics they have. Someone in power, like your professor for instance, may have more communicator reward valence than a stranger, because the professor has the power of grades and probably has more credibility for you. If someone violates our expectations, these deviations cause *arousal*, an increased attention to the deviation.[65] Cognitive arousal is mental awareness of the deviation; physical arousal involves physiological heightening. For instance, if a person stares at you, you might wonder why he's doing that (cognitive arousal) or you might start to sweat (physical arousal). Once arousal happens, threats occur. Your *threat threshold* is the tolerance you have for deviations; how threatened do you feel? Maybe you don't mind if another person stands too close; maybe you can't put up with someone staring at you. The size of your threat threshold is based on how you view the person who is deviating from your expectations; what is that other's communicator reward valence? Then you add in the *violation valence*, which consists of your positive or negative value placed towards the deviations from your expectations.

When someone violates one of your expectations (for instance, he touches you when you didn't expect it), you interpret the meaning of that violation and decide if you like it or not. If you don't like it, then the violation valence is negative; if the surprise was pleasant (even though you didn't expect it), then the violation valence is positive. The theory predicts that if a violation is ambiguous, then the communicator reward valence will influence how you interpret and evaluate the violation. If the person is someone you like, then you'll positively evaluate his violation; if you don't like him, then you'll negatively evaluate his violation. Take a simple example of how someone is dressed. On an interview, there are certain expectations of how you should look. If you go in wearing jeans and a t-shirt and the company wants its workers to wear suits,

On an interview, you want to be positively evaluated.
© iofoto, 2008, Shutterstock.

then you've violated expectancies. It's pretty likely that you don't have any power here, or any way to reward the company for hiring you. Thus, the interviewer will evaluate you negatively, feeling aroused that you didn't understand such a basic concept like appropriate attire. However, what if you are a highly sought-after, uniquely imaginative individual that the company has been pursuing? Your violation of the dress code might be seen positively; you're bold and creative, just like they thought. EVT is an interesting theory that focuses on what we expect nonverbally in conversations, as well as suggesting what happens when our expectations aren't met. It's very practical in applications across many contexts.

WHAT ARE THE KEY POINTS TO REMEMBER ABOUT NONVERBAL COMMUNICATION?

Nonverbal communication is a complex combination of behaviors that form a source of information used by other people to make sense of messages that you send. Even though much of your nonverbal behavior is spontaneous and unconscious, you should realize that it contributes a significant percentage of the meaning that people attribute to your messages. As such, you should try as hard as you can to be a good self-monitor and pay close attention to your nonverbal behaviors. However, nonverbal behavior is also a source of information for you. It can help you to more accurately interpret the communication of others, so pay attention!

Be careful to not overgeneralize the meanings of particular nonverbal cues. The specific meaning of any nonverbal behavior is typically dependent on multiple factors, including (but not limited to) culture, the relationship between the people communicating, the specific communication context, and individual characteristics of the participants. You wouldn't want others to make stereotypical assumptions about your behavior, so make sure that you don't make those same assumptions about the behavior of others. Gather as much information as possible before reaching conclusions. Sometimes a touch is just a touch!

SUMMARY

Verbal and nonverbal communication are powerful, critically important elements in the creation of shared meaning, because they have the ability to clarify your ideas to others or to confuse them. It's not always easy to use language or nonverbal behavior correctly, because both are arbitrary and ambiguous. The relationship that words or movements have with ideas is not based on a concrete characteristic; instead, you are relying on the ability of the audience to associate your symbols with their cognitions (beliefs, attitudes, and values). You've been exposed to some theoretical explanations of how these attempts to create meaning work in our lives. We interpret language and nonverbal communication because of our particular culture, which provides a frame of reference on how to assign meaning. In order to be a competent communicator, you need to remain aware that your words aren't always understood as you mean them to be and that your nonverbal behavior can supplement or contradict those words. The next chapters will let you put those meanings into action!

ENDNOTES

1. Language and Culture, Introduction, http://anthro.palomar.edu/language/language_1.htm.

2. "Internet World Users by Language," Internet World Stats, http://www.internetworldstats.com/stats7.htm (accessed Sept. 22, 2007).

3. In 1997, the Science Citation Index reported that 95 percent of its articles were written in English, even though only half of them came from authors in English-speaking countries. David Graddol, "The Future of English?" (digital edition), http://www.britishcouncil.org/de/learning-elt-future.pdf (accessed Sep. 22, 2007).

4. G. H. Mead, *Mind, Self and Society; From the Standpoint of a Social Behaviorist* (Chicago: University of Chicago Press, 1934).

5. "Top Television Buzzwords of 2007," The Global Language Monitor. http://www.languagemonitor.com/wst_pagell.html (accessed Sept. 22, 2007).

6. E. Natalle, with J. L. Flippen, "Urban Music: Gendered Language in Rapping," in Philip Backlund and M. R. Williams (ed.) *Readings in Gender Communication* (Belmont, CA: Wadsworth-Thompson, 2004), 140–149.

7. "Remarks by the President after Two Planes Crashed into World Trade Center," http://www.whitehouse.gov/news/releases/2001/09/20010911.html (accessed Sept. 22, 2007).

8. "Remarks by the President Upon Arrival at Barksdale Air Force Base," http://www.whitehouse.gov/news/releases/2001/09/20010911-1.html (accessed Sept. 22, 2007).

9. "Statement by the President in His Address to the Nation," http://www.whitehouse.gov/news/releases/2001/09/20010911-16.html (accessed Sept. 22, 2007).

10. D. Berlo, *The Process of Communication* (New York, Holt, Rinehart and Winston Inc., 1960).

11. "Adopt-a Confusion" Perspectives Press, http://www.perspectivespress.com/pjadopta.html (accessed Sept. 22, 2007).

12. Cronen, Pearce, and Snavely 1979. Vernon E. Cronen, W. Barnett Pearce, and Lonna Snavely (1979). "A Theory of Rule Structure and Forms of Episodes, and a Study of Unwanted Repetitive Patterns (URPs)," pp.225–240 in Dan Nimmo, ed. Communication Yearbook III. Edison, NJ: Transaction Books.

13. C. K. Ogden and I. A. Richards, *The Meaning of Meaning*, 8th ed. (New York, Harcourt, Brace & World, 1923), 9–12.

14. S. Trenholm, *Thinking through Communication* (Boston: Allyn and Bacon, 2000), 87.

15. L. A. M. Perry and D. Ballard-Reisch, "There's a Rainbow in the Closet," in Philip Backlund and M. R. Williams (ed.), *Readings in Gender Communication* (Belmont, CA: Wadsworth-Thompson, 2004), 17–34.

16. Bipolar.com http://www.bipolar.com/ (accessed May 1, 2008).

17. C. Kramarae, *Women and Men Speaking: Frameworks for Analysis* (Rowley, MA: Newbury House, 1981), 1.

18. Ibid.

19. J. T. Wood. *Communication in Our Lives*, 4th ed. (Belmont, CA: Thompson Wadsworth, 2006), 137.

20. Urban dictionary http://www.urbandictionary.com/ (accessed Sept. 12, 2007).

21. Lake Superior State University, "List of Banished Words," http://stuft.vox.com/library/post/lakesuperior-state-university-2007-list-of-banished-words.html (accessed Sept. 12, 2007).

22. M. Orbe and C. Bruess, *Contemporary Issues in Interpersonal Communication* (Los Angeles: Roxbury, 2005).

23. D. O'Hair, G. Friedrich, and L. Dixon, *Strategic Communication in Business and the Professions* (Boston: Houghton Mifflin, 2005).

24. K. Adams and G. Galanes, *Communicating in Groups: Applications and Skills* (Boston: McGraw-Hill, 2006).

25. R. Adler, L. Rosenfeld, and R. Proctor, *Interplay: The Process of Interpersonal Communication* (New York: Oxford University Press, 2004).

26. J. Burgoon and A. Bacue, "Nonverbal Communication Skills," in J. Greene and B. Burleson (eds.), *Handbook of Communication and Social Interaction Skills* (Mahwah, NJ: Lawrence Erlbaum, 2003).

27. F. Manusov, "Perceiving Nonverbal Messages: Effects of Immidiacy and Encoded Intent on Receiver Judgements," *Western Journal of Speech Communication* 55 (Summer 1991), 235–253. Also M. Knapp and Hall, *Nonverbal Communication in Human Interaction*, 6th ed. (2005).

28. R. L. Birdwhistell, "Background to Kinesics." *Etc.* 13, (1955), 10–18.

29. A. Mehrabian and S. Ferris, "Inference of Attitudes from Nonverbal Communication in Two Channels," *Journal of Consulting Psychology* 31 (1967), 248–252.

30. J. Shapiro, "Responsivity to Facial and Linguistic Cues," *Journal of Communication*, 18 (1968), 11–17. Also L. Vande Creek and J. Watkins, "Responses to incongruent verbal and nonverbal emotional cues," *Journal of Communication*, 22 (1972), 311–316; and D. Solomon and F. Ali, "Influence of Verbal Content and Intonation on Meaning Attributions of First-and-Second-Language Speakers," *Journal of Social Psychology*, 95 (1975), 3–8.

31. "The Kennedy-Nixon Presidential Debates, 1960," The Museum of Broadcast Communications, http://www.museum.tv/archives/etv/k/htmlk/kennedy-nixon/kennedy-nixon.htm (accessed May 1, 2008).

32. K. Drummond and R. Hopper, "Acknowledgment Tokens in Series," *Communication Reports* 6, (1993), 47–53.

33. R. Riggio and H. Freeman,"Individual Differences and Cues to Deception," *Journal of Personality and Social Psyhchology* 45 (1983), 899–915.

34. J. Burgoon, D. Buller, L. Guerrero, and C. Feldman, "Interpersonal Deception: VI, Effects on Preinteractinal and International Factors on Deceiver and Observer Perceptions of Deception Success," *Communication Studies*, 45 (1994), 263–280.

35. A. Vrij, K. Edward, K. Roberts, and R. Bull, (2002). Detecting deceit via analysis of verbal and nonverbal behavior. *Journal of Nonverbal Behavior* 24, 239–263.

36. Burgoon et al.

37. R. Birdwhistell, *Kinesics and Context* (Philadelphia: University of Pennsylvania Press, 1970).

38. P. Ekman, "Movements with Precise Meanings," *Journal of Communication* 26 (1976), 14–26.

39. A. Mehrabian and M. Williams, "Nonverbal Concomitants of Perceived and Intended Persuasiveness," *Journal of Personality and Social Psychology* 13 (1969), 37–58.

40. G. Savage (1978). Endings and beginnings: Turn taking and the small group in Wall, V. (ed.), Small Group Communication: Selected Readings (Columbus, OH: Collegiate).

41. J. Weimann and M. Knapp, "Turn Taking and Conversations," *Journal of Communication* 25 (1975), 75–92. Also M. Argyle, *Bodily Communication* (New York: International Universities Press, 1975).

42. G. Gladstone and G. Parker, "When You're Smiling, Does the Whole World Smile for You?" *Australasian Psychiatry* 10 (2002), 144–146.

43. W. Donaghy and B. F. Dooley, "Head Movement, Gender, and Deceptive Communication," *Communication Reports* 7 (1994), 67–75.

44. J. Martin and T. Nakayama, *Intercultural Communication in Contexts* (New York: McGraw Hill, 2000).

45. C. Maslow, K. Yoselson, and H. London, "Persuasiveness of Confidence Expressed via Language and Body Language," *British Journal of Social and Clinical Psychology*, 10 (1971), 234–240.

46. Knapp and Hall, 2005.

47. J. Burgoon, "A Communication Model of Personal Space Violations: Explication and an Initial Test," *Human Communication Research*, 4 (1978), 129–142. Also J. Burgoon, "Nonverbal Signals," in M. Knapp and G. Miller (eds.), *Handbook of Interpersonal Communication* (Thousand Oaks, CA: Sage, 1994); and J. Burgoon, "Spatial Relationships in Small Groups," in R. Cathcart, L. Samovar, and L. Heaman, *Small Group Communication: Theory and Practice* (Madison, WI: Brown, 1996).

48. E. T. Hall, *The Silent Language* (Garden City, NY: Doubleday, 1959); and E. T. Hall, "A System for the Notation of Proxemic Behavior," *American Anthropologist*, 65 (1963), 1003–1026.

49. I. Altman, *The Environment and Social Behavior* (Monterey, CA: Brooks Cole, 1975).

50. L. Malandro, L. Barker, and D. Barker, *Nonverbal Communication* (New York: Random House, 1989).

51. S. Lyman and M. Scott, "Territoriality: A Neglected Sociological Dimension," *Social Problems* 15 (1967), 236–249.

52. M. Knapp, *Essentials of Nonverbal Communication* (New York: Holt, Rinehart & Winston, 1992).

53. D. Morris, *Manwatching: A Field Guide to Human Behavior* (New York: Harry N. Abrams, 1977).

54. Ibid.

55. D. Katz, "The Functional Approach to the Study of Attitudes," *Public Opinion Quarterly* 24 (1960), 163–204.

56. W. Gordon, C. Teagler, and D. Infante, "Women's Clothing as Predictors of Dress at Work, Job Satisfaction, and Career Advancement," *Southern States Speech Communication Journal* 47 (1982), 422–434.

57. P. Andersen, *Nonverbal Communication: Forms and Functions* (Mountain View, CA: Mayfield, 1999). Also D. Leathers, *Successful Nonverbal Communication: Principles and Applications*, 3rd ed. (Boston: Allyn and Bacon, 1997).

58. J. Pearson, *Gender and Communication* (Dubuque, IA: William C. Brown, 1985).

59. J. Wood, *Gendered Lives: Communication, Gender, and Culture*, 5th ed. (Belmont, CA: Wadsworth, 2002), 141.

60. S. Rosenberg, S. Kahn, and T. Tran, "Creating a Political Image: Shaping Appearance and Manipulating the Vote," *Political Behavior* 13 (1991), 347.

61. S. Wallace, D. Yoder, L. Hugenberg, and C. Horvath, *Creating Competent Communication: Interviewing.* (Dubuque, IA: Kendall/Hunt Publishing, 2006).

62. Burgoon, 1994.

63. Burgoon, 1978.

64. T. R. Levine, L. Anders, J. Banas, K. Baum, K. Endo, A. Hu, and C. Wong, "Norms, Expectations, and Deception: A Norm Violation Model of Veracity Judgments," *Communication Monographs* 67 (2000), 123–137.

65. Burgoon, 1978. P. 133

REFERENCES

D. Berlo (1960). *The Process of Communication.* New York, Holt, Rinehart and Winston Inc.

S. Campo, K. A. Cameron, D. Brossard, and M. Frazer (2004) "Social norms and expectancy violations theories: Assessing the effectiveness of health communication campaigns." Communication Monographs 71, 448–470

P. Ekman and W. Friesen (1975). *Unmasking the face.* Englewood Cliffs, NJ: Prentice-Hall.

P. Ekman and W. Friesen (1969). The repertoire of nonverbal behavior: Categories, origins, usage, and coding. *Semiotica,* 1, 49–98.

R. Gass and J. Seiter (2003). *Persuasion, social influence, and compliance gaining.* Boston: Allyn & Bacon.

D. Graddol (2000). The Future of English? (digital edition). http://www.britishcouncil.org/de/learning-elt-future.pdf

J. Hornick (1992). Tactile stimulation and consumer response. *Journal of consumer research, 19,* 449–458.

L. Howells and S. Becker (1962). Seating arrangement as leadership emergence. *Journal of abnormal and social psychology, 64,* 148–150.

D. Kaufman and J. Mahoney (1999). The effect of waitress touch on alcohol consumption in dyads. *Journal of social psychology, 139,* 261–267.

C. Kramarae (1981), Women and men speaking: Frameworks for analysis. Rowley, MA: Newbury house.

R. M. Krauss and U. Hadar (1999). The role of speech-related arm/hand gestures in word retrieval. In, R. Campbell & L. Messing (Eds.), Gesture, speech, and sign (pp. 93–116). Oxford: Oxford University Press.

E. Morsella and R. M. Krauss (in press). The role of gestures in spatial working memory and speech. American Journal of Psychology. http://www.columbia.edu/cu/psychology/commlab/publications.html (retrieved Sept. 28, 2007)

G. H. Mead (1934). *Mind, self and society; From the standpoint of a social behaviorist.* Chicago: University of Chicago press.

E. Natalle and J. Flippen (2004). Urban Music: Gendered language in Rapping. In Backlund, P., and Williams, M. (ed) *Readings in Gender Communication.* Belmont, CA: Wadsworth-Thompson. 140–149.

C. K. Ogden and I. A. Richards (1923). *The Meaning of Meaning.* New York, Harcourt, Brace & World, Inc., 9–12.

L. Perry and D. Ballard-Reisch (2004). There's a Rainbow in the closet. In Backlund, P., & Williams, M. (ed.). *Readings in Gender Communication*, Belmont, CA: Wadsworth-Thompson, 2004, 17–34.

S. Rosenberg, S. Kahn, and T. Tran (1991). "Creating a political image: Shaping appearance and manipulating the vote." Political Behavior 13, 345–367 P. 347

G. Savage (1978). Endings and beginnings: Turn taking and the small group. In Wall, V. (ed). *Small group communication: Selected readings*. Columbus: Collegiate.

F. Strodtbeck and L. Hook (1961). The social dimensions of a twelve man jury table. *Sociometry, 24,* 297–415.

G. Trager (1958). Paralanguage: A first approximation. *Studies in linguistics, 13,* 1–12.

S. Trenholm (2000). *Thinking through Communication.* Boston: Allyn and Bacon.

J. Wood (2006). *Communication in Our Lives, Fourth Ed.* Belmont, CA: Thompson Wadsworth, 2006.

VERBAL AND NONVERBAL COMMUNICATION

Was anyone else confused by the Icelandic proverb at the beginning of this chapter? "Better wise language than uncombed hair." I clearly do not relate to Icelandic wisdom. Were they trying to say: "You should speak well rather than worry about looking good?"

One of the themes of this chapter is **sharing**. In the process of communication we try to share meaning. Our world is getting more complicated all the time. The authors of this chapter state there are over 5,000 languages on the planet. That means there are at least 5,000 ways to say "boy," "girl," and "Yes, we should live in peace." Some cultures have several words for the one thing. The Aleuts (Eskimos) reportedly have several words for snow. (I do not speak Aleut.) There is crunchy snow, wet snow, etc., etc. When you live in a snow-covered land, you create different words for different kinds of snow. We create new words all the time to express new ideas and define new things. Do you think your grandparents googled answers? Or did they have to look up information in a book? (Gasp!)

Then we add the channel of nonverbal communication to the verbal channel, and things get even more complex. Have you ever seen someone who looks like they are lying? A child tells a parent, "I didn't take the last cookie." But they are looking away, avoiding eye contact, searching for the right words. They have *guilty* written all over their face. Adults exhibit many of the same characteristics when we want to avoid the truth. Yet we are amazingly good at deciphering combinations of verbal and nonverbal messages that we see simultaneously. Next, we want to consider the context for these messages in different relationships.

3

INTERPERSONAL COMMUNICATION

Whether texting, talking, or tweeting, the most common form of communication you will do in your life is **interpersonal communication.**[1] Up to this point you have learned all about the theory of communication. You have defined it, seen models of it, and dissected it into verbal, nonverbal, and listening. You have even explored the inner workings of perception. Now it's time to look at the ways we actually use communication.

This course was designed to give you insight (and practice) into the three major ways people use communication: giving speeches (formal or informal), working in small groups (like campus clubs and committees), and the thing you will do most in your life, interpersonal communication (or talking with others one-on-one). Yes, you may be asked to speak in front of a group some day or present a report for your job. Yes, committees are unavoidable and it's unlikely that you will always be working with people you agree with or like. The reality is that you will deal with the day-to-day, face-to-face, and let us not forget the ever-popular electronic versions, referred to as computer-mediated communication (CMC) within the communication field, with individuals in all aspects of your life. The fact is that we use interpersonal communication to connect with others and keep those connections going through the good times and the bad. Sometimes we stay connected for decades, other times we need to find ways to "disconnect." There's an old 1960s song titled "Breakin' Up Is

©2013 by Monkey Business Images, Shutterstock, Inc.

Hard to Do." Maybe we can make connecting—or disconnecting—a little easier for you, or at least make it so you don't feel so alone in your misery.

So, what is interpersonal communication? Let's spend some time focusing on how we do what we do, why we do it, and why it sometimes goes terribly wrong. In this chapter we look at *interpersonal communication* in terms of four basic questions:

1. What is interpersonal communication?
2. How do needs and attraction impact interpersonal communication?
3. How do we accomplish interpersonal communication?
4. How do we keep interpersonal communication going (or get out of it, if desired)?

WHAT IS INTERPERSONAL COMMUNICATION?

There are two basic ways to define interpersonal communication. The simplest way is by counting the number of people. If there is only one person we call it *intrapersonal communication*. Once you add a second person it becomes *interpersonal communication*. Most scholars agree that the addition of a third person shifts things into *small-group communication*.

But merely counting heads misses many of the complexities of defining interpersonal communication. We are all aware of the vast difference in interactions between ordering food at McDonalds and a long, heart-to-heart talk with a close friend. So there must be more to defining interpersonal communication than just numbers. One way to distinguish these differences is to add the notion of **impersonal communication** to our discussion. Think about all the one-on-one interactions you have in a day and try to rank them on the following continuum.

Impersonal Communication		**Interpersonal Communication**
Role-based		Individualized
General		Specific
Highly scripted		Unique
I-It	I-You	I-Thou

Figure 3.1
Impersonal Communication

Think of the left side of the continuum as those interactions that are very general, usually based on a role being played or a task being accomplished. This would easily cover your McDonalds encounter. You are the customer, and they are the employee. Your desire is to order your food and have it served quickly and accurately. There is an expected script ("Do you want fries with that?") for both roles, and if the interaction goes well, all parties move on to the next task (you eat the food, and they serve the next customer) with little thought.

Think of the right side of the continuum as those interactions that are very specific and individualized. These are the people who know you best. They know your moods, your body language; they even know your past. They are probably your BFFs, your family members, and possibly that "one true love." Each encounter with these people is unique. Sometimes you provide support for one another and other times you simply enjoy each other's company. The scripts are loosely defined (although one classic indication of these close encounters is the "secret language" you share: the code words, nicknames, and phrases that only your best friends or family members understand).

Of course, any continuum leaves room in the middle. In this case, you have many acquaintances and friends that fall somewhere in between the ends of the continuum. The philosopher Martin Buber[2] had language to describe these differences. He referred to the range in terms of: "I–It," "I–You," and "I–Thou." I–It matches the Impersonal end of the continuum, and the I–Thou aligns with the Interpersonal end. What Buber's language adds is a category for the middle range of the Impersonal–Interpersonal continuum. The I–You refers to those acquaintances that go beyond the role-based, superficial level, but do not reach the fully personal level of the I–Thou.

Social Penetration Theory[3] would have us trade in the continuum for nesting circles. In this case, the closest relationships are shown in the innermost circle. Others are represented by the varying degrees of closeness for each outer circle. For this theory, issues of the encounter's **depth** and **breadth** are key factors. For those persons on the outer rim, a wide range of topics might be discussed, but the depth to which they go is minimal. Chatting about the weather is a classic example. For the innermost circle, those dearest to you, the range of topics may have narrowed over time, but the depth to which you will reveal your thoughts and feelings goes deep. That classic heart-to-heart talk mentioned above clearly fits this category.

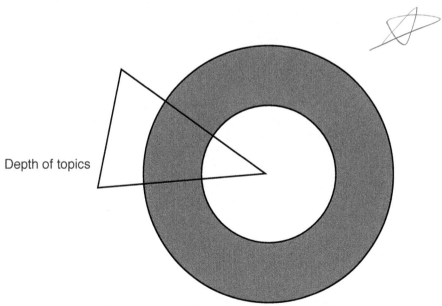

Figure 3.2
Social Penetration Theory Image

©2013 by Heider Almeida,
Shutterstock, Inc.

Defining **relational communication** is the final aspect needed for our understanding of interpersonal communication. It is important to note that when we use the term *relationship* or *relational* in this text, we are not only talking about the romantic, makes-you-feel-all-tingly-inside thing. Relational communication refers to any type of relationship: work, family, school, the guy who delivers your pizza at 2 a.m., etc.

In fact, the basis of defining relational communication stems from the notion that all messages include two levels of meaning: the **content-level** and the **relational-level**.[4] The content level meaning of any message is the "what" aspect of the message: What does the message mean? However, to figure out what a message means, you must also look at the relational level of the message, the "context" aspect. This aspect includes: who said it, to whom they said it, why they said it, where and when they said it, and how they said it.

If I go to the local bar and order a screwdriver, I will be surprised if the server brings me a Sears Craftsman tool. On the other hand, if the electrician asks you for a screwdriver while he is working on your wiring and you bring him a vodka and orange juice, he may or may not be appreciative, but certainly he will be surprised. The content-level of the word *screwdriver* in and of itself cannot provide enough information for anyone to attribute correct meaning. We are constantly deciphering the content-level of any message based on the relational-level or message context, including the sender, the receiver, the setting, etc.

Interpersonal communication occurs in specific relational contexts. As two individuals work to share their ideas through verbal and nonverbal messages, they are, in turn, developing relationships. In fact, you know well that some of those impersonal, role-based encounters you have had in your life have continued long enough to develop into acquaintances that become good friends, that quite possibly end up as best buddies. As the relational level of a message develops, so does the relationship. That is how you develop those secret code words, nicknames, and phrases. Spoken outside that particular relational context, their meanings are changed.

For the purposes of this book, *interpersonal communication* will be defined as interactions between two people that vary in depth, breath, and quality to create a variety of relational encounters.

HOW DO NEEDS AND ATTRACTION IMPACT INTERPERSONAL COMMUNICATION?

Both individual human needs and issues of attraction between people have great impact on the ways we communicate interpersonally. They motivate our behavior and help define our relationships.

Needs

Most communication scholars look to research on human needs to begin understanding why we ever started communicating with others. Beyond its basic functional purposes, like "Hey, Mac, a sabertooth tiger is about to eat you," human interactions have contributed to deeper and ever-more-important connections between people over the ages. But why did these connections come about? What did we need interpersonal communication for? Abraham Maslow,[5] the best-known scholar on the subject of needs, created an inverted pyramid to demonstrate what he called a *hierarchy of needs*. According to Maslow, we have basic needs of air, food, water, shelter, and sex. (Yes, sex is a basic need directly connected to our survival; our need to procreate; turns out it is just one of our basic biological needs playing itself out on a college campus). So, back to Maslow ... (I know it is hard to focus on this reading when — *lol* we were just talking about sex, but do your best.) Maslow believed that once you covered all the basics on the bottom of the pyramid, you now had energy to move on to other things, like "belonging."

Alfred Schutz,[6] another well-known scholar on the topic of needs laid out a simple (but much less popular) set of reasons why we need human relationships. Much like Maslow's second tier, Schulz believed that people have three basic needs with regard to interpersonal interactions: inclusion, affection, and control.

Everyone has a desire for *inclusion*, to be a part of something. Think back to your very first moments on this campus. I don't mean your campus visits when you were still in high school. Fast-forward to the point where your parents and friends drove away and left you here alone. Do you remember anything about how that moment felt? What did you do first? Where did you go? Did you immediately turn to your phone as a way to connect virtually with another person? Even "virtual inclusion" counts. With whom did you eat your first meal in convo? Was it your new roommate? Was it someone from across the hall? Some of you may have come to AU with a few friends from high school. Maybe you were even rooming with one of them. In that case, you were not as alone as you might have been. Some of you were a part of some campus organizations like the football team or the band. In that case, you probably came to campus early and you had a built-in network of upper-class students to instantly connect with. The fact is that experts know how vulnerable people feel in those moments when they are yanked away from the places where they belong and dropped into a new, unfamiliar environment. Feeling "a part of" or included somewhere is a vital human need. The first day of college is one of those rare times when you may get a glimpse of just how important that need is. To help you find new friends, campus activity boards across the nation work diligently to plan activities those first few days of college. Some of you may have been connected with your new roommate on Facebook or by email before you ever came to campus. That is not a coincidence. That is careful planning on the part of student life administrators. They want you to feel included as soon as possible, and they will go to extreme measures to ensure that it happens. They are aware of the research showing that student satisfaction with their college experience depends largely on the satisfaction students have with their campus relationships.

That first day you may have been a tad desperate. You may have gone to convo with anyone who would make eye contact and say a few words. Compared to that first meal, do you still eat with the same people? Do you still sit in the same place in convo? If you were one of the lucky ones (the band members and football players), you were guided and mentored by the older students in that group, so you may well still be doing what you did with the people you did it with. But, if you were on your own trying to navigate this new territory, there is a good chance you are no longer hanging out with that person you first befriended, and your seat choice (while always the same now) may have changed drastically. Schultz would say that is due to our second primary need: *affection*. At first you just sought out a warm body, but now that you have been here a while you can be more particular. You probably find yourself continuing to hang around the people who are nice to you.

Schutz would add one more piece to the puzzle. He would say that your journey to make friends here at AU is driven by your need for *control*. Everyone desires some level of predictability in their life. You want to know that the people you sit with in convo day after day will treat you the same basic way each day. You want to know that your circle of friends will act a certain way or think a certain way. It isn't controlling in a negative sense, but more a way to create a world that is familiar to you and comfortable. In fact, later in this chapter as we discuss conflict, you may notice that a common source of relational turbulence comes from people changing their behavior or attitudes. We humans hate change, especially change that disturbs the balance of our relationships.

Along with our individual needs, there are factors of attraction influencing our interpersonal encounters.

Attraction

People become attracted to a variety of things. We might be attracted to the color of an individual's eyes. Someone might be drawn to a person who matches their intellect and wit, or the fact that another human being on the planet actually owns the same rare album from an obscure musical group. Sometimes the hotty sitting next to you in class might be attractive to you. The reasons for attractions break into three categories: physical attraction, situational attraction, and similar interests.

©2013 by Diego Cervo, Shutterstock, Inc.

Physical Attraction: If you think back to Maslow and his hierarchy, you will remember that sex was one of the basic needs all humans' experience. Is it any wonder that physical attraction is usually the primary factor in early relationships? Each culture establishes its own parameters of beauty, and those messages are sent to children at an early age through the media, family messages, their community, and even the toys they play with. The Barbie doll has been a "blond bombshell" since her origination in 1961, and no matter how many brown-haired friends she has in her doll network, children learn from a young age that blonds do have more fun … and more boyfriends. Based on societal notions of beauty, we tune into others around us and seek out those who possess the most beauty traits. Physical fitness levels, body shape and size, hair and eye color, as well as issues of grooming and cleanliness, factor into the purely physical attraction between individuals.

Situational Attraction: Some friendships stem from the situational convenience of proximity. If you find yourself spending time with the people you work with, have classes with, or share hobbies with, you may not realize how much of the friendship is based on the mere fact that you are around that person much of the day. In fact, only time will tell if the friends you make based on physical proximity and frequent encounters will last beyond the convenience of those current situations. Once you find yourself in different classes, a new dorm floor, or away from an old hobby, you will figure out which people you truly want to seek out (as a friendship of choice) and which people you lose interest in once the circumstances that brought you together have passed.

©2013 by Jamie Roach, Shutterstock, Inc.

Similar Interests: Initially the physical features are the predominant factor in making connections, but even as children we learned that beauty is skin deep. While much of life's pleasures may be found in surface-level attraction, for most people there needs to be something of substance wrapped up in that beautiful skin. You may just as easily be drawn to individuals based on common hobbies and interests. People who work in theatre tend to be drawn to other theatrical types. Athletes share the common bond of teamwork and that camaraderie can build life-long friendships.

HOW DO WE ACCOMPLISH INTERPERSONAL COMMUNICATION?

There are many types of relationships: family, friends, work, romantic. Some you are born into, some you are placed into, and others you seek out. Some are face-to-face and others are online. We make sense of our relationships in the form of a story, "The story of us," as the song lyrics put it. As with any good story, all of our relationships have beginnings, middles, and ends. While there is always a "Once upon a time," we don't all get to the "happily ever after."

Scholars have identified common stages that most relationships go through as they develop and solidify. Many of these stages have been articulated in the shape of models that map out relationship progression. No one model is able to accommodate all the intricacies of relationship development and decline, but a few have become recognizable standards in the communication field.

One of the earliest attempts to illustrate relationship stages was Levinger's[7] simplistic ABCDE model. While missing many significant details, it did capture the essence of relationship stages clearly and succinctly. Others, most notably Knapp,[8] have built more complex models featuring the types of communication one displays during the stages of relational change. Rawlins[9] contributed by developing a model featuring stages that are unique to friendships.

Models are not perfect and no one model can capture all the details of human relations. In an effort to be clear, each model leaves many basic assumptions unstated. One of those assumptions is that no one is obligated to stay on the path. People move at their own speed, jump off the track at varying times, and often never reach stages of relationship disintegration. Only death is inevitable. Beyond that, each individual will move through his or her relationships in unique ways. Flawed as they are, models do give us language and ideas to help frame our perceptions of relationships. They categorize and compartmentalize relationship movement in useful ways.

	Levinger	Knapp & Vangelisti	Rawlins
Beginnings	Acquaintance	Initiating	Role-limited
		Experimenting	Friendly relations
	Build-up	Intensifying	Moving toward friendships
		Integrating	Nascent friendships
Middles	Continuation	Bonding	Stabilized friendships
		Differentiating	Waning friendships
	Deterioration	Circumscribing	
		Avoiding	
		Stagnating	
Ends	Endings	Terminating	

Figure 3.3
Models of Relationships

Each model describes the beginning differently, but all try to capture the spirit of those first moments, the early days when relationships are hardly even called "relationships." In that first encounter, far more is unknown than known. With every new encounter lies the potential for a sustaining relationship. The reality is that a very small percentage, maybe as few as 1 percent, of our initial interactions goes much beyond the initial engagement. We meet new people every day, at the doctor's office, holding a door for us, in the grocery store checkout line. Have you ever stopped to think about all the potential relationships you dismiss with little thought? You might chat about the weather, an upcoming holiday, or the length of the line you are standing in, but few encounters go beyond that superficial level of interactions. In any encounter, we humans have an intense need to know and understand as much as we can. We do not handle uncertainty well. It makes us nervous, causes confusion, and throws off our equilibrium. **Uncertainty reduction theory**[10] tells us that we will do whatever we can to reduce uncertainty and discover where we are and with whom we are talking. In fact, many people gravitate toward the places and people they know, in part to avoid uncertainty. Others are more comfortable with new people and new situations. Reducing that uncertainty helps us make sense of the encounter and better predict what comes next.

The models show ways in which we can move beyond initial movements to learn more about the people we are around. The world of social media provides new ways to gather basic information about a person and interact.[11] Through Facebook we can see what music they like, what school they attend, and quite literally what they "Like." In early conversations we can experiment or "try on" a relationship, by asking questions about background, activities, and interests. Each new piece of information allows us to decide whether to proceed with the relationship or abandon the cause.

One of the best ways to increase the comfort level of both people is through self-disclosure. Relationships develop almost exclusively through the sharing of ideas, opinions, and details of our lives. We call this level of personal sharing *self-disclosure*. Once the interaction moves beyond surface-level talk about weather, hometowns, and "what's your major?" people gradually share more personal information. The more you share of yourself with another person, the more the relationship has the potential to grow. Most people have an expectation of what is called **reciprocity** when they self-disclose.[12] There is an unwritten rule that any time someone shares something about themselves, the recipient will respond by sharing their information too. In most well-developing relationships this is certainly the case. However, people have varying levels of comfort when it comes to disclosing personal information. Joseph Luft and Harry Ingham[13] created a famous image called the Johari Window to display four possible categories of information between two people.

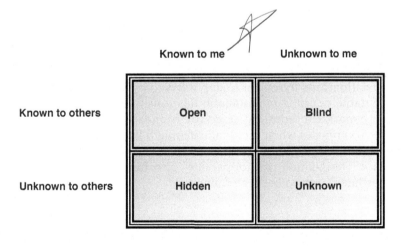

Figure 3.4
Johari Window

Information shared openly between two people fits into the Open quadrant. Our secrets belong in the Hidden. Less prominent, but there nonetheless, is information others know about us, but we cannot see ourselves. These are the things to which we are Blind. One sign of true friendship is the ability to point out the good and bad features of which our friends may be unaware. These may be as superficial as the piece of food stuck between their teeth or as intimate as their personal flaws. The Unknown category can only be known through sustained and long-term relationships. But, there has been more than one instance of romance, unknown to both parties for years, developing between longtime friends.

We all can envision our key relationships in terms of the Johari Window. It is yet another way to describe the Impersonal-Interpersonal continuum. In fact, it is a key explanation of those variations of connectedness. In our lives, we know whom we can trust enough to tell our secrets. We know when it is socially appropriate and personally beneficial to keep quiet. We also know that the lines dividing these quadrants are fluid and even changing. The high school confidant to whom you once bared your soul may have grown distant over time. Your parents, who you swore as a teen would never understand your secrets, may have become (once again) your best friends.

Whether they are based on work relationships, friendships, family, or romance, the more we self-disclose and learn to trust individuals with the parts of us we have kept secret, the more the relationship will grow. As we spend more time together, we intensify the relationship. One line of research documents key moments, called *turning points*,[14] as a way to see the progression of closeness. The classic "first 'I love you'" and "first kiss" are clear examples of a turning point. There are many other little ways in which we mark the intensity of the relationships. The first time you take someone home to meet your family, the first fight you have … and survive, the first vacation you take together; all of these moments demonstrate new levels of closeness between friends and romantic partners.

As trust builds, lives become increasingly interwoven, social circles overlap, and "coupledness" is publicly evident. This is clearly seen in romance. Couples mark their connection by holding hands, wearing the other person's clothing, or leaving personal belongings in their partner's living space. Friends can publicly mark their relationships too. We all know those inseparable friends who are rarely seen without the other. They take the same classes, work at the same job, go to the same parties, and eat at the same dining table.

Increasing levels of trust, commitment, and planning for the future move relationships into what Knapp refers to as "bonding." Marriage is the undisputable example for romantic relationships. We have fewer ways to publicly mark the bonding stage for friendships. College friends who become roommates when they graduate might be one exception. Brides and grooms publicly mark friendships with their choices of a best man or maid-of-honor. Designation of "godparents" also functions as a way to clearly demonstrate closeness between friends.

HOW DO WE KEEP IT GOING/GET OUT OF IT?

All relationships experience some level of disturbance at some time. *Relational maintenance*[15] research acknowledges the importance of studying how people weather these momentary disruptions and reconnect into a new level of comfort and security. Looking at the models, you could get the impression that "what goes up must come down." However, much of the relational work that occurs in daily life is more about maintaining the relationship. All relationships have growing pains of one sort or another. One useful model that attempts to capture the ever changing levels of connectedness is Conville's **Helical Model.**[16] Built on the metaphor of a spiral, he shows the cyclic progression we go through as we move from periods of security to times of alienation. These cycles parallel a back-and-forth movement between Knapp's earlier *integration* and *differentiation* stages. Ultimately, the model reassures us that even in times of distance, there is hope of a return to stabilization and security.

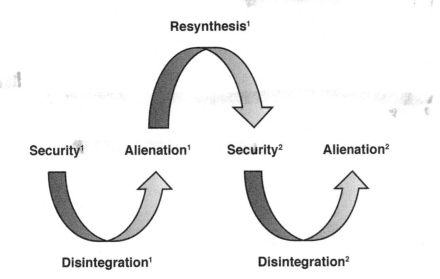

Figure 3.5
Helical Model

One example of issues that can cause problems in all types of relationships is referred to as **Dialectic Tensions.**[17] People have differing needs for things like personal space and privacy. Baxter and Montgomery found several sets of opposing needs that cover the basic differences.

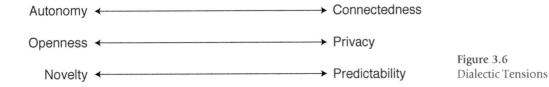

Figure 3.6
Dialectic Tensions

Even though some individuals may have higher needs for autonomy (alone time), their partners might have a higher need for togetherness. You might want to spend time alone, while your friend or romantic partner wants to spend every waking hour together. These opposing needs can create relationship tensions if unattended. Neither end of the continuum is better or worse, but perceptions of what is appropriate behavior varies greatly. Some individuals are more private, disclosing less personal information. Others disclose high levels of information and see disclosure as a primary indicator of affection and intimacy. Equally frustrating are the differing needs for planned and predictable behavior, as opposed to last-minute, spontaneous choices. The person needing more novelty might break up with someone because he or she is seen as "boring." The person needing more predictability might resent the lack of planning and ability to depend on consistent behavior from their partner. Depending on the level of needs, the tensions between individuals can mount. Think of it like rubber bands being stretched in opposite directions. Left unattended the band will snap, and so too will the bond between humans.

Several coping techniques have been identified. Relational partners can make alternating choices of whose needs will be met. Or they might decide that in certain situations, one person's needs will prevail, while in other situations the opposite need will be chosen. Sometimes partners give up their own needs entirely for the sake of the relationship. An attempt at reframing the opposing needs is an option that could bring a resolution for all parties.

Conflict is an inevitable part of all relationships. The introduction of problems, disagreements, and tension can actually be seen as a positive part of relational maintenance, depending on how that conflict is managed. Conflict introduces a dialog on issues of disagreement in order to facilitate change. Conflict management strategies have sometimes been characterized in two dimensions: cooperation and assertiveness. The image below shows a two-dimensional chart with **cooperation** and **assertiveness** on two axes. Ranking a person's willingness to cooperate with his or her partner (from high to low) and his or her need to assert individual desires (from high to low) sets forth five possible conflict management strategies.[18]

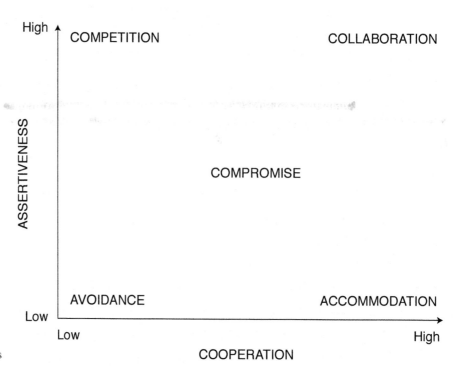

Figure 3.7
Conflict Management Strategies

Each of the five possible configurations has benefits and drawbacks given particular conflict situations. In an ideal world, everyone would have all of their needs met in harmonious **collaboration**. That storybook way of settling conflicts is rare and takes a great deal of time and discussion. It is highly cooperative and highly assertive, and unfortunately, highly unlikely. Most people support such resolutions to their conflict in theory more than in practice. It is more likely that a range of other strategies will be employed during conflict negotiations. Those who are low in both cooperation and assertiveness tend to **avoid** conflict. This choice might have advantages when engaging in the situation that is not worth the time or energy (or could result in some level of danger). However, avoiding conflicts leads to no productive change and can prolong the inevitable. On the opposite end of the cooperation continuum, those who "give in" and yield to the wishes of others may do so for strategic relational reasons. If the conflict is less important than the relationship, **accommodation** works well. On the other hand, if a person always sacrifices his or her needs, it can lead to resentment and unhealthy relationships. **Competition**, which is seen as a positive attribute in our culture, does allow an individual to get his or her needs met. However, that success might come at the detriment of the relationship. As with many "majority rule" decisions made in our culture, a common middle ground is **compromise**. While neither party may be completely satisfied with the result, all parties may be willing to live with the decision. Relationship characteristics vary in degrees of power, status, gender, and culture. Each brings with it unique expectations of social appropriateness when it comes to conflict. Partners who navigate the ups and downs of conflict effectively can use each incident as a way to grow.

Social Exchange Theory[19] has been proposed as a way to imagine the internal debate we may have as we navigate the course of relational maintenance. We are constantly measuring the costs and rewards of the relationship to decide whether we want to keep working toward a sustained connection. If there is more work involved (costs) to stay together than the benefits we reap (rewards), we might decide to enter the stages of relationship dissolution. There are probably as many ways to define relational costs as there are people in the world. Each person must make her or his own judgment on the worth of continuation. Some reasons for leaving relationships are more complicated and sensitive than others. A wide range of dysfunctional interactions within relationships, including both physical and mental abuse, have been studied under the category of the **dark side of interpersonal communication**. In such cases, the costs can weigh even more heavily on the individuals involved.[20]

Regardless of the reasons, individuals often decide not to continue in a relationship. While we see this most clearly in romance, even friends can have a falling out and family members are not above "cutting someone out of the will." Knapp's model of relationship stages, shown earlier in the chapter, indicates the progression of movement in relationship deterioration. This can involve varying periods of **stagnation**, **avoidance**, and backing away referred to as **circumscribing**. Friendships might wane, according to Rawlins model, but those endings are often less measurable.

Duck proposed a different set of stages to describe communication behaviors during relationship termination.[21] Originally, there were five steps, but later a sixth step was added to the model to allow for a resurrection of the relationship.[22]

Intrapsychic
Dyadic
Social
Grave Dressing
Resurrection

Figure 3.8
Duck's Model

When a final breakdown occurs and an individual decides to end a relationship, there is a complex set of stages still needed. People enter into an **intrapsychic** level (intrapersonal) where an internal dialogue occurs. Only when they move to a **dyadic** (interpersonal) level do they actually talk with their partner about the decision. Once a decision is made, the news has to be shared publically in the **social** phase. Just as with all losses in life, the pair also goes through a **grave dressing** (like a postmortem) process to transition to the next chapter in their lives. The added sixth stage is one we have all experienced first- or secondhand. With any termination there exists the possibility of **resurrection**. In some instances there could be many such declines that lead to rebirth of the relationship. The potential for reconnection makes it difficult to play the role of "supporting friend" when your BFF breaks up with her boyfriend. The social and grave dressing phases are necessary, but from an outsider's viewpoint, they are also sometimes difficult to navigate. The adage "Be careful what you say, it may come back to haunt you" applies appropriately here, as some supportive friends may well know.

Most people say there are only two things in life that are unavoidable: taxes and death. As you can see from this chapter, we might easily add interpersonal communication to this list. However unavoidable it may be, understanding what it is, how our needs and attractions impact it, how we accomplish it, and how we keep it going (or end it, depending on the circumstances) brings awareness that can enhance our relationships in significant and productive ways.

ENDNOTES

1   Extensive material can be found in both Knapp, M. L., & Daly, J. A. (Eds.) (2011). *Handbook of Interpersonal Communication.* (4th ed.). Thousand Oaks, CA: SAGE; Canary, D., & Dainton. M. (Eds.) (2003). *Maintaining Relationships through Communication: Relational, Contextual, and Cultural Variations.* Mahwah, NJ: Lawrence Erlbaum.

2   Buber, M. (1970). *I and thou.* New York: Scribner. (Original work published 1936)

3   Altman, L,. & Taylor, D. A. (1973). *Social Penetration: The Development of Interpersonal Relationships.* New York: Holt, Rinehart & Winston.

4   Watzlawick, P., Beavin, J. H., & Jackson, D. D. (2011). *Pragmatics of Human Communication.* New York: W. W. Norton

5   Maslow, A. H. (1943). A Theory of Human Motivation. *Psychological Review, 50,* 370-396.

6   Schutz, W. C. (1958). *FIRO: A Three-Dimensional Theory of Interpersonal Behavior.* New York: Holt, Rinehart & Winston.

7   Levinger, G., & Raush, H. (Eds). (1977). *Perspectives on the Meaning of Intimacy.* Amherst MA: University of Massachusetts Press.

8   Knapp, M. L., & Vangelisti, A. L. (2006) *Interpersonal Communication and Human Relationships* (6th ed.) Boston: Allyn and Bacon; Avtgis, T. A., West. D. V., & Anderson, T. L. (1998). Relationship Stages: An Inductive Analysis Identifying Cognitive, Affective, and Behavioral Dimensions of Knapp's Relational Stages Model. *Communication Research Reports,* 15(3), 280-287.

9   Rawling, W. K. (1992). *Friendship Matters: Communication Dialectics in the Life Course.* New York: Aldine de Gruyer; Rawlins, W. K. (2008). *The Compass of Friendship: Narrative, Identities and Dialogues.* Thousand Oaks, CA: SAGE.

10 Berger, C. R., & Calabrese. R. J. (1975). Some Explorations in Initial Interaction and Beyond Toward a Developmental Theory of Interpersonal Communication. *Human Communication, 1,* 99-112.

11 Antheunis, M. L., Schouten, A. P., Valkenburg, P. M., & Peter, J. (2012). Interactive Uncertainty Reduction Strategies and Verbal Affection in Computer-Mediated Communication. *Communication Research,* 39(6) 757–780; Gibbs, J. L., Ellison, N. B., & Lai, C. (2011). First Comes Love, Then Comes Google: An Investigation of Uncertainty Reduction Strategies and Self-Disclosure in Online Dating. *Communication Research,* 38(1) 70–100.

12 Gouldner, A.W. (1960). The Norm of Reciprocity: A Preliminary Statement. *American Sociological Review, 25,* 161-178.

13 Luft, J. (1970). *Group Processes: An Introduction to Group Dynamics.* (2nd ed.). Palo Alto: CA National Press Books; Wheeless, L. R. (1978). A Follow-Up Study of the Relationships among Trust, Disclosure, and Interpersonal Solidarity. *Human Communication, 4,* 143-145.

14 Baxter, L. A., & Bullis, C. (1986). Turning Points in Developing Relationships. *Human Communication, 12,* 469-493.

15 Canary, D. J., & Stafford, L. (Eds). (1994). *Communication and Relational Maintenance.* San Diego, CA: Academic Press.

16 Conville, R. L. (1991). *Relational Transitions: The Evolution of Personal Relationships.* Westport, CT: Praeger.

17 Baxter, L. A., & Montgomery, B. M. (1996). *Relating: Dialogues and dialectics.* New York: Guilford Press.

18 Wilmot, W., & Hocker, J. L. (2010). *Interpersonal conflict.* (8th ed). New York: McGraw Hill.

19 Thibaut. J. W., & Kelley, H. H. (1959). *The Social Psychology of Groups.* New York; Wiley.

20 Spitzberg, B. H., & Cupach, W. R. (Eds.) (2007). *The Dark Side of Interpersonal Communication* (2nd Ed.). Mahwah, NJ: Lawrence Erlbaum.; Cupach, W. R., & Spitzberg, B. H. (Eds.) (2010). The Dark Side of Close Relationship (2nd Ed.). New York: Routledge.

21 Duck, S. W. (Ed.) (1992). *Personal Relationships 4: Dissolving Personal Relationships.* London: Academic Press.

22 Rollie, S. S., & Duck, S. W. (2006). Stage Theories of Martial Breakdowns. In J. H. Harvbey & M. A. Fine (Eds.). *Handbook of Divorce and Dissolution of Romantic Relationships* (pp. 176-193). Mahwah, NJ: Lawrence Erlbaum.

INTERPERSONAL COMMUNICATION

In some ways, this is what this unit is all about: **relationships**. Humans are social animals; our lives are enriched by family and friends. There is an old saying in Communication: "You cannot **start** a relationship without communication. You cannot **maintain** a relationship without communication. It is even difficult to **end** a relationship without communication." When we try to start a relationship, we put ourselves at risk. You open up to someone, you are **self-disclosing**. The risk in this action is if the person rejects the invitation, he is not only rejecting the message, he is rejecting **you**. (You didn't really want to go out with him anyway.)

If you were successful at starting a relationship, now you have to maintain it. Friends share information and stories and do more than text each other. Have you ever seen two people grow apart? They lose interest in each other and stop sharing information about their lives. Friendships and marriages dissolve when partners stop talking to each other.

There is one other interesting point in this chapter along these same lines. **Conflict** is a natural part of all relationships. Now, we don't mean fistfights and wrestling. Everyone is unique and has her own experiences and **connotative** definitions. If two people see the world in different ways, there will be disagreements. In healthy relationships, people can learn from these conflicts. You can teach me something new. I can teach you, or we may discover a new idea by compromising. (If only politicians and countries would learn this lesson, we would all be better off.) A healthy body requires exercise. A good mind needs new information and challenges. It should be no surprise that a good relationship also requires a little work.

In the next chapter, we discuss two of the tools for a healthy relationship: understanding **perception** and learning to **listen**.

PERCEPTION AND LISTENING
DO YOU HEAR WHAT I HEAR?

LEARNING OBJECTIVES

After reading this chapter, you should understand the following concepts:

- Explain the reason humans are limited in their capacity to process information

- Distinguish between the three key perception processes

- Define the primary selectivity processes

- Describe the factors that affect the selective exposure, selective attention and selective retention processes

- Demonstrate an understanding of social identity theory

- Explain schemata and the types of information that it typically includes

- Describe the four schemata that we use to interpret communication events

- Define attribution theory and distinguish between internal and external attributions

- Explain covariation theory and the three types of information used to interpret people's behavior

- Define self-serving bias and explain how it is problematic

- Describe the fundamental attribution error

- Discuss three factors that influence our perceptions

- Distinguish between hearing and listening processes

- Identify the seven steps to effective listening

- Recall the four listening styles and identify the focus of each

- Explain the four motivations to listen and recall a potential pitfall of each

- Recognize the six common listening misbehaviors

From *Interpersonal Communication* by Kristen Eichhorn, Candice Thomas-Maddox and Melissa Wanzer. Copyright © 2008 Kendall Hunt Publishing Company. Reprinted by permission.

KEYWORDS

perception
limited capacity processors
selection
selective exposure
biased information search
proximity
utility
reinforce
selective attention
novelty
size
concrete
selective retention
primacy and recency
organization
constructivism
schemata
prototypes
personal constructs
stereotypes
social identity theory
scripts
script theory
interpretation
attribution theory
external attribution
unintentionality
intentionality
internal attribution
covariation theory
distinctiveness
consistency
consensus
self-serving bias
fundamental attribution error
rapport talk
report talk
hearing
listening
BIG EARS
paraphrasing
positive feedback
negative feedback
dual perspective taking
noise
listening styles
people-oriented
action-oriented
content-oriented
time-oriented listening
discriminate listening
appreciative listening
comprehensive listening
evaluative listening
empathetic listening
pseudo-listening
monopolizing
disconfirming
defensive listening
selective listening
ambushing

© Elena Kouptsova-Vasic, 2007,
Shutterstock.

In the *Friends* episode "The One Where Ross and Rachel Take a Break," Ross becomes frustrated by Rachel's enthusiasm for her new job. To make matters worse, Ross has also been acting jealous over Rachel's relationship with her boss, Mark. Ross tries to explain to Rachel that he wants to have a relationship with her, that he is tired of always getting her answering machine and having dates cancelled because of her work. The situation becomes a bit heated when Rachel sarcastically asks Ross if he wants her to quit her job so she can be his girlfriend full-time, with no other obligations. Rachel gets very frustrated and tells Ross that they can't keep arguing about the same thing over and over again.

Finally, Rachel suggests that maybe they should take a break. Ross understands that to mean a moment to cool off and calm down; maybe do something that will take their minds off the problem. Rachel has something else in mind: a break from the relationship.

OVERVIEW

Just like Ross and Rachel, we have all encountered situations in relationships where our perceptions have caused us to interpret messages differently than they were intended. Ross perceived Rachel's request to take a "break" to mean that she needed a temporary time-out from their discussion. In Rachel's mind, the meaning of the word "break" was much different.

Imagine a world where we could completely eliminate misunderstandings between roommates, co-workers, relationship partners, parents, children, teachers, and students. Could such a world ever exist? In this chapter we explore the reasons our messages are sometimes partially interpreted, completely misinterpreted, or even ignored by others. Two processes that play a key role in how we send and receive messages in our relationships are perception and listening. In the first part of this chapter we examine the process of perception, paying special attention to the relationship between elements of perception and their relationship to interpersonal communication. We will then turn our attention to the process of listening and how it impacts our interpersonal relationships. Can you recall a time when someone accused you of not listening? Perhaps you *heard* what the person said but did not really *listen* to what they were saying. In the second part of this chapter we will distinguish between the terms *hearing* and *listening*, and advance a number of ways to improve listening, an extremely important, yet often neglected, communication skill.

Perception and listening are so closely intertwined that it is difficult to discuss one without addressing the other. As we form relationships, our perception impacts how we view the other person as well as how we interpret their messages and behaviors. In the opening scenario Ross perceived his relationship with Rachel to be solid. Rachel, on the other hand, perceived the relationship to be on rocky ground due to Ross' jealous behavior. It is not at all unusual for two people to perceive the same relationship in very different ways. Now consider the role that perception plays on your ability to listen. It should come as no surprise that if our perception differs, our listening skills will also differ. In fact, interpretation is a common factor present in both of the processes of perception and of listening. When Rachel commented that they needed a "break," Ross' perception of their relationship caused him to listen and interpret her message in a way that was very different from what Rachel intended. If you watch reality television shows such as *Survivor* or *Big Brother*, you see numerous examples of the link between perception and listening. Since these programs involve strategy, many of the players plant "seeds of doubt" in the minds of their competitors with the hope that it impairs their perception and ability to listen and interpret messages from others. Often, the winning contestant is the player who has succeeded in impairing the perception and listening skills of the competitors.

Our hope is that once you gain a better understanding of the relationship between these two concepts, you will gain a better understanding of why individuals view relationships, people, behaviors, and messages in different ways. An awareness of the impact of perception and listening in our relationships will increase the accuracy of our interpersonal communication. Let us first focus on the primary perceptual processes and examine the relationship between perception and interpersonal communication.

PERCEPTION AND INTERPERSONAL COMMUNICATION

Perception can be best described as the lens through which we view the world. Just as your view of color would be altered if you were to wear a pair of glasses with blue lenses, our perception impacts our view of people, events, and behaviors. One definition of **perception** is that it is the process of selecting, organizing and interpreting sensory information into a coherent or lucid depiction of the world around us (Klopf 1995). Stated more simply, perception is essentially how we interpret and assign meaning to others' behaviors and messages based on our background and past experiences. The word "experience" is important in understanding the overall process of perception. Consider the role that perception has played in your college experience. Perhaps you enjoy writing and have kept a personal journal. If your English professor assigned daily journal entries in her class, you might tell others that the class was one of the most enjoyable ones you have ever taken. Based on your experience—and your love for writing and journaling—you perceived the class to be easy and enjoyable, and you looked forward to communicating with your professor during her office hours to discuss how you could improve on your writing. But suppose there is another student who has struggled with writing throughout his academic career. He might report to others that the teacher was difficult to talk with and that her assignments were unfair. Based on his perception, their conversations during office hours may have been full of criticism and confusion, and he may describe the instructor as being "uncaring" and an "impossible perfectionist." Since each student brought a unique background and set of experiences to the class, the resulting perceptions of the teacher and class were very different.

Chances are that you have learned about perception in other classes, such as psychology or sociology. Researchers from a wide range of academic fields study perceptual processes. While psychologists conducted much of the initial research in the area of perception, communication scholars have focused

Have you ever felt overwhelmed at work? © Diego Cervo, 2007, Shutterstock.

specifically on the impact of perception on the meanings assigned to messages. From a communication perspective, perception is important because we often define ourselves based on our perceptions of how others see us. Recall our discussion in Chapter Two of reflected appraisal (or looking glass self) which explains how we form impressions of ourselves based on how we think others see us. If people respond favorably toward us, we may feel more self-assured and communicate in a more confident manner. Our perception also causes us to form impressions of others which impacts how we communicate with them. How would you feel if you approached one of your classmates at a party and she ignored you? Chances are you would perceive her to be rude and would avoid subsequent interactions with her when you see her in class or on campus. But take a moment to consider the factors that might have influenced your perception. Perhaps you, or maybe even your classmate, were nervous because you have not been to many parties on campus. Maybe your classmate did not recognize you due to the fact that there are many people in the class. There are a number of factors that could alter the perception each of you has of the interaction at the party. All of our interpersonal interactions are influenced by the perceptions we form of ourselves and others. In order to fully grasp the importance of perception, let us examine how we break down bits of information from our environment and form perceptions of ourselves and others.

Lyrics from a song made popular by the group The Police illustrate a common problem most of us have experienced in our lifetime—being inundated with too much information. Have you ever felt overwhelmed because it seemed as though your professor disseminated too much information in one lecture? Or have you experienced problems at work because your manager gave you too many instructions, tasks or responsibilities at once? Perhaps you have returned to your apartment after being away for a few days only to find that your inbox is overflowing with email and your answering machine is filled with messages. If any of these situations seem familiar to you, you are not alone. On any given day, we encounter literally thousands of stimuli that bombard our senses and compete for our attention.

Social psychologist Robert Cialdini (2001) notes that we live in an extremely complicated society which he describes as "easily the most rapidly moving and complex that has ever existed on this planet" (7). Cialdini (2001) further states that we cannot analyze all aspects of our environment because "we haven't the time, energy or capacity for it" (7). If it is not possible to process and recall everything we see, hear, taste, touch, or smell, then how do we make sense of the world around us?

The way humans manage all of the stimuli encountered in the environment is to limit the amount and type of information taken in. This elimination process often occurs at a subconscious level. Thus, on any given day, we put limits on what we choose to see, hear, taste, touch, or smell. Because of the innate limitations in our ability to process information, humans are often described as **limited capacity processors**. Stated simply, we consciously and subconsciously make choices about the amount and type of stimuli we perceive. Think of a time when you were so focused on your homework that when your mother commented on how loud you were playing your music, you thought, "Wow, I can't even really hear it." To fully understand how people make sense of their environment, we need to take a closer look at three key perceptual processes: selection, organization and interpretation.

Selection

The first perception process is **selection**. While you might not always be consciously aware of the process of selection, we are continually making choices about the amount and type of information that we choose to notice. Remember our earlier discussion about our ability to be limited capacity processors? It is virtually impossible to pay attention to all the things we could possibly sense at any given time. These limitations in our ability to assimilate and interpret information prevent us from "taking it all in" and so we must select certain messages or stimuli over others. These selections we make are often done in a purposeful rather than random manner (Klopf 1995). Three primary selectivity processes which impact our perception include selective exposure, selective attention, and selective retention. The next sections provide an overview of each of these processes and discuss variables that affect them.

Selective exposure refers to the choice to subject oneself to certain stimuli. Choices regarding which messages and stimuli you will subject yourself to are made each day. You choose whether to expose yourself to the messages being sent by advertisers and newscasters when you decide whether to turn on your television or radio each morning. You choose whether to subject yourself to the messages left on your answering machine or via email. Often the choice to engage in selective exposure is based on our desire to seek information or stimuli that is comfortable or familiar to us. Culture plays a key role in determining what messages or stimuli we choose to expose ourselves to and those which we avoid. Consider the fact that some people avoid communicating with those from other cultural backgrounds. They engage in selective exposure by avoiding conversations with people from different cultures. Individuals may focus on the obvious differences of race or ethnicity and assume that they do not have anything in common with people who are so dissimilar. The choice to avoid communication may cause individuals to miss learning about all the beliefs and interests that are shared. According to Fischer and his colleagues (2005), we are most likely to seek out information consistent with our beliefs, values, and attitudes and to avoid information that is viewed as inconsistent. Our propensity to seek out certain types of information and avoid others is referred to as a **biased information search** (Fischer et al. 2005). While we might not consciously be aware of this process, each day we selectively choose to associate with particular individuals or groups of people and attend to certain types of messages in a variety of contexts. Perhaps today you chose to attend your communication class rather than going out to eat lunch with a friend. The decision to attend your communication class is yet another example of selective exposure.

There are a number of factors that affect selective exposure including, among others: proximity, utility, and reinforcement. Not surprisingly, we are most likely to selectively expose ourselves to messages that are nearby, or close in proximity. In fact, **proximity** is the number one predictor of whether we will develop a relationship with another person (Katz and Hill 1958). Consider the relationships that you formed with those who attended your high school. Proximity impacted your ability to selectively expose yourself to those in the same school and form relationships. While the Internet has

It's your choice to watch television and subject yourself to shows and advertising.
© Philip Date, 2007, Shutterstock.

changed the way we communicate and form relationships, most people still find it difficult to form relationships and communicate with those who are not physically close to them. Second, we are most likely to expose ourselves to messages that we perceive as being useful. **Utility** refers to the perception that particular messages are immediately useful; these messages have a much greater chance of being selected than those that are not seen as useful (McCroskey and Richmond 1996). Expecting an important message from your parents will influence your choice to selectively expose yourself to your email messages. If there are several messages in your inbox, a message from friend or family member is more likely to be viewed than one from the Department of Student Services at your university. Finally, most people expose themselves to messages that are consistent with their views, or **reinforce**, their attitudes and beliefs (Fischer et al. 2005). Thus, if you are strongly opposed to the death penalty, you will probably not attend a lecture delivered by a professor advocating capital punishment for convicted murderers.

Once we have made the decision to place ourselves in a position to physically receive a message, we then focus on certain aspects or elements of the message. **Selective attention** refers to the decision to pay attention to certain stimuli while simultaneously ignoring others. Factors which affect selective attention often include the novelty, size, and concreteness of the stimuli. **Novelty** refers to the tendency to pay attention to stimuli that are novel, new, or different. Novel aspects are more likely to capture our attention than those with which we are familiar. For example, we tend to notice a friend's new hairstyle almost immediately. In the *Friends* episode discussed at the beginning of the chapter, Rachel became more aware of and paid closer attention to changes in Ross' behavior. Previously, he had been secure and confident in their relationship, but as Rachel became more focused on her career, his messages communicated a new jealousy. Another factor that affects selective attention is the **size**, or magnitude, of the stimuli. We are more likely to pay attention to large items, objects, or people. It probably is not completely by chance that most Chief Executive Officers in U.S. companies are at least six feet tall and that virtually every U.S. President elected since 1900 has been the taller of the two candidates. Finally, we are more likely to pay attention to information that is **concrete**, or well-defined, than to information which is perceived as abstract or ambiguous. Individuals have an easier time attending to messages that are clear and straightforward. For example, if a manager tells an employee to "change her attitude and behavior," but does not provide specific or concrete information about how or why the attitude or behavior is problematic, the employee is likely to ignore this message (McCroskey and Richmond 1996).

Once the decision has been made to expose and attend to stimuli, the final stage in the selectivity process involves **selective retention**, which refers to the choice to save or delete information from one's long term memory. Two factors affecting the propensity to retain information include primacy and recency effects, and utility. Researchers have identified a range of variables which affect an individual's ability to retain information. When studying the type of information people are most likely to retain, researchers note that arguments delivered first **(primacy)** and last **(recency)** in a persuasive presentation are more likely to be recalled and to be more persuasive (Gass and Seiter 2003). As we form relationships, we are

What kind of an impression do you try to make in a job interview?
© Marcin Balcerzak, 2007, Shutterstock.

often concerned with the first or last impression that we make. It has been estimated that we form our initial impression of others during the first three to five seconds. Recall the last job interview that you attended. Careful attention was paid to your clothing and appearance to ensure that you would make a positive first impression that the interviewer would remember. However, if you tripped and spilled the contents of your portfolio as you exited the interview, the recency of the last impression may be imprinted on the interviewer's memory. A second important factor related to retention is **utility**, or usefulness. Almost all of us have heard the phrase, "use it or lose it." Essentially what this phrase implies is that if we do not apply the information we obtain, we may not retain it later. For example, many of you might have received training in cardiopulmonary resuscitation (CPR) at one time in your life. But if one of your classmates needed CPR, would you remember the steps? The same principle is true of the information and skills discussed in this text. It is our hope that by providing you with examples of concepts and information, you will see the usefulness of the strategies and become more effective in your interpersonal interactions with others.

Organization

Once we have selected information, or stimuli, we then begin the process of placing it into categories in order to make sense of it. **Organization** "refers to our need to place the perceived characteristics of something into the whole to which it seems to belong" (Klopf 1995, 51). Organization is the process by which we take the stimuli and make sense of it so that it is meaningful to us. Remember the earlier example of the classmate who ignored you at a party? Some of the stimuli that caused you to form your perception included her lack of eye contact and her failure to reciprocate your greeting. In the organization process, you take each of these stimuli (eye contact and lack of communication) and put them together to form an impression.

One theory that is useful in understanding how individuals organize information in meaningful ways is constructivism. Kelly (1970) developed the theory of **constructivism** to explain the process we use to organize and interpret experiences by applying cognitive structures labeled schemata. **Schemata** are "organized clusters of knowledge and information about particular topics" (Hockenbury and Hockenbury 2006, 265). Another way to describe schemata is as mental filing cabinets with several drawers used to help organize and process information. Schemata are the results of one's experiences and, therefore, are dynamic and often changing as we encounter new relationships and life experiences. Suppose your first romantic relationship was a disaster. The initial schema you formed to organize information about romantic relationships (which may have been obtained from television shows or movies) was likely altered to include this negative experience you encountered. But suppose your next romantic partner is incredibly thoughtful and romantic. New information is incorporated to your schema that now enables you to evaluate various aspects of romantic relationships based on both the positive and negative experiences you encountered in the past. Thus, we apply schemata to make sense of our communication experiences. More specifically, we apply four different types of schemata to interpret interpersonal encounters: prototypes, personal constructs, stereotypes, and scripts (Fiske and Taylor 1984; Kelley 1972; Reeder 1985).

Have you ever thought of your ideal romantic partner? What would he or she be like? **Prototypes** are knowledge structures which represent the most common attributes of a phenomenon. These structures are used to help organize stimuli and influence our interactions with others (Fehr and Russell 1991). Prototypes provide us with a "benchmark" that is the standard used to evaluate and categorize other examples that fall into the same category. Recall your initial encounter with someone you dated recently. It is very likely that you evaluated this individual's behaviors based on whether this person fit your "prototypical," or best, example of a relationship partner. If you were to make a list of the characteristics you desire in the "ideal" romantic partner, these preconceived ideas and expectations represent your prototype and affect how you will perceive each potential romantic partner encountered in the future. Research by Fehr and Russell (1991) supports the idea that we have prototypes about love and friendship. They conducted six different studies in an attempt to identify participants' prototypical examples of different types of love (e.g., maternal love, paternal love, friendship love, sisterly love, puppy love, infatuation, and so on) and the factors associated with love. Characteristics such as caring, helping, establishing a bond, sharing, feeling free to talk, demonstrating respect, and exhibiting closeness were all associated with perceptions of love. In a related study, Fehr (2004) examined prototypical examples of interactions which led to greater perceived intimacy in same-sex friendships. Fehr (2004) found that interaction patterns which involved increased levels of self-disclosure and emotional support were perceived by friends as being more prototypical of expectations for intimacy than other types of practical support. Prototype theory is extremely useful in shedding light on how we organize our thoughts about interpersonal communication and relationships.

Personal constructs serve to help you evaluate others and influence your interactions.
© Yuri Arcurs, 2007, Shutterstock.

A second type of schemata is **personal constructs** which Kelly (1955; 1970; 1991) describes as bipolar dimensions of meaning used to predict and evaluate how people behave. Personal constructs have also been described as the "mental yardsticks" that we use to assess people and social situations. Several examples of personal constructs include: responsible-irresponsible, assertive-unassertive, friendly-unfriendly, intelligent-unintelligent, and forthright-guarded. Personal constructs serve as another means of evaluating others and simultaneously influence how we approach interactions. For example, if you label your co-worker as "friendly" you may smile more at this person and share more personal information than you would with another co-worker labeled as "unfriendly." Raskin (2002) notes that we monitor our personal constructs closely and keep track of how accurately they predict life circumstances. When necessary, we revise them when we perceive them as unreliable. We tend to define situations and people based on the personal constructs that we use regularly. Thus, it is possible that we might not be aware of qualities some people possess or situations that we do not access regularly (Raskin 2002).

The third type of schema we use to help us organize information is stereotypes. **Stereotypes** are impressions and expectations based on one's knowledge or beliefs about a specific group of people which are then applied to all individuals who are members of that group. Stereotypes greatly influence the way messages are perceived. Some researchers argue that stereotypes are often activated automatically when an individual observes a member of a group or category (Carlston 1992) and we are likely to predict how that person will behave. For example, Hamilton and Sherman (1994) note that individuals' perceptions of different racial and ethnic groups are often "planted in early childhood by influential adults in their lives" (3). Influential individuals, such as family members, and the media play an important role in shaping how we define others and how we view the world.

Why do we categorize people, events, and objects? As mentioned previously, we are limited in our ability to process the sheer number of stimuli bombarding us at any given time. Thus, we identify ways to categorize and organize stimuli to enhance "cognitive efficiency," or to make information more manageable. A second explanation for our tendency to stereotype as described by Hamilton and Sherman (1994) is "categorization as self-enhancement" (6). Simply stated, we tend to evaluate those groups to which we belong more favorably than groups to which we do not belong. Recall the groups you associated with in high school. If you were a member of the student council, you may have viewed members as being strong leaders and very organized. Students who were not

If you're on a sports team, you may identify more closely with other athletes.
© PhotoCreate, 2007, Shutterstock.

members of the student council may have created their own schema for evaluating its members—they may have labeled them as being "powerhungry," or aggressive. **Social identity theory** offers an explanation for our tendency to evaluate in-groups more positively than out-groups. According to social identity theory, an individual's self-esteem is often connected to membership or association with social groups (Hamilton and Sherman 1994; Turner 1987). In an effort to maintain a positive identity, we may overemphasize or accentuate differences between in-groups and out-groups.

Can placing people into groups or categories based on particular traits or characteristics be problematic? Absolutely! For example, individuals are often categorized based on whether they have some type of physical or mental disability. Braithwaite and her colleagues found that people without disabilities often assume that individuals with physical disabilities are helpless, while this is certainly not the case (Braithwaite and Harter 2000). They conducted a number of interviews with persons with physical disabilities and found that they often received a great deal of either unwanted or unsolicited help from persons without disabilities. This example illustrates the problem of inaccurately categorizing people. In this case, persons without disabilities inaccurately categorized persons with disabilities as helpless or needy, resulting in inappropriate "helping" behavior. Suggestions for managing these interactions more appropriately will be addressed in Chapter Thirteen when we discuss interpersonal communication in health-related contexts.

People form stereotypes about individuals based on race, culture, sex, sexual orientation, age, education, intelligence, and affiliations, among other characteristics. It is crucial that we realize that stereotypes are formed as a result of our perceptions of others and, as a result, can be accurate or inaccurate. When inaccurate or inflexible stereotypes are applied to individuals, they often divide rather than unite people. Is it possible to resist the temptation to stereotype or categorize people? While the research on changing stereotypes is not extensive, much of it is promising. Stereotyping is a normal tendency. Our desire to reduce our level of uncertainty about people and situations leads us into the stereotype "trap." We are uncomfortable in situations where we have little or no information about others, and our initial tendency is to open our schematic files in an attempt to locate any information that will help us figure out how to communicate. For example, one of the authors of your textbook is a native of West Virginia. Throughout her life, she has encountered stereotypes of people from West Virginia. When she lived in California, one of her college roommates commented, "You're nothing at all what I expected someone from West Virginia to be like!" When asked to describe her expectations, the roommate described some very negative stereotypes. The two became best friends and discovered that even though one was from Texas and the other was from West Virginia, they had more in common than they thought. If you have never communicated with a person from another culture, your first tendency may be to recall any information associated with the person's culture that you have read about or seen on television. Regardless of whether this information is accurate or inaccurate, it is often used as a "guide" for our expectations and communication. The key to overcoming the negative outcomes of stereotyping is to remain open-minded and flexible. While your tendency may be to look for something to help organize and make sense of stimuli, remember that the information used to form the stereotype may be incorrect. Fortunately, there is a growing body of scholarship which suggests that the stereotypes people form can be modified over time (Hamilton and Sherman 1994).

The last type of schema we use to organize is scripts. According to Abelson (1982), **scripts** are knowledge structures that guide and influence how we process information. Abelson (1982) describes scripts as an "organized bundle of expectations about an event sequence" (134). Simply stated, we adhere to a number of different scripts throughout a day, scripts that tell us what to do and say, as well as *how* to do and say it. Very often we never notice how scripted our day-to-day interactions are until someone deviates from the expected script. A comedian makes reference to the potential embarrassment caused by scripts in his description of an encounter he had when exiting a taxi cab at the airport.

Taxi Driver: Thanks! Have a nice flight!

Comedian: You too! *(then, realizing that the taxi driver is not flying)* I mean, the next time you fly somewhere.

Another scenario, a casual conversation between two co-workers at the copy machine in the workplace, illustrates the relevance of scripts to our day-to-day functioning.

Dominique: Hi Anthony!

Anthony: Hey Dominique, how are you?

Dominique: Not so good. My arthritis is acting up and it's making it impossible for me to get any work done on this report that is due at noon. Then my son's school just called to say he's not feeling well, and I can't get a hold of my sister to go pick him up at school. It's just been one thing after another.

Anthony: *(looking at his watch)* Wow, I didn't realize it was so late! Um, yeah, well, hey, nice talking to you. I've got to go!

Did Anthony respond appropriately to Dominique's explicit description of how she was feeling? Can you explain why Anthony had to go? **Script theory** explains Anthony's reaction to Dominique's description of her arthritis and problems with child care. According to script theory, we often interact with others in a way that could be described as "automatic" or even "mindless."

Because we have repeated experience with these scripts, we are able to adhere to them in a manner described as "mindless," meaning that we are not consciously aware of the fact that we are following a script. Essentially, we rely on scripts to tell us how to proceed in situations and what to say. We enter into situations that we have been in before with a specific set of expectations and, when individuals violate our expectations by not adhering to the script, we are not sure what to do. From an interpersonal communication perspective, we use scripts to determine how to proceed during social interaction and form perceptions of others based on whether or not they are following the "script."

Interpretation

After we have selected and organized information, the final step in the perception process involves interpretation. **Interpretation is the subjective process of making sense of our perceptions.** The interpretation process is described as highly subjective because individuals' interpretations of communication events vary extensively and are influenced by a wide range of factors. The following sections serve as an overview of the dominant theory used to explain how people interpret information, discuss errors in interpretive processes, and identify factors that influence the ways we interpret information.

The dominant theory that explains how people explain their own and others' behavior is known as **attribution theory** (Heider 1958; Kelley 1967; 1971). This theory is also known as naïve psychology because people often try to connect observable behavior to unobservable causes (Littlejohn 1983). Can you recall a time when you have tried to explain a friend's unusual behavior? Perhaps she was supposed to phone you at a scheduled time, and the call never came. You may try to explain her lack of communication by theorizing that she overslept, the car broke down, or she had a fight with a significant other. All of these are causes that you have not directly observed, but they are used as potential explanations for the friend's behavior. Attribution theory is commonly applied to interpret the reasons for our own actions as well as the actions of others. According to Heider (1958) there are three basic assumptions to attribution theory: (1) that it is natural for people to attempt to establish the causes of their own and others' behavior, (2) that people assign causes for behavior systematically, and (3) that the attribution impacts the perceiver's feelings and subsequent behavior. Thus, the causes assigned to peoples' behaviors play a significant role in determining reactions to interpreted behaviors.

Maybe you visualize your friend standing by her broken-down car as a reason she didn't call you.
© Bartosz Ostrowski, 2007, Shutterstock.

According to attribution theory, people assign causes to behaviors in a fairly systematic way and typically use different types of information to make these decisions. Generally, when individuals attempt to explain behaviors, they will choose among three different explanations: the situation, unintentionality or chance, and intentionality or dispositions (Heider 1958). A person's behavior may be best explained by considering the situation and how this factor may have influenced behavior. Situational factors are often referred to as **external attributions**. For example, perhaps you are normally talkative and outgoing when in social situations. However, you go to a party with some friends and see your former relationship partner with a new "love" interest. Because you still have feelings for this person, this situation is upsetting to you, and you spend the evening moping and avoiding conversations. Hence, your behavior at the party could be best explained by situational or external attributions. The second factor typically used to explain behavior is **unintentionality** or chance, which refers to one's inability to predict whether the behaviors will be consistent in the future (Kelsey et al. 2004). For example, someone may guess several answers on a difficult test and then claim that they may or may not be able to replicate their test performance again in the future. The third factor, **intentionality**, or disposition, is also referred to as an internal attribution. Internal attributions are typically described as being stable or persistent and often refer to behaviors that are likely to be exhibited repeatedly across a variety of contexts (Heider 1958). If your friend Sally acts quiet and reserved in almost all situations, then you would explain her quiet and reserved demeanor at your birthday party based on internal attributions or personality traits. When attempting to explain her behavior, you might say "Sally is just that way," or tell others that she is normally very shy.

Harold Kelley (1973) also developed a prominent theory of attribution which attempts to explain how we formulate perceptions of others. Kelley's **covariation theory** states that we decide whether peoples' behavior is based on either internal or external factors by using three different and important types of information: distinctiveness, consensus, and consistency. In order to apply Kelley's covariation principle, we must have multiple observations of individuals to accurately explain their behavior. **Distinctiveness** refers to whether or not a person typically behaves the same way with the target, or receiver, of the behavior. When distinctiveness is high, we tend to attribute others' behavior to external causes. When distinctiveness is low, we tend to attribute others' behavior to internal causes. For example, if Professor Munhall is always pleasant and helpful toward all students, he would be exhibiting low levels of distinctiveness. In this situation, Dr. Munhall's behavior would be attributed to internal factors (e.g., he is such a caring teacher). Suppose one minute Professor Munhall snaps at Alan during class and the next minute he responds calmly to Marcus' request for clarification. In this situation, his behavior would be described as highly distinctive since he does not normally behave this way toward students. External factors would be used to explain his highly distinctive behavior (e.g., he had a bad day).

The second type of information used to attribute causes to behaviors is consistency. **Consistency** refers to whether an individual behaves the same way across contexts and at various times. For example, would the person behave the same way regardless of whether she was at a party, at work, at school, or at a bar? It is important to keep in mind that the key element here is the context or situation. When an individual acts in a highly consistent manner, we tend to attribute the individual's behavior to internal rather than external causes. Very often, we ask whether the behavior is unique or consistent in the particular context. If your friend Kaia is always loud and outgoing in social situations, and you observe her acting this way at a party, you would explain her behavior based on internal rather than external factors. That is, Kaia acted in a loud, outgoing manner because this is the way she typically behaves with most individuals and in most situations (high consistency). Conversely, if Kaia was quiet, shy, and withdrawn at the same party, you might explain her behavior by saying that the party must not have been fun (external factor) because she was acting differently than the expected behavior in social situations (low consistency).

The final factor, **consensus**, considers whether the behavior is unique to the individual or if they are behaving in the way that would be typically expected of others. We say that consensus is high when a person acts the same way that others would behave. Recall our example from the beginning of the chapter. Did Ross behave in a way that was similar to the way Joey, Chandler, or several other men would respond? The key element in this factor is the actor, or source of behavior, (as opposed to the context, which is the focus of consistency). When consensus is high, we attribute peoples' behavior to external rather than internal factors. For example, the majority of Americans say that they do not enjoy giving speeches and typically experience anxiety prior to and during the event (high consensus). Thus, we attribute Jay's speech anxiety to external (everyone is nervous about public speaking) rather than internal factors. But suppose Jay actually looks forward to the prospect of public speaking. When someone actually enjoys giving speeches (low consensus), we might explain this person's unique behavior by saying this person is highly confident and self-assured (internal factors).

Not surprisingly, we often evaluate and explain our *own* behavior using standards that are very different from those used to evaluate and explain the behavior of *others*. The two most common attribution errors people make are known as the self-serving bias and the fundamental attribution error. The **self-serving bias** states that we tend to manufacture, or construct, attributions which best serve our own self-interests (Hamachek 1992). For example, when we excel in school or sports, we often explain our success based on internal factors or causes. We might think "I am smart" or "I am an incredible athlete," both of which are internal attributions. The self-serving bias provides us with a viable explanation for the sources of student motivation in the classroom. Research by Gorham and her colleagues (1992) indicates that students view motivation in school as a student-owned trait or characteristic. Thus, when a student feels motivated to do well in school, he or she credits this intention to do well on internal rather than external factors. On the other hand, when a student feels unmotivated, or is unwilling to work hard in school, he or she is more likely to attribute the cause of this lack of motivation to the teacher's behavior (external attributions—the teacher did not explain the assignment clearly) rather than to the self (internal attributions). Why do we avoid taking responsibility for our poor performance, mistakes, or shortcomings? One explanation for attributing our failures to external causes is to save face. While our tendency to protect our own self-image is understandable, it is important to realize that these distorted perceptions of self are problematic. Falsely taking credit for accomplishments and blaming others (or circumstances) for our failures can lead to distorted self-images and inaccurate representations of ourselves during social interaction (Hamacheck, 1992).

The next question to ask is whether we attribute others' failures and successes to external or internal factors? A second common attribution error often made during the interpretation stage of perception is the **fundamental attribution error**. When attempting to explain others' negative behaviors, we tend to overestimate the internal factors or causes and underestimate the external factors or causes. Conversely, when attempting to explain our *own* mistakes or shortcomings, we tend to overestimate the external causes and underestimate the internal causes. For example, if you are driving to school and see someone speeding by you, you might say to your friend, "What a reckless driver," (internal attribution). However, if you are speeding down the same road the next day and that same friend asks you why you are in such a rush, you might respond, "I am late for work," or "I need to get a parking space," both of which are external attributions. Kelsey and her colleagues (2004) recently used attribution theory to investigate the explanations students provided for their college instructors' classroom "misbehaviors." Examples of teacher misbehaviors include boring lectures, unfair grading, and providing too much information. The researchers found that students were more likely to attribute their teachers' inappropriate classroom behaviors to internal causes (e.g., he doesn't care about teaching) rather than to external causes (e.g., she's had a bad day). It is important to understand and acknowledge that while the way we make sense of our own and others' behaviors is less than perfect, it greatly affects how we interact with others. To improve the way we select, organize, and interpret information, it is also essential to consider our individual differences and how these differences impact our perception.

INDIVIDUAL DIFFERENCES AND PERCEPTIONS

While there are numerous factors that affect the way we perceive information, in this section we focus on three widely researched and acknowledged variables related to perception. Three variables that have been identified by scholars as impacting perception are sex, age, and culture. We begin our discussion by considering how sex differences affect perception and communication.

Do you think men and women view the world differently? Deborah Tannen, a noted gender scholar and linguist, would answer this question with an unequivocal "Yes!" Tannen (1986; 1990; 1994) notes that men and women hold different worldviews and philosophies regarding how they are expected to act in society which evolve from early interactions with family members, peers, and society. Tannen and other gender scholars (see, for example, Wood 1999) assert that men and women are socialized differently and, as a result, develop different perceptions of the world and their place within it. For example, women often perceive the world as a place to connect and form bonds with others. Men, on the other hand, view the world as a place to assert their independence and autonomy. These differences in perceptions affect the ways that men and women approach social interactions. Tannen says that women often engage in **rapport talk** which is analogous to small talk or phatic communication, while men often exhibit **report talk** which involves discussions about facts, events, and solutions. The following scenario illustrates the difference between rapport and report talk.

> *Elyse and Dave got a flat tire during their drive to work. As they discuss the event with colleagues, Elyse explains various details associated with the tire episode when speaking with her friends. "It was horrible! We were driving down the freeway when all of the sudden we heard a 'thump-thump' under the car. Of course, today would be the day that we left the cell phone at home on the table! Didn't you get a flat tire about a month ago, Janelle?"*

Typically, other females respond by sharing their similar stories and experiences. Dave, on the other hand, would provide the details of the morning's event differently.

"We got a flat tire on Interstate 270 this morning. We didn't have a cell phone, but the car behind us pulled over and let me use their phone to call AAA."

It is important to note that not all men and women communicate this way. However, because men and women may see the world differently, it affects how they perceive themselves and others and ultimately impacts their interpersonal communication.

A second frequently studied variable that affects perceptions is age. Recall the last time you engaged in a conversation with older relatives, friends, or co-workers. Did you notice any differences in your perspectives on various issues? One student recently shared an example of a conversation held with her mother that illustrated the impact of age on perceptual differences. Because this female student does not like to cook or clean, her mother told her that "No man will want to marry her!" The daughter argued her "case" by explaining to her mother that times have changed and that women and men today often share domestic responsibilities in the home. This conversation between mother and daughter illustrates how age and experience impacts our perceptions. As we grow older, we tend to build on our diverse life experiences and our perceptions often change or, in some cases, become more firmly ingrained. Some research indicates that older individuals possess more consistent and stable attitudes and are more difficult to persuade (Alwin and Krosnick 1991). Other findings suggest that as people age they become more cognitively sophisticated and are better able to see the world from others' perspectives (Bartsch and London 2000). Thus, it is important to consider how age affects both our own and others' perceptions.

Finally, culture affects our perceptions of the world and simultaneously influences our communication with others. In Chapter Ten we discuss the impact of cultural differences on perceptions and interpersonal communication in greater detail. However, it is important to restate the powerful impact culture can have on our perceptions. One reason for examining cultural differences is to learn more about how socialization in different cultures affects peoples' perceptions and behavior. For example, researchers often study perceptual and behavioral differences in individualistic and collectivistic cultures. Collectivistic cultures emphasize group harmony and concern for others. An example of a collectivistic culture is found in China. Individualistic cultures, as found in the United States, tend to value individual rights, independence, and autonomy. Members of collectivistic cultures view the world much differently than individuals from highly individualistic cultures. There are numerous research examples which illustrate the difference between individualistic and collectivistic cultural beliefs, attitudes, behaviors, and values. One interesting study explored Chinese and U.S. managerial differences in attempts to influence employees (Yukl, Fu, and McDonald 2003). According to Yukl and his colleagues, "the cross-cultural differences in rated effectiveness of tactics were consistent with cultural values and traditions" (Yukl, Fu, and McDonald 2003, 68). Chinese managers rated informal strategies and strategies that emphasized personal relations as more effective than traditional Western strategies which emphasize being direct and task oriented. Swiss and American managers perceived more direct task-oriented tactics as being more effective than informal strategies and strategies that emphasized personal relations. In another study, Miller (1984) examined the impact of culture on the fundamental attribution error. She asked children and adults in India and the U.S. to provide possible explanations for pro-social (e.g., helping someone paint their house) and anti-social behaviors (e.g., engaging in aggressive behavior). Miller's findings provide valuable insight into how factors such as age and culture impact our perception. Children in both cultures offered similar attributions for the behaviors. However, adults in the U.S. were more likely than their Indian counterparts to explain events by attributing them to individual traits. Adults from India, on the other hand, focused on situational or contextual causes as possible explanations for behaviors. It is important to remember that most of us hold more favorable perceptions of the groups we belong to than those to which we do not belong. Thus, we should be cognizant of our tendency to be favorably disposed towards people, ideas, beliefs, and concepts from our culture and our inclination to be more critical of people, ideas, and concepts from other cultural perspectives.

THE LINK BETWEEN PERCEPTION AND LISTENING

By now you have a more sophisticated understanding of why some information is selected over others, how information is organized, and how messages are interpreted. Additionally, we have provided you with some information about common attribution errors that individuals make and variables that affect the process of perception. To further understand the potential implications of perception, we must consider how our different perspectives of people and messages influence and are influenced by listening. At the beginning of this chapter, we pointed out that perception and listening are closely related to one another. Our perception of others impacts both our ability and our desire to listen in social interactions.

In the *Friends* episode "The One the Morning After" Ross tries to explain to Rachel his reasons for sleeping with another woman on the same night that Rachel suggested that they take a "break" from their relationship. Ross pleads with Rachel to work through it. He tells her he can't even think of what his life would be like without her; without everything she is to him. Rachel just can't get beyond what Ross did to betray her. She tells him that he has become a completely different person to her, now that she's seen that he is capable of hurting her. Rachel believes there will never be anything he can say or do that will change the way she feels about him now.

Because her perception of Ross' commitment to their relationship has changed, so has Rachel's ability to listen to the messages he attempts to communicate. As we listen to messages communicated by others, new information is provided that may cause us to change existing perceptions or perhaps even form new ones. Listening is an essential part of effective interpersonal communication. Yet it is often understudied and underemphasized in communication courses. In the next section we make a distinction between hearing and listening, offer strategies to enhance your own listening skills, and describe the various listening styles employed by individuals.

Listening

These quotations illustrate the power and functions of listening in the communication process. Listening is a key element for acquiring information and developing and sustaining our relationships. Yet, communication practitioners often refer to listening as the "forgotten" communication skill. The fact that listening skills are often neglected or undervalued is surprising since most people engage in listening more than any other type of communication activity. For example, college students report that up to 50 percent of their time is spent listening, compared to speaking (20 percent), reading (6 percent), and writing (8 percent) (Janusik and Wolvin 2006). While colleges often require classes which emphasize competence in writing and speaking, few highlight listening as an important communication skill.

When we engage in effective listening behaviors we communicate a message that we comprehend and care about what the speaker has to say. Recall a time when you attempted to communicate with a friend or family member, only to receive a distracted response of "Yeah. Uh-huh. Mm-hmm." The lack of active listening behavior is extremely frustrating. A lack of awareness of ineffective listening behaviors has potential negative implications for both personal and professional relationships. Our goal in focusing on this topic is twofold: to assist you in understanding the listening process and to shed some light on how your own behaviors may be interpreted by others. Our hope is that after completing this chapter you will be able to evaluate your own listening skills and to implement some of our suggestions.

As stated earlier, individuals typically spend more time listening during their lifetime than any other communication activity. For many of you, this chapter will be the only formal training in appropriate and effective listening skills you will ever have. The implications of effective listening span a variety of interpersonal contexts. In the health care setting, Wanzer and her colleagues (2004) found that patients who perceived their physicians to employ effective listening skills were more satisfied with their doctor and the care provided. Research has also identified a link between one's career success and effective listening skills. Employers report that listening is a top skill sought in hiring new employees, and it plays a significant role in evaluations for promotion and incentives (AICPA 2006). As we begin our discussion of effective listening skills, it is important that we first distinguish between the concepts of "hearing" and "listening."

> Gina was cooking dinner for Joni one evening after a long day at work. As she stirred the pasta sauce on the stove, she sighed, "I just don't understand why my manager doesn't see what's happening with our latest project. Half of the team is running around clueless, and I keep getting left with their messes to clean up."
>
> Joni gave a half-hearted response while scanning her emails on her laptop. "Uh-huh," she said without breaking eye contact with the computer screen.
>
> Gina stopped cooking and scolded Joni, "You never listen when I try to tell you about my day at work!"
>
> Joni was shocked, "What do you mean? I heard every word you said!"

Marge, it takes two to lie. One to lie and one to listen.
—Homer Simpson

The most basic of all human needs is the need to understand and be understood. The best way to understand people is to listen to them.
—Ralph Nichols

Listening, not imitation, may be the sincerest form of flattery.
—Dr. Joyce Brothers

TABLE 4.1 Daily Average Hours Devoted to Communication Activities

Communication Activities	Total Number of Hours	Approximate Percentage of Time
Writing	1.82	8
Reading	1.40	6
Speaking	4.83	20
Listening*	5.80	24
Television*	2.12	9
Radio*	.86	4
CD/Tapes*	1.32	5
Phone*	1.87	8
Email	1.33	6
Internet	2.73	11
Total Listening Hours	**11.97**	**50**

Items marked with an * represent those activities which focus primarily on listening.

Gina countered, "Prove it! What did I just say?"

Joni dropped her head and apologized, realizing that while she had heard Gina talking, she hadn't really listened to a word she said.

Have you ever been involved in a situation similar to the one described above? Perhaps you have been the one who has heard the words but did not listen to what was being said. Perhaps one of the most common mistakes made in the listening process is making the assumption that hearing is the same as listening. In fact, listening and hearing are two distinct processes. **Hearing** involves the physical process of sound waves traveling into the ear canal, vibrating the ear drum and eventually sending signals to the brain. Although we often hear messages, we do not necessarily attend to them. This explains why you might be sitting in your room right now reading this text and hearing an air conditioner turn on, birds chirping outside, or friends yelling in the hallway. But while your brain has processed these sound waves, you may not have necessarily been listening for these stimuli. **Listening** not only involves the physical process of hearing, but it also involves the psychological process of attending to the stimuli, creating meaning and responding. Listening is often described as a dynamic and ongoing process in which individuals physically receive a message, employ cognitive processes to attribute meaning to the message, and provide verbal and/or nonverbal feedback to the source.

As you reflect on this definition, it should become quite apparent that listening is a highly complex process. First, listening is dynamic because it is an ongoing activity that requires an individual to be active and engaged. Unlike hearing, listening requires an individual to be mindful and aware of one's surroundings. After we physically receive the sound waves and hear the message, the next step involves employing cognitive processing to attribute meaning to the information that was received. Hopefully the steps involved in this cognitive process are familiar to you. They include: selection, organization, and interpretation. Do you recall our earlier discussion of these stages as part of the perception process? These same elements are involved in listening. We are selective in the information we expose ourselves to and attend to in the perception process; the same is true in listening. We select what sounds and messages we will listen to and which we will ignore. Have you ever encountered a mother who can carry on a phone conversation and never become distracted while children are screaming and playing in the background? The mother has selected what sounds to focus her attention on in the listening process—she has selected the message that is being received via the telephone. Just as we organize stimuli during the perception process, information is also organized as a part of the listening process. Finally, we must interpret information and assign a meaning to what we have heard while listening. The relationship between perception and listening should be even clearer—the similarities between both processes are nearly identical. The final stage of the listening process involves formulating a response, or feedback, to send to the source via verbal and/or nonverbal channels. Examples of verbal feedback may include, "You look sad," "Tell me more," or "What do you plan to do?" Some examples of nonverbal responses could include nodding your head, making eye contact, or even giving a hug.

To help you remember some of the key strategies involved in effective listening, remember the following acronym: **BIG EARS**. Each of these strategies is discussed in the paragraphs that follow.

How can you keep yourself from daydreaming during a long lecture?
© Anita, 2007, Shutterstock.

TABLE 4.2	Key Strategies for Effective Listening (BIG EARS)
B	Be open and receptive to the message
I	Interpret the message
G	Give feedback
E	Engage in dual perspective
A	Adapt your listening style
R	Reduce noise
S	Store the message

Be Open to the Message. Listening is difficult enough to begin with, but when we fail to prepare ourselves to receive messages, it becomes even more so. Effective listening requires you to employ effective nonverbal listening behaviors, control message overload, and manage your preoccupations and other distractions.

First, we need to be aware of our nonverbal listening behaviors. The next time you are sitting in class listening to a lecture, take a moment and consider the role your nonverbal behaviors play in the listening process. Do you look like you are open to receiving messages? Maintaining an open body position, engaging in eye contact, and responding to the lecture by nodding your head are all examples of nonverbal behaviors that communicate a willingness to listen.

Next, focus on ways to manage the multiple sources of information that are competing for your attention. Remember our discussion of perception and the role of selective attention and exposure? Effective listening behaviors require you to dedicate your attention to a particular message. The next time you are tempted to watch *Grey's Anatomy* while carrying on a phone conversation with your mother, think twice. One of the sources will ultimately win out over the other—will it be the television show or your mother?

Finally, identify ways to manage the multiple preoccupations and distractions that can impair your ability to listen. Look beyond superficial factors that may be hindering your ability to focus on the message. While a professor's distracting delivery style or prehistoric clothing choices may cause your attention to focus away from the lecture being delivered, these are not excuses to disregard the source's message. Remain focused on the content of the message. On average, Americans speak at a rate of 125 words per minute. However, the human brain can process more than 450 words per minute (Hilliard and Palmer 2003) and we can think at a rate of 1000–3000 words per minute (Hilliard and Palmer 2003). So what happens with all that extra time? Often we daydream or we become bored because our brain can work faster than the speaker can talk. Therefore, it is important to dedicate yourself to relating the information to existing information that you already know. While this can be challenging at times, chances are that it will prove to be extremely useful. Ask yourself questions during a conversation or lecture such as, "How will this information benefit me?" or "How will this information benefit my relationship with the source?" Being open to receiving messages is the first step to ensuring an effective listening experience.

Interpreting the Message. Interpretation refers to the cognitive processes involved in listening. Recall our discussion of the role of interpretation in perception. We pointed out that associations are often made between stimuli and things with which we are already familiar. Interpretation is also a key element in listening, and in verifying that the meaning we assigned to the message is close to that which was intended by the source. Some strategies to assist in interpretation of messages include asking questions, soliciting feedback, and requesting clarification. These strategies will help you interpret the source's message more accurately. Consider the following interaction between Maya and Raj:

Maya: I hate biology.

Raj: Why?

Maya: Well, I guess I don't hate it, but I am upset I did poorly on the first exam.

Raj: Why did you do poorly?

Maya: Because I studied the wrong chapters.

Raj: So, do you dislike the material?

Maya: Well, no, I actually enjoy the teacher and the book.

Raj: So, you like biology but you are upset you studied the wrong material?

Maya: Yes, I actually like the course; I am just mad because I know I could have received an A if I had studied the right material.

Because Raj asked Maya to provide additional information to help clarify why she hated biology he was able to interpret Maya's situation more clearly. In fact, it changed the meaning of the message entirely. Maya's initial message was that she hated biology and it turns out that she actually enjoys biology. Raj was able to accurately interpret the message because he asked questions and solicited feedback. But soliciting feedback is not the only element involved in listening. **Paraphrasing** is another useful strategy for clarifying meaning and ensuring that you have accurately interpreted a message. Paraphrasing involves restating a message in your own words to see if the meaning you assigned was similar to that which was intended. But this is still not enough. Effective listening also requires you to provide the source with feedback to communicate that you have both received and understood the message.

Give Feedback. Feedback serves many purposes in the listening process. By providing feedback to the source, we are confirming that we received the message and were able to interpret and assign meaning to what was being communicated. Feedback can be either positive or negative and communicate its own message. **Positive feedback** includes verbal and nonverbal behaviors that encourage the speaker to continue communicating. Examples of positive feedback include eye contact, nods, and comments such as, "I see," and "Please continue." **Negative feedback** is often discouraging to a source. Examples of negative feedback would be disconfirming verbal comments such as "You are over-reacting" or "I don't know why you get so upset," or negative nonverbal responses such as avoidance of eye contact, maintaining a closed body position (e.g., crossed arms), or meaningless vocalizations such as "Um-hmm." Positive feedback communicates interest and empathy for the speaker, whereas negative feedback often results in feelings of defensiveness.

Engage in Dual-Perspective Taking. **Dual-perspective taking**, or empathy, refers to the attempt to see things from the other person's point of view. The concept of empathy has been a primary focus of the listening process required of social workers and counselors. Norton (1978) explains this by theorizing that all people are part of two systems—a larger societal system and a more immediate personal system. While it is often possible to gain insight into an individual's societal system, truly understanding someone's personal system is often a more difficult task. Consider the phrase, "Put yourself in another person's shoes." Do you think it is possible to truly put yourself in another person's shoes? This would require us to be able to tap into their unique background and experiences in order to perceive things exactly as they do. But is this ever really possible? Our position is that it is not. This

What kinds of positive feedback show that you are interested and listening?
© Phil Date, 2007, Shutterstock.

Empathetic listening requires an attempt to see things from your friend's point of view.
© Galina Barskaya, 2007, Shutterstock.

may help explain why we find it difficult to respond to a friend who is going through a difficult break-up. Our initial response may be to respond with a statement like, "I know exactly how you feel. I've been through dozens of broken relationships." But this is not necessarily the best response. There is a unique history to your friend's relationship that you can never truly understand. While you cannot fully put yourself in her shoes, you can communicate empathy by attempting to see things from her point of view. Reaching into their "field of experience" (as discussed in Chapter One) and trying to understand the framework which they use to interpret the world can influence your ability to effectively listen. Dual-perspective taking requires a receiver to adapt his listening style to accommodate a variety of situations.

Adapt Your Listening Style. Effective communicators are flexible in their communication style and find it easy to adjust both their speaking and listening styles, based on the unique demands of the receiver, the material, or the situation. Duran (1983) defines communicative adaptability as a cognitive and behavioral "ability to perceive socio-interpersonal relationships and adapt one's interaction goals and behaviors accordingly" (320). Duran and Kelly (1988) developed the Communicative Adaptability Scale. Their scale suggests we can adapt our communication in six different ways which include: social composure (feeling relaxed in social situations), social experience (enjoying and participating socially), social confirmation (maintaining the other's social image), appropriate disclosures (adapting one's disclosures appropriately to the intimacy level of the exchange), articulation (using appropriate syntax and grammar), and wit (using humor to diffuse social tension). You can determine the extent to which you are adaptable on these six dimensions by completing the Communication Adaptability Scale at http://cart.rmcdenver.com/instruments/communicative_adaptability.pdf.

Reduce Noise. Noise refers to anything that interferes with the reception of a message. Recall the various types of noise that were discussed in Chapter One: physical, psychological, and physiological noise. Our job as listeners is to focus on ways to reduce the noise that interferes with the reception of messages.

Oftentimes, this is easier said than done. While we are able to control some forms of physical noise that interfere with listening (e.g., cell phones or radios), other types of physical noise may be more difficult to manage (e.g., a neighbor mowing her yard). Obviously, the less noise there is, the better our chances of effectively receiving the message. Reducing psychological and physiological noise may be more difficult. Sometimes it is difficult to listen to a professor's lecture knowing that you have a big midterm exam in the class that follows, and gnawing hunger pains that begin during your 11:00 A.M. class can impair listening as well. Consider ways to manage these potential distractions and maximize listening potential—be prepared for that exam, be sure to eat something before leaving for class. Planning ahead for potential distractions to listening can ultimately assist you in receiving a message that you can store in memory for future reference.

Store the Message. A final strategy in the listening process involves storing what we have received for later reference. This process involves three stages: remembering, retention, and recall. Have you ever been impressed with a doctor or a professor because they remembered, retained, and recalled your name? This is not an easy task. Nichols (1961) demonstrated that immediately after listening to a ten-minute lecture, students were only able to remember about fifty percent of what they heard. As time passes, so does our ability to remember. Nichols' study suggested that after two weeks, most listeners were only able to remember about twenty-five percent of what they had heard. The following are strategies that can be used to enhance message retention.

1. Form associations between the message and something you already know.
2. Create a visual image of the information you want to remember.
3. Create a story about what you want to remember to create links between ideas. *Suppose your mother asks you to go to the store to pick up soda, laundry detergent and paper cups. You can enhance your ability to remember the information by creating a story which links the ideas such as, "Sam dropped a paper cup full of soda on her jeans and now they need to be put in the laundry machine."*
4. Create acronyms by using the beginning letters of a list of words to assist your recall. BIG EARS is an example of this tool.
5. Rhyme or create a rhythm to organize information. Creating a song or rhyme that is unusual or humorous typically helps trigger recall.

Listening Styles

Reflecting on your own interpersonal relationships, did you ever notice that individuals have different listening styles? Or perhaps you have noticed that an individual's listening style changed when the topic changed. Have you considered your own listening style and how it may change with the person or topic? For example, with our friends we might pay more attention to their feelings and when we listen to co-workers we may be more focused on the content of the message. Research has identified four predominant listening styles (Watson, Barker, and Weaver 1995). **Listening style** is defined as a set of "attitudes, beliefs, and predispositions about the how, where, when, who, and what of the information reception and encoding process" (Watson, Barker, and Weaver 1995, 2). This suggests that we tend to focus our listening. We may pay more attention to a person's feelings, the structure or content, or particular delivery elements, such as time. The four listening styles are people-oriented, action-oriented, content-oriented, and time-oriented. There is no optimal listening style. Different situations call for different styles. However, it is important to understand your predominate listening style. Let us take a closer look at each of these listening styles.

People-Oriented. First, **people-oriented** listeners seek common interests with the speaker and are highly responsive. They are interested in the speaker's feelings and emotions. Research shows a positive relationship between the people-oriented listening style and conversational sensitivity (Cheseboro 1999). This makes sense since people-oriented listeners try to understand the speakers' perspective and therefore are more sensitive to their emotional needs. They are quick to notice slight fluctuations in tone and mood. For example, they may comment, "You really look upset," or "You smile every time you say her name." Although you must consider the individual and the situation, this style may work best when we are communicating with our friends or family about sensitive issues.

Action-Oriented. An **action-oriented** listener prefers error-free and concise messages. They get easily frustrated with speakers who do not clearly articulate their message in a straightforward manner. They tend to steer speakers to be organized and timely in their message delivery. They grow impatient with disorganized speakers that use ambiguous descriptions or provide unrelated details. For example, an action-oriented listener may use the phrase "Get to the point," when the speaker is telling a lengthy story or may interrupt a speaker and say, "So. . . . what did you do?" The action-oriented listening style may work best when there is little time for extra details and decisions need to be made quickly.

Content-Oriented. Unlike the people-oriented listener, the **content-oriented** listener focuses on the details of the message. They pick up on the facts of the story and analyze it from a critical perspective. They decipher between credible and noncredible information and ask direct questions. They try to understand the message from several perspectives. For example, they may say, "Did you ever think they did that because . . ." or "Another way to think about the situation is . . ." Because they analyze the speaker's content with a critical eye, the speaker may feel reluctant to share information because they do not want to hear alternative perspectives. Additionally, they may feel intimidated by the criticalness of content-oriented listeners since they are engaged by challenging and intellectual discussion. The content-oriented listening style works best in serious situations that call for vital decision-making.

Time-Oriented. Finally, **time-oriented** listeners are particularly interested in brief interactions with others. They direct the length of the conversation by suggesting, "I only have a minute," or they send leave taking cues (such as walking away or looking at the clock) when they believe the speaker is taking up too much of their time. This type of listening is essential when time is a limited commodity. Usually, time is precious in the workplace. A day can be eaten up by clients, co-workers, supervisors, and other individuals needing our attention. Time-oriented individuals protect their time by expressing to others how much effort they will devote to their cause.

Gender and Cultural Differences in Listening Styles

Some researchers suggest there are gender differences when it comes to listening styles. In the mid-1980s, Booth-Butterfield reported that "males tend to hear the facts while females are more aware of the mood of the communication" (1984, 39). Just about twenty years later, researchers' findings were consistent in indicating that men score themselves higher on the content-oriented listening style and women score themselves higher on the people-oriented listening style (Sargent and Weaver 2003). In addition, Kiewitz and Weaver III (1997) found that when comparing young adults from three different countries, Germans preferred the action style, Israelis preferred the content style, and Americans preferred the people and time styles.

Although no listening style is best, it is imperative to understand your own listening style and to recognize the listening styles of others. Depending on the situation and the goals in communicating, you may need to adjust your listening style. In addition, recognizing the listening style in others will help direct your responding messages. For example, if you notice your boss is engaging in action-oriented listening style, you may want to produce a clearly articulated message. He may become irritated if you include miscellaneous information or use confusing vocabulary.

Motivation to Listen and Potential Pitfalls

When we do anything, we have some kind of motivation, or purpose. Sometimes this motivation is driven by our goals, dreams, and interests. Other times motivation may be a result of guilt, responsibility, or shame. Consider your motive for attending school. Perhaps you are a student because you have set a goal to graduate or maybe you are motivated out of a sense of responsibility to your parents. Either way, motivation drives behavior. Have you ever considered your motivation for listening? Researchers have identified five listening motivations (Wolvin and Coakley 1988). Certain motivations for listening lend themselves to particular listening barriers. Therefore, let us examine each of these motivations independently and offer potential pitfalls for each. Table 4.3 presents some guidelines for effective listening.

TABLE 4.3 Guidelines for Effective Listening
Effective listeners do their best to avoid these behaviors:
1. Calling the subject uninteresting
2. Criticizing the speaker and/or delivery
3. Getting overstimulated
4. Listening only for facts (bottom line)
5. Not taking notes or outlining everything
6. Faking attention
7. Tolerating or creating distractions
8. Tuning out difficult material
9. Letting emotional words block the message
10. Wasting the time difference between speed of speech and speed of thought

Source: Nichols, R. G., and L. A. Stevens. 1957. *Are you listening?* New York: McGraw-Hill.

Discriminate Listening. First, we may listen for the purpose of discriminating. The purpose of **discriminate listening** is to help us understand the meaning of the message. In certain situations we want to discriminate between what is fact and what is an opinion. Or perhaps we try to discriminate between what is an emotionally-based argument and what is a logically-based argument. One example of a situation in which we might engage in discriminate listening is in the workplace when we attentively listen to how a co-worker responds to our new recommendation. Here we are trying to determine if they agree or disagree with us. Another example is engaging in listening in the classroom when the teacher suggests that portions of the lecture will be on the exam. In this example, we are discriminating between what the teacher believes is important material for the exam and what is not going to be on the exam. Furthermore, we tend to use discriminate listening when we are trying to determine whether someone is lying to us.

Potential Pitfall. Often when we are trying to discriminate between messages, we selectively listen to certain stimuli while ignoring others. For example, if someone does not maintain eye contact with us, we may jump to conclusions regarding her trustworthiness. If discrimination is your motivation, it is important to keep an open mind and attend to the entire message.

Appreciative Listening. Another motivation we have for listening is **appreciative listening**. The purpose of appreciative listening is for the pure enjoyment of listening to the stimuli. This may be listening to your favorite tunes on your iPod, attending the opera, a musical or the movies, or listening to the sounds of the waves crashing on the shore.

Potential Pitfall. With appreciative listening it is important to be proactive. In order to be successful in appreciative listening you must *decrease noise*. You can do this by controlling distractions. For example, turn off your cell phone. Sometimes you can even choose your physical environment. If you are going to the movies, you can choose a particular seat away from potentially "loud" patrons. Or you may choose to go to the movies with a partner that will not inhibit your pleasure-seeking experience by talking or asking questions throughout.

Comprehensive Listening. We also may be motivated to listen in order to grasp new information. **Comprehensive listening** involves mindfully receiving and remembering new information. When our boss is informing us of our new job duties or a friend is telling you when they need to be picked up at the airport we are engaging in comprehensive listening. Our goal is to accurately understand the new information and be able to retain it.

Potential Pitfall. Often there are several messages that the speaker is sending and it is the job of the listener to determine which messages are the most important. With comprehensive listening it is critical to *recognize the main ideas and identify supportive details*. If you are unsure, *seek feedback or paraphrase the message*. For example, you may ask, "So you are flying Southwest and you need me to pick you up at baggage claim at 10:00 P.M., correct?"

Evaluative Listening. When our motivation goes beyond comprehending messages to judging messages we are engaging in evaluative listening. **Evaluative listening** involves critically assessing messages. This occurs when a salesperson is trying to persuade us to buy a product or when we listen to political speeches. We are evaluating the credibility and competency of the speaker and the message. Our goal here is to create opinions and sound judgments regarding people and information.

Potential Pitfall. Prejudices and biases may interfere with our listening ability when we are motivated to listen for evaluative purposes. For example, individuals who identify with a particular political party are quick to judge the messages of an individual representing an alternative party. It is important to *be aware of your own preconceived notions* and not let that impede on your ability to effectively interpret the speaker's message.

Empathetic Listening. The last motivation to listen is for empathetic reasons. The purpose of **empathetic** (or therapeutic) **listening** is to help others. For example, we may meet up with our friends to discuss their most recent romantic episodes or we may help our family members make tough financial decisions. Our goal is to provide a supportive ear and assist in uncovering alternative perspectives. Often, just by listening our friends will identify their own issues or our family members will uncover their own solutions to their problems. Other times, they may ask for suggestions or recommendations.

Potential Pitfall. It is critical to distinguish if the speaker indeed wants you to be an active participant in offering solutions or if he wants you "just to listen." Sometimes we assume that solutions are being sought, but what is really wanted is someone to act as a "sounding board."

Common Listening Misbehaviors

There can be severe consequences when we choose not to listen effectively. One study found that the second most frequently occurring mistake made by education leaders deals with poor interpersonal communication skills and that the most frequent example given for this type of mistake was *failure to listen* (Bulach, Pickett, and Booth 1998). The perception that we are not listening may be because we lack appropriate eye contact with the speaker, we appear preoccupied or distracted with other issues, or because we do not provide the appropriate feedback. When we send these signals, the speaker interprets our behavior as not caring. This can damage internal and external business relationships. These behaviors can have severe consequences. Another study examined the top five reasons why principals lost their jobs (Davis 1997). The results of this study found that the most frequently cited response by superintendents focused on failure to communicate in ways that build positive relationships. The results of this study can be applied to situations outside of the educational setting. So, how do people communicate in ways that do not build positive relationships? This section will identify the six common listening misbehaviors.

Pseudo-Listening. **Pseudo-listening** is when we are pretending to listen. We look like we are listening by nodding our head or providing eye contact, but we are faking our attention. This is a self-centered approach to listening. Let us be honest, when we are pseudo-listening we are not "fooling" anyone. We are not able to ask appropriate questions and we are not able to provide proper feedback.

Monopolizing. Listeners that engage in **monopolizing** take the focus off the speaker and redirect the conversation and attention to themselves. Often, monopolizers interrupt the speaker to try to "one up" the speaker. They may try to top his story by saying "That reminds me . . ." or "You think that is bad–let me tell you what happened to me. . . ."

Disconfirming. Listeners that deny the feelings of the speaker are sending **disconfirming** messages. Recall our discussion in Chapter Four regarding the implication of sending disconfirming messages. Examples of disconfirming messages include: "You shouldn't feel bad . . ." or "Don't cry . . . there is no need to cry." This misbehavior discourages the source to continue speaking and decreases perceptions of empathy.

Defensive Listening. An individual who engages in **defensive listening** perceives a threatening environment. Defensive communication has been defined as "that behavior which occurs when an individual perceives threat or anticipates threat in the group" (Gibb 1961, 141). Defensiveness includes "how he appears to others, how he may seem favorable, how he may win, dominate, impress, or escape punishment, and/or how he may avoid or miti-gate a perceived or anticipated threat" (141). In other words, defensiveness is a process of saving "face." The issue of face is associated with people's desire to display a positive public image (Goffman 1967). An example of defensive listening is, "Don't look at me, I did not tell you to do that. . . ."

Selective Listening. **Selective listening** happens when a listener focuses only on parts of the message. She takes parts of the message that she agrees with (or does not agree with) and responds to those particular parts. We reduce cognitive dissonance or psychological discomfort, screening out mes-sages that we do not agree with, to remain cognitively "stable." For example, if we recently bought a new SUV, we may choose not to pay attention to mes-sages suggesting that SUV's are not environmentally sound. We would, how-ever, choose to pay attention to messages that suggest SUV vehicles rated higher on safety tests.

Ambushing. Ambushers will listen for information that they can use to attack the speaker. They are selectively and strategically listening for messages that they can use against the speaker. Often ambushers interrupt the speaker. They do not allow the speaker to complete his thought and jump to conclu-sions. Ambushers make assumptions and get ahead of the speaker by finish-ing his sentences. They are self-motivated and lack dual perspective.

SUMMARY

In this chapter, we explained the perception process: selecting information, organizing information and interpreting information. Additionally, we identified and explained factors related to each of the three primary selectivity processes. At this point, you should have a more detailed understanding of why certain messages or information gets selected over others. We also learned more about the four types of schema that affect interpersonal communication. Once information has been selected and organized, the final step is interpretation. The primary theory that explains how we make sense of our own behavior and that of others is attribution theory. The way that we make sense of our own and others' behavior is quite different and flawed. In the final sections we discussed the two primary attribution errors as well as factors that affect our interpretation process.

In the last section of this chapter, we explained the difference between hearing and listening. Remember, listening refers to the dynamic process in which individuals physically hear a message, employ cognitive processes to attribute meaning to the message, and provide verbal and/or nonverbal feedback to the source. Afterwards, we identified the seven steps to effective listening by using the acronym BIG EARS: Be open to the message, Interpret the message, Give positive feedback, Engage in dual perspective, Adapt your listening style, Reduce noise, and Store the message. Not only is it important to increase your listening skills, it is also crucial to recognize different listening styles. We discussed four different types of listening styles: people-oriented, action-oriented, content-oriented, and time-oriented. Then we explained why people are motivated to listen. Four motivations to listen are to discriminate, appreciate, comprehend, and evaluate. By identifying potential pitfalls for each motivation, our hope is that you can adapt your communication to the message recipient and also be aware of your own shortcomings. Finally, we recognized six common listening misbehaviors including: pseudo-listening, disconfirming, defensive listening, monopolizing, selective listening, and ambushing.

EXERCISES

Activity #1: "Chatter Matters"

Youngsters are encouraged to become little chatterboxes to promote better communication skills. Children aged three to five at Hardwick Primary School, Stockton, will receive a Chatter Matters bag each week, containing a game, book, toy, and CD designed to improve their talking, listening, and reading. Teacher Linda Whitwell said each week the children will swap bags, so they get to use a number of different devices to develop their talents. She said: "The children will be taking the bags home each week, so we are hoping to encourage parents to work with their children to improve their reading, writing, and speaking ability. It will be something fun and different for everyone to use, and hopefully it will have the desired affect." (p. 6). *This excerpt was taken from "The Northern Echo" on February 22, 2006.*

Discussion Questions:

1. What are some advantages of this endeavor?
2. What might be some limitations?
3. If you were coordinating "Chatter Matters," what would you emphasize?

From *The Northern Echo*, February 22, 2006. Reprinted with permission.

Activity #2: Practice Responding

Complete the conversation below using the prompts in parentheses.
Sample: Erica: I am really sad.
      You: *What's the matter?* (Probe to find out more.)

1. Erica: My mom just called and she sounded awful.

   You: _____ (Probe to get an example.)

2. Erica: She said that my dad is leaving her.

   You: _____ (Paraphrase what Erica just said.)

3. Erica: Well, they have not been getting along lately.

   You: _____ (Probe to find out more.)

4. Erica: I noticed they were fighting more often over Thanksgiving.

   You: _____ (Empathize with Erica.)

5. Erica: Yeah. I am totally miserable.

Activity #3: Listening Responses

Identify which listening responses are positive and which are negative by placing a "P" or an "N" on the line before the response.

_____ There is no reason to get upset.

_____ This happens to everyone.

_____ Can you give me an example? / What do you mean?

_____ Don't feel bad.

_____ So you're not getting along? / Do you mean you're arguing a lot?

_____ You're tougher than this.

_____ Snap out of it.

_____ What makes you think that? Tell me more.

_____ You must be really upset. That's terrible.

_____ She is not worth it.

_____ Get over it.

_____ It's not that bad.

Activity #4: Listening Is Work: Willingness to Listen

Often, it is not a lack of skill that makes someone a poor listener; rather it is a lack of effort on the listener's part (Richmond and Hickson 2001). Determine the extent to which you do or do not make an effort to listen to speakers by completing the Willingness to Listen Measure. This measure tells you how well you listen in public speaking situations and can be found at http://www.jamescmccroskey.com/measures/wtlisten.htm.

REFERENCES

Abelson, R. P. 1982. Three modes of attitude-behavior consistency. In M. P. Zanna, E. T. Higgins, and C. P. Herman (Eds.), *Consistency in social behavior: The Ontario symposium* (Vol. 2, 131–146). Hillsdale, NJ: Lawrence Erlbaum Associates.

AICPA. 2006. *Highlighted Responses from the Association for Accounting marketing survey: Creating the Future Agenda for the Profession—Managing Partner Perspective.* Retrieved December 22, 2006, from *http://www.aicpa.org/pubs/tpcpa/feb2001/ hilight.htm.*

Alwin, D. F., and J. A. Krosnick. 1991. Aging, cohorts, and the stability of sociopolitical orientations over the lifespan. *American Journal of Sociology, 97,* 169–195.

Bartsch, K., and K. London. 2000. Children's use of state information in selecting persuasive arguments. *Developmental Psychology, 36,* 352–365.

Booth-Butterfield, M. 1984. She hears . . . he hears; What they hear and why. *Personnel Journal, 63,* 36–43.

Braithwaite, D. O., and L. M. Harter. 2000. Communication and the management of dialectical tensions in the personal relationships of people with disabilities. In D. O. Braithwaite and T. L. Thompson (Eds.), *Handbook of communication and people with disabilities.* Mahwah, NJ: Lawrence Erlbaum Associates.

Bulach, C., W. Pickett, and D. Boothe. 1998. *Mistakes educational leaders make.* ERIC Digest, 122. ERIC Clearinghouse on Educational Management, Eugene, OR.

Carlston, D. E. 1992. Impression formation and the modular mind: The associated systems theory. In L. L. Martin and A. T. Tesser (Eds.), *The construction of social justice* (pp. 301–341).

Chesebro, J. L. 1999. The relationship between listening and styles and conversational sensitivity. *Communication Research Reports, 16,* 233–238.

Cialdini, R. B. 2001. *Influence: Science and practice.* Boston, MA: Allyn and Bacon.

Davis, S. H. 1997. The principal's paradox: Remaining secure in precarious position. *NASSP Bulletin, 81,* 592, 73–80.

Duran, R. L. 1983. Communicative adaptability: A measure of social communicative competence. *Communication Quarterly, 31,* 320–326.

Duran, R. L., and L. Kelly. 1988. An investigation into the cognitive domain of competence II: The relationship between communicative competence and interaction involvement. *Communication Research Reports, 5,* 91–96.

Fehr, B. 2004. Intimacy expectations in same-sex friendships: A prototype interaction-pattern model. *Journal of personality and social psychology, 86,* 265–284.

Fehr, B., and J. A. Russell. 1991. The concept of love viewed from a prototype perspective. *Journal of Personality and Social Psychology, 60,* 425–438.

Fischer, P., E. Jonas, D. Frey, and S. Schulz-Hardt. 2005. Selective exposure to information: The impact of information limits. *European Journal of Social Psychology, 35,* 469–492.

Fiske, S. T., and S. E. Taylor. 1984. *Social cognition.* Reading, MA: Addison-Wesley.

Gass, R. H., and J. S. Seiter. 2003. *Persuasion, social influence and compliance gaining.* Boston, MA: Allyn and Bacon.

Gibb, J. R. 1961. Defensive communication. *Journal of Communication, 11,* 141–149.

Goffman, E. 1967. *Interaction ritual: Essays on face-to-face behavior.* New York: Pantheon Books.

Gorham, J., and D. M. Christophel. 1992. Students' perceptions of teacher behaviors as motivating and demotivating factors in college classes. *Communication Quarterly, 40,* 239–252.

Hilliard, B., and J. Palmer. 2003. Networking like a pro!: 20 tips on turning the contracts you get into the connections you need. Agito Consulting.

Hamachek, D. 1992. *Encounters with the self (3rd ed.).* Fort Worth, TX: Harcourt Brace Jovanovich.

Hamilton, D. L., and J. W. Sherman. 1994. Stereotypes. In R. Wyer and T. Srull (Eds.), *Handbook of social cognition (2nd ed.).* (1–68). Hillsdale, NJ: Lawrence Erlbaum.

Heider, F. 1958. Attitudes and cognitive organization. *Journal of Psychology, 21,* 107–112.

Hockberg, J. E. 1978. *Perception (2nd ed).* Englewood Cliffs, NJ: Prentice Hall.

Hockenbury, D. H., and S. E. Hockenbury. 2006. *Psychology (4th ed.).* New York, NY: Worth Publishers.

Janusik, L. A., and A. D. Wolvin. 2006. *24 hours in a day: A listening update to the time studies.* Paper presented at the meeting of the International Listening Association, Salem, OR.

Katz, A. M., and R. Hill. 1958. Residential propinquity and marital selection: A review of theory, method, and fact. *Marriage and Family Living, 20,* 27–35.

Kelley, H. H. 1967. Attribution theory in social psychology. In D. Levine (Ed.), *Nebraska Symposium on Motivation* (Vol. A5, p. 192–238). Lincoln: University of Nebraska Press.

———. 1971. *Attribution in social interaction.* Morristown, NJ: General Learning Press.

———. 1972. Causal schemata and the attribution process. In E. E. Jones, D. E. Kanouse, H. H. Kelley, R. E. Nisbett, S. Valins, and B. Weiner (Eds.), *Attribution: Perceiving the causes of behavior* (151–174). Morristown, NJ: General Learning Press.

———. 1973. The process of causal attribution. *American Psychologist, 28,* 107–128.

Kelly, G. A. 1970. A brief introduction to personal construct psychology. In D. Bannister (Ed.), *Perspectives in personal construct psychology* (1–30). San Diego: Academic Press.

———. 1991. *The psychology of personal constructs: Vol. 1. A theory of personality.* London: Routledge. (Original work published in 1955.)

Kelsey, D. M., P. Kearney, T. G. Plax, T. H. Allen, and K. J. Ritter. 2004. College students' attributions of teacher misbehaviors. *Communication Education, 53,* 40–55.

Kiewitz, C., and J. B. Weaver III. 1997. Cultural differences in listening style preferences: A comparison of young adults in Germany, Israel and the United States. *International Journal of Public Opinion Research, 9,* 233–247.

Klopf, D. 1995. *Intercultural encounters: The fundamentals of intercultural communication.* Englewood, CA: Morton.

Littlejohn, S. W. 1983. *Theories of human communication.* Belmont, CA: Wadsworth.

McCroskey, J. C., and V. A. Richmond. 1996. *Fundamentals of human communication.* Prospect Heights, Illinois: Waveland Press.

Miller, J. 1984. Culture and the development of everyday social explanation. *Journal of Personality and Social Psychology, 49,* 961–978.

Nichols, R. G. 1961. Do we know how to listen? Practical helps in a modern age. *Speech Teacher, 10,* 118–128.

Norton, D. 1978. *The dual perspective.* New York: Council on Social Work Education.

Raskin, J. D. 2002. Constructivism in psychology: Personal construct psychology, radical constructivism, and social constructivism. In J. D. Raskin and S. K. Bridges (Eds.), *Studies in meaning: Exploring constructivist psychology (1–25).* New York: Pace University Press.

Reeder, G. D. 1985. Implicit relations between disposition and behavior: Effects on dispositional attribution. In J. H. Harvey and G. Weary (Eds.), *Attribution: Basic issues and application* (87–116). New York: Academic Press.

Richmond, V. P., and M. Hickson, III. 2001. *Going public: A practical guide to public talk.* Boston: Allyn & Bacon.

Sargent, S. L., and J. B. Weaver III. 2003. Listening styles: Sex differences in perceptions of self and others. *International Journal of Listening, 17,* 5–18.

Tannen, D. 1986. *That's not what I meant.* New York: Ballantine Books.

———. 1990. *You just don't understand: Women and men in conversation.* New York: Ballantine Books.

———. 1994. *Gender and discourse.* New York: Oxford University Press.

Turner, J. C. 1987. *Rediscovering the social group: A self-categorization theory.* New York: Basil Blackwell.

Wanzer, M. B., M. Booth-Butterfield, and M. K. Gruber. 2004. Perceptions of health care providers' communication: Relationships between patient-centered communication and satisfaction. *Health Communication, 16,* 363–384.

Watson, K. W., L. L. Barker, and J. B. Weaver Ill. 1995. The listening styles profile (LSP-16): Development and validation of an instrument to assess four listening styles. *International Journal of Listening, 9,* 1–13.

Wolvin, A. D., and C. G. Coakley. 1988. Listening. Dubuque, IA: William C. Brown, Publishers.

Wood, J. T. 1999. *Gendered lives: Communication, gender, and culture* (3rd ed.). Belmont, CA: Wadsworth Publishing Co.

Yukl, G., P. P. Fu, and R. McDonald. 2003. Cross cultural differences in perceived effectiveness of influence tactics for initiating or resisting change. *Applied Psychology: An International Review, 52,* 68–82.

PERCEPTION AND LISTENING

When I was a kid, **Big Ears** was an insult. (I will save the stories of my childhood trauma for another time.) We are not good listeners. I say: We are **not** good listeners. We have more distractions in our lives than any people in history. There are more messages, thoughts, and useless information bombarding us than ever before.

Have you ever watched a modern student write a paper? The computer screen is on. A word processing program is operating and Facebook is on another screen, music is playing, and friends are walking by talking and interrupting. Oh, and of course, the ever-present phone is open on the desk in anticipation of a text or call. OMG! Whassup? LOL.

Our messages and our attention spans are getting shorter. Some people call it multitasking but research indicates that the brain works better when it focuses on one thing. We are losing the abilities to concentrate and to listen. Businesses hold seminars to teach employees how to listen. Communication professionals hold workshops to teach nurses, doctors, and police officers how to listen more effectively. Clearly, business professionals must understand the information being communicated to them and be able to effectively translate this material to others. Do our friends and families deserve any less? Relationships are lost when people do not listen to each other. Everyone needs to work on their **perception** and **listening skills**.

DEVELOPMENT OF SELF AND INDIVIDUAL DIFFERENCES
JUST ME, MYSELF, AND I

LEARNING OBJECTIVES

After reading this chapter, you should understand the following concepts:

- Define the term self and explain why it is viewed as a complex process
- Define the term self-complexity and explain the benefits of high self-complexity
- Explain the three components of the self-system and discuss how each component affects interpersonal communication
- Discuss the development of the self with special emphasis on the individuals and groups of individuals that play important roles in the development of the self
- Explain attachment theory, including the three attachment styles that affect the way individuals view the self and others
- State the importance of direct definitions and identity scripts
- Discuss the significance of the self-fulfilling prophecy and social comparison processes for identity formation
- State the difference between state and trait approaches in studying communication
- Define communication apprehension and discuss its effects
- Discuss the way communication apprehension is typically measured and identify treatment options for individuals scoring high in communication apprehension
- Define willingness to communicate and distinguish it from communication apprehension
- Define and give examples of the two forms of destructive aggression
- Explain why some individuals are verbally aggressive
- Define and give examples of two forms of constructive aggression
- Define humor orientation
- Define affective orientation

From *Interpersonal Communication* by Kristen Eichhorn, Candice Thomas-Maddox and Melissa Wanzer. Copyright © 2008 Kendall Hunt Publishing Company. Reprinted by permission.

KEYWORDS

self
self-complexity
self-concept
public self
inner self
self-esteem
self-regulation
reflected appraisal/looking glass self
attachment theory
secure
anxious-avoidant
anxious-ambivalent
direct definitions
identity scripts
attachment security hypothesis
social comparison theory
behavioral confirmation/self-fulfilling prophecy
similarity hypothesis
perpetual conflict
state approach
trait approach
personality
communication apprehension
willingness to communicate
systematic desensitization
cognitive modification
skills training
constructive and destructive forms of aggression
hostility
verbal aggressiveness
argumentativeness
independent-mindedness
assertiveness
humor orientation
affective orientation

© amygala imagery, 2007, Shutterstock.

OVERVIEW

In an excerpt from a song by the 1980s rock band, The Talking Heads, the burning question "How did I get here?" is raised. Most of us, at one time in our lives, have asked the same question. Another profound question, "Who am I?" fixates our culture. It is asked in song lyrics from rock groups and Broadway alike, from No Doubt, Alanis Morisette, Will Smith, Elvis Presley, Seal, and the Smashing Pumpkins to the musical *Les Miserables*. The Talking Heads added another concern "How did I get to be this way?" The theme song of television's most popular show is "Who Are You?" and *CSI* and similar programs involve the audience in the weekly unraveling of someone's identity, seeking answers from his interactions with others. The preoccupying search for self is this chapter's concern. In the first half of this chapter we address these questions by discussing the process of identity formation. Special emphasis will be placed on the role that interpersonal communication and relationships play in this process. A definition of the term self is provided, along with an overview of relevant terms used to describe and explain various aspects of the self. Next, a detailed description of the development of the self is presented, with special attention given to those individuals and processes considered essential to identity formation.

In the second part of this chapter, we examine the impact of individual differences on interpersonal communication. When communication researchers want to learn more about the impact of individual differences on social interaction, they often turn their attention to communication-based personality traits. According to communication researcher John Daly (2002), "the greatest proportion of articles in our journals have explored topics directly or indirectly related to personality" (133). To learn more about how people differ in their communication patterns, we define the term personality, distinguish between trait and state approaches to interpersonal communication research, and provide explanations of a number of different communication based personality traits. While there are many traits that influence our communication with others, we focus on several that have been researched extensively. These have been identified as predispositions that can either hinder or facilitate communication with others. "Everyone thinks of changing the world, but no one thinks of changing himself," wrote Leo Tolstoy. By looking within instead of outwardly, we can choose to improve our ability to communicate.

DEFINITION OF SELF

While individuals use the term self frequently and with relative ease, it is quite challenging for researchers to offer a single consistent definition for the term (Baumeister 1998). The **self** has been defined as a psychological entity consisting of "an organized set of beliefs, feelings, and behaviors" (Tesser, Wood, and Stapel 2002, 10). Another way of understanding the **self** is as a complex system made up of a variety of interdependent elements that attain self-organization (Vallacher and Nowak 2000). In attempting to explain the self, theorists often emphasize the origins of self, noting that it emerges through communication and established relationships with others and is constantly developing and evolving (Epstein 1973; Park and Waters 1988). Take a moment to consider how your self-perceptions have changed over the years. Are you the same person you were five, ten, or fifteen years ago? You have probably changed and matured a great deal over the years and see yourself as being quite different from when you were younger. Thus, one's perception of self is often described as a process because it evolves and is largely determined by ongoing communication with significant others. This idea is further validated by social psychologist Arthur Aron (2003) who says, "What we are and what we see ourselves as being seems to be constantly under construction and reconstruction, with the architects and remodeling contractors largely being those with whom we have close interactions" (Aron 2003, 443). In later sections of this chapter we explore the specific individuals and processes that exert the greatest influence in shaping our self-perceptions.

The self is also recognized as highly complex and multidimensional. Researchers agree that there are numerous dimensions, or aspects, of the self that make up one overall perception of the self. While we might think of ourselves as relatively uncomplicated individuals, most of us are highly complex and can assume a variety of roles. For example, on any given day, you may assume the roles of student, employee, daughter, sister, friend, teammate, roommate, or resident comedian. This example illustrates how individuals vary in their **self-complexity** or number of self-aspects, also known as subselves. Individuals possessing higher levels of self-complexity reap a number of personal benefits. What does it mean to possess higher levels of selfcomplexity? Referring back to the example of the student, if she views her multiple roles (sister, teammate, friend, etc.) as separate or unique, and at the same time has encountered a number of life experiences associated with those roles, then she probably has a greater number of non-overlapping selfaspects, or higher self-complexity. On the other hand, a woman who views herself only in two closely-related roles, e.g., teammate and student, and has limited life experiences associated with these roles, will probably have fewer self-aspects, or lower self-complexity.

How does one benefit from higher levels of self-complexity? Individuals with higher self-complexity may be less prone to having mood fluctuations (Linville 1985) and may cope better with stress (Koch and Shepperd 2004). When individuals report lower self-complexity they are more likely to experience negative affect in response to a negative life event than someone who reports higher self-complexity. Individuals with lower self-complexity may not be able to separate the limited roles they assume and may experience what researchers call "spill over." Thus, a student athlete who has a bad game may not be able to separate her experience on the soccer field ("me as soccer player") from her experience in the classroom ("me as a student") and the negative affect from the soccer game will expand, or spill over, to other self-aspects (Koch and Shepperd 2004). The student athlete has a bad game, does not study for her chemistry exam because she is still angry about her performance on the field and, as a result, fails her chemistry test the next day.

How could her performance on the soccer field affect other aspects of this girl's day?
© Robert J. Beyers II, 2007, Shutterstock.

Higher self-complexity may actually act as a buffer for people by allowing them to mentally separate themselves from painful life events (Linville 1987). Furthermore, the buffer effect has direct interpersonal, or relational, implications. The buffer effect was observed for those higher in selfcomplexity faced with relationship dissolution. Individuals higher in self-complexity thought about the relationship less and were less upset about their relationships ending than individuals lower in self-complexity (Linville 1987). Familiar fictional characters demonstrate instances of high and low self-complexity following relationship disengagement. For instance, *Gilmore Girls'* Rory Gilmore, whose roles of daughter, granddaughter, friend, and student are emphasized more heavily than that of girlfriend, dealt with the end of relationships with various boyfriends by spending more time with her mother and friends, and by increasing her involvement at school. These actions served as a buffer for Rory, which kept relationship concerns from dominating her thoughts or actions. In contrast, the popular show *The O.C.* exhibited the character Marissa Cooper, who fell into alcoholism and depression after her own breakup with central character Ryan Atwood. Marissa allowed the role of romantic relationship, which she found self-defining, to affect all other aspects of her self. While typically not as extreme as these two situations, instances of lower selfcomplexity, compared to high, are more likely to produce negative effects.

Importance of Studying the Process of Identity Formation

Why should interpersonal communication scholars study aspects of the self and the process of self development? Similar to other frequently studied concepts, research and perspectives on the self are vast and vary greatly (see, for example, Tesser, Felson, and Suls 2000; Tesser et al. 2002). There are a number of terms related to self in the literature and definitions for them are often inconsistent, making it difficult to integrate and interpret research on the self (Houck and Spegman 1999). But, before we can engage in a meaningful discussion of the self and related processes, we need to offer clear definitions of terms such as self-concept, self-esteem, and self-regulation. We also need to highlight distinctions between key terms and concepts. In addition, if we want to understand how and why individuals vary in attitudes, beliefs, values, mannerisms, security, psychological states, etc., we need to take a closer look at both how and why people perceive themselves in a particular way. Exploring the communicative and relational processes that affect the development of the self either positively or negatively is important because it helps us to understand who we are and why we are this way. Once we understand differences in how individuals develop a sense of self as well as the processes associated with the development of a more positive self-perception, we can train individuals to interact more competently with those around them. As Houck and Spegman (1999) argue, "Given its manifestation of social competence, the development of the self is of fundamental importance not only to the well-being of individuals, but also to the well-being of others with whom they associate" (2).

There are three constructs related to the self that typically emerge in discussions about the self and developmental processes. These three specific aspects of the self are: self-concept, or cognitions about the self; self-esteem, or affective information related to the self; and autonomy/self-initiative, or self-regulation, processes. In order to better understand the self-system and its related components, it is important to define and distinguish between these related constructs. In this chapter, we present a detailed definition of each of these three components, offer examples of related terms used to discuss each of these key areas, and provide a brief overview of the importance of these concepts to interpersonal communication and relationships.

The Self System

Terms such as self-concept, self-esteem, self-schema, and self-regulation are used in dialogues about the self and identity development. Some of these terms have been used interchangeably and yet, as we will see, they are very different constructs.

Self-Concept/Cognitions about the Self. One term that often emerges in discussions about the self is self-concept. Houck and Spegman describe the self-concept as a cognitive construct which is a "descriptive reference to the self, or a definition of the nature and beliefs about the self's qualities" (Houck and Spegman 1999, 2). While there are a variety of other terms used when describing the self (self-cognition, self-image, self-schema, and self-understanding), self-concept is used most frequently. In the most basic sense, self-concept refers to what someone knows about himself.

Social psychologists and sociologists argue that people possess multiple perceptions of the self-concept, or different personas (Bargh, McKenna, and Fitzsimons 2002). For example, Goffman (1959) and Jung (1953) draw distinctions between a **"public"** self, or the self that we project during social interaction, and an **"inner"** self that we keep private and that may reflect how we really feel about ourselves. The public self is described as our "actual" self-concept while the inner self is presented as our "true" self. Psychologists note that individuals often project an actual self in public that is quite different from their true self. Individuals may not present their true selves for a variety of reasons. One reason could be the fear of evaluation from others. Or, in some instances, an individual may not yet fully know or understand his or her true self.

One place where individuals may feel more comfortable expressing their true selves is on the Internet (Bargh et al. 2002). According to researchers, the anonymity of the Internet gives people the chance to assume different personas and genders and to express aspects of themselves "without fear of disapproval and sanctions by those in their real-life social circle" (Bargh et al. 2002). Two different experiments were performed that used a reaction time task to access college students' perceptions of their true and actual selves. Researchers found that the true self-concept was more readily recalled during Internet interactions while the actual self was more accessible during face-to-face interactions. In a third related experiment, college students were randomly assigned to interact, either via the Internet or face-to-face. Students assigned to the Internet had an easier time expressing their true selves to their partners than those assigned to the face-to-face condition. If individuals feel more comfortable expressing their true selves during Internet exchanges, they are then more likely to establish

Why do you think some people find it easier to express their "true" selves over the Internet?
© Zsolt Nyulaszi, 2007, Shutterstock.

relationships with individuals they meet on the Internet (McKenna, Green, and Gleason 2002). This research may provide some explanation for the fact that more individuals are using the Internet to establish romantic and platonic relationships.

An individual's self-concept influences how one views or interprets social interaction, and at the same time it regulates one's involvement in the interaction. Suppose the student council president is asked to speak to the superintendent of schools to discuss student views on proposed schedule changes. Her self-confidence in her role as a student leader causes her to assert herself in the interaction and offer suggestions for an alternative plan. Research on the relationship between self-concept and interpersonal processes has explored the effects of self-concept on social perception, the relationship between self-concept and selection of interaction partners, strategies individuals use to mold and interpret communication with others, and how individuals respond to feedback that is not consistent with their self-concept. Three of these areas of research—the relationship between self-concept and social perception, self-concept and partner choice, and self-concept and interaction strategies—are particularly interesting and relevant to understanding how and why our self-concept affects our communication with others.

Much of the research on the relationship between self-concept and social perception concludes that people are likely to view others as relatively similar to themselves (Markus and Wurf 1987). When you interact with your friends, family members, and co-workers, you perceive them to be more similar than dissimilar to you in attitudes, beliefs, values, goals, and behaviors. From an interpersonal communication perspective, similarity is an important variable that affects our interactions with others and, when used strategically as an affinity-seeking behavior, can potentially increase liking between interactants (Bell and Daly 1984).

The way one sees or defines one's self also affects both the choice of relationship partners and subsequent behavior in those relationships (Markus and Wurf 1987). Research on the relationship between self-perception and relationship satisfaction indicates that individuals report greater relationship satisfaction when they choose partners that validate views of themselves (Schlenker 1984; Swann 1985). In other words, individuals attempt to find a relationship partner who expresses similar or consistent views with their ideal or desired self. Much of the research on the role of the self in social interaction has examined the process of impression management during interpersonal encounters (Markus and Wurf 1987). Not surprisingly, individuals work diligently to present a particular image of themselves to both external (Goffman 1959) and internal audiences (Greenwald and Breckler 1985). Using impression management techniques consciously and effectively is linked to heightened self-awareness (Schlenker 1985). While we may not always be aware of our impression management efforts, our day-to-day choice of dress, hairstyle, choice of words, and artifacts are selected strategically to project a specific desired image of ourselves to those around us. Think about the choices you make when deciding what to wear and how to style your hair in various social situations. It is highly likely that impression management played a role in your decisions.

Self-Esteem/Affect about the Self. Another term used frequently when discussing the self is **self-esteem**, defined as the subjective perception of one's self-worth, or the value one places on the self (Houck and Spegman 1999).

There are a number of related evaluative terms associated with self-esteem that include: self-affect, self-worth, and self-evaluation. All of these terms illustrate the evaluative nature of this concept with individuals typically experiencing either positive or negative feelings about themselves or their behavior. Self-esteem can be measured objectively, unlike self-concept. Research indicates that individuals typically vary in their reported levels of self-esteem. Those reporting higher levels of self-esteem feel more favorable about themselves and their behaviors than individuals with lower self-esteem.

How can a teacher influence a child's self-esteem?
© NorthGeorgiaMedia, 2007, Shutterstock.

According to researchers, self-esteem has become a "household" term today. Teachers, parents, therapists, coaches, and individuals that communicate regularly with children and have the potential to affect a child's self-esteem have been encouraged to focus on ways to help children see themselves more favorably (for an overview of this research, see Baumeister, Campbell, Krueger, and Vohs 2003). The previously held assumption driving these efforts was that individuals with higher self-esteem would experience a number of positive benefits and outcomes. More recently, Baumeister and his colleagues examined the extensive research on self-esteem with special attention on the relationship between self-esteem and performance, interpersonal success, happiness, and lifestyle choices (for an overview of this research, see Baumeister et al. 2003). The findings from their extensive research were unexpected. Surprisingly, there was only a modest relationship between perceptions of self-esteem and school performance. Why? According to social psychologists, high self-esteem does not necessarily cause higher performance in school. Instead, researchers suspect that solid academic performance in school actually leads to higher self-esteem. When researchers investigated efforts to boost students' self-esteem, students did not improve in school and sometimes even performed at lower levels.

Similar to findings reported in the educational context, researchers concluded that occupational success may boost self-esteem rather than self-esteem leading to greater success in the workplace. The conclusions in this area are mixed, at best, with some research illustrating a positive relationship between self-esteem and occupational success and other research contradicting these findings (Baumeister et al. 2003). By this point, you might be asking yourself, "Are there any meaningful educational or occupational advantages associated with higher levels of self-esteem?" There *are* benefits to possessing higher self-esteem; they are just not as extensive as researchers initially estimated. For example, individuals with higher self-esteem seem to be more tenacious than those with low self-esteem. Social psychologists conclude that self-esteem may help individuals continue working on a task even after they failed initially (Baumeister et al. 2003).

What is the relationship between self-esteem and interpersonal communication and relationship success? Individuals self-reporting higher self-esteem typically indicate that they are well-liked and attractive, have better relationships, and make more positive impressions on others than those reporting lower levels of self-esteem. However, when researchers further investigated whether high self-esteem individuals were perceived this way by others using objective measures, the results were disconfirmed. The researchers further explain this finding by noting that while "narcissists are charming at first," they tend to eventually alienate those around them by

Rewarding children for good behavior gives them a boost in self-esteem.
© Vartanov Anatoly, 2007, Shutterstock.

communicating in ways that are perceived by others as inappropriate and ineffective (Baumeister et al. 2003, 1). The connection between self-esteem and the quality of romantic and platonic relationships is small to moderate, at best (Aron 2003). Some research indicates that there is a small consistent relationship between self-esteem and marital satisfaction and success over time (see, for example, Aube and Koestner 1992; Karney and Bradbury 1995). Based on research conducted thus far, couples' reported self-esteem does not appear to be a major predictor of marital satisfaction or persistence.

However, in addition to tenaciousness, there are some additional recognized benefits of having higher self-esteem. For example, higher self-esteem has been linked to feelings of happiness. Individuals reporting higher self-esteem are generally happier folks than individuals selfreporting lower self-esteem and are probably less likely to be depressed. Lower self-esteem has been repeatedly linked to greater incidence of depression under certain situations or circumstances. While it is disappointing to find that programs and initiatives created to boost individuals' self-esteem were generally ineffective in doing so, it is important to emphasize specific communication patterns that might be beneficial in helping others formulate positive self-impressions. Baumeister and his colleagues (2003) note that instead of giving children "indiscriminate praise" which may lead to excessive narcissism, parents and educators should focus on "using praise to boost self-esteem as a reward for socially desirable behavior and self-improvement" (1).

As you can imagine, there is a great deal of information available on how to boost one's self-esteem in order to avoid depression, increase tenaciousness, and relate more effectively to others. Perceptions of one's self-esteem can change over time because of significant life experiences. There are

---

TABLE 5.1   Ways to Boost Your Self-Esteem

1. *Think back to when you tackled a task for the very first time.*
   Trying something for the first time can be a daunting experience. The next time you feel under-confident, recall the first time you tried something new— and succeeded! This will help you to overcome your fears.

2. *Do something you have been putting aside.*
   Once you complete this task, it will help you feel as though you can follow through on something.

3. *Work on your ability to relax.*
   There are a number of different ways to reduce anxiety and stress in your life. Consider taking exercise classes, meditating, or involving yourself in something that helps you relax.

4. *Recall all of your accomplishments.*
   Take a minute to reflect on all of the times you have succeeded at doing something that you set out to do (e.g., passing your driver's test, passing exams, putting money away for vacation).

Adapted from an article that appears on the Uncommon Knowledge website www.self-confidence.co.uk/self/esteem/tips.

Research Brief: Playing Computer Games May Boost Self-Esteem

Mark Baldwin, a psychologist at McGill University in Montreal, argues that computer games offer another less conventional and interesting way to boost one's self-esteem. While these games are not recommended for individuals with serious self-esteem problems, Baldwin and his team of researchers found that the games helped people feel better about themselves and their relationships by focusing on the positive, not the negative (Dye 2004). Visit *http://abcnews.go.com/Technology/story?id=99532&page=1* to read the entire article.

numerous websites, books, workshops, and even computer games available for individuals who want to address problems with low self-esteem. See table 5.1 for an example of the type of information currently available to help individuals combat self-esteem problems.

Self-Regulation. The third and final component of the self-system, self-regulation, is occasionally referred to in literature as self-determination, independence, self-assertion, self-control, or internalization. Self-regulation is regarded by some as a highly significant component of human existence (Bargh and Chartrand 1999). Why is self-regulation so important? Because self-regulation, defined as "the capacity to exercise choice and initiation" (Houck and Spegman 1999, 3), allows us to pursue and engage in goaldirected activity. It is important to study the process of self-regulation in order to understand how and why individuals are motivated and make choices. Research in this area examines aspects of initiative, motivation, and decision-making in relation to morality and developing a conscience. It also sets out to discover why some individuals are motivated to achieve goals and others are not. The significant process of self-regulation can occur at either a conscious or a subconscious level (Bargh and Chartrand 1999). You probably exert self-regulation, whether you are aware of the process or not.

What is the relationship between self-regulation and interpersonal communication and relationships? Baumeister and Vohs (2003) offer several examples of how the process of self-regulation is related to interpersonal communication and relationships. Problems such as interpersonal violence between relationship partners and extradyadic sexual relations are obviously linked in some way to failures in self-regulation. Self-regulation is closely related to successful maintenance of close romantic relationships (Baumeister and Vohs 2003). Related research by Finkel and Campbell (2001) indicated that individuals reporting higher levels of self-regulation were more likely to exhibit accommodating behaviors in their romantic relationships. Not surprisingly, most individuals prefer being in relationships with partners that are accommodating, or willing to compromise, to meet each other's needs.

The extent to which one communicates effectively and appropriately with others is also linked to self-regulation or initiative. Recall from Chapter One our discussion of Spitzberg and Cupach's (1984) model of communication competence and its three components. This model advances the significance of motivation or initiative in communicating effectively with others. While individuals may posses the skills and knowledge necessary for communicating effectively, if they are not motivated to do so, they will not enact the appropriate behavior. Thus, the process of self-regulation directly affects our communication abilities and the quality of interpersonal relationships.

Now that we understand the three main components of the self-system and their relationship to interpersonal communication, we move on to the discussion of the development of self. Two important questions to consider are: Which individuals or groups of individuals are most influential in forming or shaping our self-perceptions? And why? Exploring these questions in much greater detail will help to answer the questions: Who am I? And how did I become this way?

Interpersonal Communication and the Development of Self

Most scholars agree that the self emerges and develops through communication with those to whom we are close (see, for example, Aron 2003). What exactly does this mean? This statement implies that, as infants, we do not possess a sense of self, but that one develops through our interactions with significant others (Cooley 1902; Mead 1934). Cooley (1902) was the first to advance "the **looking glass self**" metaphor which describes the impact of interpersonal communication on the development of self. Researchers (Felson 1989) extended the concept of looking glass self to include the term **reflected appraisal**, referring to the tendency to view ourselves based on the appraisals of others. Who are these significant others that affect our self-perceptions? Researchers have generally studied the influence of family and other significant individuals such as peers and relationship partners as they affect the development of self. We review the importance of interpersonal communication with family, peers, and significant others as it relates to the construction and reconstruction of the self over time.

A child who feels secure in the family environment will naturally expect positive peer relationships.
© Losevsky Pavel, 2007, Shutterstock.

Family. Family plays a significant role in the development of one's identity. One theory that has received a great deal of attention from researchers studying the process of identity development is attachment theory. John Bowlby (1969, 1973) developed **attachment theory** in an attempt to explain the strong bond children form with the primary caregiver and the stress which results from separation from one another. Communication plays a pivotal role in creating the security associated with this attachment. Other theorists have expanded on the original theory advanced by Bowlby (1969) and typically recognize three different types of attachment relationships—secure, anxious-avoidant, and anxious-ambivalent (Ainsworth, Blehar, Waters, and Wall 1978).

When the primary caregiver behaves in a loving, supportive, and nurturing way towards her child, the child is likely to develop a secure attachment. A secure attachment is often "characterized by intense feelings of intimacy, emotional security, and physical safety when the infant is in the presence of the attachment figure" (Peluso, Peluso, White, and Kern 2004, 140). Because children raised in a secure environment typically have a history of responsive and supportive caretaking from their caregivers (Ainsworth et al. 1978), these experiences lead the children to believe that others will act in a supportive and caring way as well. Children who develop secure attachment styles are confident in their interpersonal relationships with their peers (Park and Waters 1988). Why is this the case? Bowlby (1973) and others (see, for example, Sroufe 1988) hold that children's first exposure to relationships is in the family context and that this experience helps them formulate expectations for subsequent relationships. Secure children, whose previous relationship experiences are generally positive, expect people in future encounters to act similarly, and therefore behave accordingly. Some research indicates that secure children recreate communication patterns and practices they experienced with their primary caregivers when interacting with peers, ultimately leading to more positive peer relationships (Sroufe 1988).

Conversely, individuals experiencing an insecure or **anxious-avoidant** attachment relationship with their primary caregiver often report trauma or neglect from their parents and exhibit significant developmental deficits (Peluso et al. 2004). Mothers of children who develop this attachment style act emotionally distant and rejecting, behaving with anger towards their children. Not surprisingly, this style of parenting can have long-term negative psychological and relational effects on individuals (Peluso et al. 2004). Unlike secure children, insecure children experience difficulty in forming relationships with others. Working from Bowlby's original theory (1973), insecure children, whose previous relationship experiences were negative, often develop a more negative "working model" of relationships and recreate negative communication patterns among peers. Some research supports this premise, with insecure children behaving more negatively and aggressively toward both known and unknown peers than secure children (Lieberman 1977; Sroufe 1988).

The third attachment style, labeled **anxious-ambivalent**, develops as a result of inconsistent and irregular treatment from parents (Ainsworth et al. 1978). Compared to secure children, those with anxious-ambivalent attachment styles experience more developmental delays, exhibit an unusual amount of conflict and confusion associated with their relationship with the primary caregiver, and are more accident prone (Ainsworth et al. 1978; Lieberman and Pawl 1988; Sroufe 1988). Both the anxious-avoidant and anxious-ambivalent attachment styles are problematic because children typically internalize perceptions of the self that are negative, which affect subsequent relationships with peers and romantic partners (Park and Waters 1988).

Communication with family members also affects how we define ourselves. Many of you have probably heard your parents describe your talents, personality traits, or other attributes in detail to other family members, friends, or even total strangers. **Direct definitions** are descriptions, or labels, families assign to its members that affect the way we see and define ourselves (Wood 2001). A child whose nickname is "slugger" may perceive herself to be an outstanding softball player. Consider the impact that the nickname "trouble" would have on a child's perception. Most of us can recall the way our family members referred to us and it is likely that many of these references were internalized. Researchers point out the significance of direct definitions by recognizing that positive labels can enhance our self-esteem while negative ones can have potentially deleterious effects on our self-perceptions (Wood 2001).

When you reflect back on your childhood, can you recall sayings or phrases that were repeated in your family? How about, "money does not grow on trees," "people who live in glass houses should not throw stones," "remember the golden rule," or "a family that prays together stays together?" Do any of these sayings sound familiar to you? Can you generate a list of phrases that were repeated in your family? These sayings are all examples of **identity scripts**, or rules for living and relating to one another in family contexts. Identity scripts help individuals to define who they are and how to relate to others (Berne 1964; Harris 1969). These phrases, which most have probably heard more than once, influence the way we relate to others and also our self-perceptions.

Peer relationships. While family relationships are important and clearly affect the development of the self, other relationships, such as peers, also play a significant role in identity development (Park and Waters 1988). The **attachment security hypothesis**, based on Bowlby's (1973) work, states that individuals are attracted to and seek out peers and relationship partners that can provide them with a sense of security. Not surprisingly, peers, like parents, can also provide a sense of security and social support for one another. Some research indicates that attachment related functions are eventually transferred from parents to peers over time (Surra, Gray, Cottle, Boettcher 2004).

Research by Meeus and Dekovic (1995) supports the significance of peer relationships later in life and indicates that peers, to a certain extent, are even more influential than parents in the identity development of adolescents. According to researchers, as young children age and mature they also begin the process of separation and individuation from their parents. Children begin to socialize more frequently with their peers, and to protest when they are separated from them. They begin to discover that most of their peer interactions are characterized by qualities such as equality and symmetry. Peer relationships, which tend to be more egalitarian, soon become more important than parental relationships and tend to influence child-parent relationship expectations. As children grow and mature, they expect to form new relationships with their parents, also based on symmetry and equality. When these relationships do not progress as expected, adolescents become frustrated and perhaps even more bonded with their peers (Meeus and Dekovic 1995). While initially researchers suspected that peers were only influential in certain areas of identity formation, research by Meeus and Dekovic (1995) illustrates the impact of peers on the formation of relational, educational, and occupational identity. Not surprisingly, best friends exerted the greatest influence on one's development of relational identity while peers or colleagues exerted the greatest influence on occupational and educational identities.

Peer relationships are also important in defining the self because individuals often use peers as a means of personal assessment. It is not unusual for individuals to compare themselves to others to determine whether they are smart, attractive, athletic or successful. When individuals compare themselves to others in order to determine their abilities, strengths and weaknesses, they are engaging in the process of social comparison. Leon Festinger (1954) developed **social comparison theory**. This theory suggests that most individuals have a basic need, or drive, to evaluate and compare themselves to those around them. Festinger holds that one of the only ways of validating an evaluation of oneself is to find out if similar others agree with it (Tesser 2003). Thus, if a student wants to evaluate his ability in school, he will typically

Have you ever compared your talents to those of your friends?
© paulaphoto, 2007, Shutterstock.

compare his abilities to those of his fellow similar classmates. How many of you immediately consult with your peers after receiving a test or paper grade?

Another way that relationships with others affect the development of self is through a phenomenon called **behavioral confirmation**, or self-fulfilling prophecy (Aron 2003). Aron (2003) defines **self-fulfilling prophecy** as a process in which people act to conform to the expectations of others (see, for example, Darley and Fazio 1980). One of the classic studies that illustrated self-fulfilling prophecy was conducted in the classroom with teachers who were randomly informed that their students were academic overachievers. Academic performances improved significantly for those average students whose teachers were told that they were high achievers. Why did the students improve academically? Because the teachers communicated with the students as if they were overachievers, the students internalized these perspectives and acted accordingly (Snyder, Tanke, and Berscheid 1977). Researchers also found that previous relationship experiences can influence our expectations of new relationship partners' behaviors (see, for example, Andersen and Berensen 2001). Thus, if an individual experienced problems in previous relationships, he or she may expect similar negative experiences in the future and may circuitously contribute to how the relationship progresses.

Relationship Partners. Over time, the bond formed between partners in a romantic relationship is sure to affect the development of the self. One particularly interesting study provides further support for this statement. Researchers found that married couples come to look more alike over extended periods of time. Zajonc and his colleagues (1987) found students were more successful in matching pictures of couples married twenty-five years compared with pictures of the same couples, newly married.

Your intimate relationships have a major influence on how you view yourself.
© Losevsky Pavel, 2007, Shutterstock.

Intimate relationships are also important to the development of the self because they influence how positively or negatively one views oneself (Aron 2003). Some recent research indicates that getting married and having children can actually increase an individual's feelings of selfworth (Shackelford 2001).

According to the **similarity hypothesis**, also related to Bowlby's research on attachment theory, we are most attracted to individuals that exhibit an attachment style similar to our own (Surra et al. 2004). Not surprisingly, researchers found that college students with secure attachment styles were more attracted to relationship partners that had also developed this attachment style. As the similarity hypothesis would predict, anxious-attachment individuals were also more likely to date anxious-attachment partners and to report being satisfied with these relationships (Surra et al. 2004). This research indicates that we often seek out individuals with similar attachment styles that also verify our perceptions of self-worth.

Relationships with family members, peers, and significant others affect the way we define ourselves and influence our evaluative perceptions of the self. Another way that we define ourselves, and simultaneously distinguish ourselves from others, is by describing our predominant personality traits.

In the second part of this chapter, we explore some of the ways people differ in how they communicate with others. While individual differences such as age, culture, ethnicity/race, sex/gender, and cognitive traits certainly affect the way we communicate. with others, interpersonal researchers have turned their attention to the powerful role that communication-based predispositions play in making sense of social phenomena (Daly 2002). In the next sections we discuss: (1) the impact of individual differences on social interaction, (2) differences between state and trait approaches to research, and (3) a number of personality traits that affect our communication with others. Because students are often interested in finding their scores on the communication-based personality instruments, we have included ways to measure many of the traits discussed in the chapter.

THE IMPACT OF INDIVIDUAL DIFFERENCES ON SOCIAL INTERACTION

Most of us have interacted with someone we might label "difficult" because of his or her communication behaviors. It is not unusual for students to share stories of the "difficult" or "less-than-popular" roommate who lives with them. This roommate is often described as difficult because he acts in a consistently problematic manner or manages regularly to offend others. Not surprisingly, this roommate's poor behavior not only impacts all of the housemates, but also affects relationship partners, friends, classmates and neighbors that must hear about and interact with the difficult roommate. A number of authors have written books about dealing with difficult people (see, for example, Keating 1984). Dealing with difficult personality types is an important and relevant topic for a number of reasons: (1) we all have to deal with difficult people, whether at home, school, or work, (2) we might be one of those "difficult people" because we have communication challenges linked to our personality, and (3) asking an individual to completely change his or her personality is unreasonable and can damage relationships. Social psychologist John Gottman (1999) describes **perpetual conflict** as disagreements between relationship partners that are often directly related to personality issues. This type of conflict is pervasive and not easily fixed because it often involves fighting over matters that cannot be easily resolved, like differences in couples' personality traits. It is very frustrating when someone tells you, matter-of-factly, to "completely change your personality" in order to become a better relationship partner. We know that this unproductive criticism is an unreasonable request.

When someone asks you repeatedly to change the same aspect of your personality, e.g., to talk more or to talk less, it is likely that this person is requesting a change in a personality trait. Much of the communication research conducted to date has adopted a trait approach to studying personality differences, which is quite different from a state approach.

A COMPARISON OF TRAIT AND STATE APPROACHES TO RESEARCH

When communication researchers investigate differences in communication behaviors, they clarify whether they are studying these behaviors from either a trait or a state approach. When they adopt a **state approach** to studying communication behaviors, they examine how individuals communicate in a particular situation or context. For example, an interpersonal communication researcher might examine how individuals feel right before they ask someone out on a date. Researchers might measure an individual's state anxiety to determine if this affects his or her ability to advance a request for a date. Thus, when researchers adopt a state approach to communication research they examine situationally specific responses (Daly and Bippus 1998).

When researchers adopt a **trait approach**, they attempt to identify enduring, or consistent, ways that people behave. If a researcher adopts a trait approach to studying communication behaviors, it means that he is interested in examining how individuals interact the majority of the time. Guilford (1959) defines a trait as "any distinguishable, relatively enduring way in which one individual differs from another" (6). Daly and Bippus (1998) identify several conclusions about traits: (1) they define ways in which people differ, (2) they can be broad or narrow in focus, (3) some address social characteristics while others emphasize cognitively-oriented variables, and (4) some can be measured using questionnaires while others are recognized by observing behaviors. Daly and Bippus comment on the distinction between state and trait approaches in research by stating, "The differences between trait and state are, in actuality, primarily differences in emphasis. Personality scholars tend to emphasize the trait over the state" (2).

Why are communication scholars so interested in studying personality traits? Communication scholars study traits because they are related to communication variables in a number of different ways. For example, in the following sections of this chapter we will learn about individuals who are highly apprehensive about communicating with others. These individuals are described as having trait-CA (Communication Apprehension) because they are consistently apprehensive about communication with others. Explained another way, high CA individuals tend to exhibit high levels of apprehension across a wide range of situations and with varied persons. Not surprisingly, research indicates that these individuals tend to exhibit a variety of behavioral disruptions when forced to interact with others (Allen and Bourhis 1996). This example illustrates the relationship between a trait (CA) and communication variables (behavioral disruptions, stuttering, pauses, etc.).

Because our **personality**, or predisposition to behave a certain way, is an important and relatively enduring part of how we see and define ourselves, interpersonal communication researchers are naturally interested in learning more about the impact of individual differences on social interaction. In addition, most researchers argue that communication behaviors linked to personality differences are explained, at least in part, by social learning; that is, we learn how to communicate by observing and imitating those around us. While a number of communication scholars have argued that one's genetic background best explains his or her personality predispositions (Beatty, McCroskey and Heisel 1998), it is still important to consider both explanations.

Finally, by learning more about how individuals with specific personality traits approach social interaction, we can advance some predictive generalizations about how they interact and plan our own behaviors accordingly. You might ask, why do communication researchers not just study self-concept? Unlike one's self-concept, which is subjective and could change from moment to moment, one's personality is relatively stable and consistent over

How is your communication affected by those around you?
© Yuri Arcurs, 2007, Shutterstock.

time. For example, if you complete one of the communication-based personality measures in this chapter today and then complete the same one a year from now, it is very likely that your scores will be highly similar or even the same. Learning more about communication behaviors that are trait-based helps researchers understand the impact of individual differences across different contexts. In the remaining sections of this chapter, we review research that adopts a trait or personality approach to studying differences in communication behaviors.

COMMUNICATION APPREHENSION AND WILLINGNESS TO COMMUNICATE

In John Maxwell's (2002) book, *The Seventeen Essential Qualities of a Team Player*, he emphasizes communication as one of the most important skills needed for succeeding in teams. Other essential skills included in his list are adaptability, collaboration, enthusiasm, and the ability to establish relationships with team members. Not surprisingly, all of these qualities also require strong communication skills. Maxwell and countless other authors from a variety of academic and professional fields emphasize the relationship between communication skills and success at work. Throughout our own textbook we continually emphasize the link between communication and relationship stability and professional success. However, what if you are not comfortable communicating with others? If you or someone you know often avoids talking in most situations and with most people, it is likely that this individual would score high in communication apprehension and low in willingness to communicate. In the following sections, we examine these two related communication-based personality traits. For each communication-based personality trait we provide a general overview of the construct, describe ways to reliably measure the trait, and discuss research on the link between the personality trait and communication behaviors. Because high levels of communication apprehension can be extremely debilitating for individuals, treatment options are also discussed.

Approximately one in five individuals in the United States is considered high in communication apprehension (McCroskey 2006). For highly apprehensive individuals, even anticipated communication with others evokes a significant amount of stress and psychological discomfort (McCroskey, Daly, and Sorensen 1976). James McCroskey (1977) conducted the seminal research in this area and defines **communication apprehension** as an "individual's level of fear or anxiety with either real or anticipated communication with another person or persons" (78). Communication apprehension (CA) can be measured in a variety of ways, but is frequently assessed using the Personal Report of Communication Apprehension (PRCA) developed by McCroskey (1978). The PRCA is a twenty-four-item five point Likert-type measure that assesses individuals' communication apprehension in general, as well as across four different areas: public, small group, meeting, and interpersonal/dyadic situations (see Applications at the end of this chapter). Individuals scoring high on the PRCA are generally quite anxious about communicating with others and will attempt to avoid interaction. Highly apprehensive individuals are less communicatively competent, less disclosive, and are more stressed and lonely than individuals low in communication

Highly apprehensive individuals are more stressed and lonely than those who are low in communication apprehension.
© Diego Cervo, 2007, Shutterstock.

apprehension (Miczo 2004; Zakahi and Duran 1985). Highly apprehensive college students are more likely to be considered "at risk" in college settings (Lippert, Titsworth, and Hunt 2005) and are less likely to emerge as leaders in work groups (Limon and La France 2005).

Willingness to communicate (WTC) is similar to communication apprehension because it also taps into an individual's propensity to avoid or approach communication with others. The willingness to communicate construct does not assess fear or anxiety, only one's tendency to approach or avoid communication in varied situations and with varied persons. McCroskey and Richmond (1987) coined the term willingness to communicate (WTC) and describe this construct as a person's tendency to initiate communication with others (McCroskey and Richmond 1998). WTC is further described as a "personality-based, trait-like predisposition which is relatively consistent across a variety of communication contexts and types of receivers" (McCroskey and Richmond 1987, 134). WTC can be measured via the WTC scale, which is a twenty-item measure that assesses an individual's willingness to interact with different individuals in different situations (see Applications section at the end of this chapter). Individuals completing the WTC scale indicate the percent of time they would choose to communicate in public, during a meeting, within a group, in a dyad, with a stranger, and in situations with acquaintances. For example, individuals are asked to indicate how often they would "talk with a service station attendant" or "talk with a physician." When individuals consistently indicate that they would not want to talk in most of the contexts listed, they are described as low in WTC. Conversely, individuals who indicate that they are willing to interact with others in a wide range of contexts are described as high in WTC.

Not surprisingly, highly apprehensive individuals are more likely to be low in WTC. Richmond and Roach (1992) summarize a significant body of research on the benefits and drawbacks for employees described as quiet, or low in WTC. First, they identify several positive factors associated with lower WTC. For example, individuals reporting lower WTC are typically less likely to initiate or perpetuate gossip and are also less likely to emerge as "squeaky wheels" within the organization. In addition, quiet individuals are less likely to take long breaks, unlike their more social high WTC counterparts. Finally, individuals with lower WTC are more likely to be discreet than more talkative individuals. Thus, organizations do not have to worry as much about quiet individuals sharing corporate secrets or new developments.

While there are some benefits of employing quiet individuals, Richmond and Roach (1992) note that, in general, quiet employees "are considered at risk in an organizational setting" for various reasons (Richmond and Roach 1992). More often than not, quiet individuals are perceived as less competent and intelligent because they do not contribute to discussions or share their accomplishments with others. Consequently, quiet employees are often mislabeled as incompetent and lacking business savvy. Research indicates that we tend to formulate negative impressions of employees who are quiet and, as a result, they are often less likely to get interviewed or considered for promotions. In research by Daly, Richmond, and Leth (1979), it was found that when individuals were described as quiet or shy in recommendation letters, they were less likely to be granted interviews than highly verbal individuals. Unfortunately, low WTC individuals may be more likely to experience the "last hired" and "first fired" syndrome than their high WTC counterparts (Richmond and Roach 1992).

What can be done to help individuals who are either high in CA or low in WTC? There is a significant amount of research that has identified treatment options for high CA individuals. Communication apprehension can be treated with methods similar to other types of phobias and neurotic anxieties (Berger, McCroskey, and Richmond 1984). According to McCroskey and his associates (1984), high levels of CA can be overcome or managed by applying three widely accepted treatment options. If these treatment options are not available, "there are other options available for individuals in the absence of these more formal treatments" (153). The three primary treatment options available for individuals high in communication apprehension are systematic desensitization, cognitive modification, and skills training.

One of the most effective means of treating high levels of CA is **systematic desensitization** (SD), a type of behavior modification derived from learning theory. Eighty to ninety percent of individuals who use systematic desensitization eliminate completely their high level or fear or anxiety. The basic premise behind systematic desensitization is that anxiety related to communication is learned and, as such, can be unlearned. **Cognitive modification**, also based on learning theory, is the second method of managing high levels of CA. "The underlying rationale for this treatment is that people have learned to think negatively about themselves, in this case, how they communicate, and can be taught to think positively" (Berger et al. 1984). The third and least successful way to treat high levels of CA is skills training. Skills training, when used as the sole method, is typically considered the least effective method for treating high levels of CA. Communication **skills training** might involve taking courses to help individuals learn to communicate more effectively. For example, individuals may take public speaking courses to improve their ability to design and deliver speeches. Experts recommend that persons with high levels of communication apprehension first employ systematic desensitization or cognitive modification as a means of reducing their anxiety and then participate in skills training courses to help manage deficient communication skills. Whether you or someone you know is highly apprehensive about communication, it is important to note that the tendency to fear communication can be treated successfully.

> And I think that those who consider disabled people 'broken' fail to see that while some of us have disabilities that are physically obvious, in truth all people are disabled in one way or another—including disabilities of character and personality.
>
> –Kyle Maynard

AGGRESSIVE BEHAVIOR

Infante (1987a) recognizes a behavior as aggressive when it "applies force . . . symbolically in order, minimally to dominate and perhaps damage, or maximally to defeat and perhaps destroy the locus of attack" (58). He further explains that there are two types of aggressive behavior; he labels them destructive and constructive. **Destructive** forms of aggression are those that can potentially damage individual's self-esteem or, to use Infante's words "destroy the locus of attack." Two widely recognized types of destructive aggression are hostility and verbal aggression.

Hostility

Hostility is defined as "using symbols (verbal or nonverbal) to express irritability, negativism, resentment, and suspicion" (Infante 1988, 7). When someone expresses hostility, he or she might say, "I am so angry I did not get chosen for the lacrosse team and I blame the selection committee!" Individuals presenting hostile personalities generally devalue the worth and motives of others, are highly suspicious of others, feel in opposition with those around them, and often feel a desire to inflict harm or see others harmed (Smith 1994). One way to measure hostility is to use Cook-Medley Hostility Scale (Cook and Medley 1954) which is one of the most commonly used means of assessing trait hostility and appears to have construct, predictive, and discriminant validity (Huebner, Nemeroff, and Davis 2005; Pope, Smith, and Rhodewalt 1990). Sample items on the hostility measure are "I think most people will lie to get ahead," and "It is safer to trust nobody." Individuals completing the hostility measure indicate the extent to which they either agree or disagree with the statements using a five-point Likert scale.

Needless to say, feeling consistently hostile toward others affects the way one views the world and impacts relationships with others. Hostile individuals tend to be quite unhappy individuals who are more likely to report depression and lower self-esteem (Kopper and Epperson 1996). From a communication perspective, researchers try to accurately identify people or communication situations that evoke feelings of hostility in order to better understand this construct. If we can identify the types of situations or people that cause others to feel hostile, perhaps we can make attempts to modify or improve these situations. Recent research by Chory-Assad and Paulsel (2004) examined the relationship between students' perceptions of justice in college classrooms and student aggression and hostility toward their instructors. As expected, when students felt instructors were not fair in regard to course policies, scheduling, testing, amount of work, etc., they were more likely to feel hostile toward their teachers. Now that we know that perceptions of injustice in college classrooms leads to greater hostility in students, we can make recommendations on how to alter these situations and to reduce hostile reactions.

Hostile individuals are more likely to experience problems in committed romantic relationships. Rogge (2006) and his colleagues examined communication, hostility, and neuroticism as predictors of marital stability and found that couples were less likely to stay together when spouses reported higher levels of hostility and neuroticism. The researchers noted that while communication skills distinguished those who were married-satisfied and those who were married-unsatisfied, they did not always predict marital dissolution. It is important to note that hostility and neuroticism "contribute to a rapid, early decline in marital functioning" (Rogge et al. 2006, 146). In addition, an inability to empathize with relationship partners and manage conflict in a productive way may negatively impact future chances at relationship success. From an interpersonal communication perspective, it is important to determine the kinds of behaviors that elicit feelings of hostility from others, to then reduce or eliminate those behaviors, and to attempt to repair the damaged relationship using relationship maintenance strategies.

Verbally aggressive attacks can permanently damage relationships.
© fred goldstein, 2007, Shutterstock.

Verbal Aggression

Another personality trait labeled difficult, or problematic, during face-to-face encounters is verbal aggression. When individuals lack the ability to effectively argue, they often resort to verbally aggressive communication. Wigley (1998) describes **verbal aggressiveness** as the tendency to attack the self-concept of an individual instead of addressing the other person's arguments. Dominic Infante (1987; 1995) identified a wide range of messages that verbally aggressive communicators use. For example, verbally aggressive communicators may resort to character attacks, competence attacks, background attacks, physical appearance attacks, maledictions, teasing, swearing, ridiculing, threatening, and nonverbal emblems. On occasion, they might also use blame, personality attacks, commands, global rejection, negative comparison, and sexual harassment in their attempts to hurt others. As Wigley (1998) notes, "there seems to be no shortage of ways to cause other people to feel badly about themselves" (192).

Infante and Wigley (1986) developed the Verbal Aggressiveness Scale, which is a twenty item self-report personality test that asks people to indicate whether they are verbally aggressive in their interactions (found in Applications at the end of this chapter). Infante and Wigley were aware of the fact that people might not self-report their use of aggression. With this in mind, the researchers designed items on the measure to make it seem like they approved of aggressive messages. The researchers developed the Verbal Aggressiveness instrument to learn more about the behavior of people who were verbally aggressive.

For those of us who have ever interacted with someone who is highly verbally aggressive, one of the more common questions is why this person acts this way. There are a number of viable explanations for why some individuals possess trait verbal aggressiveness. Individuals may be verbally aggressive because they learned this behavior from others. Thus, social learning, or modeling effects explain why verbally aggressive parents have children that also become verbally aggressive. Another explanation for this trait is that verbally aggressive individuals lack the ability to argue effectively and, as a result, are more likely to become frustrated during arguments. The inability to defend one's position is frustrating and often causes the highly aggressive person to lash out at others. In this case, trait levels of verbal aggression are linked to argument skill deficiency (ASD). Researchers note that if verbal aggression is linked to ASD, then one way to combat this problem is to train individuals in effective argumentation (Wigley 1998).

There are a number of significant negative consequences for individuals who regularly communicate in verbally aggressive ways. Verbally aggressive individuals are more likely to use a variety of antisocial behaviors and, as a result, are less liked (Myers and Johnson 2003). Research by Infante, Riddle, Horvath, and Tumlin (1992) compared individuals who were high and low in verbal aggressiveness to determine how often they used different verbally aggressive messages, how hurtful they perceived these messages to be, and their reasons for using verbally aggressive messages. Individuals who were high in verbal aggressiveness were more likely to use a wide range of verbally aggressive messages (e.g., competence attacks, teasing, and nonverbal emblems). High verbal aggressives were less likely than low verbal aggressives to perceive threats, competence attacks, and physical appearance attacks as hurtful. When high verbal aggressives were asked to explain their behavior, they stated that they were angry, did not like the target, were taught to be aggressive, were in a bad mood, or were just being humorous. Wanzer and her colleagues (1995) found that verbally aggressive individuals are less socially attractive and more likely to target others in humor attempts than to target themselves. Their inappropriate use of humor may explain why acquaintances rate them as less socially attractive.

College students scoring high in verbal aggressiveness were more likely to be considered academically at risk in college settings than students scoring low in verbal aggressiveness (Lippert et al. 2005). Lippert and his colleagues (2005) call for more research to understand why verbally aggressive college students are more academically at risk. They suspect that verbally aggressive students' inappropriate classroom behavior may lead to negative evaluations from teachers and peers. Consistently negative experiences in the classroom may contribute to verbally aggressive students' at risk status.

What can be done to help high aggressives? From a communication perspective, it is important to recognize when we are being verbally aggressive with others and to attempt to eliminate these behaviors. Recognize that when you communicate in a verbally aggressive way, others may model your behavior. Have you ever had a younger sibling mimic your verbal or nonverbal messages? There is a substantial amount of research on this trait and the potentially negative effects of high amounts of verbal aggression on relationships in married (Infante, Chandler, and Rudd 1989), family (Bayer and Cegala 1992), and organizational contexts (Infante and Gorden 1991). If you are predisposed to using verbal aggression, enroll in courses that might help you improve your ability to argue. One of the most widely recognized ways to address or treat verbal aggression is to train individuals who are skill deficient in argumentation to defend their positions more effectively.

Next, we turn our attention to several communication-based personality traits that may help individuals communicate more effectively during social interaction. More specifically, we examine argumentativeness, assertiveness, humor orientation, and affective orientation.

CONSTRUCTIVE AGGRESSIVE BEHAVIOR

Argumentativeness and assertiveness are described by Infante as constructive forms of aggression. Both of these behaviors are considered constructive forms of aggression because they are more active than passive, help us achieve our communication goals, and do not involve personal attacks (Rancer 1998). For some individuals, arguing with friends, colleagues, or family members is considered enjoyable and challenging. For others, arguing leads to hurt feelings, confusion, or even anger.

Argumentativeness

According to Rancer, individuals vary extensively in their perceptions of argumentative behavior. Infante and Rancer (1982) define argumentativeness as "a generally stable trait which predisposes individuals in communication situations to advocate positions on controversial issues and to attack verbally the positions which other people hold on these issues" (72). When individuals are argumentative, they attack issues and positions. When individuals are verbally aggressive, they attack others by using competence or character attacks, or possibly even swearing. When someone exhibits high levels of argumentativeness, they are able to both advocate and defend positions on controversial issues. Infante and Rancer (1982) developed the Argumentativeness Scale, which is a twenty-item Likert-type scale that asks people to record how they feel about responding to controversial issues. Ten items on the scale assess motivation to approach argumentative situations and ten items assess motivation to avoid argumentative situations (see Applications section at the end of this chapter).

There are a number of benefits associated with argumentativeness. Highly argumentative individuals are more effective in their attempts to persuade others. They employ a wider range of persuasion and social influence tactics and tend to be more tenacious in their persuasion attempts (Boster and Levine 1988). Highly argumentative individuals are more resistant to compliance attempts from others and generate more counterarguments in response to persuasive encounters (Infante 1981; Kazoleas 1993). Argumentative individuals are viewed as more credible and competent communicators who are also more interested in communicating with others (Infante 1981; 1985). More recently, research by Limon and La France (2005) explored communicator traits associated with leadership emergence in work groups. As predicted by their hypotheses, college student participants low in CA and high in argumentativeness were more likely to emerge as leaders in work groups than students high in CA and low in argumentativeness. These findings illustrate the significance of this communication skill as it relates to one's potential to become a leader.

As mentioned previously, the inability to argue effectively is extremely problematic for individuals and for relationships. Research by Andonian and Droge (1992) linked males' reported verbal aggressiveness to date rape, which is an especially aggressive form of interpersonal behavior. They found that males' tendency to report acceptance of date rape myths, e.g., females might say no to sexual intercourse but really mean yes, was positively related to verbal aggressiveness and negatively related to argumentativeness. Again, this study, like others, emphasizes the constructive nature of argumentativeness and the destructive nature of verbal aggression. Similarly, in the organizational setting, the best conditions for organizational communication are when managers and employees are both high in argumentativeness and low in verbal aggression (Infante and Gorden 1987; 1989). Research on the benefits of argumentativeness in organizational contexts supports the notion of **independent-mindedness**, which refers to the extent to which employees can openly express their own opinions at work (Rancer 1998). The research on the benefits of argumentativeness in different contexts illustrates the significance of this skill.

Can we train individuals to argue more constructively? A number of programs have achieved successful results in training individuals to improve their ability to argue effectively. Anderson, Schultz, and Staley (1987) implemented cognitive training in argument and conflict management to encourage individuals to argue with one another. For individuals who are low in argumentativeness, this can be a daunting task. The researchers were pleased that they were able to see results from females who were low in argumentativeness. This study, as well as others, indicates that individuals can be trained to argue more effectively.

Assertiveness

Another form of constructive aggression is **assertiveness**, which is defined as the capability to defend your own rights and wishes while still respecting and acknowledging the rights of others. When individuals act in an assertive way, they stand up for themselves and are able to initiate, maintain, and terminate conversations to reach interpersonal goals (Richmond and Martin 1998). One way to measure assertiveness is by using the Socio-Communicative Orientation Scale developed by Richmond and McCroskey (1990). This measure includes ten assertiveness items and ten responsiveness items. Individuals are asked to report how accurately the items apply to them when they communicate with others. Some examples of assertive characteristics include: defends own beliefs, independent, and forceful. Individuals use Likert-type responses to indicate whether they strongly agree or strongly disagree that these characteristics apply to them (see the Applications section at the end of this chapter).

How can assertive behavior contribute to individual success?
© Yuri Arcurs, 2007, Shutterstock.

There are innumerable benefits associated with the assertiveness trait. By acting in an assertive manner, individuals are able to defend themselves, establish relationships, and take advantage of opportunities. Richmond and Martin (1998) note that assertive communication is more beneficial than aggressive communication and can lead to "long-term effectiveness while maintaining good relationships with others" (136). Assertive individuals are perceived as more confident and self-assured and often rated as more effective teachers and managers than unassertive individuals. When it comes to practicing safe sex, sexually assertive males are more likely than unassertive males to use condoms to protect themselves (Noar, Morokoff, and Redding 2002). Researchers say that increasing sexual assertiveness in males may lead to long-term increases in safer sexual behaviors (Noar et al. 2002).

Humor Orientation

Booth-Butterfield and Booth-Butterfield (1991) developed the concept of **humor orientation** and define it as the extent to which people use humor as well as their self-perceived appropriateness of humor production. Humor orientation (HO) can be measured using the Humor Orientation Scale (found in the Applications section at the end of this chapter), which is a seventeen-item questionnaire that assesses how often people use humor in their day-to-day communication and how effective they are at enacting humorous messages. When developing the HO measure, M. Booth-Butterfield and S. Booth-Butterfield (1991) examined the different types of humorous communication behaviors people used when they were attempting to be funny. They found that individuals scoring higher on the HO measure (also called high HO's) accessed more categories of humorous communication behaviors such as nonverbal techniques, language, expressivity, and impersonation. Persons who enacted humor frequently and effectively perceived themselves as funny, and utilized a variety of humorous communication behaviors across diverse situations. Wanzer, Booth-Butterfield, and Booth-Butterfield (1995) later confirmed that high humor-oriented people were perceived by others as funnier than low HO's when telling jokes. Thus, being humorous is not simply in the eye of the high HO.

Humor can add more than just laughs to the work environment.
© Zsolt Nyulaszi, 2007, Shutterstock.

There appear to be a variety of intrapersonal and interpersonal benefits associated with the humor orientation trait. For example, high HO's are typically less lonely (Wanzer et al. 1996a), are more adaptable in their communication with others, have greater concern for eliciting positive impressions from others, and are more affectively oriented, i.e., are more likely to use their emotions to guide their communication decisions (Wanzer et. al. 1995). Honeycutt and Brown (1998) found that traditional marital types, which usually report the highest levels of marital satisfaction (Fitzpatrick 1988), were also higher in HO than other types.

When managers are perceived as more humor-oriented by their employees, they are also viewed as more likable and effective (Rizzo, Wanzer, and Booth-Butterfield 1999). Not surprisingly, there are a number of benefits for teachers who use humor effectively in the classroom. For example, students report learning more from instructors perceived as humor-oriented (Wanzer and Frymier 1999) and also report engaging in more frequent communication outside of class with humor-oriented teachers (Aylor and Opplinger 2003).

More recently, researchers have examined whether high humor-oriented individuals are more likely than low humor-oriented individuals to use humor to cope with stress and whether they benefit from this "built in" coping mechanism (Booth-Butterfield, Booth-Butterfield, and Wanzer 2006; 2005). In two different, yet similar studies, employed participants reported their HO, whether they used humor to cope with stressful situations, coping efficacy, and job satisfaction. The researchers speculated that individuals employed in highly stressful jobs, such as nursing, would: (1) benefit from the ability to cope using humor, and (2) would vary in this ability based on HO scores (Wanzer et al. 2005). Nurses who reported higher HO were more likely than low HO nurses to use humor to cope with stressful work situations and to perceive their coping strategies as effective (higher coping efficacy). In addition, humor-oriented nurses reported greater coping efficacy, leading to higher job satisfaction. Researchers found the same relationships between HO, coping and job satisfaction in a similar study of employed college students (Booth-Butterfield, Booth- Butterfield, and Wanzer 2006). These studies illustrate how humor can help individuals cope with difficult or stressful situations.

Can we train people to use humor more appropriately and effectively? Perhaps. We know that people often participate in improv classes and classes on stand-up comedy to improve their ability to deliver humorous messages. It seems likely that if people understand why certain messages are universally perceived as funny, they could be trained to improve their ability to deliver humorous messages with greater success. For now, researchers who study humor and the effects of humor recommend that individuals avoid using any type of humor based on stereotypes, or humor viewed as racist, sexist, ageist, or homophobic. Individuals need to be aware of audience characteristics that influence the way humorous content is interpreted and make attempts to use humor that is innocuous. For example, individuals who want to incorporate more humor into their day-to-day communication may use more self-disparaging humor, making certain not to overuse this type of humor as it may damage one's credibility.

Affective Orientation

Affective orientation refers to the extent to which individuals are aware of their own emotional states and use them when making behavioral decisions (Booth-Butterfield and Booth-Butterfield 1990). Individuals described as affectively oriented tend to be quite aware of their affective states and consult them before acting. Conversely, individuals described as low in affective orientation tend to be relatively unaware of their emotions and tend to reject their emotions as useful (Booth-Butterfield and Booth-Butterfield 1998). Affective Orientation (AO) can be measured via the Affective Orientation (AO15) Scale which is a fifteen-item instrument used to assess the extent to which individuals are aware of and consult their affective states and

What kind of campaign might work to persuade this individual to quit smoking?
© Serghei Starus, 2007, Shutterstock.

can be found in the Applications section at the end of this chapter. The revised fifteen-item measure "offers a more definitionally focused and concise operationalization of AO, exhibits minimal gender differences in mean scores and it is psychometrically more sound than the original AO scale" (Booth-Butterfield and Booth-Butterfield 1998, 180).

What are some of the benefits and/or drawbacks of higher AO? Individuals that exhibit higher levels of AO tend to be more nonverbally sensitive and better at providing comfort to others (Booth-Butterfield and Andrighetti 1993; Dolin and Booth-Butterfield 1993). Interestingly, individuals with higher AO also tend to utilize humor more frequently than lower AO individuals (Wanzer et al. 1995). The researchers suspect that higher AO individuals might use humor as one method of treating or managing negative affective states. From a relationship perspective, higher AO individuals tend to be more romantic and idealistic in their beliefs about intimate relationships (Booth-Butterfield and Booth-Butterfield 1994). More recent research on AO has examined the relationship between this trait and health behaviors. Specifically, researchers have been examining the relationships between AO and specific health practices such as smoking. Higher AO individuals are more likely to smoke than low AO's (Booth-Butterfield and Booth-Butterfield 1998). These findings are important and can be used to formulate successful persuasive campaigns. For example, the researchers note that since smokers are more affectively oriented, persuasive prevention campaigns should generate negative affective states (e.g., fear) and then connect them in some way to smoking (Booth-Butterfield and Booth-Butterfield 1998).

Individuals may reap a variety of personal and interpersonal benefits when they exhibit higher levels of argumentativeness, assertiveness, humor orientation, and affective orientation. While these traits are not the only ones that have proven to be beneficial for sources (e.g., cognitive complexity), they are studied frequently, and can be assessed via self-report instruments, and are linked to other positive traits and characteristics.

SUMMARY

The goal of this chapter was to help you learn more about the complex, evolving, and multidimensional nature of the self. To learn more about who we are and why we act a certain way, we explored the role of interpersonal communication and relationships in identity formation. Communication with family members, peers, and relationship partners influences how we see ourselves and how we relate to others. Our personality differences also affect the way we relate to others. In this chapter we discussed differences between state and trait approaches to studying personality and the connection between personality traits and communication behaviors. Communication based personality traits such as CA, WTC, hostility, verbal aggression, argumentativeness, assertiveness, humor orientation, and affective orientation were discussed in this chapter. Some of the behaviors associated with these communication traits can be problematic for both sources and receivers. We hope that after reading this chapter you now have a better understanding of these traits and how some can either hinder or facilitate our communication with others.

APPLICATIONS

Discussion Questions

A. Write about or discuss in small groups the person/persons that were most influential in your life. What other individuals play a role in the process of identity formation that were not identified in this chapter?

B. Visit several websites that offer suggestions for improving one's self-esteem. Critique these websites based on the following criteria: (1) Quality and quantity of information presented, (2) Inclusion of a discussion of both the pros and cons of high and low self-esteem, (3) Credentials of the individuals posting these sites, and (4) Ease of navigation of these sites. Based on your analysis of these sites, would you use these sites or send friends to these sites for information?

C. Complete one or more of the following personality measures and score them:

- Personal Report of Communication Apprehension
  http://www.hawaii.edu/gened/oc/PRCA-24.pdf
- Verbal Aggressiveness Scale
  http://commfaculty.fullerton.edu/rgass/335%20Fall2001/
  Aggressiveness%20Scale.htm
- Argumentativeness Scale
  http://commfaculty.fullerton.edu/rgass/argumentativeness_scale1.htm
- Assertiveness-Responsiveness Measure
  http://www.as.wvu.edu/~richmond/measures/
  sociocommunicative.pdf
- Humor Orientation Scale
  http://healthyinfluence.com/wordpress/2009/07/17/the-humor-orientation-scale-original-17-item-version/
- Affective Orientation Scale
  http://www.as.wvu.edu/~mbb/ao21.htm

Recruit a friend that knows you quite well to complete the measure based on how the friend perceives your communication behaviors. Next, draw comparisons between self and other reports of the communication-based personality assessments. After examining the self and other reports closely, write about the following: (1) Are there similarities in the self and other reports, (2) Are there differences in the self and other reports, (3) Are these scores valid—do they accurately explain your communication tendencies, (4) After completing these assessments, do you feel it is necessary to change any aspect of communication behaviors? Why or why not?

ACTIVITIES

Willingness to Communicate Scale (WTC)

Below are twenty situations in which a person might or might not choose to communicate. Presume you have completely free choice. Indicate the percentage of times you would choose to communicate in each type of situation. Indicate in the space at the left what percent of the time you would choose to communicate.

0=never, 100=always

_____ **1.** Talk with a service station attendant.
_____ **2.** Talk with a physician.
_____ **3.** Present a talk to a group of strangers.
_____ **4.** Talk with an acquaintance while standing in line.
_____ **5.** Talk with a salesperson in a store.
_____ **6.** Talk in a large meeting of friends.
_____ **7.** Talk with a police officer.
_____ **8.** Talk in a small group of strangers.
_____ **9.** Talk with a friend while standing in line.
_____ **10.** Talk with a waiter/waitress in a restaurant.
_____ **11.** Talk in a large meeting of acquaintances.
_____ **12.** Talk with a stranger while standing in line.
_____ **13.** Talk with a secretary.
_____ **14.** Present a talk to a group of friends.
_____ **15.** Talk in a small group of acquaintances.
_____ **16.** Talk with a garbage collector.
_____ **17.** Talk in a large meeting of strangers.
_____ **18.** Talk with a spouse (or girl/boyfriend)
_____ **19.** Talk in a small group of friends.
_____ **20.** Present a talk to a group of acquaintances.

SCORING: To calculate the total WTC score follow these steps:

Step 1: Add scores for items 3, 8, 12, and 17; then divide by 4.

Step 2: Add scores for items 4, 11, 15, and 20; then divide by 4.

Step 3: Add scores for items 6, 9, 14, and 19; then divide by 4.

Step 4: Add the final scores from steps 1, 2, and 3; then divide by 3.

>82 High overall WTC

<52 Low overall WTC

Source: Richmond, V. P. and J. C. McCroskey. 1995. *Communication: Apprehension, avoidance, and effectiveness. (4th ed.).* Scottsdale, AZ: Gorsuch Scarisbrick.

REFERENCES

Ainsworth, M. D. S., M. C. Blehar, E. Waters, and S. Wall. 1978. *Patterns of attachment: A psychological study of the strange situation.* Hillsdale, NJ: Erlbaum.

Allen, M., and J. Bourhis. 1996. The relationship of communication apprehension to communication behavior: A meta-analysis. *Communication Quarterly, 44,* 214–226.

Andersen, S. M., and K. Berensen. 2001. Perceiving, feeling, and wanting: Motivation and affect deriving from significant other representations and transference. In J. P. Forgas, K. D. Williams, and L. Wheeler (Eds.), *The social mind: Cognitive and motivational aspects of interpersonal behavior* (231–256). New York: Cambridge University Press.

Anderson, J., B. Schultz, and C. Courtney Staley. 1987. Training in argumentativeness: New hope for nonassertive women. *Women's Studies in Communication, 10,* 58–66.

Andonian, K. K., and D. Droge. 1992. *Verbal aggressiveness and sexual violence in dating relationships: An exploratory study of antecedents of date rape.* Paper presented at the annual meeting of the Speech Communication Association, Chicago, IL.

Aron, A. 2003. Self and close relationships. In M. R. Leary and J. P. Tangney (Eds.), *Handbook of self and identity.* New York: The Guilford Press.

Aube, J., and R. Koestner. 1992. Gender characteristics and adjustment: A longitudinal study. *Journal of Personality and Social Psychology, 70,* 535–551.

Aylor, B., and P. Opplinger. 2003. Out-of-class communication and student perceptions of instructor humor orientation and socio-communicative style. *Communication Education, 52,* 122–134.

Bandura, A. 1986. *Social foundations of thought and action.* New York: Prentice Hall.

Bargh, J. A., and T. L. Chartrand. 1999. The unbearable automaticity of being. *American Psychologist, 54,* 462–479.

Bargh, J. A., K. McKenna, and G. M. Fitzsimons. 2002. Can you see the real me? Activation and expression of the "true self" on the Internet. *Journal of Social Issues, 58,* 33–48.

Baumeister, R. F. 1998. The self. In D. Gilbert, S. T. Fiske, and G. Lindzey (Eds.), *The Handbook of social psychology* (680–740). New York: Oxford Press.

Baumeister, R. F., and K. D. Vohs. 2003. Self-regulation and the executive function of the self. In M. R. Leary and J. P. Tangney (Eds.), *Handbook of self and identity.* New York: The Guilford Press.

Baumeister, R. F., J. D. Campbell, J. I. Krueger, and K. Vohs. 2003. Does high self-esteem cause better performance, interpersonal success, happiness or healthier lifestyles? *Psychological Science in the Public Interest, 4,* 1–44.

Bayer, C. L., and D. J. Cegala. 1992. Trait verbal aggressiveness and argumentativeness: Relations with parenting style. *Western Journal of Communication, 56,* 301–310.

Beatty, M. J., J. C. McCroskey, and A. D. Heisel. 1998. Communication apprehension as temperamental expression: A communibiological perspective. *Communication Monographs, 65,* 197–219.

Bell, R. A., and J. A. Daly. 1984. The affinity-seeking function of communication. *Communication Monographs, 49,* 91–115.

Berger, B. A., J. C. McCroskey, and V. A. Richmond. 1984. Communication apprehension and shyness. In W. N. Tinally and R. S. Beardsley (Eds.), *Communication in pharmacy practice: A practical guide for students and practitioners* (128–158). Philadelphia, PA: Lea & Febiger.

Berne, E. 1964. *Games people play.* New York: Grove.

Booth-Butterfield, M., and A. Andrighetti. 1993. *The role of affective orientation and nonverbal sensitivity in the interpretation of communication in acquaintance rape.* Paper presented at the annual convention of the Eastern Communication Association, New Haven, CT.

Booth-Butterfield, M., and S. Booth-Butterfield. 1990. Conceptualizing affect as information in communication production. *Human Communication Research, 16,* 451–476.

———. 1991. Individual differences in the communication of humorous messages. *Southern Communication Journal, 56,* 32–40.

———. 1994. The affective orientation to communication: Conceptual and empirical distinctions. *Communication Quarterly, 42,* 331–344.

———. 1996. Using your emotions: Improving the measurement of affective orientation. *Communication Research Reports, 13,* 157–163.

———. 1998. Emotionality and affective orientation (171–190). In McCroskey et al. (Eds.), *Communication and personality.* Cresskill, NJ: Hampton Press.

Booth-Butterfield, M., S. Booth-Butterfield, and M. B. Wanzer. 2006. Funny students cope better: Patterns of humor enactment and coping effectiveness. *Communication Quarterly.* (In Press)

Boster, F. J., and T. Levine. 1988. Individual differences and compliance-gaining message selection: The effects of verbal aggressiveness, argumentativeness, dogmatism, and negativism. *Communication Research Reports, 5,* 114–119.

Bowlby, J. 1969. *Attachment and loss: Vol. 1. Attachment.* New York: Basic Books.

———. 1973. *Attachment and loss: Vol. 3. Loss, sadness, and depression.* New York: Basic Books.

Chory-Assad, R. M., and M. Paulsel. 2004. Classroom justice: Student aggression and resistance as reactions to perceived unfairness. *Communication Education, 53,* 253–273.

Cook, W. W., and D. M. Medley. 1954. Proposed hostility and pharisaic-virtue scales for the MMPI. *Journal of Applied Psychology, 38,* 414–418.

Cooley, C. H. 1902. *Human nature and the social order.* New York: Scribner's.

Daly, J. A. 2002. Personality and interpersonal communication. In Knapp and Daly (Eds.), *Handbook of interpersonal communication* (133–180). Thousand Oaks, CA: Sage Publications.

Daly, J. A. and A. M. Bippus. 1998. Personality and interpersonal communication: Issues and directions. In McCroskey et al. (Eds.), *Communication and personality* (1–40). Cresskill, NJ: Hampton Press.

Daly, J. A., V. P. Richmond, and S. Leth. 1979. Social communicative anxiety and the personnel selection process: Testing the similarity effect in selection decisions. *Human Communication Research, 6,* 18–32.

Darley, J. M., and R. H. Fazio. 1980. Expectancy confirmation processes arising in the social interaction sequence. *American Psychologist, 35,* 867–881.

Dolin, D., and M. Booth-Butterfield. 1993. Reach out and touch someone: Analysis of nonverbal comforting responses. *Communication Quarterly, 41,* 383–393.

Dye, L. 2004. Researchers design games to boost self-esteem. Retrieved on 12/20/2006 from *abcnews.go.com/Technology/print?id.*

Epstein, S. 1973. The self-concept revisited: Or a theory of a theory. *American Psychologist, 28,* 404–416.

Felson, R. B. 1989. Parents and reflected appraisal process: A longitudinal analysis. *Journal of Personality and Social Psychology, 56,* 965–971.

Festinger, L. 1954. A theory of social comparison processes. *Human Relations, 7,* 117–140.

Finkel, E. J., and W. K. Campbell. 2001. Self-control and accommodation in close relationships: An interdependence analysis. *Journal of Personality and Social Psychology, 81,* 263–271.

Fitzpatrick, M. A. 1988. *Between husbands and wives: Communication in marriage.* Newbury Park, CA: Sage.

Goffman, E. 1959. *The presentation of self in everyday life.* Garden City, NY: Doubleday.

Gottman, J. M. 1999. *The marriage clinic: A scientific based marital therapy.* New York: Norton.

Greenwald, A. G., and S. J. Breckler. 1985. To whom is the self presented? In B. R. Schlenker (Ed.), *The self and social life* (126–145). New York: McGraw-Hill.

Guilford, J. P. 1959. *Personality.* New York: McGraw-Hill.

Harris, T. 1969. *I'm OK, you're OK.* New York: Harper & Row.

Honeycutt, J., and R. Brown. 1998. Did you hear the one about?: Typological and spousal differences in the planning of jokes and sense of humor in marriage. *Communication Quarterly, 46,* 342–352.

Houck, G. M., and A. M. Spegman. 1999. The development of self: Theoretical understandings and conceptual underpinnings. *Infants and Young Children, 12,* 1–16.

Huebner, D. M., C. J. Nemeroff, and M. C. Davis. 2005. Do hostility and neuroticism confound associations between perceived discrimination and depressive symptoms? *Journal of Social and Clinical Psychology, 24,* 723–740.

Infante, D. A. 1981. Trait argumentativeness as a predictor of communicative behavior in situations requiring argument. *Central States Speech Journal, 32,* 265–272.

———. 1985. Inducing women to be more argumentative: Source credibility effects. *Journal of Applied Communication Research, 13,* 33–44.

———. 1987. Aggressiveness. In J. C. McCroskey and J. A. Daly (Eds.), *Personality and interpersonal communication* (157–192). Newbury Park, CA: Sage.

———. 1988. *Arguing constructively.* Prospect Heights, Illinois: Waveland Press.

———. 1995. Teaching students to understand and control verbal aggression. *Communication Education, 44,* 51–63.

Infante, D. A., and W. I. Gorden. 1987. Superior and subordinate communication profiles: Implications for independent-mindedness and upward effectiveness. *Central States Speech Journal, 38*, 73–80.

———. 1989. Argumentativeness and affirming communicator style as predictors of satisfaction/dissatisfaction with subordinates. *Communication Quarterly, 37*, 81–90.

———. 1991. How employees see the boss: Test of an argumentative and affirming model of superiors' communicative behavior. *Western Journal of Speech Communication, 55*, 294–304.

Infante, D. A., and A. S. Rancer. 1982. A conceptualization and measure of argumentativeness. *Journal of Personality Assessment, 46*, 72–80.

Infante, D. A., B. L. Riddle, C. L. Horvath, and S. A. Tumlin. 1992. Verbal aggressiveness: Messages and reasons. *Communication Quarterly, 40*, 116–126.

Infante, D. A., and C. J. Wigley. 1986. Verbal aggressiveness: An interpersonal model and measure. *Communication Monographs, 53*, 61–69.

Infante, D. A., T. A. Chandler, and J. E. Rudd. 1989. Test of an argumentative skill deficiency model of interspousal violence. *Communication Monographs, 56*, 163–177.

Jung, C. G. 1953. *Psychological reflections.* New York: Harper and Row.

Karney, B. R., and T. N. Bradbury. 1995. The longitudinal course of marital quality and stability: A review of theory, methods, and research. *Psychological Bulletin, 118*, 3–34.

Kazoleas, D. 1993. The impact of argumentativeness on resistance to persuasion. *Human Communication Research, 20*, 118–137.

Keating, C. 1984. *Dealing with difficult people: How you can come out on top in personality conflicts.* New York: Paulist Press.

Koch, E. J., and J. A. Shepperd. 2004. Is self-complexity linked to better coping? A review of the literature. *Journal of Personality, 72*, 727–760.

Kopper, B. A., and D. L. Epperson. 1996. The experience and expression of anger: Relationships with gender, role socialization, depression and mental health functioning. *Journal of Counseling Psychology, 43*, 158–165.

Lieberman, A. F. 1977. Preschooler's competence with a peer: Relations with attachment and peer experience. *Child Development, 48*, 1277–1287.

Lieberman, A. F., and J. H. Pawl. 1988. Clinical applications of attachment theory. In J. Belsky and T. Nezworski (Eds.), *Clinical implications of attachment* (327–351). Hillsdale, NJ: Erlbaum.

Limon, S. M., and B. H. LaFrance. 2005. Communication traits and leadership emergence: Examining the impact of argumentativeness, communication apprehension and verbal aggressiveness in work groups. *Southern Communication Journal, 70*, 123–133.

Linville, P. W. 1985. Self-complexity and affective extremity: Don't put all your eggs in one cognitive basket. *Social Cognition, 3*, 94–120.

———. 1987. Self-complexity as a cognitive buffer against stress-related illness and depression. *Journal of Personality and Social Psychology, 52*, 663–676.

Lippert, L. R., B. S. Titsworth, and S. K. Hunt. 2005. The ecology of academic risk: Relationships between communication apprehension, verbal aggression, supportive communication, and students' academic risk. *Communication Studies, 56*, 1–21.

Markus, H., and E. Wurf. 1987. The dynamic self-concept: A social psychological perspective. *Annual Review of Psychology, 38*, 299–337.

Maxwell, J. C. 2002. *The seventeen essential qualities of a team player.* Nashville, TN: Thomas Nelson Publishers.

McCroskey, J. C. 1977. Oral communication apprehension: A summary of recent theory and research. *Human Communication Research, 4*, 78–96.

———. 1978. Validity of the PRCA as an index of oral communication apprehension. *Communication Monographs, 45*, 192–203.

McCroskey, J. C. 2006. Personal communication with the author.

McCroskey, J. C., and M. J. Beatty. 1984. Communication apprehension and accumulated communication state anxiety experiences: A research note. *Communication Monographs, 51*, 79–84.

McCroskey, J. C., J. A. Daly, and G. A. Sorensen. 1976. Personality correlates of communication apprehension. *Human Communication Research, 2*, 376–380.

———. 1995. Correlates of compulsive communication: Quantitative and qualitative characteristics. *Communication Quarterly, 43*, 39–52.

———. 1998. Willingness to communicate. In McCroskey et al. (Eds.), *Communication and personality* (119–132). Cresskill, NJ: Hampton Press.

McCroskey, J. C., and V. P. Richmond. 1987. Willingness to communicate. In J. C. McCroskey and J. A. Daly (Eds.), *Personality and interpersonal communication* (129–156). Newbury Park, CA: Sage.

McKenna, K. Y. A., A. S. Green, and M. E. J. Gleason. 2002. Relationship formation on the Internet: What's the big attraction? *Journal of Social Issues, 58,* 9–31.

Mead, G. H. 1934. *Mind, self, and society.* Chicago: University of Chicago Press.

Meeus, W., and M. Dekovic. 1995. Identity development, parental and peer support in adolescence: Results of a national Dutch survey. *Adolescence, 30,* 931–945.

Mizco, N. 2004. Humor ability, unwillingness to communicate, loneliness, and perceived stress: Testing a security theory. *Communication Studies, 55,* 209–226.

Myers, S. A., and A. D. Johnson. 2003. Verbal aggression and liking in interpersonal relationships. *Communication Research Reports, 20,* 90–96.

Noar, S. M., P. J. Morokoff, and C. A. Redding. 2002. Sexual assertiveness in heterosexually active men: A test of three samples. *AIDS Education and Prevention, 14,* 330–342.

Park, K. A., and E. Waters. 1988. Traits and relationships in developmental perspective. In S. Duck (Ed.) *Handbook of personal relationships: Theory, research, and interventions* (161–176). Chichester: John Wiley & Sons Ltd.

Peluso, P. R., J. P. Peluso, J. F. White, and R. M. Kern. 2004. A comparison of attachment theory and individual psychology: A review of the literature. *Journal of Counseling and Development, 82,* 139–145.

Pope, M. K., T. W. Smith, and F. Rhodewalt. 1990. Cognitive, behavioral and affective correlates of the Cook and Medley Hostility Scale. *Journal of Personality Assessment, 54,* 501–514.

Rancer, A. S. 1998. Argumentativeness. In McCroskey et al. (Eds.), *Communication and personality* (149–170). Cresskill, NJ: Hampton Press.

Richmond, V. P., and D. K. Roach. 1992. Willingness to communicate and employee success in U.S. organizations. *Journal of Applied Communication,* 95–115.

Richmond, V. P., and J. C. McCroskey. 1990. Reliability and separation of factors on the assertiveness-responsiveness measure. *Psychological Reports, 67,* 449–450.

Richmond, V. P., and M. M. Martin. 1998. Sociocommunicative style and sociocommunicative orientation. In McCroskey et al. (Eds.), *Communication and personality.* Hampton Press: Cresskill, NJ.

Rizzo, B., M. B. Wanzer, and M. Booth-Butterfield. 1999. Individual differences in managers' use of humor: Subordinate perceptions of managers' humor orientation, effectiveness, and humor behaviors. *Communication Research Reports, 16,* 370–376.

Rogge, R. D., T. N. Bradbury, K. Halweg, J. Engl, and F. Thurmaier. 2006. Predicting marital distress and dissolution: Refining the two-factor hypothesis. *Journal of Family Psychology, 20,* 156–159.

Schlenker, B. 1984. Identities, identifications and relationships. In V. Derlega (Ed.), *Communication, intimacy and close relationships.* New York: Academic Press.

–––. 1985. Identity and self-identification. In B. R. Schlenker (Ed.), *The self and social life* (65–99). New York: McGraw-Hill.

Self-Improvement. (n.d.). Retrieved September 29, 2005, from *http://www.mygoals.com/content/self-improvement.html.*

Shackelford, T. K. 2001. Self-esteem in marriage. *Personality and Individual Differences, 30,* 371–391.

Smith, T. W. 1994. Concepts and methods in the study of anger, hostility, and health. In A. W. Siegman and T. W. Smith (Eds.), *Anger, hostility, and the heart* (23–42). Hillsdale, NJ: Erlbaum.

Snyder, M., E. D. Tanke, and E. Berscheid. 1977. Social perception and interpersonal behavior: The self-fulfilling nature of social stereotypes. *Journal of Personality and Social Psychology, 35,* 656–666.

Spitzberg, B. H. and W. R. Cupach. 1984. *Interpersonal communication competence.* Newbury Park, CA: Sage.

Sroufe, L. A. 1988. The role of infant-caregiver attachment in development. In J. Belsky and T. Nezworski (Eds.), *Clinical implications of attachment* (18–38). Hillsdale, NJ: Erlbaum.

Surra, C. A., C. R. Gray, N. Cottle, and T. M. Boettcher. 2004. Research on mate selection and premarital relationships: What do we really know? In A. L. Vangelisti (Ed.), *Handbook of family communication* (53–82). Mahwah, NJ: Lawrence Erlbaum.

Swann, W. R. 1985. The self as architect of social reality. In B. R. Schlenker (Ed.), *The self and social life* (100–126). New York: McGraw-Hill.

Tesser, A. 2003. Self-evaluation. In M. R. Leary and J. P. Tangney (Eds.), *Handbook of self and identity.* New York: The Guilford Press.

Tesser A., J. V. Wood, and D. A. Stapel. 2002. Introduction: An emphasis on motivation. In A. Tesser, D. A. Stapel, and J. V. Wood (Eds.), *Self and motivation: Emerging psychological perspectives* (3–11). Washington, DC: American Psychological Association.

Tesser, A., R. B. Felson, and J. M. Suls (Eds.). 2000. *Psychological perspectives on self and identity.* Washington, DC: American Psychological Association.

Vallacher, R. R., and A. Nowak. 2000. Landscapes of self-reflection: Mapping the peaks and valleys of personal assessment. In A. Tesser, R. B. Felson, and J. M. Suls (Eds.), *Psychological perspectives on self and identity* (35–65). Washington, DC: American Psychological Association.

Wanzer, M. B., and A. B. Frymier. 1999. The relationship between student perceptions of instructor humor and student's reports of learning. *Communication Education, 48,* 48–62.

Wanzer, M. B., M. Booth-Butterfield, and S. Booth-Butterfield. 1995. The funny people: A source orientation to the communication of humor. *Communication Quarterly, 43,* 142–154.

———. 1996. Are funny people popular? An examination of humor orientation, verbal aggressiveness, and social attraction. *Communication Quarterly, 44,* 42–52.

———. 2005. "If we didn't use humor, we'd cry:" Humorous coping communication in health care settings. *Journal of Health Communication, 10,* 105–125.

Wigley, C. J. 1998. Verbal aggressiveness. In McCroskey et al. (Eds.), *Communication and personality* (191–214). Cresskill, NJ: Hampton Press.

Wood, J. T. 2001. *Interpersonal communication: Everyday encounters. (3rd ed.)* Belmont, CA: Wadsworth Publishing Company.

Zajonc, R. B., R. K. Adelmann, S. B. Murphy, and R. N. Niedenthal. 1987. Convergence in the appearance of spouses. *Motivation and Emotion, 11,* 335–346.

Zakahi, W. R., and R. L. Duran. 1985. Loneliness, communication competence, and communication apprehension: Extension and replication. *Communication Quarterly, 33,* 50–60.

SELF-IDENTITY

Who are you? It is a simple question. You have been answering it since you were able to talk. My name is David. On the other hand, this is one of the most difficult and important questions that we will face throughout our lives.

Who are you now? How do you feel about yourself? Are you happy, successful, comfortable? Are there things you would like to change about yourself? College is a time when many people define themselves for the first time. You are away from home. You are no longer the child of Homer and Marge Simpson. You are you. You can dye your hair purple and call yourself Raoul (at least until the next break when you return home). **Self-identity** and **self-esteem** are two of the most critical components of communication. If you feel good about yourself, you are likely to take a few chances and open up to people. On the other hand, if you are having a bad hair day, you are less likely to ask out that cute guy in your biology class. How you see yourself and how you define yourself can shift from day to day or even hour to hour. A professor tells you that you have written a really good paper. The most wonderful person in the world tells you that he loves you. Because you are brilliant and lovable, you feel really good about yourself and are likely to risk talking to someone new.

Unfortunately, a bad paper or a rejection from a significant other can have the opposite effect. **Who are you** is and will remain a fundamental question in the process of communication. The next chapter complicates matters even further by exploring your **cyber-self** and **cyber-communication**.

From Face-to-Face to Cyberspace
Forming Relationships Online*

LEARNING OBJECTIVES

After reading this chapter, you should understand the following concepts:

- Discuss how relationships developed prior to the Internet
- Explain how the evolution of the Internet has changed the way people develop interpersonal relationships
- Discuss factors of online attraction
- Explain the differences between face-to-face and computer mediated communication
- Identify the benefits and drawbacks of forming relationships via CMC
- Identify and explain the two factors individuals should consider when forming online relationships
- Identify cues that may indicate deception in online communication

KEYWORDS

social networking
self-disclosure
hyperpersonal model of CMC
active vs. passive communication activity
reduced social cues theory
flaming
detachment
informal vs. formal language style
synchronous
asynchronous
media richness theory
social presence theory
digital divide
gender-bending
coup de foudre
time and behavioral factors

OVERVIEW

The process of initiating relationships has evolved. Online social networks such as Facebook and MySpace have created opportunities for individuals to research other people and decide whether they want to pursue a relationship. Even dating practices have changed over the last few years. No longer do we have to count on friends to introduce us to someone they think is perfect for us or to frequent singles bars to look for love. Thanks to the Internet, we can find our perfect mate by posting a list of personal interests or by completing online personality profiles and allowing sites such as eHarmony and match.com to find a match.

Examples of the connection between Computer Mediated Communication (CMC) and relationship development are identified and discussed throughout this book. In Chapter Six we discussed the role of CMC in the initiating stages of relationship development. In Chapter Seven, we discussed how CMC is used to help us maintain relationships. In this chapter, we focus

*Chapter Contributions by Mary Mino

© Franz Pfluegl, 2007,
Shutterstock.

exclusively on research, theories, and constructs related to CMC and relationship development processes. In addition, we take a much closer look at how the use of this medium has altered interpersonal communication and the process of relationship development.

Online dating is one of the many ways in which people use online communication to build and sustain relationships. While mediated matchmaking is not necessarily a new phenomenon (Ellison, Heino, and Gibbs 2006) it certainly has changed and increased in popularity. Ellison and her colleagues describe the evolution of mediated matchmaking and note that as early as the mid-nineteenth century, singles placed ads in the newspaper to find a perfect mate (Ellison, Heino, and Gibbs 2006). Decades later, in the 1980s, singles used video dating services to meet potential mates. Today, a significant percentage of single persons turn to the Internet to help them find their "perfect match" (Lenhart and Madden 2006a). Nearly thirty-seven percent of single people state that they have visited Internet dating sites in the pursuit of romance.

Interpersonal scholars Mark Knapp and John Daly (2002) encourage researchers to study CMC because of its impact on face-to-face communication and relationship development processes. As we have stated throughout this text, communication competence is essential to building and maintaining effective relationships. Individuals require knowledge, skill, and motivation to communicate effectively and establish rewarding relationships. The same is true in the context of online communication.

This chapter addresses competent online communication by providing an overview of existing research on CMC that explains why online communication has become so prevalent and how to use it effectively and appropriately to establish relationships. The prospect of forming interpersonal relationships through CMC poses a multitude of questions. Will these relationships be similar to those formed via face-to-face interaction? What are the positive and negative aspects of forming a relationship through CMC? What are some suggestions for establishing successful online relationships? How has the Internet altered the way people establish, maintain and terminate relationships? In the first section of this chapter, we briefly discuss the methods used in the past in developing interpersonal relationships. Next, we focus on positive and negative aspects of interpersonal relationships formed through CMC. In the final section, we offer suggestions for using CMC as a means of developing interpersonal relationships.

Since the early 1990s, communication scholars have written about how online relationships are developed and maintained (see, specifically, Wildermuth 2001; Rumbough 2001; Parks and Roberts 1998; Parks and Floyd 1996; Walther 1996; Walther 1995; Walther, Anderson, and Park 1994; Walther 1993; Walther 1992; Walther and Burgoon 1992). However, communication researchers are not the only ones studying the development of online relationships. Researchers from academic fields such as computer science, behavioral science, psychology, sociology, and business have written about the impact of CMC on social interaction (see, for example, Nie 2001; Conley and Bierman 1999; Capulet 1998; Gwinnell 1998; Tanner 1994). At the end of 2004, more than an estimated 945 million people worldwide were participating in some form of online communication (Cyber Atlas 2005),

A significant number of single people turn to the Internet to find their "perfect match."
© Yuri Arcurs, 2007, Shutterstock.

and that number continues to increase. In fact, due to the prevalence of CMC, Steve Jacobs, cofounder of Apple Computer, made the recommendation that "personal computers be renamed 'interpersonal computers'" (Adler and Towne 2003, 20).

To better understand the how and why of relationships initiated and maintained online, let us first look at some comparisons between relationships that form via face-to-face communication (hereafter referred to as FTF) and those that form through CMC.

METHODS OF DEVELOPING INTERPERSONAL RELATIONSHIPS

In previous chapters, we have explored the ways in which individuals initiate, maintain, and terminate all types of relationships. It is important to note that the majority of the research conducted to discover how and why people come together and grow apart in relationships was in FTF contexts. Because we know that the communication situation, or context, greatly affects how messages are sent and received, it is important to consider how communication and relationship development processes may differ when individuals use CMC as a primary means of interaction. Before we identify the differences between FTF and CMC, let us examine some of the ways relationships began prior to the introduction of CMC.

ESTABLISHING RELATIONSHIPS: BEFORE THE INTERNET

Take a minute and imagine how your relationships with friends and family members would change if you did not have access to the Internet or a cellular phone. Would it be possible to establish and maintain relationships with others without this technology? Of course, it would be possible! But prior to the introduction of these technological advancements, the ways people communicated in relationships were very different. In the following sections, we discuss some of the different methods individuals used to establish and maintain their relationships prior to the development of the Internet.

Family and Community

Stated simply, social networking refers to the process of connecting with others to form different types of relationships. Before the Industrial Revolution in 1760, families functioned as independent economic units and served as the primary source of social networking for most individuals. People relied almost exclusively on FTF interactions with others in their community as the primary means of establishing relationships. The family played a significant role in the socialization of its members and was most likely to interact with other families that lived in close proximity. During this era, many relationships initially formed due to convenience. Relationships also developed through family members' involvement in church activities or arrangements made among families and friends (Rogers 1997).

How would your personal relationships change if you couldn't use a cell phone?
© Leah-Anne Thompson, 2007, Shutterstock.

Advances in Transportation

The Industrial Revolution, which occurred from 1760–1830, transformed the family and resulted in drastic changes in social network systems. Advances in transportation such as the rail system and automobiles increased options for the formation of interpersonal relationships. Individuals could now leave their hometowns and travel across the country to establish relationships with people hundreds of miles away. As society became more mobile, individuals were no longer restricted geographically in their choices of relationship partners. Individuals could establish and even maintain long distance relationships with greater ease (Rogers 1997).

Letter Writing and Telephone Use

Prior to the invention of the telephone, writing letters was the primary means of establishing and maintaining interpersonal relationships. Written correspondence provided a method of remaining faceless and allowed intimacy with a reduced amount of risk (Pratt et al. 1999). The number of couples who fell in love through written correspondence peaked during World War II as women began to write to soldiers overseas. Gwinell (1998) points out the significance of letter writing by noting that it served as a means of helping individuals with similar backgrounds communicate across greater geographic distances. While letter writing was an important means of communicating with friends, relatives, and relationship partners, the feedback from receivers was limited to textual information only and the rate of receiving feedback was extremely slow.

The telephone, created in 1876, drastically altered the way individuals communicated with one another on a day-to-day basis. Unlike letter writing, the telephone allowed individuals to send verbal and nonverbal messages and the feedback was immediate. Today we use cellular phones that provide us with the ability to communicate with virtually anyone, anywhere, and anytime! While cellular phones offer the convenience of being able to communicate with our friends, family, and significant others, they also can be a source of frustration and annoyance. In a recent *20/20* survey, eighty-seven percent of Americans indicated experiencing rude cell phone behavior that included people talking on cell phones in public places in loud voices (Cohen and Langer 2006).

Singles Clubs

During the last few decades, individuals have flocked to bars and singles clubs in order to meet the "right person." Not only has the singles scene replaced the family's influence on interpersonal relationships, but Rogers (1997) also contends, "The singles scene replaced the church social as one of the chief places to meet a member of the opposite sex" (1). Many agree that even today bars and clubs remain a common place to meet people (DeGol 2003). Think about how relationship initiation is portrayed in many television shows. Aside from on *Seventh Heaven*, no relationships are forming at church socials. Rather, Dr. McDreamy and Meredith Grey begin their relationship over drinks at the local bar in *Grey's Anatomy*, and the main characters in sitcoms such as *How I Met Your Mother* and *30 Rock* vainly attempt to forge connections with other singles at bars or clubs.

Mediated Matchmaking

While mediated matchmaking "is certainly not a new phenomenon" (Ellison, Heino, and Gibbs 2006, 416) it has evolved and, more recently, has increased in popularity. Ellison and her colleagues describe the evolution of mediated matchmaking and note that as early as the mid-nineteenth century, singles placed ads in the newspaper to find a perfect mate (Ellison, Heino, and Gibbs 2006; Schaefer 2003). Later, in the 1980s, singles used video dating services to meet potential mates (Woll and Cosby 1987; Woll and Young 1989).

During the late 1970s and early 80s, some individuals used dating services to help them find the perfect match (Jedlicka 1981). These singles agencies typically advertised in magazines and promised to match individuals using sophisticated computer technology. Singles using these services typically paid between fifteen and thirty dollars and then completed a questionnaire that asked for a variety of information such as physical appearance, race, age, religion, and hobbies. Once individuals submitted this information to the agency, they were matched with someone who scored similarly or who was deemed a good match. Jedlicka (1981) notes that "the computer's ability to evaluate and suggest alternatives is limited" (374). At the time, research on this type of mediated matchmaking was significant because it illustrated both the potential and limitations of computers as a means of social networking in the early 1980s.

With advances in technology, individuals have been able to increase the ways in which individuals establish and maintain their relationships. While many of the communication channels and forms of social networking mentioned in this section are still used, the arrival of the Internet has had a significant impact on the way we communicate with one another and the methods used to develop and maintain our relationships.

ESTABLISHING RELATIONSHIPS: THE INTERNET ERA

The birth of the Internet in the late 1960s resulted in electronic mail, or email. Originally, researchers used email to correspond with one another, but this technology rapidly moved beyond the research setting and became available for the general population (Lerner Productions 2003). For example, from 1995 to 1998, the number of people using email increased by fifty percent and by the year 2000, seventy-eight percent of the people online reported using the Internet specifically for email. This statistic is staggering—nearly three-fourths of online users depend on the medium to communicate via email (Boneva, Kraut, and Frohlich 2001).

Have any of your current relationships been established through email?
© Juriah Mosin, 2007, Shutterstock.

Because of its popularity and immediacy, email has evolved into a common form of CMC. In fact, many of today's interpersonal relationships are established through email. Friendships form in MySpace or Facebook communities instead of at local community socials and events. Romantic relationships form because of connections made through Match.com or Yahoo!

In today's world, people can video conference with colleagues and clients across the globe.
© Andresr, 2007, Shutterstock.

Personals as opposed to meeting at church socials or in high school classes. As Pratt and his co-authors (1999) have contended, the use of CMC as a form of correspondence in interpersonal relationships is merely the natural evolution of interpersonal relationships beyond face-to-face interaction.

The Internet has become one of the most rapidly growing technologies in the world. In 1997, over 50 million people utilized Internet services and almost half of them described the Internet as an "indispensable" part of their day-to-day lives (Miller and Clemente 1997). Although defining the Internet as "indispensable" may seem extreme, this medium has certainly added convenience to communication. With the click of a mouse, individuals can access a multitude of services from email to stock quotes. One can simply go to eBay to purchase a car, a rare collector's issue of *Sports Illustrated*, or the latest Fendi purse that has sold out in all the stores. Co-workers can easily access databases from all over the world or have a video conference with a client on the other side of the globe. In fact, research has suggested that the Internet is replacing other more traditional media (La Ferle, Edwards, and Lee 2002; Althaus and Tewksbury 2000; Johnson and Kaye 1999).

With all of these services, it seems logical that people turn to the Internet as a source of social networking. Today, a significant percentage of single persons are turning to the Internet to help them find their "perfect match" (Lenhart and Madden 2006a). Nearly thirty-seven percent of single people state that they have visited Internet dating sites in the pursuit of romance (Lenhart and Madden 2006b). Specifically, some people choose to use the Internet as a source for seeking out and developing interpersonal relationships. Yet many romantic partners are reluctant to admit to others that they met online. Why does this stigma of online romance exist? Individuals may be reluctant to admit meeting a relationship partner online because the use of CMC as a means of establishing relationships continues to be somewhat of an anomaly. Because many individuals meet their relationships partners through FTF encounters, using CMC to establish relationships is often regarded as nontraditional (Emmers-Sommer 2005) or somewhat unusual. However, we speculate that meeting partners online will be viewed differently over time as more singles use Internet services to "shop" for the ideal mate. After all, individuals use the Internet to shop for everything from cars to clothes online (Conley and Bierman 1999), why not "shop" for relationship partners as well?

Online Dating

Technological advancements such as cell phones and computers have certainly altered the way we communicate with others during the initial stages of relationship development. Recall our discussion of "silent dating" practices in Chapter Six. With the advent of cell phones, individuals can now send multiple text messages first to gauge whether the other party is interested in furthering the relationship. Today, individuals that are interested in establishing a relationship will often "text" and "IM" one another prior to advancing to that first phone call or going on that first date.

It is also more common today for individuals to use CMC to meet, maintain, and terminate romantic relationships. As interpersonal relationships form because of connections made via the Internet, numerous online dating sites assist people in their search for similar relationship partners. Recall our earlier discussion of the role that similarity plays in deciding whether to initiate a relationship with someone. In cyberspace, the search for similarities in age, cultural background, sexual orientation, religion, educational level, interests, and likes and dislikes is easier. Many sites, such as eHarmony, Match.com, or Yahoo! Personals provide users with the opportunity to enter preferences for a variety of demographic categories. Some sites have even targeted specific audiences: silversingles.com for seniors; eSPIN-the-Bottle for tweens and older; Jdate for singles of the Jewish faith, and a few off-the-garden-path varieties, including gothicmatch.com and several variations thereof. Books such as *The Complete Idiot's Guide to Online Dating and Relating* (Swartz 2000) offer popular Internet sites that fulfill a variety of interpersonal needs and requirements. Many of these sites are increasing in popularity when it comes to initiating relationships because they provide more information than can be included in a written personal ad and they allow people to correspond anonymously for longer periods of time (Scharlott and Christ 1995). Consider the popularity of the online dating service, match.com. The website was created in 1995 and advances "a simple mission: to take the lottery out of love" (www.match.com). The creators of this website boast that use of their site has resulted in over 250,000 marriages per year! With over 15 million members, match.com offers a significant amount of choices in potential relationship partners. Individuals simply log on to the site and begin viewing portraits and reading descriptive information about the members of this online community. If members are uncomfortable posting personal information, they can use the alternative online dating service known as chemistry.com. Individuals choosing to use this online dating service allow others to do the "searching and matching for them."

As the demand for online dating websites increases, the services offered by these sites have become more sophisticated and now cater more specifically to users' needs. If a person is concerned about the honesty of a potential date, there are even sites such as true.com that conduct background checks on its members. Criminal background investigations and public record screenings are conducted to ensure that members are not married and are free of criminal charges. If an online dater is still uneasy about a potential date, sites such as truedater.com allow him to read reviews posted by others who have met the potential date through a dating website. Truedater.com claims to provide an objective review of how honestly someone has portrayed himself in his online profile by allowing others to comment on experiences with the person.

Individuals also use CMC to maintain their relationships. As mentioned in Chapter Seven, individuals send emails and use IM (instant messenger) to correspond regularly with friends, family members, and relationship partners. One of the most frequently used relationship maintenance strategies, labeled "mediated communication," involves the use of computers to stay in touch with significant others and sustain the quality of the relationship.

Not surprisingly, CMC can also be used to terminate relationships with significant others. Individuals can use the Internet to learn more about how to end a relationship and they can use email and Instant Messenger (IM) as a means of terminating the relationship. For example, individuals can use

The convenience of CMC can help family members stay in touch more often.
© Zsolt Nyulaszi, 2007, Shutterstock.

There are Internet sites available for children to chat with other kids from all over the country.
© Jacek Chabraszewski, 2007, Shutterstock.

Positively Passionate Inc. (*www.positively.biz*), an Internet break-up service, to end an unwanted relationship. For $200 this company will call or send an email to your partner and terminate the relationship for you. This website also offers a variety of relationship-related information and services.

Online Social Networks

Just as online dating sites have gained in popularity, so have online social networking sites. Online social networking sites provide people with a place to come together to identify and discuss common interests or causes. The network expands as users add or invite "friends" to the site. Currently, some of the more popular social networking sites are MySpace, Facebook, and Xanga. For those who wish to share audio or video files, sites such as YouTube and Flickr provide a forum for distributing personal recordings to online friends. Children with Internet savvy visit sites such as clubpenguin.com, which allow them to chat with other children from around the country. While the social aspects of these sites have broadened our opportunities for forming friendships with those who may live thousands of miles away, there are also new "uses" for these sites.

Not only are Harry Potter and Rolling Stones fans seeking one another in online social networks, marketers, scammers, predators, and even journalists are reviewing these sites to gain information about individuals. A 2006 study conducted by Purdue University found that many employers report using online social networks for background checks of potential employees. Nearly thirty-five percent of the employers surveyed reported that they use search engines such as Google to locate information on potential hires, thirteen percent check social networking sites such as Facebook and MySpace, and an additional fifteen percent search for personal blogs posted on the Internet.

As the number of people forming relationships via online dating sites and social networking sites increases, so does the need to understand the appeal of these sites for connecting individuals.

WHAT ATTRACTS PEOPLE TO ONE ANOTHER ONLINE?

When answering the question "What attracts people to one another online?" we discover qualities and characteristics that are similar to those that attract us to others in FTF relationships. Physical attractiveness and social attractiveness are still paramount. Recall our discussion of the importance of physical and social attractiveness in Chapter Six. If you have ever glanced at an online profile, you probably noticed that most individuals highlight their physical characteristics. A unique aspect of initiating relationships online is that individuals also spotlight factors of social attractiveness in their list of desired qualities in a potential mate. Background, attitude, and demographic similarities—information that often requires extensive small talk on a first date—can easily be determined by browsing an online profile.

Earlier in the text, we discussed the importance of self-disclosure in achieving intimacy in relationships. **Self-disclosure** involves divulging personal information to another individual and is usually delivered through face-to-face or computer-mediated channels. Consider the rate at which self-disclosure occurs in FTF relationships compared to CMC. When scholars compare FTF with online relationship development processes, they note quite significant differences. Walther (1996) advances a **hyperpersonal model of CMC**, noting that online communication often facilitates relationship development and perceptions of intimacy. Walther further explains his hyperpersonal model of CMC based on the following factors:

1. *The sender's ability to construct a specific and desired image of him/herself.* The sender can create an image that reflects an "ideal" versus the "real" self if he or she chooses. Unlike in FTF interactions where physical flaws or idiosyncratic personality traits may be readily apparent, a person's weaknesses are not on display or are often omitted from the personal description in computer-mediated contexts.
2. *The sender's ability to alter any message content prior to sending them.* The sender can create messages, review them, and then alter them as needed when using computer-mediated channels of communication. This process may improve the quality of the information exchanged and elicit more favorable responses from receivers.
3. *The receiver's propensity to create positive impressions of the partner.* Because the sender has created an ideal or desired image and has carefully monitored and edited the information exchanged, the receiver is likely to form more favorable impressions via CMC than through FTF contexts.
4. *The increased depth and breadth of self-disclosure exchanged between the relationship partners.* Similar to FTF interactions, if the initial exchanges between individuals are positive, this leads to increased disclosure. In CMC the rate at which individuals exchange private information tends to be much faster than in FTF contexts (Walther 1996; Anderson and Emmers-Sommer 2006).

Walther (1996; 1997) and other scholars agree that greater levels of intimacy can be established through CMC than in similar types of FTF interactions. Follow-up research has substantiated this claim, noting that intimate relationships often develop in computer-mediated contexts faster than in FTF contexts because of the higher frequency of interaction (Hian, Chuan, Trevor, and Detenber 2004).

If you are one of the millions of students who have created an online social profile on a site such as MySpace, think about how much personal information you have disclosed on the Internet. A twenty-year old woman named Sami posted one profile on MySpace.com. Sami is a college graduate and is employed as a dental assistant. She enjoys wakeboarding, jet skiing, and going to the mall to hang out with her friends. She has a countdown on her profile that informs us how soon the day of her wedding to David will arrive. In case we might question how she and David feel about one another, she posts a video clip of the two of them locked in a passionate embrace. For those of us who want to know her likes and dislikes, Sami posts a survey that details this information. We know how many tattoos and piercings she has and that she is right-handed. After only five minutes, we learn Sami's full name, birth date, and hometown, her weight, her eye color, her weaknesses and goals, how many CDs she owns, where she wants to visit abroad, and that she wants to have children. We also know what high school and college she attended and where she works. Sami also blogs her daily itinerary as well as her current "mood" status, and everyone can learn where she and her friends will be on Friday night. In less than ten minutes, you may know more about Sami than you know about classmates you have known since first grade! As you can see from this example, individuals tend to open up in the online environment more quickly than they do in FTF interactions. Information that one might typically keep "private" until a friendship or romantic relationship develops is posted on a site for the entire world to see. What are the benefits of this online disclosure? It has made it easier for people to "cut to the chase" in identifying similarities. A simple glance at an online profile allows us to determine whether we have anything in common with the other person.

What are some of the pitfalls associated with Internet disclosure? Perhaps the biggest concern with online disclosure of information is safety. Not surprisingly, people differ in the amount and type of information they disclose on these Internet sites. In a 2006 study of 487 teenagers who reported having an online profile posted on a site, gender differences emerged when comparing the types of information boys and girls disclosed online. See the findings at http://www.pewinterest.org/. Select "teens", then search for Privacy and Online Social Networks. Select article: Online Privacy: What Teens Share and Restrict in an Online Environment.

Boys and girls were similar in their willingness to share first names, school names, or IM screen names. However, females indicated a tendency to post more photos (both of themselves and of their friends) than males, while boys were more likely to post videos or to reveal their hometowns and last names in their online profile. Thus, there appears to be subtle gender differences in the type of information disclosed online.

How Do FTF and CMC Differ?

Now that we have examined the transformation in relationship development because of the introduction of the Internet, let us focus on the distinctions between FTF and CMC and how these differences affect relationship development. Table 6.1 highlights the distinctions between these two forms of communication.

Level of Communication Activity. The vast majority of our FTF interactions require us to be **active** participants in a conversation. Of course, there are times when someone may engage in **passive** communication behaviors (e.g., responding "uh-huh" to a question while watching a game on television), but our physical presence typically requires us to be engaged in an interaction. In the CMC environment, the level of communication activity can range from active to passive. Active participation occurs when one sends an instant message (IM) to a friend or posts a response to an online chat room. Examples of passive activity are often less obvious and include "lurking," or viewing posts made on a discussion board or chat forum without responding. Since there are often several people engaged in chat room discussions, many who are unknown to the "regulars" participating in the online conversation, this passive behavior often goes unnoticed. This behavior is in stark contrast to social expectations in the FTF environment. If one were to stand by and listen in on a conversation without responding, others would

TABLE 6.1 Comparisons of FTF and CMC Qualities

Qualities	Face-to-Face (FTF)	Computer-Mediated Communication (CMC)
Level of communication activity	Active	Passive (lurking, viewing) Active (source of message)
Nonverbal cues	Real	Artificial
Language style	Elaborate and more formal	Restricted and less formal
Synchronicity	Synchronous	Asynchronous and synchronous
Richness of interaction	High	Low
Social presence	High	Low

perceive the behavior as strange or threatening. The person that was not participating in the conversation would probably be asked if he or she had something to contribute.

Nonverbal Cues. In cyberspace, the rules for nonverbal communication are drastically different from the rules in face-to-face interactions. One theory developed to explain the absence of nonverbal cues in online interactions is **reduced social cues theory** (Sproull and Kiesler 1986). According to this theory, humans depend on social cues such as a person's appearance, attire, facial expressions, and gestures to help interpret received messages. Many of the social cues that we depend on in FTF interactions are absent in CMC. One look at another person's face reveals a myriad of cues about the mood or intent of a message. During FTF interactions, we often check to see whether the other person is smiling, whether he or she looks confused, or if the person is focused on the message. The absence of cues makes the process of managing and interpreting online interactions much more difficult. As a result, alternative forms of nonverbal cues compensate for the lack of social cues: Emoticons are used to communicate emotion, capital letters are used to indicate the severity of the message, and acronyms or abbreviations are inserted in messages to indicate a playful or informal tone. Examples of these artificially created nonverbal cues are included in Table 6.2.

Several outcomes are associated with the reduction in social cues. Because we cannot see the expressions or responses of others in the online world, the social norms and constraints that typically guide our behavior are modified. In essence, our interpersonal behavior becomes "deregulated." In the absence of cues, people have a greater tendency to use "flaming" in their online communication. **Flaming** refers to aggressive attacks made against another person. An example of flaming would be the excessive use of capital letters in an attempt to scold a person. Another consequence of reduced social cues is the

Passive behavior online often goes unnoticed by active participants.
© Romanchuck Dimitry, 2007, Shutterstock.

TABLE 6.2 Examples of CMC Nonverbal Cues

Emoticons	Smiling	☺ or :-)
	Bad hair day	&:-)
	Laughing	:-D
	Kissing	:-*
	Giving a rose	@-}—
Capital Letters	I WISH YOU WOULD STOP POSTING MESSAGES TO MY BULLETIN BOARD!	
Acronyms	AWHFY	Are we having fun yet?
	ROTFL	Rolling on the floor laughing
	CYAL8R	See you later
	EMFJI	Excuse me for jumping in
	HAK	Hug and kiss

tendency for **detachment**. In CMC environments, participants may perceive themselves to be less connected to the conversation. As a result, a person may exit a chat room discussion abruptly and without warning or they may deliberately ignore attempts by others to communicate. In an FTF conversation, most people would make some indication of their intention to leave a conversation rather than simply walking away.

In FTF interactions, one look at someone's face can tell you how that person is reacting to your message.
© Galina Barskaya, 2007, Shutterstock.

Language Style. Think about the last email you sent to a close friend or family member. Chances are the style of language was less formal than language typically used in your FTF conversations. Due to the tedious nature of typing, it is often easier to take "short cuts" when composing written messages. As a result, our CMC messages are often more **informal** in terms of language style compared to the more elaborate and **formal** nature of FTF messages. For example, one friend might say to the other, "Are you okay? You seem to be upset about something," in an FTF conversation. If the same interaction occurred via email or text message, the interaction might look more like this: "RUOK? U seem 2B upset . . ." For some Internet users, this informal language style has found its way into their written communication. Some faculty members report that students who engage in frequent online communication tend to use poor grammar in their academic writing. Lee (2002) points out that teachers are frustrated by student papers that include shortened words, improper capitalization and punctuation, and the erratic use of characters such as & and @.

Synchronicity. Another notable distinction between FTF and CMC interactions involves the synchronicity, or the rate at which responses occur in the exchange of messages. In FTF interactions, the sending and receiving of messages is **synchronous**, or occurs in real time, or simultaneously. At the same time a source sends a message, feedback cues are being received to help interpret the receiver's response. When you ask a friend to comment on your outfit, and you notice an odd look on his face while you are asking the question, feedback is being received while the message is being communicated. The source and the receiver are sending cues to one another simultaneously, thus synchronous communication occurs. Online environments can provide opportunities for synchronous communication in forums such as chat rooms or via instant messaging. The expectation is that once a message is received, an immediate response will be provided.

Asynchronous communication involves a time lapse between when a message is received and when a response is made. Asynchronous CMC messages are typically in the form of emails or discussion board postings. We do not expect a friend to respond immediately to an email that we send and often several days may pass between the time when someone posts a message to an online discussion board and others post responses.

Richness of Interaction. **Media richness theory** (Daft and Lengel 1984) describes the capability of a communication channel to convey a variety of cues. By information richness, or media richness, we refer to the channel's level of synchrony, the availability of social cues, the ability to use natural language (as opposed to text or symbols), and the ability to convey emotions using the channel. As CMC lacks social cues and nonverbal expressions and uses text language instead of natural language, it is typically judged as being "less rich" on the media richness continuum although it spans across varying levels of richness. Emails are low in richness due to the lack of nonverbal cues. However, suppose you were to have a conversation with a friend using a web camera attached to your computer. The camera allows you to observe a number of your friend's nonverbal cues and increases the level of media richness.

FTF interactions are the richest communication channel on the continuum. Recall some of the cues you received in the last conversation you had with your best friend. Not only did you receive the actual words of the message, you could also sense the mood through tone of voice, facial expressions, and posture.

Social Presence. Short, Williams, and Christie (1976) created **social presence theory** to describe the perceived psychological closeness that occurs during a FTF interaction. Earlier chapters have discussed the concept of immediacy. Social presence focuses on the immediacy that occurs when we communicate with others. In a FTF conversation, there are numerous cues that cause us to feel psychologically closer to the person. A lingering glance or a forward lean accompanied by a smile can make a person feel connected to the other. The absence of nonverbal cues in email or chat room interactions results in low levels of social presence.

Using a web camera can heighten interactive richness because you can see the other person's nonverbal cues.
© Supri Suharjoto, 2007, Shutterstock.

In a FTF conversation, when you see a smile it makes you feel more connected to the other person.
© Tomasz Trojanowski, 2007, Shutterstock.

WHO IS ONLINE AND WHY?

Parks and Roberts (1998) found that the most desirable online relationships center on developing close friendships and finding romance. When seeking interpersonal relationships online, the majority of users interact more often with members of the opposite sex. However, even though men and women use the Internet equally, they use it for different reasons. Boneva and his colleagues (2001) concluded that women spend more time using email to correspond with relatives and close friends. On the other hand, Scharlott & Christ (1995) found men are more likely to "maximize the number of contacts, presumably to increase their chances of finding someone interested in a physically intimate relationship" (198). Interestingly, women and men achieve different levels of success with their online relationships goals. Women who are looking for friendship achieve their goal thirty-three percent more often than men who are seeking romantic and sexual relationships (Scharlott and Christ 1995). In some instances, individuals may initially use the Internet as a means of establishing friendships, but these relationships eventually transform into something different over time. Consider the following example:

Posted on December 1, 2003

Margaret wrote: Wanted to share my internet romance. Back in May of 2001 I went on to an over 40's chat out of curiosity. I was not looking for anybody. I met a man through the chat who also was not on the lookout. I guess in the way I was talking, it caught his eye and he asked if he could e-mail me as a friend. We both stated from the beginning that it was nothing more than friendship. The more we talked, the more things began to change.

He sent me his photo and I sent him mine. He expressed his feelings of love for me and I did the same in return. On September 20th he came to Canada to visit me (he is from the U.S.) and we knew even before the visit we would be attracted to each other. As soon as we met at the airport we knew it! We had such a great time together. He kept telling me how much he loved me, he held my hand constantly as we walked around seeing the sights and the kisses were certainly there as well. On the 23rd he told me that he had to have me and asked me to be his wife. I immediately responded with a yes.

For all you that may think we might be very young people, this is not the case. I'm 42 and he is 51. I work for a police agency and he is in state government. My son and I are now flying down to his state for the American Thanksgiving and to meet his family, friends, and co-workers. He has already started with the immigration papers (which we are truly hoping) will not become a big headache or a long wait. We speak to each other every day either by computer or by telephone expressing our love for each other. In the future, when I have been given permission by immigration to be married, I will then move to the States and we will be married in his home state. I never thought in my wildest dreams that this kind of situation would ever happen to me.

I have heard the negative feedback on internet dating but on the other hand, I've heard more positive coming out of it. I already know—2 girls in my office are successfully internet dating—one with someone in Canada and the other with someone in the U.S. Good luck to everybody who goes this route.

—http://www.internetdatingstories.com/

This example illustrates how rapidly relationships can evolve through CMC as well as the variety of ways that individuals use the Internet. Margaret states that she initially used the Internet because she was "curious," not because she was looking for a mate. She mentions that her online relationship started out as platonic but then quickly transformed into a romantic connection. This example also illustrates the hyperpersonal model of CMC discussed earlier in the chapter.

In addition to sex differences in Internet use, Nie (2001) established a correlation between income and education and the use of the Internet. College graduates are more likely to use the Internet consistently. Furthermore, research indicates that the average age of Internet users is under forty and that these individuals have an average yearly income of $55,000 (Suler 2002). With regard to Internet use among persons of various ethnic and racial backgrounds, research has found that nearly eighty percent of English-speaking Latinos, seventy-four percent of Caucasians, and sixty-one percent of African-Americans use the Internet (Marriott 2006). These demographic statistics support the presence of a **digital divide**, or a gap, between those who have access to the Internet and those who do not. With so many people turning to the Internet as the primary channel for communication and information, the notion of a digital divide is one that demands attention by researchers. The question of "power" becomes an issue as we analyze the accessibility of CMC.

EFFECTS OF CMC RELATIONSHIPS

The social dynamics and venues created by the Internet generate both opportunities and risks for developing interpersonal relationships (Parks and Floyd 1996). Over the years, our students have shared both success and horror stories about friends, family members, co-workers, or acquaintances who have established romantic relationships and friendships online. Students often recount stories about individuals who travel across the country to meet a "true love," only to find that the person has completely misrepresented him- or herself online. We suspect that the media may also play a role in shaping our students' negative opinions of online relationships. Perhaps the stories of healthy relationships that have developed online are not as newsworthy as those that end in heartache or disappointment. While the media may depict a relatively one-sided view of online relationships, much of the literature on forming online relationships focuses on both positive and negative aspects of communicating online.

Positive Aspects

An article published in *Time* magazine (Kirn 2000) compared the initiation of online relationships to dating practices of the past. "In many ways this is courtship as it once was, before the advent of the singles bar. There is plenty of conversation but no touching" (73). Communicating online may allow people to gradually build their level of intimacy before they meet, which may result in more meaningful relationships.

Several authors have discussed other positive aspects of using CMC to form interpersonal relationships: less chance of face-to-face rejection, less geographic limitations, less confrontation with unwanted admirers, and more potential relationship prospects (Anderson and Emmers-Sommer 2006; Walther 1993; 1996). Rabin (1999) also feels that there are benefits associated with the use of CMC to establish relationships. Rabin (1999) claims:

> "The risks involved in making an impression in an appearance-obsessed world and the embarrassment of face-to-face rejection are perils that don't affect the cyberflirt . . . Flirting online frees you from a host of offline pitfalls, including shyness . . . incompatibility (Poof! Mr./Ms. Wrong is gone just like that!) and geographic limitations (Stuck in a small town? Not any more.)" (2).

Other positive aspects include developing an initial interest without a major emphasis on physical appearance and an increased level of familiarity. Cooper and Sportolari (1997) contend that

> "In FTF [face-to-face] interaction, people make quick judgments based on physical attributes. . . . People who may have FTF encounters unwittingly keep themselves from intimate relationships by being overly focused upon or critical of their or others' physical appearance are freed up online to develop connections" Furthermore, "frequent contact with others is possible with little inconvenience or cost from the comfort and safety of one's own home" (9).

The concept of the importance of frequent contact supports Hendrick and Hendrick's (1983) contention that individuals who communicate on a more consistent basis tend to develop a stronger attraction to each other.

Negative Aspects

Studies often describe the physical dangers involved in forming online relationships, but there is an equal amount of danger present during face-to-face interactions (Conley and Bierman 1999). However, there are other negative aspects of forming relationships online.

Lack of Technical Knowledge and Absence of Social Context Cues.
A lack of technical knowledge and the absence of social context cues may impede some individuals from using the Internet to communicate effectively. Rintel and Pittam (1997) contend, "users must not only come to terms with the basics of interaction management vis-à-vis the technical commands necessary to communicate, but also the curtailment of the social context cues that are used in managing interactions and establishing interpersonal relationships" (530–531). In other words, those who choose to communicate via the Internet have to learn not only the technological aspects of interaction, but also how to compensate for the lack of social cues available in electronic messages. If a friend sends you an email, there is some technical knowledge required to access that message. Not only do you have to know how to "log on" to your email, there are probably also passwords and user identification codes that have to be entered in order to access your online mailbox. Once

the message is accessed, the next task involves interpreting the emoticons and language that is used to communicate emotions and feelings. Specifically, Parks and Floyd (1996) have asserted, "Relational cues emanating from the physical context are missing, as are nonverbal cues regarding vocal qualities, bodily movements, and physical appearance. Thus, CMC is judged to have a narrower bandwidth and less information richness than face-to-face communication" (81). In essence, there is a new level of knowledge and skill required to effectively communicate online. Unfortunately, some individuals lack online competence. Emails that fail to address the other person by name or that include one-word responses are often perceived as being rude. Given that many email addresses are abbreviations or codes, sending emails without signing your name can also be confusing. After all, how is a receiver supposed to know that js123456@ohiou.edu is Jane Smith if she fails to sign her email? Failure to employ proper online etiquette can result in potential communication breakdowns and misunderstandings.

Anonymity. Anonymity when communicating online may also pose problems. Rintel and Pittam (1997) have shared Kiesler, Seigel, and McGuire's (1984) fears that "the increased anonymity [of] CMC leads to uninhibited behavior . . . by some users to try extreme and (risky) attention-getting strategies to initiate interactions . . ." (531). This anonymity or pseudonymity allows individuals to communicate more openly and, in some cases, individuals may feel that they can get away with using exaggerated, deceptive, manipulative, or abusive communication. These risky behaviors "fail to establish new relationships and sometimes result in retaliation rather than interaction" (Rintel and Pittam 1997, 531).

Deceptive Behavior. Furthermore, online anonymity may lead to an increase in deceptive behavior. Deceptive behaviors include misrepresenting personal attributes, failing to share important personal information such as existing interpersonal relationships with a spouse, an over reliance on an "online" persona, or accelerated intimacy. Greenfield (1999) has discussed the misinformation often shared during online interactions. He has observed:

> There are some estimates that between thirty-three and fifty percent of individuals on the Internet are lying about some aspect of who and what they are. Some people have been found to represent themselves as members of the opposite sex! There is undoubtedly a considerable amount of lying about marital and financial status along with portraying one's personal characteristics as being more desirable than in reality. Everyone online weighs less than the real-time scale indicates! People become actors and actresses, allowing their innermost fantasies to become expressed online (30).

In addition, lying online allows individuals to create a new identity, an online persona. As Cooper and Sportolari (1997) have warned, "rather than using the net as a way to work on inhibited or conflictual aspects of the self, people may instead (consciously or not) use online relating to further split off unintegrated parts of themselves, leading to a compulsive and destructive reliance on their screen personae and relationships" (12). Individuals can create online personas that differ greatly from their real self-presentation. For example, those that want to experience what it is like to be the opposite sex may engage in a practice described as online **gender-bending** (Slagle 2006).

This deceptive practice often involves presenting oneself as the opposite sex in chat rooms or online video games to experience what it is like to be a man or woman. One man interviewed about his gender-bending practices admitted to adopting a female superhero persona named Robotrixie when participating in online games. A female that participates in similar online games stated that she has figured out how to identify males that are engaging in online gender-bending: "The fact that they are scantily clad is a huge clue" and "often the bigger the breasts, the more likely it's a guy" (Slagle 2006).

Internet Addiction. Although some psychologists believe that excessive reliance on the Internet should not be defined as an addiction because substance abuse is not involved, research has categorized what is considered an excessive amount of Internet use as Internet addiction. According to one study (Young 1998), Internet addiction is characterized by spending six hours or more online at a time, craving online interaction, and feelings of anxiousness and irritation when offline. Furthermore, Young (1998) has contended that Internet addiction can affect an individual's life in many areas, including family and relationships, as it often leads to individuals becoming more involved with their virtual life and less involved with reality.

Accelerated Intimacy. If used effectively, CMC can allow a relationship to form gradually. However, Trafford (1982) and Greenfield (1999) have both called attention to a phenomenon they often observe in online relationships known as **coup de foudre** (bolt of lightning), or accelerated intimacy. When comparing individuals that establish relationships online to those that establish their relationships via FTF communication, those establishing relationships online often experience significant increases in the amount of intimate information exchanged. Trafford (1982) and Greenfield (1999) agree that the accelerated amount of intimacy experienced in online relationships may not always benefit individuals or relationships. Most interpersonal researchers agree that it takes a great deal of time and effort to establish trust and intimacy in relationships. Individuals may need time to process information about the relationship partner, observe the relationship partner for consistency in their behaviors, and then determine whether there is the potential for the relationship to move forward.

FORMING SAFE AND MEANINGFUL ONLINE RELATIONSHIPS

Books such as *Putting Your Heart Online* (Capulet 1998), which details the process involved in forming an online relationship, devote pages to developing effective interpersonal relationships online and emphasize that the Internet offers a new framework in which to create meaningful interpersonal relationships. With the emergence of the Internet as a popular social network, there is a need for students of interpersonal communication to examine this form of communication. Thus, we believe that it is important to offer suggestions for forming safe and meaningful relationships online. Two important areas to consider when developing online relationships are time factors and behavioral cues.

Time Factors

Researchers emphasize the importance of taking the necessary time to develop meaningful online relationships (Walther 1992; Rintel and Pittam 1997). Given that many individuals post in-depth personal information on social networking and dating sites, we may think we have achieved intimacy in an online relationship when in fact, it may not be as intimate as we imagine. The information is available—personal likes, dislikes, hopes, and aspirations are posted for all to see. Similar information would typically be revealed only after multiple face-to-face conversations. Ample time for forming CMC relationships and allowing for adequate impression formation is critical.

Walther, Anderson, and Park (1994) applied Walther's (1992) social information processing perspective to analyze the impact of time factors in CMC relationships. This perspective acknowledges that, due to cue limitations of CMC, the medium cannot possibly convey all the task-related information (or the social information) in as little time as multi-channel FTF communication. While the personal information posted in an online profile may cause us to feel like we know a person, it is important to take into consideration that the lack of nonverbal cues may inhibit accurate impression formation. Consider the following example:

> Angela was eagerly anticipating her first face-to-face meeting with Marin. The two had met on Facebook and exchanged emails for the past three weeks. Angela's friends laughed when she said she was "in love," and they pointed out that it wasn't possible to fall in love so quickly. But they just didn't understand. Through their countless emails, they had shared so much information—much more than Angela had ever shared in any of her previous relationships that she developed via FTF interactions. They finally decided to meet in person. From the first awkward hug at the entrance to the coffee shop, Angela began to second-guess things. While they talked, she became annoyed when Marin kept glancing around the room while she was talking, causing Angela to feel as though she really wasn't listening to what she was saying. As the conversation continued, Angela found that she was bothered by the critical tone and negative facial expressions that Marin made when talking about things around campus. At the end of the evening, Angela was crushed—what had happened to the relationship? Things had gone so well when they communicated online, so why did everything fall apart when they finally had the chance to meet?

At the beginning of the example we learn that Angela has been exchanging emails with Marin for three weeks and feels that she may be "in love" with Marin. When Angela says that she has shared more information with Marin online than she has ever shared in her previous FTF relationships, she illustrates the hyperpersonal nature of CMC described earlier in the chapter. This example illustrates the tendency for some individuals to self-disclose at greater depths and at a faster rate in CMC contexts than in FTF contexts. Additionally, this scenario reinforces the importance of spending time with individuals in FTF interactions in order to form more accurate perceptions of their attitudes, beliefs, values and behaviors. Walther, Anderson, and Park (1994) agree that time is an important factor when forming accurate impressions in online relationships. Specifically, they believe that the critical difference between FTF and CMC relationship formation is the rate at which perceived intimacy is achieved. While they acknowledge that we are certainly capable of achieving intimacy in CMC relationships, time is a critical factor.

Based on this research, we encourage students that want to develop relationships online to pay thoughtful attention to time factors. Take time to get to know one another, and recognize the potential value of social cues that are sometimes are only available through a face-to-face meeting. Beebe, Beebe, and Redmond (2002) have asserted, "The key to success [when developing online relationships] is to apply the same skills that you would in a face-to-face relationship" (384). Think about the additional information obtained in a FTF conversation—the tone of voice, nonverbal behaviors, and other cues that offer additional insight about the other person. Just as you would devote a significant amount of time and energy to relationships developed via FTF communication, the same would hold true for relationships developed online.

While we are unable to pinpoint exactly how much time it should take to develop a successful online relationship, we can offer another suggestion related to time. Beware the **coup de foudre**, or being "struck" by the "lightning" pace of a relationship! If you feel that a relationship is moving along too quickly, it probably is.

Behavioral Cues

In addition to considering the time factor, understanding **behavioral cues** is essential when forming online relationships. Ellison, Heino, and Gibbs (2006) conducted a study of the self-presentation strategies, or behaviors, used by online dating participants. Ellison and her colleagues interviewed thirty-four individuals that were currently active on a large online dating site to learn more about how they managed their online impressions. Participants indicated that they often paid close attention to small or minute online cues that they and others sent. For example, one participant described the significance of profiles that were well-written, stating "I just think if they can't spell or . . . formulate a sentence, I would image that they are not that educated" (Ellison et al. 2006, 10). Another participant commented that she did not want to come across as at all sexual in her profile because she "didn't want to invite someone who thought I was going to go to bed with them [as soon as] I shook their hand" (Ellison et al. 2006, 10). Individuals indicated that they also tried to be brief when responding to potential partners so as not to appear "too desperate for conversation" (Ellison et al. 2006, 10). All of these examples illustrate how individuals monitor behavioral cues to display a certain image online. Individuals must not only understand how to use effective behavioral cues, but also how to assess the behavioral cues of others. When communicating online, there are several strategies to use to maximize effective online communication.

Being honest is the first guideline to follow for effective online communication. Conley and Bierman (1999) contend that honesty is a crucial component of successful online relationships. One should not exaggerate personal attributes and must always be specific about self-attributes and the desired attributes one is looking for in others. Ellison (2006) describes the tendency for people to describe their ideal self, not their actual self, when attempting to find a relationship partner. For example, one woman using online dating services noted that the picture she posted on her profile was from five years ago and that the picture depicted her as a thinner version of her current self (Ellison et al. 2006). Because the picture was dated and depicted her ideal, not actual self, the woman expressed a desire to lose weight so that her online and FTF personas were consistent. This example illustrates the relationship between online behavior, FTF interactions and the potential for relationship development. When individuals are deceptive online about aspects of their appearance, likes, dislikes, or hobbies, they risk being "caught" in a lie once actual FTF interactions occur. Inconsistencies between the ways that individuals present themselves online and in FTF contexts could affect the potential for the relationship to develop further.

Secondly, Swartz (2000) discusses the importance of safety when forming online interpersonal relationships. Specifically, it is important to maintain a degree of anonymity by revealing personal information gradually. He observes, "many times because of loneliness, sexual desire, or desperation we might go against our better judgment" and warns not to "jump headlong into a relationship using a rationalization along the lines of 'you've got to take risks to succeed'" (24).

Moreover, Gwinnell (1998) has emphasized the importance of being very inquisitive during online interactions and has strongly suggested asking the following questions:

1. Are you seeing anyone now?
2. How many online relationships have you had?
3. Why did your last relationship end?
4. How many times have you been married?
5. What would your ex tell me about you?
6. How do you deal with everyday life issues such as cleanliness, religious preference, and use of alcohol and drugs?
7. Is there someone I can contact who can offer his or her personal opinion of you? (78–81). (See also Capulet 1998, 121–127).

While these questions may seem somewhat intrusive, it is important to learn as much as you can about this individual prior to meeting FTF.

In addition to being inquisitive, one must be alert to the possibility of deception. Beebe, Beebe, and Redmond (2002) believe "the detection of deception in face-to-face encounters is aided by the presence of nonverbal cues. However, online such deception is almost as easy as simply typing the words" (389). Thus, one must "be cautious in forming relationships with Internet strangers" (Beebe et al., 2002. 389). Detecting the warning signs of deception is paramount. Swartz (2000) provides one of the most comprehensive discussions of "red flags" for detecting deception. Specifically, he advises one to look for signs of vagueness or non-responsiveness, which may indicate the person is hiding something. Swartz also recommends that individuals pay attention to whether or not the person goes offline or disappears for days or weeks at a time. Consider when the individual seems to be the most available to communicate. If he or she seems to be getting online at odd hours or odd times of the day, this may indicate that the person is concealing something from you. Another warning sign to consider is the individual's tendency to form quick online emotional attachments. Finally, Swartz encourages online users to focus on the other person's knowledge of current or historical events, which may indicate actual age or specific gender information. In the same way that we attempt to identify red flags during initial FTF encounters, we can use these guidelines to monitor the quality of online interactions.

SUMMARY

An article in *Newsweek* (Levy 1997) describes the surge of consistent Internet use as an "indelible feature of modern life" (52). Those who support forming relationships online also believe that CMC is not necessarily a replacement for face-to-face interactions; rather, CMC can provide an option that allows people to be more selective when searching for interpersonal relationships. However, before using CMC individuals must possess the knowledge, skills, and motivation needed to communicate effectively using this medium. This chapter offered an overview of how the Internet has changed the way we establish relationships with others.

In the past, FTF communication with family and community members was the primary means of networking with others to establish platonic and romantic relationships. Today, individuals can connect with others through CMC and establish romantic or platonic relationships with individuals from all over the world! Of course, there are both benefits and drawbacks associated with CMC. We hope that individuals will adopt the suggestions offered in this chapter for communicating effectively online. By following the experts' guidelines and paying attention to any red flags that may indicate deceptive online behavior, we hope that our students will establish safe and rewarding relationships.

APPLICATIONS

Discussion Questions

1. Discuss the different communication channels used to interact with your friends and family. On any given day, which communication channel do you use the most? Explain why.
2. Discuss the pros and cons of using social networking sites such as Myspace and Facebook. Why do you think college students use these sites so often?
3. Do you feel that individuals are more willing to self-disclose private information through computer mediated communication than FTF communication? Why do you feel that this is/is not the case? Support your position with specific examples.
4. How is the *coup de foudre* phenomenon that often results from developing relationships via CMC problematic for individuals? What suggestions could you offer someone that chooses to establish an online romantic relationship?

REFERENCES

Anderson, A. T., and T. M. Emmers-Sommer. 2006. Predictors of relationship satisfaction in online romantic relationships. *Communication Studies, 57,* 153–172.

Althaus, S. L., and D. Tewksbury. 2000. Patterns of Internet and traditional news media in a networked community. *Political Communication, 17* (1), 21–45.

Adler, R. B., and N. Towne. 2003 *Looking out, looking in.* (10th ed.).Belmont, CA: Wadsworth.

Beebe, S. A., S. J. Beebe, and M. V. Redmond. 2002. *Interpersonal communication: Relating to others.* (3rd ed.). MA: Allyn & Bacon.

Boneva, B., R. Kraut, and D. Frohlich. 2001. Using e-mail for personal relationships: The difference gender makes. *American Behavioral Scientist, 45,* 530–549.

Capulet, N. 1998. *Putting you heart online.* CA: Variable Symbols, Inc.

Cohen, J., and G. Langer. Poll: Rudeness in America, 2006. Retrieved from abcnews.go.com June 6, 2006.

Conley, L., and J. Bierman. 1999. *Meet me online: The #1 practical guide to Internet dating.* NC: Old Mountain Press, Inc.

Cooper, A., and L. Sportolari. 1997. Romance in cyberspace: Understanding online attraction. *Journal of Sex Education & Therapy, 22* (1), 7–14.

Cyber Atlas. 2005. Geographics: Population explosion http://cyberatlas.internet.com/big_picture/geographics/article.

Daft, R. L., and R. H. Lengel. 1984. Information richness: A new approach to managerial behavior and organization design. *Research in Organizational Behavior, 6,* 191–233.

DeGol, T. (Executive Producer). (2003, February 13). *WTAJ Channel 10 News* [Television broadcast]. Altoona, PA.

Ellison, N., R. Heino, and J. Gibbs. 2006. Managing impressions online: Self-presentation processes in the online dating environment. *Journal of Computer-Mediated Communication, 11,* 1–28. Retrieved online June 19, 2007 from *www.blackwell-synergy.com.*

Emmers-Sommer, T. M. 2005. Non-normative relationships: Is there a norm of (non) normativity? *Western Journal of Communication, 69,* 1–4.

Greenfield, D. N. 1999. *Virtual addiction: Help for netheads, cyberfreaks, and those who love them.* CA: New Harbinger Publications.

Gwinnell, E. 1998. *Online seductions: Falling in love with strangers on the internet.* NY: Kodansha America, Inc.

Hian, L. B., S. L. Chuan, T. M. K. Trevor, and B. H. Detenber. 2004. Getting to know you: Exploring the development of relationship intimacy in computer-mediated communication. *Journal of Computer-Mediated Communication, 9,* Retrieved June 24, 2007 from http://www.ascusc.org/jcm/vol9/issue3/detenber.html.

Hendrick, C., and S. Hendrick. 1983. *Liking, loving and relating.* CA: Brooks/Cole.

Jedlicka, D. 1981. Automated go-betweens: Mate selection of tomorrow? *Family Relations, 30,* 373–376.

Johnson, T. L., and B. K. Kaye. 1999. Cruising is believing? Comparing Internet and traditional sources on media credibility measures. *Journalism and Mass Media Quarterly, 75* (12), 325–340.

Kiesler, S., J. Seigel, and T. W. McGuire. 1984. Social and psychological aspects of computer mediated communication. *American Psychologist, 39,* 1123–1134.

Kirn, W. 2000. The love machines. *Time, 155,* 73.

Knapp, M. L., and J. A. Daly (Eds.). 2002. *Handbook of interpersonal communication.* (3rd ed.). CA: Sage.

La Ferle, C., S. M. Edwards, and W. N. Lee. 2000. Teens' use of traditional media and the Internet. *Journal of Advertising Research, 40* (3), 55–66.

Lee, J. 2002. I Think, Therefore IM. *New York Times,* September 19, p. G.1.

Lenhart, A., and M. Madden. 2006a. Teens, Privacy, and Online Social Networks, PEW Internet and American Life Project. http://www.pewinternet.org/report_display.asp?r=211. Accessed May 26, 2007.

———. 2006b. "Online activities and pursuits," PEW Internet and American Life Project. http://www.pewinternet.org/PPF/r/177/report_display.asp. Accessed May 28, 2007.

Lerner Productions. 2003. *Master the basics: Birth of the net.* http:// www.learnthenet.com.

Levy, S. 1996/1997. Breathing is also addictive. *Newsweek,* December/January, 52–53.

Marriott, M. 2006. Digital Divide Closing as Blacks Turn to Internet. *New York Times,* March 31.

Miller, T. E., and P. C. Clemente. The 1997 American internet user survey: Realities beyond the hype. NY: Find/Svp, Inc. [On-line]. Available: http://www.findsvp.com/.

Nie, N. H. 2001. Sociability, interpersonal relations, and the internet: Reconciling conflicting findings. *The American Behavioral Scientist, 45,* 420–435.

Parks, M. R., and K. Floyd. 1996. Making friends in cyberspace. *Journal of Computer Mediated Communication, 46* (1), 80–97.

Parks, M. R., and L. D. Roberts. 1998. 'Making MOOsic' The development of personal relationships on line and a comparison to their off-line counterparts. *Journal of Social and Personal Relationships, 15* (4), 517–537.

Pew Research Center. 2006. Pew Internet and American Life Project. http://www.pewinternet.org

Pratt, L., R. L. Wiseman, M. J. Cody, and P. F. Wendt. 1999. Interrogative strategies and information exchange in computer-mediated communication. *Communication Quarterly, 47* (1), 46–66.

Rabin, S. 1999. *Cyberflirt: How to attract anyone, anywhere on the world wide web.* NY: Penguin Putnam, Inc.

Rintel, S. E., and J. Pittam. 1997. Strangers in a strange land: Interaction management on internet relay chat. *Human Communication Research, 23* (4), 507–534.

Rogers, R. M. 1997. *Looking for love online: How to meet a woman using an online service.* NY: Simon & Schuster Macmillan Co.

Rumbough, T. 2001. The development and maintenance of interpersonal relationships through computer-mediated communication. *Communication Research Reports, 18,* (3), 223–229.

Scharlott, B. W., and W. G. Christ. 1995. Overcoming relationship-initiation barriers: The impact of a computer-dating system on sex role, shyness, and appearance inhibitions. *Computers in Human Behavior, 11* (2), 191–204.

Short, J. A., E. Wiliams, and B. Christie. 1976. *The social psychology of telecommunications.* New York, NY: John Wiley & Sons.

Slagle, M. August 2006. Gender-bending proves popular in online games. Retrieved July 16, 2007 from Hamptonroads.com http://content.hamptonroads.com/story.cfm?story=109533&ran121532

Sproull, L., and S. Kiesler. 1986. Reducing social context cues: Electronic mail in organizational communication. *Management Science, 32,* 1492–1512.

Swartz, J. 2000. *The complete idiot's guide to online dating and relating.* IN: Que Corporation.

Suler, J. 2002. Internet demographics. In *The Psychology of cyberspace,* www.rider.edu/suler/psycyber/basicfeat.html (article orig. pub.1999).

Trafford, A. 1982. *Crazy time: Surviving divorce.* NY: Bantom Books, Inc.

Tanner, W. 1994. Gender gap in cyberspace. *Newsweek,* May, 52–53.

Walther, J. B. 1992. Interpersonal effects in computer-mediated interaction: A relational perspective. *Communication Reports, 19,* 52–90.

———. 1993. Impression development in computer-mediated interaction. *Western Journal of Communication, 57,* 381–389.

———. 1995. Relational aspects of computer-mediated communication: Experimental observations over time. *Organization Science, 6,* 186–203.

———. 1996. Computer-mediated communication: Interpersonal, intrapersonal, and hyperpersonal interaction. *Communication Research, 19,* 52–90.

Walther, J. B., J. F. Anderson, and D. W. Park. 1994. Interpersonal effects in computer-mediated interaction: A meta-analysis of social and antisocial communication. *Communication Research, 21* (4), 460–487.

Walther, J. B., and J. K. Burgoon. 1992. Relational communication in computer-mediated communication. *Human Communication Research, 19,* 50–88.

Wildermuth, S. M. 2001. Love on the line: Participants' descriptions of computer-mediated close relationships. *Communication Quarterly, 49* (2), 89–96. Belmont, CA: Wadsworth.

Woll, S. B., and Cosby, P. C. (1987). Videodating and other alternatives to traditional methods of relationship initiation. In W.H. Jones and D. Perlman (Eds.), *Advances in Personal Relationships* (Vol. 1, pp. 69–108). Greenwich, CT: JAI Press.

Woll, S. B., and Young, P. (1989). Looking for Mr. or Ms. Right: Self-presentation in videodating. *Journal of Marriage and the Family, 51*(2), 483–488.

Young, K. S. 1998. *Caught in the net.* NY: John Wiley & Sons, Inc.

COMPUTER-MEDIATED COMMUNICATION

Most of the people in this classroom were born in the Internet Era. You have grown up in the shadow of Facebook, Google, and Twitter. No technology has impacted social relationships as much as the computer and social media.

Your parents and grandparents witnessed the advances of television and the telephone. I am almost embarrassed to admit that the first computer I saw was in 1974, and it occupied an entire room. Mobile phones were as big as a walkie-talkie, and we carried our music around with boom boxes the size of a small suitcase. (They invented dirt just a few years before I was born.)

Now we are all wired. On Facebook, 900 million "friends" coexist, the third largest "nation" on the planet. Students sleep with their phones for fear of missing a message. The pace of change occurs faster than ever, and consumers are forced to upgrade technologies more often just to keep up with the pace of change. The ultimate question is: **How will all this technology impact our human communication?**

College is an incredibly social time. We are surrounded with people our own age and invited to participate in numerous classes, clubs, and activities. Have you seen the movie *The Social Network*? It suggests that Mark Zuckerberg's failure to stay in a relationship or join the right social clubs was his impetus to create Facebook. The social media is a cyberversion of a college campus. Who is in a relationship? What are you doing right now? Are there any pictures? What music are you listening to? What groups have you joined? Questions you might ask when you meet someone new on campus are being answered on their Facebook page. Will social media replace social interaction? Are cyber friends different than human friends? Do we present ourselves the same way online as we do in real life? Is our self-disclosure different?

At this point in the research, there are many more questions than answers. Businesses exploit social media to determine our tastes in products and how to sell products to networks of friends. It is a brave new world with new challenges for our relationships. Now is a good time to stop for a moment and think about the consequences of technology and the future of human relationships. The possibilities sound almost like futuristic science fiction. (Maybe my avatar will meet your avatar in cyberspace some day. The question is, Will it be by our choice or theirs?)

From the outer reaches of cyberspace to the realm of the small group, life's complexities are forcing us into small decision-making collectives. In business or in life, it is rare that anyone has all the answers. To promote a product today, you need a research and development team, a sales staff, a marketing team, lawyers, and a public relations staff. Gone are the days of a solitary inventor introducing her product to the world. Fears of copyright litigation, product safety, and start-up financing costs require a number of specific people with specific talents. Most of us have done group projects in other classes. Did you enjoy them? Traditionally, the answer is 50 percent Yes and 50 percent No. Some enjoy the social nature of the project, the shared labor, the creativity of teamwork; while a few enjoy watching others do all the work. Conversely, others hate the loss of control, the difficulty in scheduling meetings, having to compromise with others, and knowing that some are watching them do all the work while earning the same grade.

Regardless of which camp you fall into, groups are a part of our modern world. We need others to complete complex tasks. Love them or hate them, groups are more popular (and necessary) than ever before. Where there are groups, there must be leaders. The following two chapters explore the function of groups and group leadership. The hope is that a little understanding of how effective groups operate will motivate the "observers" to get more involved and teach the "dominators" a little tolerance.

It is like our earliest lessons in grade school: We need to learn how to work and play well with others. Of course, the consequences of these lessons are job performance and maintenance of social relationships in voluntary organizations. The dollars and common sense of group performance and leadership will impact us all of our public and professional lives.

SMALL GROUP COMMUNICATION

LEARNING OBJECTIVES

After reading this chapter, you should understand the following concepts:

- Identify the unique characteristics of groups and how they affect what any group can accomplish.
- Distinguish the main formats of group presentations.
- Evaluate the benefits and risks of enlisting a group for task or social purposes.
- Devise ways to maximize group cohesiveness while avoiding groupthink.
- Use the deliberative problem-solving method for groups to accomplish task-oriented goals.

This chapter and the next focus on group communication processes. Think of these two chapters as a treatment of groups on the macro and the micro level. This chapter operates on the macro level, orienting you to the nature and functions of groups as a whole, concentrating on the process of group decision making. The next chapter examines groups on the micro level, unpacking the ways that various group members perform their roles during the group process.

You know other people by the company they keep. That statement points to the centrality of groups—not just as a classroom exercise but as a basic constituent in who we are and how we appear to others. Since we participate in a mosaic of groups, we need to understand how they work. Employers expect this ability to work collaboratively. Almost every job description includes in the list of desired qualifications phrases such as "works well with others," "contributes positively to a team," "feels comfortable in a collaborative environment." Even our kindergarten report cards included a category labeled "plays well with others" or the equivalent.

Many students groan or grumble at the mention of "group work" or a "group project," usually because of some experience with malfunctioning groups. Equipped with a clearer idea of how to operate within a group, we can approach group collaboration as an opportunity to make headway rather than headaches.

This chapter begins by recognizing the scope and variety of groups that play a part in various aspects of our lives. Then we turn to the pros and cons of groups so we can prepare for the ups and downs of collaborative efforts.

Next, we explore how groups operate, focusing on how to maximize perform-ance and personal satisfaction. Finally, we travel through a systematic process of group decision making.

NATURE AND FUNCTIONS OF GROUPS

Groups, like relationships, don't simply happen. Just any random assembly of strangers does not constitute a group. For a collection of people to qualify as a group, they must develop certain characteristics. These characteristics transform a bunch of individuals into a group that can plan and act coopera-tively. Since groups are made and don't blossom spontaneously, we should determine what factors go into creating them. Aside from providing a defini-tion of groups, these features also identify some of the standards for measur-ing whether a particular group is coalescing or disintegrating.

What Makes a Group?

The classic definition of a group is a collection of people possessing the fol-lowing qualities (Cartwright & Zander, 1968):

- *Definable membership* (Examples: Eenie, Meanie, Mai Ni, and Moe who sit together at lunch daily; supporters of Scooter Smartiepants for student body president; students assigned to collaborate on a group project)
- *Group consensus or collective perception of unity and identity* (Examples: our lunch crowd; the folks who want to elect Scooter and are willing to actively seek that goal; he's on our project team)
- *Sense of shared purpose; shared goals or ideals* (Examples: avoid having to sit alone and be vulnerable to bullies; get Scooter elected as student body president; complete a project and get an "A" doing so)
- *Interdependence in satisfaction of needs*; to get what the members of the group want, the members have to cooperate with one another (Examples: be on time for lunch; get the flyers printed; put time and energy into the group project)
- *Interaction* that includes communicating, exerting influence, being sup-portive and sensitive to the individuals who make up the group (Exam-ples: not texting other friends when meeting with the lunch group; letting other members of the committee know your preferences; carefully listen-ing to the ideas of others in regard to the project)
- *Can behave as a single organism*—for better or worse (Examples: "Sorry, there's no room at this table"; "We will all stand in the front row at the rally"; "We accept no other conclusion than the ones we've come to while doing our project—we are right and all others are wrong")

Given this definition, you probably can list at least ten groups to which you belong. Groups include families, play groups, athletic teams, committees, work teams, clubs, gangs, religious organizations, social organizations, volun-teer organizations, etc., and all of these can possible have subgroups—starters separating themselves from benchwarmers, minority factions on committees, cliques within social groups. Whether we like it or not, others will place us in groups as well: demographic groups, groups based on our performance, phys-ical location, heritage, or other factors.

Groups also serve many purposes in the counseling/therapy arena. Guidance groups led by counselors bring people together to work on career decisions or work together to learn new personal or interpersonal skills. Therapy groups led by psychotherapists aim at helping people move through complex emotional issues. Peer support groups help people going through shared experiences: grief, chronic illnesses, divorce, crises, and trauma.

Take a minute right now and actually list ten groups you belong to. Your list should look something like the sample in Table 7.1. Try to list groups that fulfill several functions so you get an idea of the range of groups that can count you as a member.

Now review your list. First, examine the list of groups. You will find that some of these groups are quite formalized, with membership dues, inductions, and formal business meetings. The level of formality among groups varies widely. Some groups are very well-entrenched, yet they have few identifiable procedures and their membership may vary. Still, you probably count them as groups that include you.

Now move to the second column. You should notice that the declared purpose of a group may not match your reasons for becoming and remaining a member. For example, membership in Lambda Pi Eta, the national undergraduate honor society in Communication Studies, represents an academic honor. All members share two characteristics: their major and their excellent academic record. Many students, however, participate in the organization for other reasons as well: the opportunity to perform public service projects, the

TABLE 7.1 Sample List of Groups I Belong To

Nature or Name of Group	Purpose of Group
Ridgemont High School Alumni Association	Stay in touch with classmates (social) Maintain networks (professional)
Delta Tau Chi fraternity	Honor society to recognize dental excellence (personal fulfillment)
Bodybuilding.com	Shared interest in fitness (hobby)
Sunday dinner gang	Have fun by sampling various cuisines (social)
AmeriCorps	Public service (civic responsibility)
Lambda Pi Eta	Undergraduate honor society for Communication majors (academic)
Weekend bicycle buddies	Physical fitness (personal well-being)
Interfaith religious study group	Discuss holy books of various faiths (spiritual)
Neighborhood Watch	Maintain neighborhood security (safety)
Group project in Speech Communication class	Complete task (such as solving a problem) assigned by instructor (academic)

ability to form professional connections, or the support and friendship of people with similar academic interests. Any group can serve many functions, and the same group may fulfill different desires for different members. For instance, almost every group generates some level of social benefits for members, since the group provides an opportunity to make and maintain friendships. At the same time, almost all social groups confront tasks they need to accomplish. Usually we will find a large portion of our enrichment in the many sectors of our lives—professional, social, civic, academic, physical, spiritual, etc.—relies on participating in groups.

Finally, consider the list of groups as a whole. Looking at the entire list, you will realize that group membership can be voluntary or involuntary. Some groups, such as academic honor societies, select their members on the basis of eligibility criteria. In other cases, the members actively seek the group rather than the group soliciting the members. Generally, voluntary groups gain new members by some mutual attraction between the existing group and the prospective members.

Sometimes we find ourselves placed in groups by others or by default. Your instructors regularly include group projects, sometimes determining membership and at other times letting students select the groups for themselves. Don't mope and complain if you find yourself placed in a group you didn't choose. One reason so many instructors (and higher education accreditation agencies, for that matter) mandate groups is to encourage development of cooperative skills with a variety of people. Of course, all of us would prefer to work and socialize only with our closest friends. Involuntary groups, however, nudge us toward expanding our collaborative skills. The most effective communicators can function smoothly in groups because they form positive relationships based on the group's shared goals and functions.

Group Size

The title of this chapter specifies *small* group communication. What is the difference between a group and a small group? Groups are considered "small" in the sense that everyone should be able to communicate directly and collaborate with all other group members. The typical size for a small group is no fewer than three members up to approximately a dozen. A collection of only two people qualifies as a **dyad**, and communication is dyadic in one-on-one pairs such as a personal interview or a conversation with a friend. There is no magical number of members perfect for every group. The upper size limit remains a bit flexible, but group interaction starts to suffer when membership of a "small" group grows too large.

Think about the optimum number of players in a video gaming situation. Although thousands of people may be logged in to an online game, your immediate group of team players (known in many role-playing games as a "party") rarely exceeds about seven to 10 members. Small group researchers usually place optimal membership between seven and 12, with some theorists classifying a group as small with up to 15 members (Weinberg & Schneider, 2003). On the low end, small groups require more than two people because the social relationships change when communication extends beyond a pair (Forsyth, 2006). With many more than 10 to12 people, groups often have trouble gaining full participation and maintaining communication among all members. As a group's membership expands, it may need to divide into smaller groups to maintain member satisfaction and prevent splintering into factions.

Some research has recommended the optimal size for student learning groups as only four or five members (Davis, 1993). I have served on university faculty committees that are so large they cannot even schedule a time for all the members to meet simultaneously. If a group finds its members cannot consistently meet together or communicate effectively with each other, then it may be time to consider reducing its size to improve interaction.

Virtual Groups

Once upon a time, every definition of a small group presumed that the group members could or would interact face to face. Not today. Increasingly, businesses, academic institutions, governments, and other organizations are using **virtual groups**, which perform the functions of groups without all the members being present at the same time or place (Hodgetts & Hegar, 2008). Technology forms an essential part of virtual groups, as the members interact through communication tools such as teleconferencing, online chats, online discussion boards, or interactive video. Some virtual groups may exist entirely through technological connections. For example, an online Alzheimer's support group may enable correspondence among members who never meet personally, but they regularly gather for online chats. Virtual group interactions often supplement personal group meetings, enabling members to collaborate despite different schedules or locations. Many co-authorships among scholars may have begun with some personal meetings at conferences, but their primary interaction may occur through collaborative Web authorship tools and e-mails.

Because they save time and reduce the need for travel, virtual groups can save money and conserve the group's energy. Many virtual group meeting tools allow members to focus more on their tasks instead of constantly worrying about the logistics of physical meetings (travel time and expense, location, refreshments, room conditions, juggling schedules).

Virtual groups can pose special challenges. With face-to-face groups, any members who attend can be included in the group's discussions. With virtual groups, everyone must constantly reassert their membership by making the effort to log on and offer some sort of tangible contribution to receive notice (White, 2002). It becomes very easy for virtual group members to fade into the background by not participating. The saying "Out of sight, out of mind" has particular relevance to virtual groups whose members may vanish into cyberspace. In a geographically unified group, absent members create a tangible void. I recall several group meetings where members temporarily departed to retrieve their absent colleagues and restore them to the group.

Ethical and security issues with virtual groups also cause concern. Many virtual group technologies, especially text-only tools such as chats and discussion boards, provide few ways to confirm the communicator's identity. How do you know the group's participants actually are the group's legitimate members? Concern about sexual predators and stalkers impersonating young children has directed greater attention to the ways information can be gathered and verified online. The Internet's relative lack of content restriction allows enormous freedom of expression. This same freedom, however, also makes virtual groups an attractive means of communication for hate groups, terrorists, or other fanatics (Bowers, 2004).

Tech Talk: Effectively Managing Online Chats or Teleconferences

Online group chats (such as the chat features embedded in courseware) or teleconferences (via platforms such as Elluminate, Skype, or Wimba) can be helpful to groups, since they allow members to participate even when they are physically far away from one another. But these virtual interactions quickly can degenerate into chaos unless they are managed properly. If you participate in or moderate an online group interaction, the following guidelines should help everyone get the most out of the experience.

1. Specify who you are addressing.
   Chats and conferences often contain several simultaneous lines of conversation. Begin each comment by naming the person(s) you are addressing. Example: "Elvis, the answer to your question is..."
2. Invite participation.
   Chats and teleconferences easily allow people to become **lurkers**—passive observers who do not participate in discussion. The group needs every member's contribution. If you notice someone has not participated, invite that person by name. Example: "Gaga, what's your opinion on the proposal?"
3. Keep up with discussion.
   The more participants, the quicker the comments pile up. Stay focused so you don't miss the input of group members or ask questions that have been answered already. Getting distracted might mean you overlook important contributions to the conversation. Online group conferences are not good times to have five different programs and a television show running simultaneously.

Members of virtual groups—or anyone who communicates online—should recognize that disclosure in cyberspace carries risks. Assume that electronic communication, such as discussion board posts to other group members, can become public. Avoid disclosing personal information that might be misused beyond the group.

Group Formats

Different formats of groups generate different communication patterns. A **panel** showcases a small number of featured speakers that appear in front of an audience. The panelists may make individual presentations, and the audience offers comments or questions. A panel format allows the panelists to set the theme for the discussion, since the range of panelists determines the focus of the topic. Panels are the standard format for many television and radio talk shows. *The Diane Rehm Show*, aired on National Public Radio for more than 25 years, uses panels. One day, for example, two diplomatic reporters and one researcher discussed the legacy of United Nations Secretary General Kofi Annan. After their comments, listeners called in to ask questions to the panelists. A reverse example of a panel is the television program *Meet the Press*, where individual guests face a group of reporters, each of whom asks a series of questions (as in the panel interviews discussed in Chapter 14). Panel formats are good choices when a specific theme needs to be presented in a way that allows for audience interaction. Most academic conventions use panels extensively, clustering several presentations on a theme and then opening the panel for questions from the audience. Panelists generally are experts on the topic.

In a **roundtable**, often called a roundtable discussion, participants are arranged so that they can address each other directly. The interaction has minimal formal structure, with each participant able to speak to any other member. A facilitator might be present to keep the discussion orderly and focused. Roundtables are very useful for encouraging input from as many participants as possible. Their main limitation is that the number of participants has to remain fairly small to enable orderly interactions where everyone can be heard. Many committee meetings are roundtables, with all group members exchanging ideas.

More formal, prepared communication may appear as a **symposium**. This format dates back to the time of Socrates (c. 470–399 BCE) and originally was a display of oratory by several speakers on a single theme—at a drinking party. Today the wine has evaporated, but the basic format remains: a series of speakers making formal speeches on one topic. Modern symposia are very common on political and scientific topics. A host usually introduces the speakers and fills the gaps between presentations. Symposia provide depth of coverage because one theme is approached from several angles.

With a **forum**, the audience controls the flow of communication. A panel is assembled, but instead of the panel directing messages to the spectators, the audience takes the initiative with comments and questions. Forums commonly occur when a community wants to obtain more information about an event. For example, on October 6, 2006, a hazardous waste disposal facility exploded in Apex, North Carolina. More than 17,000 people had to be evacuated (Associated Press, 2006). Later the town held a forum to answer residents' questions about compensation and cleanup. Many online news sites include forums where visitors post comments that develop into ongoing discussions.

Figure 7.1 diagrams the basic group formats and their communication patterns. These formats are not absolutely distinct, although they stress different patterns of interaction. They may combine to form other formats, such as a symposium followed by a forum or a panel that becomes a roundtable after the audience departs. Student groups in this course have developed all sorts of original formats whenever they make group presentations. Some examples include skits, game shows, videos, and combinations of the four formats discussed in this section.

WHY GROUPS?

The previous sections of this chapter show how we are intertwined in networks of groups. These groups sometimes conflict, complement, or overlap with each other. Collectively, much of our identity consists of our group membership. How often have you defined people based on their group affiliations? We often hear about "guilt by association" or we gauge social status by the groups someone belongs to. The entire field of sociology is dedicated to the study of groups. So, it is not a matter of "Do I want to belong to a group or not?" Rather, it is a matter of "How much do I want to get out of the groups I belong to?" The answer depends on how much you are willing to

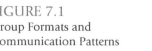

FIGURE 7.1

Group Formats and
Communication Patterns

Panel
A panel includes audience input to the panelists
after their presentation.

Roundtable
A roundtable enables interaction among all
participants.

Symposium
In a symposium, each group member makes a
formal presentation.

Forum
In a forum, the audience initiates communication
between the group and themselves.

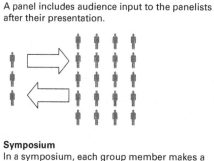

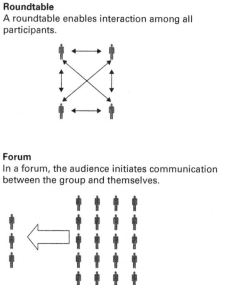

put into those groups in terms of presence (physical or in cyberspace), energy—whether it be intellectual, physical, and/or emotional—and some level of commitment at least for a given time.

Potential Advantages of Groups

We often seek or find ourselves in groups because collectively we can achieve more than we can accomplish individually. A supportive group enables individual members to excel beyond their own capacity and to extend the scope of their accomplishments (Turner & Pratkanis, 1998). By pooling the talents of several people, groups can perform tasks more creatively than individuals working alone. Typically, in a group setting, people expand on and modify each other's ideas. If you had to solve a problem working alone, you might run out of ideas and get frustrated after a few minutes. But if you had other people offering productive suggestions, you could spin ideas off of other ideas, stimulating your own creativity. This pooling of talent explains why writers improve their craft by attending workshops. A central activity of such workshops is the perspective each writer can bring when discussing another writer's work. You may have found that a productive class discussion leaves you with an enriched understanding of an assignment that you found incomprehensible before the conversation. That's a benefit of getting the perspectives of others.

Groups also can take on more complex projects than individuals can address alone. Any complex task may call for a range of skills that extend beyond those of any one person. Involvement with a group offers members the opportunity to utilize the diversity of the group's members. The familiar aphorism "Two heads are better than one" definitely applies here, especially when members can contribute different viewpoints and backgrounds that broaden the group's range. For example, when the United States government was seeking ways to address the problems in Iraq following the removal of Saddam Hussein's regime, they commissioned the Iraq Study Group. The ten-member group formed in March 2006. Its final report submitted in December contained 79 recommendations, some with as many as ten sub-points (Barrett, 2006; James A. Baker III Institute, 2006). Consider how difficult it would have been for any individual to formulate that many distinct policy options.

Groups introduce checks and balances that can improve outcomes. By commenting on, evaluating, extending, supporting, or critiquing each other's contributions, a group can improve the quality of decisions and increase satisfaction with outcomes (McCauley, 1998). Reckless or poorly planned actions become less likely when members of a group can contribute diverse viewpoints. Groups provide another benefit: shared responsibility and mutual support in case things go wrong (McCauley, 1998).

The energy and creativity of group members can create a multiplier effect, so the collective efforts add up to more than the sum of each member's individual capacity (Schweiger & Sandberg, 1989). In a properly functioning group, the whole is greater than the sum of the parts. This multiplier effect is known as synergy. The ripples of synergy circulating through a group can operate positively or negatively (Salazar, 1995). With **positive synergy**, each group member's enthusiasm, energy, creativity, and dedication amplify the same qualities in other members, taking the group to higher levels of performance. You might have participated in positive synergy during your own experience with groups. Sometimes you feel the energy a group generates and you recognize it by making comments such as, "The enthusiasm is contagious."

Potential Limitations of Groups

Negative synergy also can spread through a group. In these cases, groups impede individual accomplishments and underperform compared to solo efforts. Instead of enthusiasm, uncooperative behaviors or attitudes become contagious. For example, pessimistic feelings that the group cannot complete a task can demoralize members. The negativity intensifies, reducing the group's effectiveness. With negative synergy, the sum of the group's work is *less* than what each individual could accomplish.

Negative synergy brings us to some of the more specific disadvantages of groups. Because of their complexity, groups often require a substantial time commitment. Arranging meetings, sharing reports, and reviewing the activities of other members can create a heavy workload. Decisions usually take longer to render because they involve the input of several people. One way of minimizing this problem is to clarify all group member schedules and contact information immediately when the group forms. Members can quickly begin to anticipate optimal meeting times and establish lines of communication.

Groups can handle their workload by using some tactics to increase efficiency. For example, establish due dates much earlier than those the instructor sets. One excellent technique some students in this course used was to set the deadline for completing each step of the project several days before the actual due date set by the instructor. This tactic allowed group members to discuss progress with the instructor and make revisions throughout the project without falling behind schedule (Schwartzman, 2006).

Another technique to stay on schedule is to establish due dates for various portions of the group project in addition to the final due date. Having these progressive deadlines reduces procrastination and allows the group to check its progress periodically. The intermediate deadlines also prevent the group from reaching the final due date only to discover that its entire approach was misguided. Some research suggests that a group's decision making becomes poorer as its level of anxiety increases (Chapman, 2006), so don't add to the group's anxiety by procrastinating.

Since groups require balancing multiple relationships and personalities, they introduce complex interpersonal dynamics absent from individual activity. Inevitably, you will encounter situations that require you to collaborate with people you may not like. Instead of labeling some group members as problematic, uncooperative, or lazy, refocus on the larger issue: the group's overall objectives or tasks. While you do not need to become best friends with all the other members of your group, you must develop enough collegiality to put aside your differences for the sake of assisting the group as a whole.

Avoiding groups is not an option. We will participate in groups, so we need to anticipate their benefits and pitfalls. Table 7.2 assists in that process by providing a list of several pros and cons associated with groups.

HOW GROUPS WORK—AND WHY THEY SOMETIMES DON'T

All the way back in Chapter 1, we noted how meaning operates on two levels: informational and relational. Groups also operate along two corresponding dimensions: task and social. The task dimension of a group covers how

TABLE 7.2 Some Advantages and Disadvantages of Groups

Potential Advantages of Groups	Potential Disadvantages of Groups
1. Division of labor; shared work versus having to do it all alone	1. Coming to agreement regarding an approach to an issue can be time consuming
2. Possibility of more resources in terms of skills and knowledge	2. Possibility of duplicating efforts if there is not sufficient coordination and communication among members
3. Possibility of improved solutions or products due to combining all members' ideas	3. If leadership is lacking or is too lax, the group may accomplish nothing or accomplishments are poor quality
4. Possibility of providing a sense of belonging and identity	4. If task functions are ignored, little gets done or it gets done poorly
5. Possibility of providing support in difficult situations versus feeling isolated and "crazy"	5. If social (maintenance) functions are ignored, hurt feelings, disenchantment with the group and the project, or disengagement in what is needed to reach goals can occur
6. Possibility of social interaction and fun—laughter tends to occur more when there are others with whom to share humor	6. Individual uniqueness may be suppressed to achieve conformity with the group (to the point of groupthink)

effectively it meets its objectives. The **task dimension** measures a group's actual progress toward its goals. Ideally, a group should accomplish its task on time and correctly, achieving all its objectives. The result of this dimension is called **productivity:** how much the group is able to accomplish in a specified amount of time. But productivity alone does not make a group fully functional. You probably know people who work in very productive settings but detest their groups because the group members are miserably unhappy. That's where the second dimension of group functions comes into play.

When we operate in a group, we want and need to feel satisfied with the process. Aside from doing the work, any group also needs to fulfill certain social needs. The emotional aspect of groups comprises the **social dimension** (also known as the maintenance dimension). Even if we participate in the most productive group imaginable, we will feel dissatisfied if the interactions among group members are unpleasant. The most satisfying groups you experienced probably were not only productive, but resulted in the members feeling good about each other as well as themselves. Generally, people seek several social benefits from groups (Robbins & Finley, 1995, pp. 17–18),particularly:

- Affection: The sense that group members genuinely care about each other
- Affiliation: The feeling of belonging
- Appreciation: Knowing that you and the work you do are valued
- Recognition: Giving and receiving credit for accomplishments
- Open Exchange: Learning from others and willingness of others to learn from you

The early, formative stages of any group tend to gravitate toward social issues, such as understanding what the group members have in common (aside from membership in the group) and getting oriented to the personalities of members (Tuckman, 1965). Throughout any group's life, both the task and social dimensions are vital, although one may assume greater priority at a given time.

The social dimension has special importance for groups, since it promotes group **cohesion**. Group cohesiveness describes how groups begin to "gel" together as a unit. They begin to develop a collective identity, a sense of mutual trust, and gain greater ability to influence each other. As a group becomes more cohesive, it can operate more effectively, coordinating responsibilities and cooperating to achieve shared goals as long as it stays focused on its tasks (Lea, Spears, & Watt, 2007). Cohesive groups tend to feel united and stick together to pursue their goals (Cota et al., 1995). The more cohesive a group becomes, the more the members will value each other (Lea, Spears, & Watt, 2007) and establish a sense of interdependence.

Cohesion is responsible for much of the emotional reward that results from working in groups. "Several decades of group research have shown that members of cohesive groups feel a strong attachment to each other and a commitment to maintain membership with others in their group" (Holtz, 2004, p. 123). I remember an especially cohesive group from one of my classes. We enjoyed working together so much that we continued meeting to discuss our project for an entire semester after the original course. That kind of prolonged interaction signifies cohesion by preserving a group beyond what the immediate task requires.

Groupthink: Cohesion Gone Bad

Cohesion sounds wonderful, but like a lot of wonderful things (such as cheesecake or key lime pie, at least to me), it works best in moderation. Excessive cohesion can make a group so mutually supportive that its members simply accept what each other says without much discussion or question. We now encounter one of the most severe problems that plagues groups: the phenomenon known as **groupthink**. Originally popularized by social psychologist Irving Janis in the 1970s, groupthink describes a group's tendency to focus on agreement among its members more than the quality of the group's work (Janis, 1972). In other words, groupthink allows cohesion to crush creativity and critical thinking. Researchers have traced several major policy blunders to their roots in groupthink, such as failure to prepare adequately for the 1941 attack on Pearl Harbor, the failed U.S. invasion of Cuba at the Bay of Pigs in 1961, escalation of the Vietnam War in 1964 (Janis, 1972), the Watergate scandal and coverup that led to President Nixon's 1974 resignation (Janis, 1982; Raven, 1998), the 1986 *Challenger* space shuttle disaster (Feynman, 1999), and the decisions that led to the 2003 invasion of Iraq (U.S. Senate, 2004).

You probably know about groupthink already, even if you don't recognize its name. As the deadline for a group project nears, the group members begin agreeing with whatever suggestions anyone makes. Anything will do—just finish and get the job done. The result is often superficial and sloppy. Or maybe fatal. On January 28, 1986, the space shuttle *Challenger* exploded just after takeoff, killing all seven people aboard. Careful analysis of communication patterns within NASA revealed that one cause of the engineering defects was groupthink. The scientists and engineers were so eager to meet deadlines and look impressive that they ignored flaws in the shuttle design (Feynman, 1999; Whyte, 1989).

Group members don't need to be alike or always agree for the group to function well.

© 2010 Tomasz Trojanowski. Used under license of Shutterstock, Inc.

Symptoms of Groupthink

What signs indicate that positive cohesion has begun to morph into destructive groupthink? Let's breathe some life into groupthink by applying it to some concrete examples. In July 2004, a Senate Select Committee on Intelligence released a report that explicitly labeled the intelligence failures preceding the invasion of Iraq an example of groupthink (U.S. Senate, 2004). The report exactly parallels our discussion, even citing Irving Janis, the theorist who popularized the term "groupthink." The report's third conclusion blames a "'group think' dynamic [which] led Intelligence Community analysts, collectors and managers to both interpret ambiguous evidence as conclusively indicative of a WMD [weapons of mass destruction] program as well as ignore or minimize evidence that Iraq did not have active and expanding weapons of mass destruction programs" (MSNBC, 2004; U.S. Senate, 2004).

Many examples of groupthink symptoms deal with the Iraq war and subsequent insurgency. These examples were invoked by the Senate report on military intelligence dealing with Iraq (U.S. Senate, 2004) and have been examined repeatedly (Greenhalgh, 2004). The examples do not demonstrate any particular argument about the propriety of the war (a topic best left to discussions that go far beyond communication techniques). Instead, our discussion reveals how poor group deliberation and decision making can lead to poor policies regardless of how just or unjust the cause may be.

Eight classic symptoms point to the emergence of groupthink (Janis, 1972, 1982; Janis & Mann, 1977).

1. *Illusion of invulnerability:* The group may believe it cannot render bad decisions. This overestimation of the group's own ability can lead to reckless or premature behavior. Example: The military strategy initially employed in the invasion of Iraq was labeled "Shock and Awe," as if merely witnessing America's military might would intimidate enemies enough to surrender. The ongoing assumption was that U.S. and coalition forces would be welcomed as liberators, not attacked as a hostile occupying force.

2. *Collective rationalization:* Members focus on justifying their own decisions, ignoring or discounting contrary evidence. Instead of reconsidering basic assumptions or learning from past mistakes, the group continues to promote its own course of action. Example: The Senate investigation of intelligence on Iraq specifically charged the intelligence community with collective rationalization (U.S. Senate, 2004). Intelligence analysts tended to "ignore or minimize evidence" that did not conform to pre-existing beliefs about the status of Iraq's weapons programs (MSNBC, 2004; U.S. Senate, 2004). "In accusing the CIA and its top leaders of engaging in a 'group think dynamic,' the committee said analysts and senior policymakers never questioned their long-held assumption that Iraq possessed weapons of mass destruction" (Branigin & Priest, 2004).

3. *Belief in the group's inherent morality:* The group believes its cause is just, so it does not consider ethical consequences. Example: If military and government leaders believe they are defending liberty against enemies of freedom, they might use this noble cause to justify using torture to extract information from prisoners or suspected terrorists.

4. *Stereotyping outsiders:* By treating outsiders as too evil to respond to reason or too incompetent to deserve serious consideration, the group insulates itself from genuine opposition (Yetiv, 2003). Opponents are designated as "the enemy," "traitors," or other derogatory out-group terms. The group deems these outsiders biased, perverse, foolish, or otherwise unworthy; therefore the group need not take them seriously. Example: A group labels its opponents "ill-informed cowards," discrediting them and dismissing their ideas as ignorant and immoral.

5. *Pressure on dissenting members:* Members may feel compelled to go along with the group's decisions. The pressure can be direct coercion, such as threat of retribution (physical harm, losing a job, etc.) or it may be indirect, such as fearing loss of status or being ostracized by the group. Opposition equals disloyalty, so anyone who wants to remain in the group keeps their objections to themselves. Example: Members of a group must cast their votes publicly, with dissenters stigmatized as "traitors."

6. *Self-censorship of dissenting views:* Instead of responding to direct pressure, members might silence their own views to avoid the shame, ridicule, or awkwardness of opposing the group. Example: A student has important points to make in class but remains silent for fear of being labeled a "know-it-all."

7. *Illusion of unanimity:* The majority or the leader believes everyone agrees with viewpoints or decisions. Often a group will proceed by assuming unanimous agreement, never checking for opposing views. Interpreting silence as assent, the group might not even take votes but simply render decisions that supposedly reflect the collective will. Example: A university's governing board may make decisions supposedly reflecting the will of the university without soliciting input from the university community.

8. *Self-appointed "mindguards":* Members may "protect" the group from information that might challenge their views or call them into question. Typically, these mindguards selectively report information to the group, including only material that confirms the group's outlook. These omissions may be justified by lofty motives such as a desire to prevent panic or to avoid alarming the group. Example: The treasurer of a student organization reports to the officers only the profitable aspects of annual financial reports.

Behavioral Outcomes of Groupthink

Exactly what negative behaviors arise from groupthink? The results emerge most clearly in decision making, although similar problems can arise in various kinds of groups. The poor group deliberation methods include the following behaviors (Hogg & Hains, 1998; Janis & Mann, 1977).

- Discussion focuses on only a few alternatives. Example: A group assignment requires formulating at least three possible solutions, so the group develops only three possible solutions. Result: The group misses important options.

- The group does not question or challenge its original preferences. Example: The group favors the first suggestion as the best, perhaps believing "You shouldn't question your first impression." Result: The group becomes committed to an outcome too soon and too rigidly, ignoring alternatives.

- The group does not reconsider ideas rejected earlier. Example: An excellent idea is dismissed as too radical and receives no further attention. Result: The group's actions do not adapt to changing information or situations, so good ideas prematurely drop out of consideration.

- The group does not seek advice from experts. Example: A student group working to improve safety on campus relies only on members' experiences rather than inviting representatives of campus police or student affairs to discuss proposals. Result: The group may develop false confidence in its own decisions and opinions, not knowing whether they are misguided or even feasible.

- Group members selectively seek advice that confirms their pre-existing biases. Example: The group systematically researches only sources that support a given viewpoint and consults only people who support that view. Result: The information the group obtains is slanted or incomplete, rendering conclusions unreliable.

- Members neglect to prepare for possible failure or negative reaction to the group's decisions. Example: The group fails to develop a back-up plan. Result: If the group's preferred course of action does not work, they have not anticipated the setback and cannot react appropriately.

- The group limits its objectives only to those that are the most convenient and agreeable. Example: A group interprets its assignment as narrowly and literally as possible. Result: The group may not meet all its goals or duties because it avoids any that are uncomfortable or challenging.

Once groupthink sets in, the group tends to exhibit a high degree of **group solidarity,** which describes the tendency of a group to act as a single unit instead of as a collection of individuals with diverse ideas. The motto of the Three Musketeers pinpoints the concept: "All for one, and one for all." Group solidarity serves some important purposes. It reinforces loyalty to the group because everyone feels there is mutual support among group members. Solidarity also reduces the development of factions. A group is less likely to splinter into antagonistic camps if the members feel allegiance to the group as a whole.

Group solidarity becomes a problem when the group lets solidarity prevent serious examination of the group's own relationships and procedures. For example, a dysfunctional family may never try to improve its destructive internal communication patterns. If the family interprets every expression of concern as a threat, then the family insulates itself from self-examination and becomes immune to change. If family members automatically reject any questions about its procedures by responses such as, "Be quiet; we're a family and this is our way of doing things," then group solidarity fuels group dysfunction.

Several telltale signs can indicate that group solidarity has begun to slide into groupthink. Whenever you are involved in a group project, you and your fellow group members should periodically ask the following kinds of questions. The more you answer "never" or "rarely," the more your group has embraced groupthink.

- How often do members express different opinions on an issue?
- How often are there split (not unanimous) votes on decisions?
- How often do members take positions that differ from a designated group leader?
- How often does the group re-examine a decision once it has been made?
- How often does the group endorse more than one option when making a decision?
- How often does the group seriously consider what to do if its preferred course of action fails?

Remedies for Groupthink

Fortunately, the prognosis for groups turns out not to be as bleak as these lists make it seem. When Irving Janis (1972, 1982) conducted his research on groupthink, he also devoted attention to groups that successfully avoided this problem. Groups can take definite measures to prevent groupthink from spoiling their effort. Many groups routinely incorporate these measures in their procedures.

Keep leaders impartial. The pressure to conform can distort decisions. Members may disproportionately agree with the leader and avoid stating their own viewpoints or advocating a different position. When leaders express a preference, they may (intentionally or unintentionally) sway the group in a particular direction. Leaders should solicit opinions, ideas, or proposals from all group members before presenting their own (if they present their own views at all).

Designate devil's advocates. To actively discourage groupthink, a group could designate one or more people to advocate positions that differ from the rest of the group. Injecting these opposing viewpoints into the group's discussions can open everyone's eyes to a wider range of ideas and options. The U.S. Senate (2004) criticized intelligence agencies for not assigning devil's advocates to challenge long-held presumptions about Iraq having weapons of mass destruction. Left unchallenged, these unproven but deeply held assumptions turned out to be incorrect. Of course, the devil's advocate tends not to be the most popular member of a group. For this reason, the devil's advocate duties should rotate among group members so no one person constantly becomes the dissenting voice.

Bring in unbiased outside experts. Groups that insulate themselves from outside scrutiny often fall into groupthink. Sometimes a group gets so locked into its customary ways of thinking that it cannot break out of its established thought patterns—even when they no longer work. Outside experts offer a "reality check" to see whether the group actually is making progress. Consider who you might invite to attend a group meeting. Your choice should be someone familiar with the topic and who has genuine credentials for offering the group some productive suggestions. The outside expert also needs to be someone who will address the group openly and honestly converse with the group. The group members also must be willing to listen to the outside guest, maintaining enough flexibility to alter the group's plans in response to the expert's input.

Divide the group into smaller, separate groups dealing with the same issue. If excessive cohesiveness leads to groupthink, then interrupting some of that cohesiveness might prevent groupthink from arising. Just as a teacher might physically separate students who copy each other's work, a group can encourage independent thought by splitting its membership into two or more subgroups. By having different combinations of people assigned to the same task, new forms of synergy can arise. Different mixes of people can generate different group dynamics, which can spark creative new results. After the subgroups have completed their work, the entire group can reconvene and discuss the outcomes. Usually this technique yields several ideas beyond what the larger group had considered.

Actively seek and deal with rival ideas or proposals. A shrewd company always has an eye on its competition. It recognizes that it can learn from competitors. A skillful athlete will treat other athletes not just as opponents, but as potential teachers who can lend new insights about athletic techniques. A group's ideas will not have merit unless the group consistently weighs them against other ideas, such as those attempted in the past or those being discussed by other groups working on the same project.

When appropriate, encourage members to interact with trusted associates beyond the group. Members of a group need some reference points beyond the group itself. To understand why, imagine yourself without any knowledge or experience of any cultures aside from your own. You would expect everyone and everything to obey your narrow expectations. Presumably everyone talks like you, thinks like you, looks like you, and shares your values. But one day you venture beyond your cultural cocoon and find that you must re-evaluate your assumptions. Groups can behave the same way, and some cults actively sequester their members so they have no contact with anyone outside the cult (Pratkanis & Aronson, 2001). With no outside contact, members have no reference points for critically evaluating the group and possibly revealing its shortcomings.

Consulting with people beyond the group requires some discretion. If the group is dealing with confidential information, preserve confidentiality beyond the group. You don't want to sacrifice someone's privacy. You might be able to discuss the group's work in ways that preserve anonymity, such as using hypothetical situations or not mentioning names.

Require criticism, evaluation, challenges, questions, and alternatives. A group can make formal provisions for introducing different viewpoints. Regularly reserving some time for questions and different (or opposing) views can prevent the group from automatically gravitating toward one point of view. One method for introducing different ideas is to require the group to consider "what if" scenarios. What if the group cannot implement its preferred solution? What if the group's proposal fails? What if one of the group's basic assumptions turn out to be wrong? What if the presumed budget vanishes?

Allow members a chance to reconsider important decisions. Anybody can make a bad decision. But the harm of a bad decision multiplies if it goes uncorrected. The group needs to remain open to correcting past mistakes before they expand into egregious errors. Reversing previous decisions or redoing work the group thought it completed will take extra time. But this delay is time well spent if it keeps the group from taking ill-informed actions. Too often, a group member realizes a mistake occurred, but suppresses this knowledge, assuming that "it's too late." So the group proceeds on the basis of the erroneous information or bad decision, piling mistake on mistake. Allowing group members a second chance can dramatically improve the quality of the group's work, and it introduces a self-correcting mechanism into the group process.

Deadlock: Group Paralysis

We have spent a lot of time discussing groupthink because it arises so often in student groups. But the opposite challenge also can appear. The problem of **deadlock**, sometimes called **gridlock**, arises when a group does not function as a unit but instead fails to progress because its membership gets embroiled in petty disputes, splinters into antagonistic camps, or simply cannot reach a decision. Sometimes deadlock occurs because group members defend their opposing ideas so passionately that they cannot cooperate to accomplish a task. In these cases, deadlock reflects a failure to employ effective conflict management. To escape from deadlock, group members must be willing to address their differences even if they cannot reach ultimate agreement.

In deadlocked groups, members typically place their own interests above the welfare of the group. To function optimally, groups must avoid the excessive cohesion that leads to groupthink. They also must steer clear of the excessive self-absorption that generates deadlock. The path to effective group operation navigates between the extremes of groupthink and deadlock (Kowert, 2002). Table 7.3 illustrates the differences between groupthink and deadlock.

Deadlock has received the most attention in its other label as gridlock, especially as applied to political inaction. Often the opposing political parties in the U.S. Congress are accused of engaging in gridlock, failing to pass important legislation (such as the nation's budget) while preoccupied with partisan squabbles. The terminology has become so customary that a company called Political Gridlock markets t-shirts and posters that poke fun at politicians. The United States has no monopoly on deadlock. The United Nations, with its huge membership and enormous intragroup cultural differences, provides fertile ground for deadlock. The U.N. talks on global climate change, for example, have a dismal record of ending without constructive results (Dvorsky, 2010). Different nations and various competing interests within each nation (corporations, environmentalists, scientists, etc.) often pursue their own agenda, leaving larger issues unresolved.

GROUP DELIBERATION

Many kinds of groups have a specific task they must perform, and this mission may actually be the reason for the group's existence. Any group that assembles to complete a specific task and render a decision is traditionally called a **problem-solving group**. Unfortunately, the conventional terminology is somewhat narrow. Problem-solving groups may not simply convene because something is wrong. The task may involve improving or building upon something already successful, or it may seize an opportunity and make the most of a positive situation. Consider problem solving in the broad sense of a mathematical problem: solving a puzzle and justifying the solution.

TABLE 7.3 Groupthink Versus Deadlock

	Groupthink	Deadlock
Major causes	High cohesion Time pressure to complete task	Low cohesion Poor conflict management skills
Indicators	Lack of substantive disagreement Considering few options	Antagonistic factions or members Minimal constructive engagement among opposing views
Decision method	Mainly unanimous agreement (consensus)	Mainly deeply split votes or inconclusive outcomes
Outcomes	Very rapid but usually incomplete or poor quality	Very slow; indefinite or no resolution of issues

Contrast this sense of problem with a complaint, which expresses dissatisfaction with a problem but offers no productive solution.

Regardless of the specific task, all so-called problem-solving groups *render reasoned decisions* to complete their work. This feature clearly distinguishes problem-solving groups from support groups, for example, which need not take specific actions to function. Problem-solving groups plan and act systematically to recommend courses of action. By contrast, we can (and often do) get meaningful support from others without them advising us how to act. Purely social groups also lack this action orientation. If asked what they do with their groups of friends, most people would answer simply "hang out," proving that any decisions are far less important than the fact of being together.

Just as in solving mathematical problems, arriving at the answer isn't enough— you must show your work. In other words, you must show you understand the process of reaching a solution. With groups, you must understand and practice the method for reaching decisions. The rest of this chapter guides you through that process.

Group decision making is quite common, and it may or may not involve the entire group in making a formal presentation. Group members interact with each other to reach an outcome. After the decision is made, it may be presented by an individual or by a group. The actual decision-making process is separate from the presentation to an audience beyond the group. A jury renders a verdict, and then the verdict is announced. A fundraising committee discusses the alternatives, and then presents them to the entire organization for a vote. Coaches devise a game plan, then they present that plan to the players.

If a group is charged with making a decision, their decision is only as good as the method they use to reach it. If the process of deciding is disorganized, full of personal animosity, or has no clear objective, the decision itself probably will be poor. The consequences of poor decisions can be devastating. A sloppily formulated verdict of a jury could unjustly condemn someone to prison or death. A fundraising committee could lead an organization to bankruptcy. Inadequate preparation for crucial sports games could spell the end of a coach's contract or the demise of the entire team.

Despite the variety of decisions groups can make, the basic process of decision making has remained relatively constant for the past century. In 1910 the philosopher and educational theorist John Dewey (1910/1991) explained the five steps that he considered crucial in all logical thought. With minor changes, the same system Dewey elaborated is used as a basis for decision-making seminars conducted by major corporations throughout the world. Dewey outlined several steps that have become the accepted gospel for solving problems. These steps have been revised and expanded a bit to make them more applicable to situations you will encounter.

Step 1. Define the Problem or Issue

First, the group must agree that an issue or need exists. Just because a group has been assembled to find a solution does not mean that the problem is real. Sometimes a few people might mistakenly perceive a problem where none actually exists. For an issue to be genuine, there must be widespread agreement that the situation should be addressed at all.

Once a need is recognized, the group must determine its nature. The definition of the problematic issue must be specific and factual. Do not assign blame for problems. At this stage, the group's task is purely descriptive. Several questions can keep the group's attention focused on description. The group might consider the following lines of inquiry:

- When and did the issue first arise? How did it happen?
- Is it a problem, an opportunity for improvement, or some other type of challenge?
- What is its history? When does it improve or get worse?
- Who does this problem affect? How are they affected?
- Who has an interest in solving or not solving the problem?
- What is the significance of this problem? How severe is it? How widespread is it? What are its effects?
- When must the problem be solved? Is there an absolute or target deadline? (Just establish the time frame now, since the actual solutions and their implementation schedule will be handled later.)
- What other information is needed to understand the problem? What more does the group need to know before it can proceed?

Answering such questions should yield exact specifications of the problem. Notice the difference between the pairs of outcomes listed in Table.7.4

The outcomes in column A might show that a problem exists, but they fail to find the cause or symptoms of the problem. They remain vague and very subjective. Different people will define "stinks" and "awful" in different ways, so their assessments of the problem will vary. The outcomes in column B offer exact sites where the problems lie. By explaining the nature of the problem very narrowly, the group can address the roots of those difficulties.

The outcome of the first step should be a precise, factual description of the situation the group faces. Going into the second step, the entire group should agree on exactly what the problem is. Decision making should not proceed until the group reaches consensus on defining the problem. You might find the first step to be time-consuming and tedious. Typically, a group will spend most of its time on defining the problem. Effort at this stage, however, pays off. Without a clear and specific identification of the problem, no proposed solution can be entirely effective.

Troubleshooting Step 1: Too often, groups zoom through step 1 only to find much later that a poorly defined problem has led to vague or ineffective solutions. You can't solve what you don't know. *Research* the nature of the

TABLE 7.4 Outcomes of Step 1 in Problem Solving

Step 1, Outcome A	Potential Disadvantages of Groups
Employee morale stinks.	Employees don't want to work on weekends. Employees want longer lunchtimes.
Our history professor is awful.	The history professor does not keep scheduled appointments with students. No woman has passed any of this professor's courses in ten years.

issues. Who says the issue or problem is what you think it is? Are there several issues that need to be addressed instead of just one?

Step 2. Establish Criteria for Solutions

Before diving right into considering solutions, the group needs to decide the ground rules that govern acceptable solutions. The guidelines enable the group to determine the best solutions later (Step 4). Typically, several considerations might apply when setting the boundaries for acceptable solutions. Depending on the task at hand, a group might emphasize some of these factors more than others.

The list in Table 7.5 is only representative of the criteria a group may choose. In addressing its task, each group must devise its own criteria, and those criteria may look very different from the items listed here. The group should determine which criteria are required and which are desired. Required criteria are standards that any potential solution absolutely must meet. Desired criteria are those that the group prefers a solution meet, but that permit some compromise. For example, a required criterion might be that the solution must be fully implemented within three years. A desired criterion might be that a solution could be put into place within one year.

Troubleshooting Step 2: This step is often overlooked or not taken seriously because groups may not appreciate its importance. Step 2 establishes ground rules for which of the proposed solutions should be kept or discarded later in the process. This step also provides the basis for evaluating solutions. For example, you might discard a solution because it does not meet budget criteria. Be careful not to jump ahead with suggesting possible solutions yet—that will come in the next step. At this point, you should just focus on what the potential solutions should or should not do.

TABLE 7.5 Sample Decision Criteria

Stakeholders
Who should the solutions take into account? Do some people or organizations deserve more benefits than others?

Precedent
Should the solutions be things that have been tried before (so there is a track record for evaluation), or does the group want totally new ideas (to encourage originality but at the risk of untested solutions)?

Time Frame
How long should solutions take to implement? What is a reasonable time frame?

Logistics
What financial resources will be available? Will solutions have to operate within a budget?
What personnel will be available? Where and how will personnel be acquired?

Constraints
Are certain alternatives automatically ruled out? What sorts of solutions are off limits and why? Specify any relevant constraints on resources and options.

Step 3. Identify Solutions

After the group defines the problem and establishes criteria, it can consider potential solutions. This step involves generating as many ways of coping with the problem as possible. At this stage, the group should concentrate on producing ideas. Quantity should be the goal. The quality of these ideas will be discussed in the next step.

Groups often prove especially adept at generating ideas for solving problems. It is a common and serious mistake to try to identify solutions individually. Working collectively, you should be able to generate more suggestions, formulate more original ideas, uncover errors that you or others made, offer and receive encouragement if you run short of ideas, and escape from "conditioned thinking" that restricts your repertoire of solutions (Beveridge, 1957, pp. 84–85). Even if no one person generates many suggestions, group members can stimulate each other's creativity by making connections between ideas and using someone else's input as a springboard for more proposals.

Brainstorming to Find Solutions

One specific way that groups can produce innovative ideas is through **brainstorming**. The objective of brainstorming is to generate in a criticism-free environment as many ideas as possible. Many methods of brainstorming exist, but here are some suggestions to make your brainstorming sessions effective.

Solicit input from each group member. Group members should offer ideas freely, without feeling pressure to contribute. The brainstorming session should allow everyone some opportunity to contribute. Quiet members might require verbal encouragement from the rest of the group. Group members should feel they are being invited, not forced, to participate (Foss & Griffin, 1995). All ideas should be accepted without fear of judgment. Invite group members to be creative, crazy, and outlandish in their ideas—sometimes these "strange" ideas end up being the best.

A designated person records all ideas. Record every idea. Since the list of ideas will be narrowed and evaluated later, do not limit the range of contributions. Sometimes ideas that seem irrelevant or impractical can serve as springboards for other actions or concepts later. The ideas should be listed so that all group members can refer to them. A chalkboard, whiteboard, or flipchart comes in handy here. Having everyone's input ready at hand frees participants from having to remember everything that has been said. When the suggestions are available for examination and review, previously unnoticed relationships among them may arise, stimulating more input.

Accept ideas at face value. Brainstorming generates ideas, but does *not* weed out or alter ideas. That process occurs later, after brainstorming is complete.

Circulate a list of ideas generated. As quickly after the meeting as possible, all group members should receive a complete list of the ideas the group generated. Timing is important, because the list should be received while the ideas are fresh in everyone's mind. Individuals might think of new suggestions while they review the list. Make sure all proposed solutions were recorded. At this point, duplicate ideas are deleted and the group might organize the suggestions so they can be examined easily.

Tips for Identifying Solutions

Brainstorming is easily mistaken for haphazard and cursory invention of ideas. That characterization applies only to poorly conducted brainstorming sessions. For brainstorming to be effective, it should conform to the following guidelines.

- Brainstorm more than once. You can't always expect brilliant ideas to emerge from just one attempt. Several sessions might be necessary to generate enough proposals to proceed to Step 4.
- Invite diversity. Varying the mix of participants will supply fresh ideas. If a group has worked together a long time, the participants might need new input to escape from a rut of the same old suggestions.
- Keep your brainstorming sessions short. Take a break from brainstorming when no one has any more suggestions or when input gets repetitive.
- Divert your attention between brainstorming sessions. If you keep racking your brain for solutions to a problem, you tend to repeat the same patterns of thought. Diversion can give you fresh insight when you resume the decision-making process. After escaping from the issue at hand for a while, "we can then see it in a fresh light, and new ideas arise" (Beveridge, 1957, p. 88). Our friends (and my great-grandmother) may have been right when they recommended that we reconsider solving a problem "after getting a good night's sleep."

As the group assembles its list of possible solutions, remember to include an option that always remains, even if only as a default: maintaining the status quo by doing nothing. This option serves two purposes: (1) It provides a benchmark for comparison to other solutions so you can definitely decide whether other options actually improve on the current situation. (2) It reminds the group that even though the status quo might not be maintained in its entirety, some components of the present system could be incorporated into the group's preferred solution.

Troubleshooting Step 3: In step 3, discussion sometimes slips ahead into the evaluation stage (step 4). The next step (Evaluate Solutions) allows you to critique the suggested plans, so save your judgments of solutions until then. The important priority now is to generate a large number of potential solutions. One way to generate more and better solutions is to combine or divide proposals that have been suggested, creating new combinations of ideas.

Step 4. Evaluate Solutions

When the group is satisfied that it has proposed as many solutions as possible (not just "good" solutions), evaluation begins. Organization of the suggestions will allow the group to see how ideas cluster or differ. When discussing the merits and drawbacks of each idea, record the results so everyone can refer to them. The designated recorder should list the strengths and weaknesses of each suggestion so that the options can be compared easily. One method for doing this is the simple chart that Benjamin Franklin used when he had to make a difficult decision. He would list each option, and then list the advantages and disadvantages in separate columns. Table 7.6 shows an example of a balance sheet like the ones Franklin used.

The group must go beyond merely counting the advantages and disadvantages—look at the *impact* of the pros and cons. The crucial questions in the evaluation step for each proposed option are:

TABLE 7.6	Balance Sheet to Evaluate Proposed Solutions	
	Advantages	**Disadvantages**
Proposed Solution 1	1. 2. 3.	1. 2. 3. 4. 5.
Proposed Solution 2	1. 2. 3. 4.	1. 2. 3.

- Do the advantages outweigh the disadvantages?
- Which options carry the greatest benefits with the least drawbacks?

To make these determinations, the group can subject each option to the following kinds of questions. These questions are designed to reveal the pros and cons of suggested solutions.

1. What are the short-term and long-term benefits?
2. What are the short-term and long-term drawbacks?
3. What are the intangible costs (time, effort) as well as the financial costs?
4. When will the costs and benefits be realized?
5. Which parts of the problem are solved by this proposal?
6. Which parts of the problem remain after this proposal is implemented?
7. Where have similar proposals been tried? How have they worked in those situations?
8. How will others outside the group react to the proposal? How readily will they endorse the option?

The preceding list offers suggestions for stimulating group evaluations of solutions. You may find that your group devises its own set of questions as the decision-making process continues. Regardless of the questions you use, make sure that you evaluate each option fairly and carefully.

To examine proposals impartially and rigorously, all group members must concentrate on evaluating the ideas instead of whoever proposes or supports them. Discussion should remain issue-centered, not people-centered. Personalized criticisms can cause discord within the group and prevent participants from reaching decisions. The leader and other group members can prevent animosity in at least two ways. First, discussion could focus first on a proposal's advantages and *then* on its disadvantages (Osborn & Osborn, 2000). Such an organizational pattern prevents participants from too hastily criticizing an option. Second, participants should depersonalize the options by separating the person from their proposal (Schwartzman, 1994). Whenever the group discusses a suggestion, participants need not mention who thought of the idea. Comments then focus on the idea itself, not on the person who offered it.

The fourth step in decision making should end with one or more solutions that the group endorses. The endorsement need not be unqualified support, but the group as a whole should be convinced that its proposed solutions represent the best available options.

Troubleshooting Step 4: Don't settle for vaguely labeling proposed solutions as "good" or "bad." If you completed step 2 carefully, you already constructed a basis for evaluating the solutions in step 4. Refer to your criteria in step 2 for elements that might play a role in your evaluation of solutions: feasibility (including cost, personnel, and time to implement), impact on stakeholders, moral concerns, etc. The ability to see both the pros and cons of solutions allows the group to anticipate and correct any problems with implementing a solution.

Step 5. Select the Best Solution(s)

Now it's decision time. A very important aspect of choosing solutions is to set up and follow through with a specific method for making decisions. The group must—read that again: MUST—explicitly employ a method for reaching decisions. Everyone in the group should understand the group's method of decision making. Votes should be taken when needed and recorded in case questions arise later. Some of the more common methods of reaching decisions are:

Consensus: For a solution to be selected, all group members must agree. Although it sounds ideal, consensus may prove difficult or impossible to reach. Furthermore, false consensus might arise due to groupthink. Group members may simply agree because they don't want to dissent (and not because they endorse the solution).

Majority Rule: The group votes on solutions and selects the solution(s) with the most votes. Some groups establish rules for a "super majority," such as three-fourths of group members, to assure more support for final decisions. For example, the U.S. Congress can override a presidential veto only with a two-thirds or greater majority vote. Majority rule is useful when differences of opinion remain. The main problem is that the minority gets left out unless they present a **minority report,** which explains dissenting views (Robbins & Finley, 1995). Whenever the U.S. Supreme Court renders a verdict that is not unanimous, justices will issue majority and dissenting opinions to justify their decisions.

Authoritarian Rule: A person decides on behalf of the entire group. Often people assume this method means that a leader does all the work and everyone else shuts up. Definitely not. All the steps in the deliberative method remain intact. Authoritarian rule simply means that one person shoulders responsibility for rendering the decision, taking into account the ideas and opinions of other group members. The authoritarian approach sometimes works well in online groups when it becomes impractical to get everyone to participate or render a decision. This method also saves time because disagreements among group members don't delay decisions. Although efficient, authoritarianism can leave group members feeling excluded from final outcomes that don't "belong" to the entire group. For this method to work well, the person making the decision must be highly competent, allow others to participate in the deliberative process, and take responsibility for the ultimate decision. Other group members contribute to the process, but one person generates the ultimate outcome. For example, academic departments and committees recommend professors for hire, but the chief academic officer makes the actual academic appointment. Table 7.7 summarizes the features of the three major decision methods.

Troubleshooting Step 5. Too often, groupmembers simply express individual opinions about solutions and consider that a decision. There needs to be some indication of how the group arrives at its selection of solutions. If using an authoritarian system, clearly establish who is responsible. For majority votes, decide on the minimum number of members who need to participate. A "majority" vote of 3-1 with three more people not voting does not constitute a genuine majority. To avoid false consensus, each participant should justify the choice of a solution. What rationale can you offer for choosing one option as opposed to others? This justification of decisions reduces chances of passive agreement.

Step 6. Implement and Test Solution(s)

The final stage is most often overlooked or given inadequate attention by student problem-solving groups in this course. Work does not end when a solution has been selected. Your group now has reached the stage for putting proposals into practice. In deciding how to implement what the group has endorsed, consider these issues:

- Who is responsible for implementation? Must the person (or people) who supervises implementation also monitor outcomes?
- When will implementation occur? When should it begin? When should it be completed?

TABLE 7.7 Comparison of Decision Methods

	Consensus	Majority	Authoritarian
Inclusiveness of group members	Most	Somewhat	Least
Accountability for decisions	Shared by all group members	Shared by the majority	Assumed by decision maker alone
Efficiency	Least	Moderate	Most
Advantages	Builds cohesiveness, since all members rally behind decisions; Maximizes input, improving diversity of ideas	Allows input and some satisfaction when group cannot reach consensus; Closes discussion definitely	Effective for apathetic or deeply divided groups; Enables quick decisions with definite resolutions
Limitations	Difficult within short timeline; Risk of hasty agreement due to groupthink	Minority may be dissatisfied, leaving group divisions; Solution may only have partial group support	Group members can feel alienated from decisions they don't contribute to; Members may have minimal interest or dedication regarding outcomes

- How long will adoption of the plan take? Will the solution be adopted all at once or will it be phased in?
- What resources are required for the solution to take effect? What are the minimum resources needed? What resources would be most desirable?

Typically, a solution goes into effect according to a timetable that allows people who are affected to anticipate change. When Congress passes a law, the new regulation usually takes effect after a sufficient time elapses for people to be notified of the change.

Sometimes a group will find that an excellent option encounters insurmountable problems in the implementation phase. For example, a clothing company may decide to increase the price of shirts it manufactures to cover the increased cost of raw materials. If customers refuse to pay the higher cost or if retailers refuse to change the prices of the shirts, the solution cannot take effect. In cases where the desired option cannot take effect, the group must return to Step 4 and evaluate other possible solutions.

Throughout the implementation process and afterwards, the group must monitor the progress of its solution. You probably are saying: "But our solution hasn't gone into effect yet!" Exactly. Successful group deliberation includes predicting possible outcomes of solutions so you can prevent setbacks. For example, a food manufacturer doesn't simply stop as soon as a new product hits the market. The manufacturer has developed detailed plans to measure success and anticipate ways to improve. Essentially, the testing part of step 6 requires answering a simple but vital question: How would you know whether the solution worked? Phrased another way: How do you define success? You need to look at where similar solutions have succeeded or failed, using this research as a basis for predicting what your solution will accomplish. Most important, in this step you need to determine how you will know whether the group's solution(s) will work and how you will monitor progress.

To decide whether the solution actually works, the group should answer the following kinds of questions:

- What are identifiable or measurable ways to identify success? Here the group should refer back to the criteria for evaluating solutions (step 2).
- When will the effects be realized?
- How often should the solution be monitored and assessed?
- Who ultimately determines whether the solution has succeeded?
- What alternatives exist if this solution fails?

Preparing answers to the final question involves the group in **contingency planning**. Whenever solutions are implemented, some back-up solutions should be prepared just in case the preferred solution does not work. Contingency planning is common in military operations. Commanders devise a first choice for a military campaign. If that choice proves unsuccessful, they resort to their second choice, a plan that would not have the same disadvantages. Contingency plans allow groups to implement new solutions quickly in case of an emergency without having to go through the entire decision-making process from the beginning.

HIGHLIGHTS

1. Although many people are skeptical about group work, groups form an important part of our lives.
2. Groups differ from random aggregates by having several characteristics:

    a. Definable membership
    b. Collective identity
    c. Shared purpose
    d. Interdependence
    e. Direct interaction
    f. Ability to behave as a single organism

3. Small groups range in size from at least three to about 12 members.
4. Virtual groups allow support and collaboration across time and distance, but they do carry risks of invading privacy and identity manipulation.
5. Groups make public presentations in several formats.

    a. Panels include presentations by experts with opportunities for audience reactions.
    b. Roundtables are minimally structured discussions among all participants.
    c. Symposia are a series of formal speeches on one theme.
    d. In forums, the audience controls the flow of communication with comments and questions to speakers.

6. Advantages of groups include positive synergy that allows groups to accomplish more than individuals, pooling talent to maximize diverse input, and ability to deal with complex issues.
7. Disadvantages of groups include negative synergy of spiraling demoralization, substantial time expenditure, and challenges of reconciling relationships among members.
8. The task dimension of groups, measured by productivity, deals with how well the group accomplishes its duties.
9. The social (or maintenance) dimension of groups, measured by personal satisfaction, deals with the group fulfilling emotional needs of members.
10. Cohesion describes the tendency of members to bond and consider themselves a unit.
11. Excessive cohesion can lead to groupthink, with members ignoring opposing ideas and agreeing uncritically simply to reach a decision.
12. Groupthink can be avoided by taking measures that inject different opinions and perspectives.
13. Deadlock paralyzes groups when members refuse to collaborate or place the group's welfare above self-interest.
14. Problem-solving groups focus on resolving puzzles and providing options for decisions.
15. Group deliberations should follow an orderly process.

    a. Define the problem, recognizing its extent, severity, and history.
    b. Establish criteria (required and desired) for solutions.
    c. Identify as many solutions as possible. Brainstorming is a useful technique to stimulate ideas.

    d. Evaluate solutions by listing the advantages and disadvantages of each proposal.

    e. Decide on the best solution or solutions, using a definite decision method.

- Consensus requires agreement from all group members.
- Majority rule opts for the preference of most group members.
- Authoritarian rule assigns one person the task of deciding based on input from the group.

    f. Explain how the solution(s) will be put into effect and how to define success.

APPLY YOUR KNOWLEDGE

SL = Activities appropriate for service learning

▣ = Computer activities focusing on research and information management

🎬 = Activities involving film or television

♫ = Activities involving music

1. Think about one of the groups you listed at the beginning of this chapter. Respond to each of the following questions as it relates to that group.
   A. On a scale from 1 to 10, with 10 being the most cohesive, how cohesive is the group?
   B. In what ways has cohesion been built in the group?
   C. What would you suggest the group do to build better cohesion? (Remember: "Better" is not necessarily "more.")

2. ♫ Musical groups provide some fascinating examples of group dynamics in action. Identify a band that has stayed together a long time. How do you explain the group's longevity? How does a band regroup after losing one or more of its members? How has the band addressed their group identity musically?

3. A saying popular during the 1960s was: "If you aren't part of the solution, you're part of the problem." Think about a situation where you were dissatisfied but you either did nothing or did not get a satisfactory solution. Working with other students, convert this experience to a problem-solving activity by brainstorming as many different potential solutions as possible. How did this brainstorming work in generating ideas?

4. SL If you collaborate with a community service organization, you'll probably be asked to help solve a problem. Ask your community partner to identify one or more significant challenges it faces. Team with classmates and community members to discuss these issues. Meetings can be organized according to a suitable group format: roundtable, panel, symposium, or forum. What did you discover about the background of the problem that your library research and textbooks did not reveal?

5. 💻 An important function of virtual groups is their role in connecting people who may have had to face adversity alone. Surf the Internet and visit some online support sites for people with various injuries or ailments. Select one of these sites based on a condition you would like to learn about. (For instance, one of my students has diabetes, so I might select a site devoted to that illness.) Monitor the site over a period of time and discuss the following issues: How do you see visitors and the website itself building cohesiveness? Connect these methods to the chapter on interpersonal relationships. Do you see people developing intimacy online the same ways they do in person? Why or why not?

6. 🎬 Watch the film *Twelve Angry Men* (1957), *Mean Girls* (2004), or *Brazil* (1985). What signs of groupthink do you identify? How does groupthink enable bad decisions to continue? What specific measures would you suggest as ways to prevent the consequences of groupthink from becoming so severe?

REFERENCES

Associated Press. (2006). Hazardous waste plant fire in N.C. forces 17,000 to evacuate. *FoxNews.com*. Retrieved December 12, 2006, from http://www.foxnews.com/story/0,2933,218177,00.html#

Barrett, T. (2006, March 15). Congress forms panel to study Iraq war. *CNN.com*. Retrieved December 11, 2006, from http://www.cnn.com/2006/POLITICS/03/15/iraq.study/

Beveridge, W. I. B. (1957). *The art of scientific investigation*. New York: Vintage.

Bowers, F. (2004, July 28). Terrorists spread their messages online: A growing number of Al Qaeda websites offer instructions for kidnapping and killing victims. *Christian Science Monitor*, p. 3. Retrieved January 16, 2005, from Newsbank Info Web.

Branigin, W., & Priest, D. (2004, July 9). Senate report blasts intelligence agencies' flaws. *Washington Post*. Retrieved April 30, 2006, from http://www.washingtonpost.com/ac2/wp-dyn/A38459-2004Jul9?language=printer

Cartwright, D., & Zander, A. (Eds.). (1968). *Group dynamics: Research and theory* (3rd ed.). New York: Harper and Row.

Chapman, J. (2006). Anxiety and defective decision making: An elaboration of the groupthink model. *Management Decision, 44*, 1391–1404.

Cota, A. A., Evans, C. R., Dion, K. L., Kilik, L., & Longsman, R. S. (1995). The structure of group cohesion. *Personality and Social Psychology Bulletin, 21*, 572–580.

Davis, B. G. (1993). *Tools for teaching*. San Francisco: Jossey-Bass.

Dewey, J. (1991). *How we think*. Buffalo, NY: Prometheus. (Original work published 1910)

Dvorsky, G. (2010, January 8). *Five reasons the Copenhagen climate conference failed*. Institute for Ethics and Emerging Technologies. Retrieved March 28, 2010, from http://ieet.org/index.php/IEET/more/dvorsky20100110

Feynman, R. (1999). Richard P. Feynman's minority report to the space shuttle *Challenger* inquiry. In *The pleasure of finding things out* (pp. 151–169). Cambridge, MA: Perseus.

Forsyth, D. R. (2006). *Group dynamics* (4th ed.). Belmont, CA: Thomson Wadsworth.

Foss, S. K., & Griffin, C. L. (1995). Beyond persuasion: A proposal for an invitational rhetoric. *Communication Monographs, 62,* 2–18.

Greenhalgh, T. (2004, September). Grappling with groupthink. *Accountancy,* 146.

Hodgetts, R. M., & Hegar, K. W. (2008). *Modern human relations at work* (10th ed.). Belmont, CA: Thomson South-Western.

Hogg, M. A., & Hains, S. C. (1998). Friendship and group identification: A new look at the role of cohesiveness in groupthink. *European Journal of Social Psychology, 28,* 323–341.

Holtz, R. (2004). Group cohesion, attitude projection, and opinion certainty: Beyond interaction. *Group Dynamics, 8,* 112–125.

James A. Baker III Institute for Public Policy. (2006). *The Iraq Study Group report.* Retrieved December 11, 2006, from http://www.bakerinstitute.org/Pubs/ iraqstudygroup_findings.pdf

Janis, I. (1972). *Victims of groupthink.* Boston: Houghton Mifflin.

Janis, I. (1982). *Groupthink: Psychological studies of policy decisions and fiascos* (2nd ed.). Boston: Houghton Mifflin.

Janis, I. L., & Mann, L. (1977). *Decision making: A psychological analysis of conflict, choice, and commitment.* New York: Free Press.

Kowert, P. A. (2002). *Groupthink or deadlock: When do leaders learn from their advisors?* Albany: State University of New York Press.

Lea, M., Spears, R., & Watt, S. E. (2007). Visibility and anonymity effects on attraction and group cohesiveness. *European Journal of Social Psychology, 37,* 761–773.

McCauley, C. (1998). Group dynamics in Janis's theory of groupthink: Backward and forward. *Organizational Behavior and Human Decision Processes, 73,* 142–162.

MSNBC. (2004, July 9). *Full text: Conclusion of Senate's Iraq report.* Retrieved June 1, 2007, from http://www.msnbc.msn.com/id/5403731

Osborn, M., & Osborn, S. (2000). *Public speaking* (5th ed.). Boston: Houghton Mifflin.

Pratkanis, A. R., & Aronson, E. (2001). *Age of propaganda: The everyday use and abuse of persuasion* (Rev. ed.). New York: Owl.

Raven, B. H. (1998). Groupthink, Bay of Pigs, and Watergate reconsidered. *Organizational Behavior and Human Decision Processes, 73,* 352–361.

Robbins, H., & Finley, M. (1995). *Why teams don't work.* Princeton, NJ: Peterson's/Pacesetter.

Salazar, A., J. (1995). Understanding the synergistic effects of communications in small groups. *Small Group Research, 26,* 169–199.

Schwartzman, R. (1994). The winning student: Dividends from gaming. *Communication and Theater Association of Minnesota Journal, 21,* 107–112.

Schwartzman, R. (2006). Virtual group problem solving in the basic communication course: Lessons for online learning. *Journal of Instructional Psychology, 33,* 3–14.

Schweiger, D. M., & Sandberg, W. R. (1989). The utilization of individual capabilities in group approaches to strategic decision-making. *Strategic Management Journal, 10,* 31–43.

Tuckman, B. W. (1965). Developmental sequence in small groups. *Psychological Bulletin, 63,* 384–399.

Turner, M. E., & Pratkanis, A. R. (1998). Twenty-five years of groupthink theory and research: Lessons from the evaluation of a theory. *Organizational Behavior and Human Decision Processes, 73,* 105–115.

U.S. Senate Select Committee on Intelligence. (2004, July 7). *Report on the U.S. intelligence commu-nity's prewar intelligence assessments on Iraq.* Senate Report 108–301. Retrieved July 7, 2006, from http://frwebgate.access.gpo.gov/cgi-bin/getdoc.cgi?dbname=108_cong_reports&docid=f:sr301.108.pdf

Weinberg, H., & Schneider, S. (2003). Introduction: Background, structure and dynamics of the large group. In S. Schneider & H. Weinberg (Eds.), *The large group revisited: The herd, primal horde, crowds and masses* (pp. 13–28). London: Jessica Kingsley.

White, D. (2002). *Knowledge mapping and management.* Hershey, PA: Idea Group.

Whyte, G. (1989). Groupthink reconsidered. *Academy of Management Review, 14,* 40–56.

Yetiv, S. A. (2003). Groupthink and the Gulf crisis. *British Journal of Political Science, 33,* 419–432.

GROUP ROLES AND BEHAVIORS

LEARNING OBJECTIVES

After reading this chapter, you should understand the following concepts:

- Recognize the characteristics of effective leadership.

- Distinguish between the task, social, and self-serving roles group members may enact.

- Identify the five stages of group development.

- Specify ways to cope with social loafing and group polarization.

- Enact the qualities of a responsible group member.

- Develop and execute a plan for a small group meeting.

- Demonstrate how groups can interact using nontraditional formats and computer-mediated communication.

A group is the sum of the roles and behaviors its members enact. From a communication perspective, a group is not just a collection of individuals, but rather a web of relationships. Placed within a group, each of us plays various roles and fulfills functions that affect ourselves and others. This dynamic dance of roles, rules, and skills makes the study of groups endlessly interesting—and challenging. Because it is so challenging, we must continue to work for effective and efficient group communication by recognizing what is occurring and then working for continuous improvement.

In this chapter, we continue our consideration of groups, focusing on task-oriented groups that you may join in this class and others (many beyond your college education). We begin by clarifying the idea of leadership, considering two perspectives on what leadership entails. Next, we concentrate on the roles we assume within groups. Typically, we assume several roles, but if we understand them and manage them properly, we can occupy roles that fit our skills and contribute to the group's well-being. Next, we cover the process of group development and address potential threats a group must address to assure its progress. We then move to an overview of group meetings, where we examine proper conduct and some formats that can enrich the group's interactions.

GROUP LEADERSHIP

Imagine that an alien lands in your front yard and demands, "Take me to your leader!" Wanting to show nice earthly hospitality, you want to comply. But where would you take our extraterrestrial visitor? To the President or someone else with a powerful title? Let's suppose that you did identify "your leader." The more important question for us is: "What makes this person a leader and what are leadership skills?" While a leader is generally considered to be a person, the concept of leadership is much different. We can understand **leadership** as the interpersonal influence that guides a group toward accomplishing its goals and building a pleasant interpersonal climate. New fads of leadership theories come and go almost weekly. The definitions of leaders and leadership suggest several implications.

- *Leadership deals with functions,* so leaders are not identical with people. In other words, don't always equate the term "leader" with the same person all the time. "The leader" is "misleading" because it need not be just one person or the same person for every task. "Leader" describes a set of functions taken on by one or more people within a group.
- *Leadership is very issue-specific.* Even within the same group working on the same task, leadership may shift among different people during different stages of the project.
- *Leaders are made, not born.* Effective leadership depends on the dynamic among the group members. The search for a uniform set of qualities that make up "natural-born leaders" has proven frustrating (although the search continues).

Studies that claim to reveal leadership traits, or consistent personality characteristics that leaders exhibit, have generated widely different results. One review of this research concludes: "(1) on scientific ground no trait or traits are found which are universally related to leadership, (2) traits of leaders cannot explain organizational effectiveness" (Andersen, 2006, p. 1089). Beyond just a set of traits, leadership involves a more complex interplay of how people manage the situations they confront (Chemers, 1997). Very little research shows that certain traits correlate with effective leadership (Northouse, 2010), but one ability seems clear. Good leaders adapt to the needs of the group and to the requirements of the situation.

So, what impact does the study of leadership have for your group work? First, groups need to recognize that leaders can arise in two ways. **Designated leaders** are elected or appointed to fulfill leadership roles. A sports team, for example, might select a team captain. **Emergent leaders** assume leadership roles not through formal selection, but by demonstrating their efficacy or influence in the group. Emergent leaders often appear when some group members demonstrate a special skill that serves the group. For example, an effective researcher might set a high standard for information gathering although no one has designated this member "chief researcher."

Next, groups should understand that leadership does not mean simply telling other people what to do. Leaders derive their influence from power that they can accrue from several sources (Erchul & Raven, 1997; French & Raven, 1959). We discussed these powers in Chapter 13, and now we should consider how they apply to the group context.

- *Coercive power:* Others comply from fear of punishment. Example: "We'd better complete this proposal before the meeting tomorrow, or the boss may fire us." [responds to the boss's coercive power]

- *Legitimate power:* Leadership comes from a person's position of influence. Example: "I guess we'll do what you say. After all, you're the club's president." [election to the office entitles the officer to exercise power]

- *Expert power:* Knowledge or skill accounts for leadership. Example: "Since you've worked in fundraising for ten years, we'll listen to your suggestions about how to raise money." [professional experience may qualify someone as a leader]

- *Reward power:* Compliance yields benefits for those who follow. Example: "If we can accomplish our agenda today, I'll take everyone out for pizza instead of us meeting again tomorrow." [provides an incentive to accomplish the goal or fulfill the request]

- *Referent power:* Arises from trust and connection based on admiration, respect, and trust (Raven, 1992). Example: "You have given so much to our group and worked so hard that we have confidence in what you recommend." [leadership acquired through a positive track record]

In the following section, we discuss exactly what leaders do within a group and how they do it.

Now that we know a bit about how leadership works in groups, let's consider leadership communication style. You might naturally prefer to use one style over another; however, you need to consider other factors. Adaptive leadership (as illustrated in Figure 8.1) acknowledges that leaders must take into account and adapt to their own nature and preferences, the characteristics of the group members, and the context surrounding the group's operation (Tannenbaum & Schmidt, 1957).

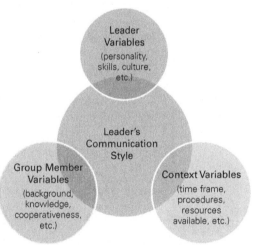

FIGURE 8.1
Factors in Adaptive Leadership

Authoritarian, Democratic, and Laissez-Faire Leadership Styles

One perspective suggests that a leader's communication ranges along a scale of types labeled as authoritarian, democratic, and laissez-faire, as shown in Figure 8.2 (Lewin, Lippitt, & White, 1939). Consider first the authoritarian style. If you find yourself creating policies on your own, controlling and dominating discussions and interactions, and believe strongly in directly supervising members of your group, you might exhibit an authoritarian leadership style. The democratic style is based on the assumption that group members can make effective decisions with guidance and facilitation. Democratic leaders commonly ask for ideas and suggestions from the group and then to put these suggestions into practice (Hackman & Johnson, 2009). Finally, the laissez-faire leadership style (named after a French term that roughly translates "let it be") is characterized by lack of leader involvement. The extremely laissez-faire leader may be completely absent from the group's

The three leadership styles are not totally distinct alternatives, but represent points on a continuum:

More Laissez-Faire   More Authoritarian

Laissez-Faire	Democratic	Authoritarian
Members control	Shared control	Leader controls
Least structure	Moderate structure	Maximum structure
High individuality	High collaboration	High conformity
"Do it yourself"	"Let's do things together"	"Do things my way"
Emphasizes freedom	Emphasizes mutual responsibility	Emphasizes efficiency
Presumes self-motivated, skillful, involved group members	Presumes partnership between leader and members of group	Presumes competent, vigilant leader
Each group member knows best	Entire group knows best	Leader knows best
Learning method: student-run seminar	Learning method: interactive discussion	Learning method: teacher lectures
Lead best by staying out of the way	Lead best by participating	Lead best by directing
Requires group to take initiative	Requires willingness by all to get involved	Requires group obedience

FIGURE 8.2

The Continuum of Authoritarian, Democratic, and Laissez-Faire Leadership Adapted from Tannenbaum & Schmidt (1957); Rees & Porter (2008)

process and will give followers total autonomy to do whatever they want. This leader is likely to avoid conflict, rarely intervene in the everyday operations of the group, and only provide input when specifically asked (Giri & Santra, 2010; Hackman & Johnson, 2009).

When might you use authoritarian, democratic, or laissez-fair leadership? First, consider cultural factors. You probably noticed that these leadership styles map nicely onto the power distance dimension of culture. Higher power distance cultures gravitate to more authoritarian leadership, while lower power distance cultures are inclined to more democratic or laissez-faire leadership. As mentioned earlier, there might be particular situations when each is appropriate; however, there are a few common pros and cons associated with each style (Hackman & Johnson, 2009).

Highly authoritarian style can cause group members to become aggressive or dissatisfied because they may feel excluded from major decisions (Lewin, 1944). If you like to work independently and express your individuality, authoritarian leadership style might feel oppressive and controlling. Typically, followers of authoritarian leaders will become more dependent on the leader and are less likely to express individual ideas (White & Lippitt, 1968). Some research on athletes shows that authoritarian coaching style, when not offset by personal regard for athletes, hastens exhaustion and burnout (Chee et al., 2007).

While authoritarian leadership might seem oppressive, some circumstances make it the most desirable choice (Bass & Bass, 2008). When a crisis arises that requires immediate action, autocratic leadership can get things done quickly. If a classmate collapses while displaying symptoms of a heart attack, you want rapid response: Call emergency services, administer CPR, notify the person's family. The decisions cannot wait for a group discussion and vote. Sometimes a situation requires unpopular decisions, so an authoritarian leader might step up and take actions that the group finds unpleasant. The best decision is not necessarily the one the group as a whole approves. If the task is simple and the leader is knowledgeable, an authoritarian style might prove to be especially efficient or productive (White & Lippitt, 1968). A well-qualified leader can dispatch tasks that might take a lot longer if done by an entire group.

Laissez-faire leadership style might not look like leadership at all. If group members are very motivated and experts in their field, they might embrace a laissez-faire leadership style. Most groups, however, operate better with more guidance than a laissez-faire approach offers. "Generally, laissez-faire leadership has been found to be negatively related to outcomes such as effectiveness and satisfaction in organizations" (Northouse, 2010, p. 198). "Laissez-faire leadership has been consistently found to be the least satisfying and least effective management style" (Bass & Bass, 2008, p. 145). The results have appeared across many types of groups, including government, education, corporate, and military.

What explains these findings? The problem seems to lie with leader non-involvement setting a tone of apathy or disregard for the group. Laissez-faire approaches apparently reduce a group's morale by demonstrating a leader's disconnection from relationships and tasks. Consider how you would feel about a course with no assignment guidelines or instructor input aside from the first class session and the final grade. If you believe you would flounder with such minimal supervision, you probably prefer more active leadership than the extreme laissez-faire approach.

Democratic leadership style can generate high productivity, commitment, and participation (Bass & Bass, 2008). Democratic leaders are often able to create a comfortable atmosphere supporting each person's value (Hackman & Johnson, 2009). By distributing power throughout a group's membership, democratic leadership enables each individual to feel capable of contributing to the success of the whole (Woods, 2005).

You might be asking yourself: "So, what's the catch? Why wouldn't I always try to use democratic leadership style?" Although democratic leadership seems ideal, we have already noted how it might not be the best choice in some situations. In addition, democratic leadership requires time and skill to develop. Implementing democratic leadership requires a foundation of mutual respect and trust to develop (Bass & Riggio, 2006). Everyone must feel capable and willing to contribute to the group—and trust others to do the same.

Furthermore, democratic leaders need to enact communication skills we have encountered in our discussions of listening, interpersonal relationships, and intercultural competence. Democratic leadership highlights listening and responding to group members. This style of leadership requires high emotional intelligence (EI) to foster "teamwork and collaboration" (Goleman,

Boyatzis, & McKee, 2002, p. 69). The democratic leader tries to acknowledge and incorporate what others think and feel, displaying empathy for their points of view.

That's Debatable

Try to identify a situation in which you have taken on each of these leadership communication styles. What helped you to determine which style was best? Have you ever chosen a style that failed miserably with your followers? If so, why did this style fail? Offer a case for or against employing each of the major styles in your examples.

Task and Social Leadership

A second leadership perspective deals with task and social dimensions of leadership. Most researchers agree that effective leadership must deal with the group's work and the relationships among the people who do it (Hackman & Johnson, 2009). These two dimensions explain the core concepts of this view. Your leadership style might be more focused on the job at hand (**task orientation**) or it might be more focused on the people involved (**social orientation**). Effective leaders should have the skill to move back and forth between these dimensions depending on the group's needs. Ernest Stech (1983) identifies patterns associated with each dimension.

If you exhibit task-oriented leadership, then you are likely to focus primarily on productivity and logistical aspects of the task. You might also be more likely to provide explicit directions and information for group members, communicate primarily through writing, and require that tasks be completed.

If you exhibit social-oriented leadership, you are more likely to ask for opinions and ideas from group members, communicate primarily through spoken word, and request that tasks be completed. The bottom line for interpersonally oriented leaders is that they focus on the people and the environment more than the task.

While these differences may be subtle, they are certainly important. The task-oriented leader may tend to be more authoritarian, and the social-oriented leader may tend to be more democratic (Hackman & Johnson, 2009). The task dimension becomes important if the group is approaching a critical deadline soon and needs to ramp up its productivity. The social dimension can help a group function smoothly as a unit if their team spirit has begun to crumble. As we move into our section on group roles, keep the task and social orientations in mind. You will see that various group members might exhibit leadership in either or both of these dimensions.

Morality Matters

Make a list of people throughout history that you consider the world's best leaders. Now make a second list consisting of people you consider the worst leaders in world history. What leadership characteristics did the people on both lists share? Exactly what in the way they led distinguishes the "good" leaders from the "bad" leaders? From your reflections, what kind of moral advice can you offer someone who wants to be a leader?

GROUP MEMBER ROLES

As we just learned with leadership, group interaction occurs on two levels: task and social. The same holds for all group members. The task function encompasses everything related to a group's productivity. But the harder a group pushes to accomplish its work, the more strain it exerts on group members. The social function includes the interpersonal factors that lead to group cohesiveness and development of a healthy group climate. But here's the tricky part: Every group must balance the tension between its task and social functions. Groups constantly strive to accomplish their work (task function) while maintaining satisfactory emotional and interpersonal conduct (social function) among group members. A group that accomplishes its task at the cost of bitter animosity among the members cannot qualify as successful. Taking some liberty with a familiar maxim, all work and no play makes a dull group. On the other hand, a group whose members become best buddies without accomplishing their collective goals also has failed. An ongoing party makes great fun, but little gets done. A successful group produces high-quality decisions from its members *and* high-quality relationships among its members (Oetzel et al., 2001).

During group interactions, a group's members assume roles that help or hinder the group's attempts to accomplish tasks and foster relationships (Bales, 1950). These roles fall into two main categories, according to the group functions they affect (Bales, 1958). **Task roles** contribute to the group's productivity. **Social roles** build the personal connections that bond the group's members. A third category describes roles that undermine task and social functions. These **self-serving roles** inhibit the group's collective function, disrupting progress or damaging interpersonal relationships. The basic distinctions between task and social functions have stood up well over half a century of testing, proving that groups and their leaders should attend to both areas (Friedman & Podolny, 1992; Poole, 1999).

Before discussing the specific roles that group members assume, several points require attention. These observations should clarify how to enact and interpret behaviors within groups.

- *Healthy groups include diverse roles.* Each task and social role serves important purposes for the group. Although any one group might not find members exhibiting every role, there certainly should be some mix among the various roles over time. This rotation adds to creativity and avoids the group's becoming too skewed toward producing or socializing. In a study of 13 Fortune 500 corporate team leaders, *every* leader identified a group with diverse viewpoints and approaches as crucial for creative output (Egan, 2005).
- *Roles are dynamic.* One person is not equivalent to one role (Poole, 1999). During the course of a group's interactions, the same person may occupy several roles—sometimes within the same meeting. Several people might share a single role, especially during complex tasks or serious relational tensions. Most groups find it healthy for members to transition through more than one role to keep the group fresh and to generate new ideas.
- *Roles may emerge rather than appear ready-made.* Instead of coming to meetings with pre-scripted roles, members often assume roles in response to what other members do (Turner, 2001). Many groups may have no idea which roles they need to fill until the members interact for

a while and notice the functions they need to fulfill relative to what other members are doing. Example: An athlete who joins a college team may not know which position to play until the coach notices gaps in the current lineup.

- *Roles are situational.* Different group activities often require different combinations of roles (Hare, 2003). A short timeline might see group members clustering around task roles to get the job done quickly while sacrificing some of the time-consuming social roles. A group split by internal conflicts might focus on social behaviors to restore cohesiveness before serious work can proceed.

Overall, no single task role or social role always qualifies as the "best one" at all times (although the self-serving roles almost always harm the group). Group members need to determine which roles serve the group best at a given time. With these reminders in place, we can proceed to the roles themselves.

Group member roles have been classified using all sorts of systems, but the one originally proposed by Kenneth D. Benne and Paul Sheats back in 1948 still holds up well as a description of how people act in groups (Mudrack & Farrell, 1995). Their category scheme (Benne & Sheats, 1948) forms the basis for the roles that we examine now, although some of the roles and their descriptions have been modernized. Depending on how we use it, any task or social role can help or hinder group interaction.

Task Roles

Task roles (see Table 8.1) keep the group moving forward toward its work-related objectives. While it is natural for someone to gravitate toward some roles because they feel more comfortable, it is also important for all group members to be willing to step into various roles as the need arises. Some of the roles come in pairs (such as information seeker and information giver), which presumes that multiple roles work together to satisfy the group's needs (Turner, 2001).

Initiator

The **initiator** starts discussion, either by suggesting new ideas or getting the group moving in a new direction. Initiators get the ball rolling, starting the group's positive momentum toward progress. You have encountered initiators in class when a student starts a line of discussion or makes a comment that triggers a chain reaction, with other students contributing their ideas, and a lively conversation builds. You also know what happens without an initiator. In the classroom without an initiator, you cover a topic that might develop into something interesting, but no one wants to begin. Everyone sits there in dead silence: no conversation, no learning. Group members often mistakenly believe that someone else will emerge as the initiator, so they shy away from getting the group moving. Lack of an initiator can plague groups that start slowly or have reached a sticking point. Without someone willing to suggest new ideas and directions, the group will stagnate and keep going over the same ground. Since initiators can break the group's focus on a single issue or reliance on a single approach, they help prevent groupthink.

TABLE 8.1 Task Roles in Groups

Social Role	Definition	Example	Uses and Limitations
Initiator	Begins discussion	First person to post in an online group discussion	Useful for breaking the ice in quiet groups; risks interrupting group's momentum by going in new directions
Information Seeker/ Information Giver	Requests/provides knowledge	Member asks for or locates relevant research	Beneficial for grounding group's ideas in reality; potential to overwhelm group with data
Opinion Seeker/ Opinion Giver	Requests/provides evaluations	Member asks for or offers reasons for liking an idea	Helpful when deciding among options; may slow progress with constant commentary
Discussion Enhancer 1. Coordinator 2. Elaborator 3. Orienter-Clarifier	1. Connects previous ideas 2. Expands ideas of others 3. Summarizes prior discussions and conclusions	1. "Darth, your suggestion has a lot in common with what Yoda advocated..." 2. "Let's take your proposal a step further..." 3. "So far, the group seems to agree on these points..."	Can push group past sticking points; simply repeats previous ideas if done poorly
Evaluator-Critic	Rationally judges ideas relative to clear standards	Member examines costs and benefits of a planned course of action	Can prevent poor decisions; might generate animosity if criticisms get personal
Procedural Technician	Enables group to interact smoothly and preserve group memory	Note taker or parliamentarian	Aids in orderly meeting conduct; danger of getting caught up in technical details

As helpful as initiators can be, sometimes the group needs to limit their influence. Constantly initiating new ideas and taking the group down new paths can divert the group from tasks that require immediate attention and follow-up. Often a group needs to check to make sure it finishes a pending task before taking a new direction. An oversupply of initiators can result in a group that starts all sorts of interesting projects without completing any of them. The group may need to depend on other members to follow through with the ideas.

Information Seeker and Information Giver

The complementary roles of information seeker and information giver address the group's need to know. The **information seeker** identifies and asks for research, experiences, and supporting materials that can assist the group. When we seek something, we presume we can find it; the game of hide and seek makes no sense if a player can simply vanish. If we want information, we anticipate finding it; the **information giver** serves that function. Information seekers and givers maintain a healthy connection between the group's discussions and concrete evidence that can support the group's actions or decisions. Information seekers ask questions such as: "How do we know that?" "Has that been proven?" "What evidence will confirm or deny that point?" "How do we test that?" Information givers conduct the research or provide the insights that can answer these questions.

Information seekers and givers play an especially vital part in identifying and defining the problem for problem-solving groups. A problem-solving group cannot begin its work until it gathers data about what the problem is, how it became a problem, and how serious it is. Some members qualify as information givers based on their experience or background, perhaps a job or family connection.

Too much information seeking and information giving can prove detrimental. A group needs to recognize when it can stop seeking and start acting. Obsession with gathering information explains why a lot of "fact-finding commissions" and "study groups" accomplish little. They get so consumed by collecting information that they lose track of what to do with it. Groups need to determine when they have enough information to proceed. A pre-set timeline ("After noon tomorrow we must move on…") can keep information manageable. Otherwise, you may find yourself in a group that always interrupts its progress by stopping to consider "just one more thing."

Opinion Seeker and Opinion Giver

The opinion seeker and opinion giver form another connected pair of group roles. The **opinion seeker** probes the group's values, usually trying to reach some evaluations of ideas or actions. Typically, an opinion seeker asks questions such as: "What do you think of that idea?" "How do you react to that?" The **opinion giver** states feelings and beliefs to aid the group in judging the members' positions on relevant topics. Opinion seekers and givers work well determining where group members stand on an issue. This pulse-checking function becomes most important whenever the group needs a formal vote. In other circumstances, opinion seekers and givers can furnish valuable feedback on member beliefs and attitudes. If members do not invite and air opinions, dissatisfaction or confusion might seethe unnoticed—and later erupt in destructive conflicts.

Opinion seeking and giving do have limits. Members of a group may need to keep their opinions in check if the group simply needs data. If I ask you to loan me a pen to sign a receipt, I don't want a critique of the pen's aesthetics—I just need the tool to do the job. Excessive exchange of opinions can cost a group time and energy that it could invest more wisely in getting information or performing a task. Unchecked sharing of opinions also easily becomes unproductive venting. As long as everyone is entitled to his or her own opinion, differences of opinion get aired but may not get resolved. Consider working with your group to reserve opportunities for seeking, giving, and acting upon opinions that the members provide.

Discussion Enhancer

Several specific functions combine under the broader category of **discussion enhancer,** or striving to extend and improve the content of a group's interactions. I repeatedly encounter this question from students: "What do I do if I have nothing to say?" My response is that everyone can contribute something, and input does not need to take the form of a totally original, brilliant insight. Your group can benefit from all sorts of participation. If you can't think of a brand new idea, consider contributing one or more of the following types of input:

- **Coordinator:** Discuss the connections between ideas that have been discussed. Point out relationships between what other group members have said. Coordinators perform a valuable service when the group cannot resolve differences about an issue. By observing how ideas connect with each other, a coordinator can help the group move toward combining ideas or compromising as a way to manage conflict. Example: "Winona, I've noticed that your plan has some important similarities to what Naomi proposed."
- **Elaborator:** Extend and expand on ideas others have stated. Suggest additions and amendments to their suggestions. In online group discussions, identify whose ideas you are extending so others can connect your comments with the appropriate group members. Example: "I'd like to add to what Snuffy was saying...." An elaborator actually adds to what other members have said instead of just repeating previous comments. Groups quickly tire of "fake" elaborators who merely parrot what others say without adding their own ideas.
- **Orienter-Clarifier:** Summarize part of the discussion to make sure everyone understands. Pinpoint the position of the group, especially in relation to its goals. For online discussion boards, provide a summary post that states decisions the group has made up to this point and where the major issues stand now. Typically, the orienter-clarifier answers questions such as: "Where do things stand now?" "What have we done so far?" "What comes next?"

All these functions can enhance discussion, but only if they truly add content rather than rehash the same points. To contribute fully, discussion enhancers must listen carefully to the group's discussions, keeping track of ideas they might revive or expand. If a group's discussion stalls due to confusion, running out of ideas, or reluctance to participate, some coordinating, elaborating, or orienting-clarifying might renew group activity.

Evaluator-Critic

The **evaluator-critic** plays the essential role of judging the group's ideas and actions against a standard. Think of an evaluator-critic as a skillful grader. The evaluator-critic, like the grader, offers thoughtful feedback and suggestions on how to do better within the guidelines of the assignment. Many group members misunderstand the evaluator-critic, assuming that it describes a complainer who only injects negativity into the group. Quite the contrary: An evaluator-critic always stands ready to scrutinize ideas fairly and rationally. Sometimes this analysis will show the group is progressing well; other times the scrutiny reveals the group is heading in the wrong direction. Evaluator-critics emerge most clearly in problem-solving groups when they state advantages and disadvantages of every proposed solution. The evaluator-critic always gives reasons for judgments, and this key quality distinguishes this role from the self-serving role of blocker (described below). An effective evaluator-critic will not let the group make important decisions without examining them carefully, so this role may offer the best antidote to groupthink.

Evaluator-critics must remain impartial; otherwise, they threaten the group's progress and satisfaction. If an evaluator-critic systematically favors some group members' ideas over others (always evaluating the same people's ideas positively or negatively), the favoritism could cause discontent in the group. Furthermore, an evaluator-critic should balance positive and negative assessments. Constantly evaluating everything as wonderful can give the group a false sense of confidence that will plunge it into groupthink. Nonstop negativity can discourage the group and reduce motivation to continue work.

Procedural Technician

Members who play **procedural technician** roles perform concrete tasks that smooth the group's function: preparing handouts, reserving meeting space, arranging the room, handling refreshments, or keeping records. One of the most important procedural roles is the **recorder**, who serves as the "group memory" (Benne & Sheats, 1948, p. 44) by taking notes and recording decisions. Many organizations appoint an officer whose main duty consists of recording, usually carrying the title of secretary. If procedural technician roles go unfilled, the group may find it has no place or time to meet, no record of its progress, and no agenda for its meetings.

Procedural roles enable the group to do its work, but they can limit the individual contributions of group members. For example, recorders often become so engrossed in taking notes that they contribute little to the discussion. Procedural technicians might get so involved with meeting the physical requirements of the group (meeting space, refreshments, technological issues, etc.) that they may sacrifice other duties. To maximize the contributions of all group members, procedural roles could rotate among several group members.

Social Roles

Groups cannot thrive on tasks alone. Social roles (see Table 8.2) help groups function smoothly as a unit, building cohesion and respect that make group work a satisfying joint effort instead of a cutthroat competition. For quite a while, research has revealed that cooperative groups perform better than competitive groups. The summary of this research is remarkably clear: "Large-scale field studies as well as experimental studies in laboratories show the same findings: Cooperation achieves better results than does competition because it creates greater total, coordinated, motivational forces" (Likert & Likert, 1976, p. 281). The lackluster performance of the United States basketball team in the 2004 Olympics demonstrates this point. Unquestionably the U.S. team had the best individual players. Still, less talented teams beat them—several times—because those teams played better together as a unit. Instead of five star players each trying to showcase their individual skills, the other national teams played as a single mutually supportive group with each member trying to enhance the performance of the overall team (Griffin, 2006).

TABLE 8.2 Social Roles in Groups

Social Role	Definition	Example	Uses and Limitations
Encourager	Provides positive reinforcement to group	Reassuring group it can accomplish its goals	Fosters positive self-esteem and confidence; risks reducing criticism of bad ideas/behaviors
Harmonizer	Manages conflicts among members	Shifting discussion away from personal insults and toward analysis of the issues	Helps reduce divisiveness in groups; may stifle helpful conflict if desire for harmony prevents dissent
Compromiser	Negotiates among different positions	Incorporating parts of several different proposals into a single plan	May increase buy-in to group decisions and reduce animosity; danger of sacrificing principles if too ready to compromise
Gatekeeper	Controls flow of communication	Refocuses discussion on topic at hand when members digress	Keeps interactions efficient; can bloat or overly constrict discussion
Follower	Carries out the will of others	Implements ideas others originate	Can convert plans into actions; unquestioning obedience can enact poor decisions
Tension Reliever	Performs actions that reduce anxiety and strain	Suggests breaks or diversionary activities	Reduces stress; could distract group

Encourager

Discouragement can haunt groups, especially when confronting a challenging task. Time limits may seem unreasonably short, the group may feel unequal to its task, or individual members may not get along. The **encourager** builds the group's morale by praising others, offering warm and positive reactions to them and to their contributions. Encouragers play the same role in groups as cheerleaders do for fans at a sports event: stir up enthusiasm to press onward toward success. Everyone needs to feel appreciated. Encouragers fulfill this need, helping the group feel good about itself.

Encouragers help a group immensely, but they can go too far. A group consisting entirely of encouragers qualifies as practically the definition of groupthink. Everyone thinks everything is wonderful, so no one scrutinizes anything. Encouragement without critical evaluation assures sloppy decisions. Sometimes a group needs a coach more than a cheerleader. Group members need to know when to cheer and when to chastise. Praising poor performance reinforces the behaviors that led to it, and the last thing a group needs to do is encourage bad behaviors. Encouragement also must be genuine. Insincere praise raises questions about the encourager's trustworthiness, arousing suspicion among group members.

Harmonizer

If conflicts are bound to appear in interpersonal relationships, then they are guaranteed to arise within the complex dynamics of groups. As we discovered in the previous chapter, conflicts can serve a very positive role by preventing groupthink and inviting genuine discussion of ideas. Whenever conflicts arise, they carry the risk of injured feelings that might cause lasting animosity among group members. The **harmonizer** eases tensions within a group by preventing or dissipating conflicts and generally smoothing the interactions among members. Harmonizers act as the goodwill ambassadors within the group, keeping any animosity among members from affecting the group's progress.

In fulfilling their role, harmonizers also must understand when to allow conflict to run its course. Sometimes the disagreements within a group arise from legitimate causes, such as different opinions about whether a proposed solution would work. A group too willing to harmonize will fall straight into groupthink, sacrificing open discussion to achieve apparent harmony. But groups can (and should) operate harmoniously while disagreeing vociferously—as long as the disagreements don't get personal. A thoughtful, honest group will experience some conflicts as members passionately argue for their positions. These sorts of conflicts clarify ideas and subject them to more rigorous scrutiny. The definition of harmony is to combine discordant notes into a pleasing sound, not to silence the differences altogether.

Compromiser

The question isn't whether conflict will occur, but how to cope with it. The **compromiser** approaches group conflicts prepared to yield somewhat to the group instead of defending a personal position to the end. A compromiser recognizes that not every group member will get everything he or she wants from a conflict. Compromisers bring the realistic attitude that they usually will have to give something to get something. A compromiser does not antagonize the group, but argues firmly for a desired position. Compromisers maintain group harmony by their willingness to set aside ego-involvement in an idea and consider other perspectives, including the possibility that they might be wrong. You probably have encountered many effective compromisers as the "deal makers" who can negotiate mutually satisfying agreements. Compromisers play key roles in international treaty negotiations, assuring that each side can claim some benefit from the settlement.

Although compromisers keep conflicts from flaring up into battles, they can cause some problems. Members who are too ready to give in to other viewpoints may not advocate their own positions forcefully. Willingness to compromise too soon can result in the loss of good ideas. Compromise also can complicate discussions of issues that require only a simple yes-or-no type of decision. Compromise can take time. Prolonged negotiations about relatively minor decisions can frustrate the group and delay its progress.

Gatekeeper

Group members feel comfortable in a group when they feel fully included, and the **gatekeeper** role maximizes member participation. The name of this role illustrates its function. Gatekeepers regulate the flow of communication. Just as a gate keeps some things in and others out, the gatekeeper keeps communication channels open to allow full participation, but restricts discussion when it wanders too much. If you have ever attended a meeting that moved quickly while still leaving all members with the feeling they participated fully, you can probably thank the gatekeepers. A member serves a gatekeeping function by inviting member input, especially soliciting the ideas of members who have remained in the background. A skillful gatekeeper also monitors the quality of communication, rechanneling discussion if someone makes an inappropriate comment or moving discussion along if the group bogs down. Gatekeepers might propose methods for regulating communication, such as time limits or content guidelines. Gatekeepers can prevent boredom in meetings by keeping discussions on track.

The gatekeeping function requires a delicate balance between opening and closing the gates that regulate communication. Always inviting more participation can exhaust group members and unnecessarily prolong meetings. Trying to micro-manage communication, however, can unduly restrict discussion by imposing too many rules that limit participation.

Follower

Every group needs a **follower** at times, someone who will perform requested actions and support whatever the group does. The follower serves as the mirror image of the initiator. While the initiator starts things moving, the follower obediently carries out instructions and works on assigned tasks. Followers also provide an audience for group members to air their ideas, since followers likely will not rush to initiate a new line of thought. A good follower in a group performs promptly and reliably. One could say that a follower "follows through" by carrying out the will of the group. Active followers provide important resources for the group; they are the "doers" who assist in accomplishing the work. That's the positive side of followers.

Unfortunately the follower easily becomes a passive, detrimental role. Followers who never question, never offer their own ideas, and never innovate provide the breeding ground for groupthink. A group of passive followers makes easy prey for incompetent or perverse leaders who may take the group in undesirable directions. Several of the Nazi defendants at the war crimes trials in Nuremberg after World War II claimed as their defense, "I was just following orders." Enthusiastic obedience can lead to moral blindness. This extreme version of following has earned the name "the Nuremberg defense." Followers often invoke this defense when they want to avoid responsibility for their actions—or inactions (Minow, 2006).

Tension Reliever

Have you ever been in a group that becomes stressed and irritated because you are so focused on the task at hand? This is when the tension reliever, or member willing to provide lighthearted and temporary diversion—often in the form of humor—from the situation, must step in to help. The tension reliever is often one of the first roles to emerge in a group and often keeps the group upbeat throughout their collective experience. Without this relief, groups may not be able to move forward. Tension relievers can provide physical as well as emotional relief, sometimes simply by proposing a break for the group. One member of a group I belong to serves as a tension reliever by occasionally guiding the group through yoga stretches during long meetings.

If a tension reliever becomes far more focused on fun than the group's problem-solving objectives, this "joker" or "clown" can divert the group from what it needs to accomplish. Temporary distractions can freshen and enliven a group. If these entertaining interludes draw more of the group's attention than the group's objectives, productivity could suffer.

Self-Serving Roles

In contrast to the task and social roles, self-serving roles (see Table 8.3) hurt the group's productivity and relationships. Self-serving roles do serve some purpose for the person assuming them. These roles fulfill some personal need, such as the desire to feel important, but at the expense of the group. Since the self-serving roles occur for a reason, the group needs to recognize their presence, not ignore or ban them (Benne & Sheats, 1948). Self-serving roles provide a wake-up call to the group to determine why the behavior occurs and how to prevent it in the future. For example, dysfunctional behavior might arise from a member's poor interpersonal skills, something the group has done to alienate the member, structuring meetings in ways that stifle full expression, or many other causes. A group should beware of hastily excluding or expelling any group member. Every participant has something important to offer the group—if the group can find a way to stimulate functional participation.

Aggressor

The **aggressor** uses communication tactics such as insulting or devaluing others, disparaging the group, and verbal attacks. Aggressors act as the verbal bullies in a group. Remember how students reacted to bullies in school? Reactions generally took the form of avoidance (in groups, stifling discussion) or fights (in groups, verbal sparring). Neither reaction helps a group. Reasons for aggression vary, but group members should avoid returning aggression with more aggression. Aggression is very contagious and can spread quickly throughout a group, fragmenting collective efforts.

Several communication techniques can prevent aggression in groups or reduce the likelihood of it escalating (Bach & Deutsch, 1971).

- *Avoid blame.* Recognizing accountability for mistakes is fine, but try not to point fingers. Instead, focus constructively on how to avoid the same sort of problem from occurring in the future.
- *Maintain a courteous rather than a sarcastic tone.* Sarcasm personalizes and intensifies conflict, inviting more aggressiveness.
- *Avoid labeling other people.* Aggressive communicators quickly resort to labels, which come across as personal attacks. Sweeping, generalized labels such as "You're the laziest person in this group" can have lasting consequences for group cohesiveness.

Review the discussions of assertiveness versus aggressiveness in Chapter 12 and conflict management strategies in Chapter 13. You have many options when you encounter aggression, so you need not choose to meet it with more aggression.

Blocker

The **blocker** is the naysayer in a group, stubbornly opposing suggestions, rejecting ideas, or introducing procedural complications. In a word, the

TABLE 8.3 Self-Serving Roles in Groups

Self-Serving Role	Definition	Example	Uses and Limitations
Aggressor	Uses verbal attacks to bully others	Ridicules the person making the proposal instead of examining the proposal's pros and cons	Don't respond aggressively; refocus on ideas, not people
Blocker	Obstructionist who prevents things from getting done	Rejects every proposal regardless of its merits	Convert blockers to evaluator-critics who provide reasons
Recognition-Seeker	Calls attention to self; brags about accomplishments	Demands credit for every good idea	Offer rewards for contributions to group
Self-Confessor	Discusses personal matters rather than group issues	Uses meetings to self-disclose instead of collaborate	Set aside forums for personal discussions
Dominator	Minimizes input from others; often controls by intimidation	Monopolizes meetings; interrupts or talks over others	Offer a limited task to lead; structure interactions to allow for everyone's input
Shirker	Does not fulfill obligations to group; fails to complete tasks	Ignores instructions; expects others to take up the slack	Make each member accountable for his or her own work

blocker serves as the obstructionist. The difference between blockers and their productive next-of-kin, opinion-givers and evaluator-critics, is that blockers resist beyond apparent reason. The U.S. Senate has a policy that invites blockers. It's the filibuster, which allows one or more senators to speak as long as they want and say whatever they want unless 60 percent of the Senate votes to close discussion. Hopefully your own groups will not allow filibusters, which have been known to extend for days or weeks without interruption.

The blocker seems to take a perverse pleasure in halting a group's forward momentum. This ability to single-handedly stall the group gives the blocker a sense of self-importance. Groups need to find ways to engage the blocker's critical tendencies in a productive fashion. If possible, blockers can put their analytical tendencies to productive use by converting to evaluator-critics. The group could acknowledge the blocker's contributions and benefit from the member's evaluative skills by assigning a suitable task. Example: Find at least two disadvantages to each of the group's proposed solutions, providing reasons for each of your points. That's a homework assignment most blockers would embrace. If a blocker continues to be unreasonable, then the group could establish ground rules for discussion, such as providing reasons for opinions.

Recognition-Seeker

Have you ever worked alongside a person who takes all the credit others deserve? You might have encountered a **recognition-seeker:** a show-off who tries to grab all the attention, hogging the glory and trying to reap all the rewards. Of course, we all enjoy praise, but the recognition-seeker distracts the group by tales of personal accomplishments that may bear no relevance to the group's activities. Recognition-seekers fuel resentment in the group, especially since they actively discourage or disparage any attempt by other group members to share the spotlight. Recognition-seekers think, "It's all about me," when in reality "It's all about *us*—the entire group."

Recognition-seekers and encouragers can form a perilous pair. If an encourager keeps praising a recognition-seeker, it fuels the cycle of recognition, inviting more recognition-seeking behavior. Groups can satisfy recognition-seekers by providing an outlet for ego-stroking behavior. As long as other group members get recognized as well, allocating a specified time or space for recognition (e.g., posting accomplishments on a group's Facebook page) can boost morale and satisfy the recognition-seeker. Another tactic might be to defer recognition until the end of the group's work, using recognition as a reward for accomplishing the group's objectives.

Self-Confessor

The **self-confessor** directs the group toward her or his own feelings or experiences, disrupting the group by substituting personal concerns for the group's agenda. Self-confessors may use inappropriate self-disclosure to avoid participating in the group's discussion. Self-confessors run rampant in student group projects. After only a few minutes of many group meetings, I hear at least one participant redirect discussion with a commentary about personal matters such as relationship issues, plans for the next weekend, or a tale of hardship (often a family crisis or personal illness). Not wishing to appear insensitive, the other group members veer off track, abandoning more pressing topics to relate their own stories or comment on the one they just heard. Does that pattern sound familiar, maybe like a typical group study session?

Groups should exercise caution when dealing with self-confessors. Since they are airing personal feelings, attempts to stifle them might seem like a personal affront, as if the group does not value them as people. An excellent way to accommodate self-confessors while retaining them in the group is to reserve some time outside formal meetings for self-talk among group members. A bit of designated social time can furnish an appropriate setting for the self-confessor to disclose without infringing on the group's meeting agenda.

Dominator

While leaders try to maximize the productive input of all group members, **dominators** try to control the group by imposing their will on others. A dominator may attempt to manipulate a group to achieve personal goals. Typical dominator behaviors include not letting other members participate, dictating orders to other members, interrupting them, or dismissing their contributions. The dominator treats the group as a personal domain, with the group members serving the dominator. Left unchecked, a dominator can silence other group members. If challenging the dominator doesn't work, most group members probably will withdraw from active participation.

Dominators can prove difficult to manage, but a group can harness their positive qualities. Since dominators like being in the spotlight, they might find initiator functions agreeable—as long as the group places limits on authority. Since a group probably can't simply eliminate the dominator's need to control, offer the dominator a specific sphere of activity to call his or her own. Place the dominator in charge of a task, since the dominator already likes to take charge. I have seen many group dominators become valuable contributors when they find an area they can control. A dominator can convert into a full-fledged group member by transferring the focus away from controlling other *people* and toward controlling one's own *tasks*.

Shirker

The final self-serving role describes a broad range of behaviors that impede group progress. The **shirker** avoids or neglects functional participation in the group. Shirkers come in many varieties, and surely you will recognize one or more of them from your own experience in groups. Typical behaviors that indicate shirking include the following:

- Failure to attend meetings, showing up late, or leaving early.
- Showing up to meetings unprepared.
- Not completing assigned tasks on time.
- Withdrawing from discussions, offering no input or responses.
- Violating group expectations.
- Apathy or negativity toward the group's members and their work.
- Distracting the group with disruptive behavior.
- Long delays in posting to online discussions.
- Not replying to contact (phone calls, e-mails, etc.) in a timely manner.

All of us have exhibited a few of these behaviors occasionally, but when they become a regular pattern, you might suspect shirking. Be careful in trying to identify shirkers and deciding to abandon them. If you encounter someone who appears to be shirking responsibilities, first try to discuss the matter with the person privately. Investigate *why* the shirking behaviors appear. The supposed shirker may be unaware of how the behaviors affect other group members. The member may have personal issues that legitimately restrict participation. Aside from these issues, some people engage in shirking behavior as a sign of dissatisfaction with the group. Probe what you and other group members might do to reclaim this person as an important part of the group. Sometimes shirking behaviors vanish after the group becomes more welcoming and inclusive toward the wayward member.

Given the wide variety of motives for shirking instead of working, it's tough to offer advice on how to deal with people who exhibit this behavior. We can, however, confront the problem of group work becoming less productive and fulfilling than individual work. By understanding how groups develop, we can make them function more smoothly.

GROUP DEVELOPMENT

If you're like most students, your experiences with group work have been thrilling or chilling. While each group experience is different, groups typically follow a similar developmental process. In this section, we will consider the stages of group development. When you receive an individual assignment, you probably think about it a while, then do it. When groups form, they go through a more elaborate process. Groups often undergo stages of development before diving into their duties. These stages have been labeled forming, storming, norming, performing, and de-forming (Tuckman, 1965; Tuckman

& Jensen, 1977). Not all groups undergo all the stages or proceed through them in the same order (Bonebright, 2010). Some groups, for example, may dissolve after one or two stages. This five-stage process depicted in Table 8.4 does, however, closely match the developmental cycle of groups that form in college courses (Myers & Anderson, 2008).

Forming

Most of us feel a little apprehensive when we first enter a group setting, especially if the group is assigned rather than one we chose. "How do I fit into this group?" "What should I expect from the group members, and what should they expect from me?" "What will the task require, and how will we work together to accomplish it?" These are just a few of the questions that might enter your mind during the forming stage of group development. When a group forms, members may be hesitant to fully express their ideas and may be just trying to figure out how they should act. Forming involves a process of testing both the relationship and task expectations in a group. During forming we often look for boundaries and try to determine what can and can't be done. While groups are forming, the members try to resolve confusion and uncertainty by seeking more information about: (a) the group's purpose, (b) other members, (c) how to proceed (Maples, 1988). A group forms as the members begin to get oriented to the people and the process of the group. Through this process, a collective unit emerges.

Storming

"Why do I have to answer all the questions?" "Why do you always get to make the final decision?" "Were you really listening to me when I explained the project or were you just focused on texting?" While you might not say these questions aloud, many of us have had similar thoughts. These questions represent the storming stage of group development. After the initial honeymoon experienced during the forming stage, group members become more comfortable with one another, begin to recognize differences, and conflicts begins to emerge. The storming stage is characterized by the clash of differing beliefs and perspectives. Emotional resistance may arise to tasks or to other members of the group (Bonebright, 2010). Storming actually can represent progress in a group's development, since the members feel secure enough to air their differences honestly. The storming stage "may even be necessary for progress to occur and for problem solving to take place [because] . . . once negative feelings and disharmony have been expressed (i.e., storming), the path becomes more accessible to positive interactions . . ." (McMorris, Gottlieb, & Sneden, 2005, p. 222). By practicing many of the effective communication techniques we have discussed so far, you should be able to move through the storming stage and begin to develop more stable patterns of interaction.

Norming

Typically, groups begin to establish some regular patterns of interaction. When your group settles on fairly consistent roles, reliably abides by accepted communication behaviors, and begins to become more cohesive, you are

TABLE 8.4 Stages of Group Development		
Stage	**Explanation**	**Interaction Issues**
1. Forming	Individuals identify as a collective unit, get oriented to group's processes and people Characteristics: testing, questioning, experimentation	What is the group's purpose? How do we contact each other? How and when will we group meet? What are we expected to accomplish?
2. Storming	Intra-group tensions develop; resistance to collaboration Characteristics: confrontation, conflict, opposition	What causes relational tensions? How do conflicts affect group progress and morale? How do members channel emotions productively?
3. Norming	Group establishes guidelines for tasks and interactions; behavioral pattern develop that the group authorizes Characteristics: sense of group identity and culture	What constructive habits or rules advance the group toward its goals? What destructive rules and habits should the group alter?
4. Performing	Group addresses tasks together, converges toward collective outcomes Characteristics: shared stake in group outcomes, mutual support	How can the group maximize efficiency and satisfaction? How can group members maintain high standards for its work?
5. De-forming (adjourning)	Group dissolves as an entity Characteristics: members go their own way, join other groups, maintain potential for future collaboration	How can the group break up without animosity? How can the group learn from its shared experiences? How (if at all) could the group re-form, perhaps with different members or new tasks?

probably experiencing norming. Over time, groups develop **norms**, defined as rules or accepted traditions that govern interaction. Norms can be very formal, such as written procedural guidelines, or they can emerge more informally as customs. Norms can cover almost any aspect of the group's activity, although they most commonly deal with conduct in meetings and the responsibilities of group members. Norms often emerge as a way to prevent tensions within the group that might arise from confusion about interpersonal or procedural issues (Johnson & Long, 2002).

Many groups make the mistake of neglecting norms, eager to jump straight toward their task. That approach causes problems. Groups need to establish clear expectations so members know how to proceed. Often these expectations arise from observing what happens within the group. Example: A group repeatedly does nothing but exchange gossip during every meeting, so a destructive norm develops for group meetings not to accomplish task-related work. Example: A group habitually checks each member's progress every day after class, so that time becomes a constructive norm for everyone to "check in" and verify what he or she has been doing.

All groups face the challenge of developing norms that improve rather than impede the group's interactions. The earlier a group develops healthy norms that contribute to its goals, the sooner it can begin to perform its tasks—and perform them well. While the forming stage of development is characterized by posing many of the following questions, the norming stage will bring fairly stable answers. These answers can help establish clear, consistent norms that pave the way to better performance.

- How often, when, and where should the group meet formally?
- What are the expectations for attendance and conduct at meetings?
- What are the expectations for performing assigned duties? What are the consequences for not performing them?
- What procedures govern meetings? What kind of agenda will be prepared?
- How will roles or assignments be divided?
- Who will preside during a given meeting? Who will serve as recorder?
- What time frames do members expect for responding to phone calls, e-mails, or online discussion board postings?

Norming adds to group cohesiveness, since the interactions among group members become more familiar and predictable (Tuckman, 1965). These shared standards bond group members, as they now have something in common other than the coincidence of belonging to the same group.

Performing

With its norms developed, the group can concentrate on the task. In the performing stage, efforts of members synchronize as the entire group moves ahead to accomplish shared objectives. Members become interdependent; they can rely on each other to assist in accomplishing tasks and getting along (McMorris, Gottlieb, & Sneden, 2005). The group manages conflicts, members are comfortable with expectations, and members adapt to the various roles they need to play. Everyone in the group can fulfill his or her responsibilities and work toward productive decisions. Performing often involves the group presenting its work to outside audiences, such as a presentation to a class.

De-forming

The final stage has been called many names—such as termination, adjourning, or mourning (to capture the sense of loss when a group dissolves)—but all the labels point to ending the group's status as an entity. The breakup of a group can occur as part of a planned process. For example, a project the group was convened to complete finally ends, and the group disbands with the completion of its task. A group might disintegrate gradually as members move on and the group loses cohesiveness.

Whatever the rationale for de-forming, a group's termination should preserve the possibility of future collaboration. As with any relationship, animosity can spoil the opportunity to reconnect should the need arise. A group might reconstitute in the future, as we see quite often with musical bands that re-form with a different lineup of performers. Collegiate sports teams and campus clubs reinvent themselves as new group dynamics develop whenever key players/members graduate or transfer.

To review the group development stages, let's consider a class example. Recently I taught a seminar-style course that lasted three hours every Monday evening. The students and I had questions about what we could accomplish. We were not used to the course format, and we couldn't hit a rhythm (forming). The first few class meetings were rough (storming). Several students dropped the course. The class spanned the dinner hour, so everyone was hungry and cranky. After a few weeks, we gradually developed norms that established some predictability and improved our interactions (norming). A different person each week took responsibility for bringing food. We established a set time and duration for breaks. We also settled into a routine for covering course content, beginning with a summary of the previous week's discussion. As a result, participation increased and the class became more rewarding for everyone (performing). Eventually the course concluded (de-forming), but some of the students continued working with me on academic projects after this course had adjourned. In the next section, we diagnose why groups may stumble—and how to lend them a hand so they can move ahead.

EFFECTIVE GROUP INTERACTION

Hopefully you now know a bit about your group's development, but what about those ever-present group problems that make you wish you could just work alone even if it means having to do more work? This section addresses some of those recurring problems and suggests a few ethical commitments that may help all members to interact effectively—and ultimately be more satisfied with the group process.

Social Loafing

Trying to grade group projects used to drive me nuts. Invariably students would approach me after the project and complain that at least one group member didn't work as hard as the others and deserved a poorer grade. I knew they were right. The hard-working group members and I constantly felt frustrated by those who didn't contribute fully to the group. Many of these students performed admirably on individual tasks. They also liked their fellow group members, so these weren't just cases of trying to sabotage the group. What happened?

The student complaints identified a crucial group phenomenon, one that can send a group into a tailspin. To understand what happened, consider the following situations:

- You applaud much more quietly in a group than with just one or two people.
- If you have to lift a heavy object along with several other people, you don't lift quite as hard as you would if lifting it alone.
- When playing tug-of-war, you pull the rope harder if playing alone than when playing as part of a team.

The last example actually stems from a 1913 study, making **social loafing** one of the oldest scientifically documented group behaviors (Kravitz &

Martin, 1986). Social loafing describes the tendency of individuals not to work as hard in group tasks as they do individually. This pattern occurs across a wide variety of groups and activities (Hart et al., 2004). The rationale for social loafing can get complex, but the basic problem is that the social loafer believes other group members will take up the slack of the loafer. As long as the loafer believes others will "cover" for inactivity or that the loafing will remain unnoticed, loafing will continue.

To maximize individual effort within the group, we need to minimize social loafing. Fortunately, social loafing is one of the most widely studied and thoroughly documented aspects of group behavior. Decades of experience and experiments have arrived at several ways to reduce the chances of social loafing.

Make each member's contribution unique and identifiable (Levine & Moreland, 1990). If each member maintains a clear connection with a contribution, then each person becomes accountable for a portion of the project. I have seen several group projects in the course you are taking identify each contribution a group member makes in the final report, including the research conducted and the portion of the report each participant wrote. By taking responsibility for specific components, each group member demonstrated his or her own effort. Identification of specific contributions makes it impossible for loafers to hide in the background (Hare, 2003).

Maximize the urgency and attractiveness of the task. Some loafing stems from simple boredom. No one rushes to contribute to a task he or she finds boring or irrelevant. Even if the group's task is assigned, members can search for an angle on the topic that connects with them. As a group, consider the stake each member holds in the group's task. If every group member believes the project matters to them, then each will expend more effort (Williams & Karau, 1991).

Minimize group size, maximize group cohesiveness. As a group becomes larger or less cohesive, social loafing increases (Liden et al., 2004). You can observe this phenomenon in the classroom. Larger classes often have far less student participation. Lost in a sea of other students, each student feels less significant and thus may decide to fade into anonymity. The larger the group, the more a social loafer can lurk in the background, doing nothing. If your group already is small, try assigning specific duties to individuals or subgroups so everyone has a responsibility to fulfill. Since social loafing sometimes arises because a member feels irrelevant, a personalized responsibility can restore meaningful contributions to the group. Cohesiveness reduces social loafing by creating an "all for one, one for all" attitude. If each member considers the entire group's efforts and results his or her own, each will be more apt to shoulder responsibility.

Optimize communication, especially beyond formal group meetings. Lack of contact among group members can lead to social loafing. Non-participants often complain of inadequate contact with other group members, especially in online groups without personal interaction (Thompson & Ku, 2006). Even in groups of only two people, lack of communication causes social loafing because one person believes the other doesn't care about the collaboration (Bacon, 2005). Lack of contact is an interpersonal, not a technical, problem. Don't always wait for a formal meeting or an impending deadline to touch base with each other. Use e-mail, phone calls, online discussion boards, online chats, texting, or personal contact to check on group progress and morale. Between formal meetings of the entire group, you can conduct mini-meetings among a few group members to deal with issues that might not require the entire group.

Hold each member accountable. Loafing will continue as long as loafers believe it has no consequences. Instead of covering for a loafer and doing the person's work for them, establish clear penalties for not fulfilling obligations to the group. For example, I found the level of participation skyrocketed after I started grading each individual member's work on a group project instead of simply assigning one grade to the entire group.

Cultural factors also seem to affect the likelihood of social loafing. Women overall exhibit far less social loafing than men, perhaps because many women are socialized into more collaborative, networking roles within families and peers (Karau & Williams, 1995). As we discovered in Chapter 2, members of collectivistic cultures—more common in Eastern nations such as China, Japan, and Korea—understand their identity in terms of a larger social group. By contrast, members of more individualistic cultures—common in the United States—define themselves more independently of others. Not surprisingly, members of collectivistic cultures demonstrate less social loafing because they more likely place the group's concerns above their own (Karau & Williams, 1995). In individualistic cultures, each person tends to answer to his or her own beliefs and values above those of a larger group.

Group Polarization

Have you ever noticed that you might do crazy things with a group of friends—things you never would consider doing alone? Or maybe you do exactly the opposite: Your originality and daring shrivel when among a group, and you become more timid and cautious than you ever imagined. Although these experiences differ, they form part of the same phenomenon, known as **group polarization**. Groups sometimes seem to shift member behaviors toward extremes: either very risky or very cautious (El-Shinnawy & Vinze, 1998). What causes this push toward extremities?

You might suspect the shift toward greater risk results from daring leaders who push members toward radical action, but the behavior does not stem mainly from leader influence (Hoyt & Stoner, 1968). Polarization also does not result simply from the majority imposing its will on a minority (Moscovici & Zavalloni, 1969). Instead, people may move toward extreme behaviors because they want to distinguish themselves as enthusiastic group members, not just conforming to the average. One study found that when racially prejudiced students group with like-minded students, the individual levels of racism increased (Myers & Bishop, 1970). Fortunately, the same effect occurred when less prejudiced students grouped together: Each student's level of racism declined. Example: Members of a military unit may exhibit reckless behavior in battle because they want to prove themselves as braver than the rest of the group. In addition, repeatedly hearing and stating arguments on a position might drive someone toward more extreme position. Example: If you hear others state their dislike of cats and you keep talking about your own dislike of cats, you might become more prone to go on a cat-hunting spree.

Group polarization poses grave dangers. Shifts toward risk can move the group toward rash actions because the enthusiasm of individual members builds momentum. Careful deliberation might give way to ill-considered, hasty acts. Shifts toward caution can paralyze a group, leading members to avoid making any decisions for fear of doing too much.

Polarization can prove difficult to stop because it often creeps up unnoticed. Within the group, everything might seem normal because group members reinforce each other's daring or timidity. Polarization becomes less likely if members can maintain some time outside the group. Some respite from the group can calm emotional tidal waves that drive a group toward extremes. It also might help to engage in group discussions most vigorously before members form firmly entrenched positions on topics (Myers & Bishop, 1970). The group interaction then becomes more of a mutual exploration of ideas than an exercise in proving how far one can go (or refrain from going) with an idea.

Become a Responsible Group Member

As we discussed earlier, it is important for groups to find common ground and experience norming before they can perform at their best. When teaching classes that incorporate group communication, I commonly find that while every student in the group may want to "get an 'A'" on the project, not all group members are willing to commit the same amount of time and/or effort to achieve this goal. Membership in a group means that you acquire responsibilities that extend to the group as a whole. You may remember the ethical principles from the National Communication Association that appeared in Chapter 1. The additional responsibilities you assume as a group member reflect your commitment "to responsible thinking, decision making, and the development of relationships and communities" (National Communication Association, 1999). These ethical principles suggest the following responsibilities for all group members.

Cultivate Trust

Without mutual trust, group members might withhold information or mislead each other. To develop trust, you must demonstrate your own trustworthiness. Establish yourself as a reliable group member who completes assignments, supports cohorts, and models productive group roles. If you promise to do something for the group, follow through.

Trust refers to the group's atmosphere as well as to member behavior. Do your part to make the group a safe area for honestly sharing information, ideas, and opinions. Trust develops with the assurance that each member can be valued. Honest, open discussion in a group occurs only when everyone gives and receives respect. This shared respect and the knowledge that each person will serve the group reliably build the foundation for trust.

Make and Meet Commitments

Cragan, Kasch, and Wright (2009) discuss several commitments students should make when operating in small groups. These commitments describe obligations all ethical communicators assume, but they become magnified in group settings. The ethical commitments apply to yourself and to your behavior toward other group members.

- *Commit to collaborating* with group members, not trying to outdo them or shame them into performing well. Provide group members with information that might help them to move forward. Do not withhold information or arguments that might assist the group. Remember the kindergarten lesson of "sharing"? The "information giver" is usually one of the most common roles in a group.
- *Commit to planning and preparing* so you can be ready when the group needs you. The more prepared you are, the better you can follow through and show you are trustworthy.
- *Commit to excellence.* The group deserves your best work, since you now have an obligation to other students as well as to yourself. Remember that you can excel without making others look bad.
- *Commit to learning from others* by listening to their contributions. Groups can provide great learning opportunities because every group member can teach you something. Practice active listening to get the most from the knowledge others can provide.

Embrace Differences

Have you ever wished that your group members could be more like you? Have you ever thought, "We just aren't a strong group because we don't have anything in common"? Actually this statement couldn't be more mistaken. A group does not exist simply to confirm each person's preconceptions, but to enrich members by exposure to different perspectives. If you never encountered anything new, you would never learn.

Typically, groups with greater diversity are actually more effective than groups with limited diversity or whose members are homo-geneous (Shaw, 1976). Groups with diverse ideas and perspectives will have a variety of proposals or suggestions and recognize factors that might otherwise be overlooked. Now, here is the challenge: While group diversity does usually make a group more effective by enhancing a group's problem-solving skills, it often threatens the trust among group members (Oetzel, 2002). Here is where it becomes particularly important for all members to respect and appreciate diverse viewpoints. Encouraging diverse personal ideas will stimulate innovative thinking and encourage considering the different views that lead us to "achieve the informed and responsible decision making fundamental to a civil society" (National Communication Association, 1999).

EFFECTIVE MEETINGS IN SMALL GROUPS

Across every type of organization most work gets done in meetings, yet almost everyone complains about the misery of meetings (Mosvick & Nelson, 1996). Just ask your friends and co-workers. They will grumble about the same things managers deplore: Meetings start late, last too long, are disorganized, or accomplish nothing. The problem may not lie with meetings themselves but with how poorly we plan, conduct, and use them (Mosvick & Nelson, 1996). In this section, we consider a few ideas that may help your small group meetings to run smoother and—most importantly—help your group become more productive.

Before a Meeting

Meet for a Reason

"Any meeting worth holding is worth planning" (Streibel, 2003, p. 10). Every meeting (except for emergencies) should be planned in advance, with definite goals and desired outcomes. If your group cannot decide what a meeting should accomplish, then do not meet until you can commit to at least one objective. If a group meets without a reason, the time likely will be wasted with idle chatter. Before scheduling a meeting, figure out why you are meeting in the first place. The clearer the purpose, the more the group will become motivated to attend and contribute ideas.

> Example (poor reason): It's Wednesday, so let's meet.

> Example (better reason): We need to divide up the topics to research, so let's meet.

Determine the Mode of Meeting

Face-to-face meetings of an entire group cost valuable time, effort, and resources. You also need to find suitable space conducive to getting things done. These personal meetings often prove necessary for socializing members into the group climate and for stimulating discussion. Other modes of meeting can speed the group's progress. Online discussion boards and social networking sites do not require everyone to be in the same place at the same time, so they work well when members' schedules conflict. A phone call might provide a quick answer to a question. Sometimes only a few members working on the same task might meet, then report to the entire group. You should not feel constrained always to meet only as an entire group at a certain time and place.

Schedule the Meeting

Settle on a definite time, place, and length of the meeting. For online work, set a deadline for posting comments. After you schedule the meeting and determine its format, confirm everyone's attendance. Send reminders to assure that everyone remembers to attend or makes provisions to catch up on what they will miss.

> Example (poor schedule): Let's meet next week for a while in the hall sometime after class.

> Example (better schedule): Let's meet next Thursday at noon for one hour in Tweedle's Coffee Shop.

Establish Clear Expectations

What should each member bring to the meeting? What will each person be expected to do in the meeting? Who will be responsible for leading the meeting? Who will be making a report to the rest of the group? Who will take notes and how will they be circulated to the group? If each person has an active role, there will be more motivation to contribute.

Set an Explicit Agenda

To prevent the meeting from becoming chaotic, share beforehand a detailed agenda. List the issues the meeting will cover, and plan on how much time each item should take. Invite all members to contribute to the agenda so everyone feels included in the group's plans. In addition to listing the meeting's topics in a definite order, the agenda should clarify items that require a vote or other group action. Don't wait until the meeting to circulate the agenda. Everyone needs to know what to expect in order to arrive properly prepared.

During a Meeting

Strive for Participation, Not Simply Attendance

Everyone shares the responsibility for making a meeting work (Doyle & Straus, 1982). Within the meeting, try to contribute something positive. Everyone should enter a meeting determined to put something into it as well as get something out of it. The commitment to participate especially holds for online meetings and teleconferences. Add to the conversation by speaking or posting, especially if you need clarification or if the meeting has not addressed an issue you consider important.

Practice Active Listening

We keep returning to active listening, since we learned in Chapter 3 that it is such a crucial communication skill. Every meeting provides an opportunity for group members to educate and help each other. Devote your full attention to what other group members are saying. Let others have their say so you can learn from them. Consider how the comments and information from others might relate to what you are doing in the group. Members will contribute to a group only if they believe others are willing to understand (Kausen, 2003). Willingness to understand lies at the core of active listening.

Keep the Meeting on Track

Always have the goals for meeting in mind. Tie the content of the meeting to the group's objectives. If the meeting strays too far from its goals, remind the group of what the meeting should accomplish. Focus on making relevant, helpful comments that will assist the group in accomplishing its goals for the meeting. A properly controlled meeting enables open expression but keeps channeling participation toward achieving the goals of the meeting (Kirkpatrick, 2006). One key way to keep the meeting on track: Stick to the agenda.

Fill Key Group Roles

Each group will organize meetings its own way, but meetings often run more smoothly if specific people bear certain responsibilities. Make sure a note-taker is designated so the group has a record of what was done in the meeting. Someone also should lead the meeting. This meeting leader (who may or may not be the designated leader of the group overall) can change as you switch to different items on the agenda, but someone should shoulder responsibility to keep the meeting organized and keep discussion going. These leadership roles should be settled in advance to save time during the meeting. The leaders who volunteer or are selected should encourage participation, move toward accomplishing tasks, and maintain a positive relational atmosphere (Kirkpatrick, 2006).

Assign Homework

Everyone should leave a meeting with a clear idea of what he or she needs to do next. The "to-do" list should include tasks, people, and time frames. What needs to get done? Who might help get it done? When should it be done? One reason many meetings fail is that the attendees leave without any direction, no sense of what they should be doing for the group. Before the meeting concludes, each group member needs to verify what job he or she needs to do. What needs to be completed by the next meeting? What progress does the group expect on key tasks?

After a Meeting

Assess Success

The group needs to know what worked in its meeting and what failed. Afterwards, take an inventory of how well the meeting fared in accomplishing its task and social goals. Which agenda items were accomplished? Which items still need work? What remains to do? How much closer is the group to accomplishing its objectives? Try to diagnose what trouble spots arose for the group. How might the group cope with these obstacles? As for relationships, what troublesome or helpful behaviors did members display? How could these behaviors be prevented or encouraged? Who should be working more closely together in the future? Who shows good leadership potential? Assessing a meeting allows the group to improve future group interactions. By correcting interpersonal or task-related problems that arose, upcoming meetings can become more productive and pleasant.

Follow Through

A responsible group member treats the end of a meeting as the beginning of an assignment. Use the time between formal meetings to accomplish tasks. The more you do between meetings, the more you can contribute to each meeting. What will you do after the meeting to move the group toward accomplishing its goals? Remember that being a responsible group member involves earning trust of the group by demonstrating reliability. If the group depends on you to get something done, make the effort to do it well.

Prepare for the Next Meeting

Each meeting sets the stage for future interactions. As soon as possible after a meeting, members need to know when to expect another gathering. Essentially, the group begins the "Before the Meeting" cycle of planning, which enables members to reserve time for the group and anticipate when their work will be due.

SPECIAL GROUP FORMATS AND TOOLS

If you have been a part of a group with dedicated, collaborative members but the group still has trouble getting its job done, you are certainly not alone. In

Chapter 15, you learned about the group deliberation process and the technique of brainstorming; however, sometimes groups find that when they meet and try to follow the "normal" or "natural" flow of the group process, they can't accomplish what needs to be completed. To assist you and your group in making effective and efficient decisions, this section offers two specific decision-making formats and two computer-mediated communication tools that you might find valuable when focusing on the groups' tasks. These techniques are used commonly in professional settings, especially when issues become too complex to resolve by standard group meetings alone.

Nominal Group Technique

The **nominal group technique** (NGT) offers a useful way to generate ideas quickly, with each group member offering input individually. Because its primary purpose is to produce ideas, NGT most often emerges as a brainstorming method (e.g., a group trying to propose possible solutions to a problem) or as a way to gather feedback from all group members (e.g., a group of employees offering input on a new health insurance plan).

NGT begins with an issue presented to the entire group. In our example, the group is considering how to minimize college tuition increases. The method proceeds through the following steps (Castiglioni et al., 2008):

1. *Invite ideas:* Each group member independently and without discussion contributes an idea. Sometimes these ideas are written or sent electronically to preserve confidentiality. Example: Each member silently writes several potential solutions, in effect conducting an individual brainstorming session.

2. *Record:* All ideas are recorded for examination by the entire group. Members can present their own ideas, or a member (leader or recorder) can record the ideas without attribution if members prefer confidentiality. Example: In our meeting, each member selects one potential solution from his or her own list. Each potential solution is recorded on a whiteboard for all members to examine.

3. *Clarify:* The group discusses the ideas that have been offered. Discussion follows time limits and a set procedure to maintain focus on the ideas under consideration. Discussion is not the time for debating the ideas, but for clarifying the ideas that have been generated. Clarification enables the group to agree on whether to combine or rephrase some suggestions. Example: Members ask questions and offer feedback to clarify the possible solutions. The solutions are not evaluated yet! The group only wants to decide which solutions it will consider for evaluation later.

4. *Vote:* Members then rank each idea in order of preference or importance. The rankings are tallied to reach an overall group decision about preferences or priorities among ideas. Example: Selecting the choices from the list on the whiteboard, group members rank their preferred solutions from best to worst, assigning numbers to indicate rank order (such as 1 = most preferred, etc.).

Additional rounds of the procedure can occur as tasks become more complex. This technique has been used frequently to gather input about methods of health education, obtain consumer feedback on problems and products, and develop plans for organizational development (Tuffrey-Wijne et al., 2007).

NGT offers several advantages. With every group member developing ideas privately and guaranteed input, NGT minimizes opportunities for dominating or blocking (Sarre & Cooke, 2009). Another benefit is that since each member bears responsibility for contributing ideas, social loafing becomes less likely (Asmus & James, 2005). The method also can generate lots of ideas quickly, and the ranking system can produce group decisions that reflect contributions from all members.

The structure of NGT also can limit its effectiveness. Because members generate their ideas individually, the method sacrifices the dynamic interplay that can fuel creativity. Ideas don't "spin off" each other, so they might not be as rich as the outcome of group brainstorming. NGT also relies on a fertile set of ideas from members who enter the process. If each member already has exhausted his or her own ideas on an issue, NGT will not spawn many new insights.

Delphi Technique

The **Delphi technique** enlists experts who do not meet together physically, but who independently contribute their input on an issue. For example, we might want to develop a new graduate degree in communication studies based on the expertise of communication department chairs across the country. Since the participants do not need to be in the same place, the method can work quite well in online settings. Here is an abbreviated version of a typical Delphi approach (Clayton, 1997).

1. *Decide on who should participate.* Ordinarily a Delphi approach recruits experts who can offer the most thoughtful insights about an issue.
2. *Develop a statement of the problem or issue along with questions or a survey.* This material is distributed to the selected participants. Set limits on the type and amount of responses you want. Make absolutely clear what kind of input the respondents should offer. Otherwise you will drown in an ocean of data.
3. *Each participant responds individually.* Responses can be gathered in a variety of formats: written, e-mailed, or video. Electronic exchange of information definitely is quickest. Keep a reliable record of each participant's input in case questions of accuracy arise.
4. *Collect the responses* and assemble them into a report that summarizes all the relevant input.
5. *Distribute the report* to all participants, asking them to offer comments, responses, or suggestions on a certain number of points. (This process works best when your report has a concise list of points and you specify how many points each participant should discuss.) The participants select the most important points and send their feedback.

The process continues until the participants agree that only the best ideas have been included in the report. The report-feedback-revise cycle continues as many times as necessary for participants to endorse the final product.

The Delphi method has several advantages. Since the participants can be anywhere, it eliminates the need to arrange meetings. Since a large number of people can participate, the Delphi approach can include a wide range of input. With each member working independently, the chance of groupthink reduces dramatically and no one automatically dominates the discussion (Garavalia & Gredler, 2004). The technique offers an excellent way to approach very controversial issues when personal interaction might mire a group in bitter conflicts. Aside from offering an independent format for group work, the Delphi technique could enhance a traditional group's efforts. If a group needs a variety of input about complex issues, the Delphi technique could generate important information that the group could use.

The Delphi technique also has limitations. The biggest challenge for such groups is time. The process relies on coordinated responses from participants, and participants may drop out as the report-feedback-revise cycles increase. Time lags in getting responses can stall a Delphi process. Another issue for Delphi groups is whether participants will remain satisfied with the proportion of their ideas that make their way into the final report. Finally, the Delphi method requires some clear-cut standard for when a final decision is reached. The larger the number of participants, the less likely a Delphi approach will achieve consensus. Must all participants agree with everything in the final report? If not, how much agreement by how many participants will signify closure? Some critics note that the Delphi technique does not offer the most effective way to reach consensus or render definite decisions (Goodman, 1987).

Online Group Tools

Now that we have considered two decision-making techniques that you might consider, we explore two types of online tools that might assist greatly with group work. Online **discussion boards,** often called **threaded discussions,** allow members to post contributions by topic (also known as a "thread")—so any member can follow the group's progress by checking what everyone has said about particular issues. By tracing the thread of discussion (the development of ideas about a topic), members can quickly determine where things stand. To maximize the effectiveness of discussion boards, clearly label the topic of your post and make sure you post responses under the correct topic area. If not, important contributions could get lost because they aren't where group members expect to find them.

Online discussion boards have benefits and drawbacks. Since members can post when they choose, discussion boards provide an **asynchronous** tool: The participants can post at different times. This asynchronous quality can have huge benefits. I have taught online courses where group members are separated by thousands of miles and time zones that span several hours. Without asynchronous discussion, it would have been impossible for all members to gather online simultaneously. Online discussion also overcomes special barriers, since a group member can participate from any location that provides online access. Discussion boards also make the group's work transparent. A social loafer becomes readily apparent by the lack of posts. Everyone can view the work that each member contributes to the collective effort.

The main drawback of discussion boards is that since they are asynchronous, long gaps might separate posts. This "login lag" can frustrate groups, especially when they need to make decisions or process information quickly (Schwartzman, 2006). Unless members check the discussion board diligently, some posts may not get a prompt reply. To prevent login lag, end important posts with a timeline for response. Then follow up your important posts with an e-mail or text message to group members, notifying them that you have added new material to the discussion board.

Tech Talk

What has been your experience with online discussion boards and chat rooms? What factors contributed to these tools working well or breaking down as ways for groups to interact? What hints would you offer to make online group interaction successful?

Online chats provide another method of group interaction by allowing members to converse from various locations at the same time. Whether text, audio, or video, online chats overcome physical impediments to meetings. For example, one of my online students had mobility limitations that prevented her from making regular trips to campus. Her regular interactions with the group through chats allowed her to contribute as much as any member, and the group conducted its business entirely through these virtual meetings.

Chats offer several advantages but also have limitations. In addition to overcoming physical challenges, chats can get things done quickly. A small number of group members, such as a subcommittee, can interact and overcome a sticking point without having to go through the hassle of finding a place for the entire group to meet. You also could explore the possibility of inviting your instructor to one or more group chats to provide the group with another source of input.

Chats, however, do not magically solve everything for groups. Because participants must be online at the same time, chats can work only when participants have similar schedules. Another limitation of chats is that the format of instant response puts participants in "instant message mode," offering very brief, telegraphic comments. Each written posting in a chat usually is only a few lines long; the medium is not friendly to detailed discussions. Chats also are tough for members to navigate after the fact. Unlike threaded discussions that neatly organize posts according to the categories you provide, chats get recorded as lists of dialogue. It takes a long time to scroll through pages of dialogue just to find one comment. Finally, chats become more chaotic the more participants they include. You may spend a lot of chat time scanning the chat log to rediscover who said what. Whenever you engage in a chat with several other people, identify who you are addressing

TABLE 8.5 Uses for Special Group Techniques and Tools

Nominal Group Technique	Delphi Technique	Online Discussion Board	Online Chat
• Group needs lots of ideas quickly • Group needs to bypass dominators and minimize social loafing • Group wants a way to reach decisions quickly	• Group needs to consult experts beyond immediate group • Group needs large amount of input • Group must have lots of time to get feedback and assemble reports	• Group members separated in time and space • Contents available to entire group • Often enables sharing of files	• Enables group members to meet quickly (such as getting a vote) • Group members separated in space but can meet at same time • Usually allows chats to be archived for reference

by name so everyone else knows who is talking to whom. Example: "Snoopy, I agree with your viewpoint. Lassie, the answer to your question is: not yet." Table 8.5 summarizes some ways you can use the techniques and tools discussed in this section.

HIGHLIGHTS

1. Leadership describes a set of functions that can guide a group. Leadership is not a unique property limited only to certain people.
2. Leaders exercise influence by acquiring and using power, which can come from fear, position, knowledge, perceived rewards, or reputation.
3. The three basic leadership styles are authoritarian, democratic, and laissez-faire. Leaders need to remain flexible in matching leadership styles to the group's needs.
4. Leadership includes task-oriented and socially oriented dimensions.
5. Effective group interaction depends on maintaining a balance among the various roles members can assume.

   a. Task roles contribute to the group's accomplishing its productivity goals.
   b. Social roles contribute to the group's building pleasant relationships and high morale.
   c. Self-serving roles undermine the group's efforts by engaging in behaviors that serve the individual instead of the group.

6. Groups develop in stages.

   a. Forming establishes the orientation period for a group to consider itself a unit.
   b. The storming stage is marked by internal conflicts, tensions, and oppositions.
   c. Norming establishes procedures and guidelines that set a group's interaction and work patterns.
   d. Performing is the stage when members converge to collaborate on meeting the group's goals and achieve shared outcomes.
   e. In de-forming (adjourning), the group dissolves but may remain open to regrouping.

7. Social loafing, the tendency for individuals to exert less effort when they serve in a group, requires the group to involve each member fully.
8. Group polarization describes the tendency for people to move toward extreme opinions or actions (more risky or more cautious) when in groups.
9. Becoming a responsible group member requires earning and showing trust, meeting ethical commitments to the group, and embracing differences among group members.
10. Effective group meetings require all group members to plan carefully, practice courteous communication, and fulfill their responsibilities in contributing to the group.
11. The nominal group technique helps stimulate groups to generate large numbers of ideas and render decisions efficiently.

12. The Delphi technique enlists experts who offer insight on a topic and enables group members to collaborate regardless of physical location.
13. Online group tools such as threaded discussions and chats can minimize spatial or scheduling problems that could prevent effective meetings.

APPLY YOUR KNOWLEDGE

SL = Activities appropriate for service learning

⌨ = Computer activities focusing on research and information management

🎬 = Activities involving film or television

♫ = Activities involving music

1. Attend a meeting of a campus or community organization. Identify specific examples of task, social, and self-serving roles played by participants in the meeting. What impact did each role have on the group's communication? What roles were needed but were under-represented?

2. 🎬 Watch one of the following movies and note how the group portrayed in the film develops over time. What is responsible for the group developing the way that it does (either for the better or for the worse)? Pay particular attention to the group communication concepts listed alongside each film.

   a. *Twelve Angry Men* (1957): groupthink
   b. *The Breakfast Club* (1985): movement from storming to norming and performing
   c. *Lord of the Flies* (1990): group polarization
   d. *Apollo 13* (1995): fulfilling ethical commitments to the group

3. Observe someone who holds a leadership position in your community or at your school. After observing how that person leads, ask some other members within the same organization to describe this person as a leader. Based on your observations and the input of others, what kinds of power does this leader exercise and when? Which style (or styles) of leadership do you believe this person exhibits and why is this effective?
   SL Alternative: Perform the same exercise, but observe people serving in leadership roles for your community partner. (Remember: The designated "head" of an organization is not the only leader.)

4. ⌨ Identify a public figure you admire as a leader. Research the biography of this person as well as what other people say about this person's leadership skills. If this person were conducting a training seminar for future leaders, what advice would she or he offer? How does this advice connect to the content of this chapter?

5. Many communication researchers find the family a rich environment for observing communication in action. Families enact complex and significant group dynamics. Carefully consider the relationships among your family members.

   a. If you had to cast each family member (including yourself) in one or more of the group roles described in this chapter, who would occupy the roles and why? Justify your "casting" by explaining the behaviors each family member performs that qualifies for the roles.

b. What norms has your family developed? How have these norms changed over time? How do they vary according to the family members involved? What functions do the various norms serve within the family dynamic?

REFERENCES

Andersen, J. A. (2006). Leadership, personality and effectiveness. *Journal of Socio-Economics, 35,* 1078–1091.

Asmus, C. L., & James, K. (2005). Nominal group technique, social loafing, and group creative project quality. *Creativity Research Journal, 17,* 349–354.

Bach, G. R., & Deutsch, R. M. (1971). *Pairing.* New York: Avon.

Bacon, D. R. (2005). The effect of group projects on content-related learning. *Journal of Management Education, 29,* 248–267.

Bales, R. (1950). *Interaction process analysis: A method for the study of small groups.* Reading, MA: Addison-Wesley.

Bales, R. (1958). Task roles and social roles in problem-solving groups. In E. E. Maccoby, T. M. Newcomb, & E. L. Hartley (Eds.). *Readings in social psychology* (3rd ed.; pp. 437–447). New York: Holt.

Bass, B. M., & Bass, R. (2008). *The Bass handbook of leadership: Theory, research, and managerial applications* (4th ed.). New York: Free Press.

Bass, B. M., & Riggio, R. E. (2006). *Transformational leadership* (2nd ed.). Mahwah, NJ: Lawrence Erlbaum Associates.

Benne, K. D., & Sheats, P. (1948). Functional roles of group members. *Journal of Social Issues, 4,* 41–49.

Bonebright, D. A. (2010). 40 years of storming: A historical review of Tuckman's model of small group development. *Human Resource Development International, 13*(1), 111–120.

Castiglioni, A., Shewchuk, R., Willett, L., Heudebert, G., & Centor, R. (2008). A pilot study using nominal group technique to assess residents' perceptions of successful attending rounds. *Journal of General Internal Medicine, 23*(7), 1060–1065.

Chee, L., Ying-Mei, T., Lung Hung, C., & Ying Hwa, K. (2007). The influence of paternalistic leadership on athlete burnout. *Journal of Sport and Exercise Psychology, 29,* 183.

Chemers, M. M. (1997). *An integrative theory of leadership.* Mahwah, NJ: Lawrence Erlbaum Associates.

Clayton, M. (1997). Delphi: A technique to harness expert opinion for critical decision-making tasks in education. *Educational Psychology, 17*(4), 373–386.

Cragan, J. F., Kasch, C. R., & Wright, D. W. (2009). *Communication in small groups: Theory, process, skills* (7th ed.). Boston: Wadsworth Cengage Learning.

Doyle, M., & Straus, D. (1982). *How to make meetings work.* New York: Jove.

Egan, T. M. (2005). Creativity in the context of team diversity: Team leader perspectives. *Advances in Developing Human Resources, 7,* 207–225.

El-Shinnawy, M., & Vinze, A. S. (1998). Polarization and persuasive argumentation: A study of decision making in group settings. *MIS Quarterly, 22,* 165–198.

Erchul, W. P., & Raven, B. H. (1997). School power in school consultation: A contemporary view of French and Raven's bases of power model. *Journal of School Psychology, 35,* 137–171.

French, J. R. E, Jr., & Raven, B. H. (1959). The bases of social power. In D. Cartwright (Ed.), *Studies in social power* (pp. 150–167). Ann Arbor, MI: Institute for Social Research.

Friedman, R. A., & Podolny, J. M. (1992). Differentiation of boundary spanning roles: Labor negotiations and implications for role conflict. *Administrative Science Quarterly, 37,* 28–47.

Garavalia, L., & Gredler, M. (2004). Teaching evaluation through modeling: Using the Delphi tech-nique to assess problems in academic programs.*American Journal of Evaluation, 25*(3), 375–381.

Giri, V., & Santra, T. (2010). Effects of job experience, career stage, and hierarchy on leadership style. *Singapore Management Review, 32*(1), 85–93.

Goleman, D., Boyatzis, R., & McKee, A. (2002). *Primal leadership: Learning to lead with emotional intelligence.* Boston: Harvard Business School Press.

Goodman, C. M. (1987). The Delphi technique: A critique. *Journal of Advanced Nursing, 12,* 729–734.

Griffin, D. (2006, 23 February). Olympic "teams" are a joke. *The Stanford Daily.* Retrieved May 2, 2007, from http://daily.stanford.edu/article/2006/2/23/olympicTeamsAreJoke

Hackman, M. Z., & Johnson, M. E. (2009). *Leadership: A communication perspective* (5th ed.). Long Grove, IL: Waveland.

Hare, A. P. (2003). Roles, relationships, and groups in organizations: Some conclusions and recommendations. *Small Group Research, 34,* 123–154.

Hart, J. W., Karau, S. J., Stasson, M. K., & Kerr, N. A. (2004). Achievement motivation, expected coworker performance, and collective task motivation: Working hard or hardly working? *Journal of Applied Social Psychology, 34,* 984–1000.

Hoyt, G. C., & Stoner, J. A. (1968). Leadership and group decisions involving risk. *Journal of Experimental Social Psychology, 4,* 275–284.

Johnson, S. E., & Long, L. M. (2002). "Being a part and being apart": Dialectics and group communication. In L. R. Frey (Ed.), *New directions in group communication* (pp. 25-42). Thousand Oaks, CA: Sage.

Karau, S. J., & Williams, K. D. (1995). Social loafing: Research findings, implications, and future directions. *Current Directions in Psychological Science, 4,* 134–140.

Kausen, R. C. (2003). *We've got to start meeting like this: How to get better results with fewer meetings.* Trinity Center, CA: Life Education.

Kirkpatrick, D. L. (2006). *How to conduct productive meetings.* Alexandria, VA: ASTD Press.

Kravitz, D. A., & Martin, B. (1986). Ringelmann rediscovered: The original article. *Journal of Personality and Social Psychology, 50,* 936–941.

Levine, J. M., & Moreland, R. L. (1990). Progress in small group research. *Annual Review of Psychology, 41,* 585–634.

Lewin, K. (1944). A research approach to leadership problems. *Journal of Educational Sociology, 17,* 392–98.

Lewin, K., Lippitt, R., & White, R. K. (1939). Patterns of aggressive behavior in experimentally created "social climates." *Journal of Social Psychology, 10,* 271–299.

Liden, R. C., Wayne, S. J., Jaworski, R. A., & Bennett, N. (2004). Social loafing: A field investigation. *Journal of Management, 30,* 285–304.

Likert, R., & Likert, J. G. (1976). *New ways of managing conflict.* New York: McGraw-Hill.

Maples, M. (1988). Group development: Extending Tuckman's theory. *Journal for Specialists in Group Work, 13*(1), 17–23.

McMorris, L., Gottlieb, N., & Sneden, G. (2005). Developmental stages in public health partnerships: A practical perspective. *Health Promotion Practice, 6*(2), 219–226.

Minow, M. (2006). What the rule of law should mean in civics education: From the "following orders" defence to the classroom. *Journal of Moral Education, 35*(2), 137–162.

Moscovici, S., & Zavalloni, M. (1969). The group as a polarizer of attitudes. *Journal of Personality and Social Psychology, 12,* 125–135.

Mosvick, R. K., & Nelson, R. B. (1996). *We've got to start meeting like this: A guide to successful meeting management* (Rev. ed.). Indianapolis, IN: Park Avenue Productions.

Mudrack, P. E., & Farrell, G. M. (1995). An examination of functional role behavior and its consequences for individuals in group settings. *Small Group Research, 26,* 542–570.

Myers, D. G., & Bishop, G. D. (1970, August 21) Discussion effects on racial attitudes. *Science, 169*(3947), 778–779.

Myers, S. A., & Anderson, C. M. (2008). *The fundamentals of small group communication.* Thousand Oaks, CA: Sage.

National Communication Association. (1999). *Credo for ethical communication.* Retrieved March 11,2010, from http://www.natcom.org/nca/index.asp?bid= 514Template2.asp?bid=514NCA

Northouse, P. G. (2010). *Leadership: Theory and practice* (5th ed.). Thousand Oaks, CA: Sage.

Oetzel, J.G. (2002). Explaining individual communica-tion processes in homogenous and heterogen-eous groups through individualism-collectivism and self construal. *Human Communication Research, 25,* 202–224.

Oetzel, J. G., Burtis, T. E., Chew Sanchez, M. I., & Pérez, F. G. (2001). Investigating the role of communication in culturally diverse work groups: A review and synthesis. In W. B. Gudykunst (Ed.), *Communication yearbook 25* (pp. 237–270). Mahwah, NJ: Lawrence Erlbaum Associates.

Poole, M. S. (1999). Group communication theory. In L. R. Frey, D. S. Gouran, & M. S. Poole (Eds.), *The handbook of group communication theory and research* (pp. 37-50). Thousand Oaks, CA: Sage.

Raven, B. H. (1992). A power/interaction model of interpersonal influence: French and Raven thirty years later. *Journal of Social Behavior and Personality, 7,* 217–244.

Rees, W. D., & Porter, C. (2008). *Skills of management* (6th ed.). London: Cengage Learning.

Sarre, G., & Cooke, J. (2009). Developing indicators for measuring research capacity development in primary care organizations: A consensus approach using a nominal group technique. *Health & Social Care in the Community, 17*(3), 244–253.

Schwartzman, R. (2006). Virtual group problem solving in the basic communication course: Lessons for online learning. *Journal of Instructional Psychology, 33,* 3–14.

Shaw, M. E. (1976). *Group dynamics: The psychology of small group behavior.* New York: McGraw-Hill.

Stech, E. L. (1983). *Leadership communication.* Chicago: Nelson-Hall.

Streibel, B. J. (2003). *The manager's guide to effective meetings.* New York: McGraw-Hill.

Tannenbaum, R., & Schmidt, H. S. (1957, March-April). How to choose a leadership pattern. *Harvard Business Review, 36,* 95–101.

Thompson, L., & Ku, H.-Y. (2006). A case study of online collaborative learning. *Quarterly Review of Distance Education, 7,* 361–375.

Tuckman, B. (1965). Developmental sequence in small groups. *Psychological Bulletin, 63,* 384–399.

Tuckman, B., & Jensen, M. (1977). Stages of small-group development revisited. *Group and Organization Studies, 2*(4), 419–427.

Tuffrey-Wijne, I. I. , Bernal, J., Butler, G., Hollins, S., & Curfs, L. (2007). Using nominal group technique to investigate the views of people with intellectual disabilities on end-of-life care provision. *Journal of Advanced Nursing, 58,* 80–89.

Turner, R. H. (2001). Role theory. In J. H. Turner (Ed.), *Handbook of sociological theory* (pp. 233–254). New York: Kluwer Academic/Plenum.

White, R., & Lippitt, R. (1968). Leader behavior and member reaction in three "social climates." In D. Cartwright & A. Zander (Eds.), *Group dynamics* (pp. 318-335). New York: Harper & Row.

Williams, K. D., & Karau, S. J. (1991). Social loafing and social comparison: The effects of expectations of co-worker performance. *Journal of Personality and Social Psychology, 61,* 570–581.

Woods, P. A. (2005). *Democratic leadership in education.* London: Paul Chapman.

CULTURE AND COMMUNICATION

We live in a global society. Even in quiet little Ashland, Ohio, a famous local company, Archway Cookies, is now owned by a French corporation. International students and faculty teach and study at Ashland University.

The current student body has traveled more, experienced more, and interacted with more groups of people than any previous generation. The words **culture** and **diversity** frighten some older Americans because they imply change. A culture is a living organism. If elements within the culture change, the culture must change as well. In other words, the changes we have seen in technology, politics, economics, gender roles, music, and so on have all contributed to changes in our cultures. The speed of change must occur to accommodate human adaptation.

Young people have adapted to technology more quickly than their elders, but the challenge to adapt is ongoing. As soon as you become comfortable with the world as you know it, you fall behind. For example, the Kodak Company made the best film in the world. More Pulitzer Prize–winning photographers used Kodak film than any other brand. Unfortunately, the Kodak Company was either unaware or unprepared for the advance of digital photography. Have you been to the Walmart in Ashland lately? Most of the signs in the store are printed in English and Spanish. The fastest-growing segment of the American population are people of Hispanic heritage. Businesses that are unprepared for this growing market will suffer the consequences.

The language of a people must also adapt to cultural changes. The term digital photography is an example of a concept that did not exist a generation ago. But once it became a reality, we had to create a name for it. One of the reasons languages die out is because they cannot adapt. A short while ago, I read a newspaper story about Yiddish scholars who were trying to create terms for modern products like hip-hugger jeans and skateboards. This may sound trivial, but if a language cannot adapt to modern culture it is doomed to the realm of dead languages, like Latin.

The one constant in the human experience is change. Our cultures and languages must reflect that reality.

CULTURE AND COMMUNICATION

Culture. You have probably heard this word used in a lot of different contexts and in a lot of different ways. We encounter the word "culture" on the news, in classes, in conversations, in newspapers, magazines, and books, on the radio, etc. In short, it seems like this society is deeply concerned with issues of culture. But what is culture? This chapter will explore this concept and its relationship to the study of human communication. Before diving into a definition of culture, we'll first discuss some of the reasons why it is important to study culture. A discussion of what comprises culture will follow along with some ways that we can see and hear culture in our own lives. We'll also discuss what intercultural communication is and some of the experiences you are likely to have if you choose to encounter different cultural systems. This chapter will conclude with a discussion of some of the things that we should be aware of when confronted by cultures that are different from our own.

REASONS TO STUDY CULTURE

The world, as you probably know, is filled with all sorts of different people. It probably comes as little surprise that humans differ in the way they approach the world. People speak different languages, eat different foods, worship differently, and basically lead vastly different lives. All of this difference can be summed up in the term diversity. The fact that the world is diverse is enough for many people to take an interest, but that fact alone is not the only reason we should be interested in the world around us.

Consider how the world has changed in your lifetime alone. There have been enormous advances in both communication and transportation technologies (Martin and Nakayama, 2004). Many of you probably couldn't picture your life without use of the Internet or a cell phone of some sort, even though these technologies are quite new. With the increased access given to us through these technologies, we now live in a world where we can communicate with people from different parts of the world and different cultures instantly. One example that comes to mind is the relationships that I maintain with colleagues and friends in Finland, France, Japan, and the Canadian Arctic. All of this is done now via e-mail. Likewise, our ability to travel to other places within the space of days or hours is a relatively recent phenomenon. Did you know that it was only in 1959 when jet service was introduced into the aviation industry making flying much more accessible to large numbers of people (Petzinger, 1995)? Because of these advances in technology, we often hear that the world is getting "smaller." One effect of this is that

people from vastly different cultures now find it easier than ever before to interact with one another. Studying intercultural communication will help us in these interactions.

Although our ability to access diverse places in the world has increased dramatically, this is not the only reason to be concerned with issues of culture. You do not even need to leave your place of residence to encounter other people who are culturally different. In fact, just by being in this class and a student at this university, you are confronted with cultural difference on a weekly if not daily basis. Here in the U.S., we live in a culturally diverse society. As you are well aware, every ten years the U.S. government takes a census. This is done for a number of reasons including the apportionment of congressional seats as well as being valuable data to determine how federal dollars should be spent. One of the things the government measures is diversity of ethnic and racial groups. According to the 2000 U.S. census, diversity increased in every single state in the United States (U.S. Census Bureau, 2006).

Intercultural scholars Judith Martin and Thomas Nakayama (2004) write that there are at least six different reasons why we should study intercultural communication. They call these reasons imperatives suggesting that we should not just be concerned with intercultural communication, but that it is necessary. Aside from the technological and changing demographic imperative discussed above, they also discuss an economic imperative, a peace imperative, a self-awareness imperative, and an ethical imperative. The economies of different nations are becoming increasingly interdependent with one another (a phenomenon known as globalization) which leads to potentially increased contact. Without an understanding of different cultural systems, this contact can potentially lead to global conflicts. Thus, the economic and peace imperatives are increasingly important. The self-awareness imperative suggests that studying intercultural communication can also be rewarding in the sense that we can grow in our understandings of ourselves. Personally, I have realized much about myself after traveling abroad and believe that these experiences have greatly enriched my life. Finally, the ethical imperative teaches us that through a careful study of intercultural communication we will be better able to resolve the inevitable ethical conflicts that arise whenever humans interact. Martin and Nakayama list these six imperatives as reasons for studying intercultural communication; however, there are other reasons as well. Hall (2005) argues that through the study of intercultural communication one is more likely to develop rewarding and fulfilling relationships. There are likely as many reasons for studying intercultural communication as there are those who study it. I invite you to consider the ways that understanding different cultures can enrich your life. The remainder of this chapter will provide some background information that will help as you begin this journey.

DEFINING CULTURE

As mentioned above, our society seems to use the term "culture" a lot. This leads us to ask what culture actually is. You may be surprised to learn that there are many different definitions of culture. In 1952, anthropologists Kroeber and Kluckohn attempted to catalogue all the different definitions of culture in order to provide some clarity of the concept. They cited 150 different definitions. One would assume that a work of this scope would be sufficient for moving us forward. This assumption, however, is incorrect. Scholars from numerous disciplines continue to this day to debate the concept. In 2006, for example, Baldwin, Faulkner, Hecht, and Lindsley published an edited text that tries yet again to provide some clarity on the concept of culture. Each definition of culture has its strengths and weaknesses. Some definitions highlight certain aspects, while hiding from view other aspects. Because of this, the definition of culture that we will use is one that is firmly grounded in communication. Bradford Hall (2005), defines culture as a "historically shared system of symbolic resources through which we make our world meaningful" (pg. 4). A more detailed definition, and the one that we will operate with throughout the remainder of this chapter is that culture is a complex system of symbolic resources, worldviews, values, and norms of appropriate enactment. This is a complex definition, but one which allows us the best opportunity to explore the richness of culture. In order to better understand this definition, I'll discuss the different aspects.

Symbols

Symbolic resources represent the "stuff" of culture in this discursive perspective (Carbaugh, 1990; Geertz, 1973; Hall, 2005; Hymes, 1972; Morgan, 2002; Philipsen, 1992). They are what people use to make sense of the world. In order to understand symbolic resources, we first should understand what symbols are. Symbols, very simply, are anything that stands for something else (Hall, 2005). Flags are good examples. A flag is normally a piece of cloth with a design of some sort on it. This cloth, however, represents something. Sometimes, they represent nations, sometimes states or provinces, sometimes cities, sometimes organizations, and sometimes military units. The point is that the cloth represents something else. The flag is a symbolic sign that something else is being represented. Words are also symbols. Whenever we use a word to refer to something, that word is symbolically representing something else. More specifically, the word is representing a thought or idea. In this way, symbols are meaningful. In fact, symbols are "infinitely rich in significance" (Colapietro, 1993, pg. 191).

This brings us to two important characteristics of symbols; arbitrariness and conventionality (Hall, 2005). A commonly heard description of symbols is that they are arbitrary in their meanings. This means that there is not really any natural reason why a symbol needs to represent what it does. For example, there is no real reason why the particular design of the U.S. flag has to represent the nation-state of the United States of America. Rather, people throughout the world have generally agreed that it does. A good way to demonstrate the arbitrariness of symbols is to look at different languages. The Merriam-Webster On-line Dictionary (2006) defines a table as a "piece of furniture consisting of a smooth flat slab fixed on legs." In Spanish, this same piece of furniture is labeled "mesa." Neither label is more correct than the other. In fact, there is nothing about the words themselves that must mean a slab fixed on legs. Rather, people who speak these languages generally agree that they do. This notion of general agreement is referred to as conventionality. Conventionality simply means that a relatively large group of people agree that a certain symbol will refer to a thought concept. Often times, these concepts are real objects in the world, but not always. For instance, because we have these symbols, we are able to refer to more abstract entities like freedom, liberty, or spirit. Because symbols are conventional, they tend to be relatively stable within groups. You can't just go about making up new symbols for things in the world and have anyone understand you.

Symbolic Resources

A resource is anything that people use. One example of a *natural* resource is water. People throughout the world need to use water in order to survive. Because of this, people have created societal institutions to ensure the availability of water and its distribution. Another example of a resource is oil. Oil is used to create energy to power vehicles, heat homes in many parts of the world, create plastic, among many other things. Because of its many uses, oil is highly valued as a resource. Perhaps a more important resource, however, are symbolic resources. People use symbols to refer to objects, to express emotions, to create and maintain groups, and generally to make the world around us meaningful. Without symbols, we could not coordinate our actions to use any other type of resource, like oil. In other words, we have to be able to refer to oil, and generally share the same conception of what it is if we want to be able to drill for it, refine it, transport it to your local gas station, and pump the gas into your vehicle.

Differences in the systems of symbolic resources lead to differences in cultural groups. Different people use different symbols to do different things. For example, in spoken American English, it is common to hear "Hey, what's up?" as a greeting. Speakers of this language know that this question is not really a request to inform the speaker of what is above her or him, rather, they understand that it is a greeting. Often times, speakers of different languages in the U.S. for the first time become confused by the use of this symbolic resource. These international visitors might mistake the greeting for an actual question, thus causing some confusion. In this case, there is simply a difference in understanding how these symbolic resources are to be used. The same American who says "what's up?" may be confused if confronted with the Korean phrase, "odi-ga-seyo." Literally, translated, this means, "where are you going?" It functions the same way as saying "How are you?" or "What's going on?" in English (Hall, 2005). The expectation is not that the person being asked tell the speaker where she or he is going, but rather to engage in a greeting.

Historically Shared

Now that we know a bit about symbols and how they are used as resources, we can discuss how it is that these symbols are transmitted across time. To say that culture is historically shared is to say that the systems of symbolic resources and the meanings they represent will be passed on from generation to generation. How is it that we share culture? One way that culture is shared is through families. As children grow up, they are taught the system that allows them to appropriately communicate. This includes learning the language as well as the rules for appropriate use of language and the rules for understanding what certain symbolic resources mean. Many children learn this from their parents and other extended family members. I'm fortunate to have two nieces and two nephews. They range in age from five to twelve years old. Over the past seven years I have watched and engaged in the instruction of appropriate language and communication use for my nieces and nephews. I'm always fascinated by how quickly they learn words. This learning process, at least for the variety of English that my family members and I are teaching, consists of pointing out objects in certain contexts and then saying the word. In doing so, we are teaching the children the meaning of certain symbolic resources.

Another source of cultural learning is from our peers. In the United States, many children are exposed to schooling at increasingly young ages. Throughout our educational lives, we learn from others in similar positions. For example, you may have learned how to play schoolyard games from your friends at school. You also learn how to appropriately (and sometimes inappropriately) act with others of a similar age. Our peer groups exert enormous pressure on us to conform to particular ways of being and acting. Everything from how to talk, to how to dress, to the music we listen to, and the activities we engage in is influenced by our peers.

Yet another source of cultural learning is from other societal members who may not be peers. An example is perhaps the best way to explain this concept. I grew up in the southwestern United States. When I was in my mid-20's I moved to New England. I had been to big cities before, but I had never had to navigate one on a daily basis until I moved there. One of the things I learned was how to ride the subway system in Boston. I learned this by watching others. From observing, I knew that I had to purchase a token, quickly move through the turnstile, and wait patiently for a train. While on the train, I learned the rules for where and how to sit and even how to look at people. Not looking at people seemed to be a crucial aspect of appropriately riding the subway, especially when it was crowded. No one ever explicitly told me these rules. Rather, I learned them from the members of society who were more experienced at riding the subway.

An important source of cultural knowledge is the media. The influence of the media on people's behavior is a well researched topic. Perhaps the most comprehensive program of study is the work done by George Gerbner and his colleagues (see Morgan and Shanahan, 1996 for a comprehensive review). This program of study is broadly known as the cultural indicators project. Scholars in this tradition work hard to determine the effects that media, particularly television, has on people. One theory that these scholars have developed is cultivation analysis. The basic argument of this theory is that the media cultivates particular attitudes, which lead to a shared way of perceiving the world (Littlejohn and Foss, 2005). For instance, they have found that heavy viewers of television tend to see the world as a more violent and gloomy place. This is known as the "mean world syndrome" (Signorelli, 1990). The point here is that the media provide us with an understanding of the cultural worlds in which we live. I recently watched a season of the popular television show *Friends* on DVD. I was struck by the types of messages that were communicated through this sitcom. While I enjoyed the humor, I also realized that powerful cultural messages about relating to one another, what counts as humorous, and how life "in the big city" went were being portrayed. Try watching your favorite television program while thinking about the cultural messages that are being communicated. You may be surprised at the types of understandings you have because of this.

THE COMMUNICATION OF CULTURE

The previous section discusses some of the sources of cultural knowledge and learning. Even if you travel to a different country as an adult, you will likely turn to peers, other societal members, the media, and sometimes family for cultural understanding. This section discusses how culture is communicated to us more specifically through narratives and rituals.

Like Hall (2005), I believe that culture is transmitted primarily through the stories that people tell each other. These stories are referred to as narratives. A narrative, according to Hall (2005), is a retelling of events from a specific point of view. We tell narratives to one another all the time. As children, we are often told narratives that are important to our families. Perhaps it was the story of how your family came to live where they do, or perhaps it was a story about your crazy uncle who got into trouble. Regardless, these narratives teach us about culture. If you've ever asked a friend to tell you how his or her weekend was, you've just asked for a narrative. We also learn culture through broad narratives that many people share. Stories like fairy tales and legends communicate important cultural messages. In short, narratives are an important aspect of our daily communicative lives. They are particularly important because they function to do at least four things.

Hall (2005) argues that there are four functions of narrative. The first function of narrative is that they provide us with information about our place in the world relative to society and other people. In this way, narratives help us shape our identities. Second, narratives tell about how the world works in both general terms and in particular contexts. Third, narratives tell us how to act in the world. Finally, narratives tell us how to evaluate the world around us in terms of good and bad, right and wrong.

Throughout my childhood, I was told the story of how my mother's side of the family came to live in New Mexico. My grandfather was one of 11 children who grew up in Alabama on a farm. When he was 14, my great-grandparents lost the farm and ended up traveling to Arkansas. At a very young age, my grandfather struck out on his own trying to find work as a farm laborer. His situation was made all the more difficult because of the Great Depression. Anyway, he met and married my grandmother in Arkansas and they sought to make a living in California. By this time, World War II had broken out, and there was word that work could be had for ship laborers in San Francisco. They journeyed to the San Francisco Bay Area and my grandfather worked in the ship yards. He was too old to join the military by this time, but he was still in need of a job. After the war, one of his brothers was hired on as a miner in Carlsbad, NM. My grandfather packed up the family and moved to Carlsbad in hopes of finding work. They arrived, but due to an injury sustained in the shipyards, my grandfather was unable to work the mines. He was a carpenter by trade, so he sought work in this area. It soon became clear that more opportunity existed for a carpenter just north in the town of Artesia. So the family moved to Artesia where my grandfather worked as a carpenter for many years.

What types of lessons might I learn from this story? Well first, it tells me about who my family is and by extension who I am and where I fit in society. The family was not wealthy which meant that they had to travel in order to find work to survive (place in the world). Second, the narrative teaches me that the world, at least at that time, required people to sacrifice for the war effort and labor in any way they could. I also learned that finding work could be difficult (how the world works). Third, the story teaches me to work hard and eventually life will become more comfortable (how to act in the world). Finally, the story teaches me that working hard and continually striving to be better is a good thing. I could relate any number of stories by way of example, but I believe it would be more beneficial if you were to do this yourself. At the end of this chapter, you will find an exercise that asks you to analyze an important narrative from your own life. I hope you find it enlightening.

Rituals

Culture is performed constantly. Every action we perform is influenced in some way by culture. Oftentimes these actions are structured and performed repeatedly. When this occurs, we are dealing with rituals. A ritual, according to Hall (2005) is a sequence of events that functions to "celebrate" an important cultural value or aspect. Rituals are important to understand because they remind us what our cultural systems value. Charles Frake (1990) writes about an interesting ritual that he analyzed when he worked with the Subanun in Zambrano Province in the Philippines. He recounts that the structure of drinking is an important ritual that allows the group to resolve disputes and reaffirm their sense of community. The drinking ritual occurs when a status superior invites others to partake in the drinking of gasi. *Gasi* is a rice fermented beverage that is drunk from a jar with a straw. Apparently, according to Frake, the liquid packs quite a punch if one drinks a lot of it. Anyway, after the invitation to drink occurs, there will be a series of rounds in which people drink from the same jar one after the other. Over the course of the drinking ritual, there is a structured way of communicating. First, the invitation is provided and permission is granted to drink. During the initial rounds, the people involved engage in small talk. In later rounds, group disputes are brought up, discussed and eventually resolved. Finally, the drinking ritual concludes with a number of competitions. Frake notes that this is a general order, although each of these elements will be present in all drinking rituals. This is far different than the "drinking" rituals found on college campuses throughout the U.S., as you might imagine.

Another good example of ritual comes to us from Tamar Katriel (1990) who writes about "griping" among some Israelis. According to Katriel, groups of Israelis will gather on Friday evenings and discuss the Situation (note: Situation is capitalized here because it refers to the situation in which everyday Israeli citizens find themselves by virtue of living in Israel.) The discussion takes on the character of griping and is only conducted with other Israelis. If one finds him or herself with close friends, then he or she will begin griping about specific situations and move to more general situations. With acquaintances, precisely the opposite occurs. The structure of the ritual sees people engaging in turns at griping where one person will begin and everyone in the group will then take a turn at griping. What is being reinforced here is a sense of community that is unique to Israelis. As with narratives, we could go on all day about different rituals from different cultures; however, it will be more meaningful if you analyze one of your own rituals.

WORLDVIEWS, VALUES, AND NORMS

Now that we discussed some ways that culture is communicated, let's turn our attention to some other aspects of culture. Recall the definition of culture used in this class. It is an historically shared system of symbolic resources, worldviews, values, and norms for behavior. The following discussion will explain what is meant by worldviews, values, and norms. An extended example from my research in the Canadian Arctic will follow in order to illustrate how these differ cross-culturally. Studying culture, however, reminds us that people's assumptions about the world can be wildly different.

Worldviews

A worldview is a deeply felt assumption or basic premise about the way the world is. People differ in their orientations to the world at fundamental levels. Where some people will orient to the world as perhaps an evil place, others, may orient to the world as a fundamentally good place. This diversity is often hard to grasp, because we tend never to question our assumptions about the world. The world simply is the way it is for many people.

Investigating differences in worldviews has been the hallmark of most cultural research. Cultural researchers are interested in documenting the variation in humanity's take on the world. Hall (2005), for instance, argues that there are at least eight different worldview dimensions which can be used to analyze the diversity of cultural groups. Each of these worldview dimensions describes the answer to some fundamental question. The worldview dimensions and their questions, along with some other clarifying questions are as follows:

Individualism–Collectivism
>   *Basic Question:* Who am I?
>   *Clarifying Questions:* Am I an individual first and foremost or am I a member of a group first and foremost?

Ascription–Achievement
>   *Basic Question:* How do people gain their position in society?
>   *Clarifying Questions:* Are people given their positions in society or do they have to work for and achieve their position in society?

Egalitarian–Hierarchical
>   *Basic Question:* How is society organized?
>   *Clarifying Questions:* Is society comprised of equals or are there basic differences between types of people?

Good–Evil
>   *Basic Question:* What is the basic nature of people?
>   *Clarifying Questions:* Are people basically good or are people basically bad?

Mastery–Adaptive
>   *Basic Question:* How do people orient to the natural environment?
>   *Clarifying Questions:* Do people shape the environment to meet their needs or do people adapt to the environment and live according to its rhythms and patterns?

Information–Social Lubricant

Basic Question: What is the fundamental purpose of language?

Clarifying Questions: Is language primarily a tool for providing and sharing information or is language primarily used for facilitating relationships between people?

High Context–Low Context

Basic Question: Where does meaning lie?

Clarifying Questions: Does meaning come mostly from the context in which people find themselves or does meaning come from the explicit verbal message?

Polychronic–Monochronic

Basic Question: What is time?

Clarifying Questions: Do people see time as progressing in a linear fashion with things happening one after the other or does time flow in a more circular fashion with multiple things occurring simultaneously?

Cultural groups will normally share a general sense of the answers to these questions. The system of meaning for each cultural group organizes the answers to these fundamental questions. The result is a cultural worldview. For instance, many U.S. Americans fundamentally believe that people are individuals who should work hard to achieve their position in society. This is possible because all people are fundamentally equal. Nature is seen as something that should be mastered in order to best serve the needs of society. Language is a primary tool for exchanging information, and is, therefore, the primary way that meaning is shared. Time is normally conceived of as linear and events and tasks are normally accomplished one after the other.

Other researchers and cultural scholars argue that there are only five different basic premises which can be used to describe the enormous variation of human culture (Carbaugh, 1996; Morgan, 2002; Fitch, 1998). These scholars refer to these worldview dimensions as *cultural premises*. The five basic premises are personhood, feeling, acting, relating, and dwelling. They too refer to basic assumptions about the way the world is. Personhood refers to fundamental assumptions about what a person is. This would encompass both the individualism-collectivism dimension and the good-evil dimension discussed above. The cultural premise of feeling describes the different ways that people experience emotion. The cultural premise of acting describes the culturally viable ways that people can act in the world. Relating refers to the cultural premise of how relationships between people are accomplished. Finally, the cultural premise of dwelling describes the different ways people inhabit the earth.

Each perspective on worldview is useful for describing and understanding the diversity of humanity. People across the globe, are members of cultures that fundamentally differ in the ways these premises and dimensions are patterned. It is important to realize that because worldviews and cultural premises are assumptions, they are rarely, if ever, questioned by members of cultural groups. In fact, these assumptions form a lens through which cultural members see the world. This lens is particular to a cultural system. When confronted with a different lens, many people can sometimes feel threatened and therefore judge alternative lenses as inferior. This is a phenomenon known as *ethnocentrism*. Ethnocentrism literally means understanding one's own group as the "center" of the world. This can sometimes lead to members of cultural groups believing that their group is superior to other cultural groups. This belief in the superiority of one's own group defines prejudice and can lead to discrimination of others who operate with a different cultural lens on the world. It is impossible to escape ethnocentrism, but we can be vigilant in suspending our judgments of right and wrong, better and worse, when it comes to interacting with others from different cultures. This is particularly true when it comes to ethically interacting with others who may differ in terms of values.

Values

A value is a belief about how the world should be (Hall, 2005). Values differ from worldviews in that these are often discussed among people, sometimes debated, and held up as ideals to which people should aspire. Values arise from worldview assumptions or cultural premises. A value can sometimes be related to worldviews in seemingly contradictory ways; however, from a cultural standpoint, worldviews and values will always be consistent. Take the worldview topic of good and evil, for example. Many people believe the world is a bad place filled with bad people. Because of that, people *should* value honesty in order to make the world a better place. People within the same cultural system can disagree as to specific values; however, it is unlikely that people within the same cultural system will hold vastly different worldview assumptions about the world.

Norms

A norm is a behavior. It isn't just any behavior though, it is a typical behavior that conforms to, and therefore, reinforces values (Carbaugh, 1990). I'm sure you've noticed that people act in patterned ways. It would be an odd sight indeed to see a complete stranger come into class completely nude and start yelling. In fact, I would wager, that you have never seen this occur. This is because such a behavior would not make cultural sense. Oh, there would be culturally patterned ways that we make sense of such an act, but the behavior itself is outside the *norms* of culture. As a rule, we tend not to act in random ways or in ways that others around us wouldn't understand. This is because our behaviors are culturally grounded in notions of appropriateness. Every time we engage in a behavior, we do so in such a way that reinforces our cultural system. If a behavior does not make sense, then a lot of "work" goes into finding out how we can make sense of the behavior.

An Arctic Interlude

One way we can really start to see just how different cultures are and how certain behaviors are made sense of differently is to travel abroad. During my travels and study in Arctic Canada, I routinely acted in ways that did not make cultural sense to the people living there. This was simply because I did not know enough of the cultural system of symbolic resources, worldviews, values, and norms in order to act in a culturally appropriate way. Several incidences come to mind which highlight how these aspects of culture operate.

I had arrived in the town of Iqaluit, Nunavut, Canada, full of excitement and wonder about the place I would be living for awhile. It was my first time "north of 60" (north of 60 degrees N latitude) and I was ready to live the life of an arctic adventurer. I was planning to spend awhile in Iqaluit talking to people and researching how the establishment of the territory of Nunavut was impacting the cultural ways of life of people who lived there. During those days I made a number of friends both Inuit and non-Inuit. One evening I was sitting with some Inuit friends learning how to carve soapstone. The conversation turned to what I would be doing the next week and I casually said, "I'm going out on the land." When I said this, the gentleman who asked me the question paused in his sanding of the stone, looked at me quizzically, and muttered, "huh?. eeeeeee huh. O.k." The other folks around looked at each other and smiled. I knew I had said something that didn't quite make sense. This came as a bit of a surprise to me because I had heard a lot of people say the phrase "on the land." I assumed that the phrase was just the way to refer to camping or backpacking, which was the activity I was going to do. I had even seen the phrase in the newspaper! We went back to sanding our soapstone in silence. I was confused because I really wanted to share my excitement about my upcoming trek with these folks, but they seemed profoundly uninterested. Finally, one of the men looked up at me and said, "you have a gun?" "Nah." I replied. He shrugged his shoulders and said, "you want, you can take mine." I shrugged, and with furrowed brow, replied, "nah. I think I'm good." There were general shrugs all around.

The next day I was having lunch with another Inuk friend of mine. She asked what I was doing over the next couple of weeks. Still not knowing much, I replied with, "I'm heading out on the land." She looked at me with a startled expression and said, "huh?" I repeated that I was going "out on the land" thinking that perhaps she hadn't heard me the first time. While I was expecting the next question to be, "where are you going" I was surprised when she replied with, "uh. o.k. . . . (long pause) . . . you taking a gun?" You can imagine my surprise when she said this. I replied that I did not have a gun and that some other folks asked me the same question. She shrugged as if she expected that response and said, "you want to take mine?" This came as a total surprise, but I was trying to be nonchalant as an insider would and simply replied, "nah. I think it will be too heavy." She shook her head slightly and said that I should call immediately upon my return in a couple weeks or she would call the RCMP (Royal Canadian Mounted Police) to come find me. We finished our lunch and I wandered off confused by the entire exchange. I knew by this time that I was clearly saying something wrong, but I wasn't clear yet that it was the phrase "on the land." Things became a bit clearer a few days later.

I was sitting outside watching the sun low in the sky light up the bay and the clouds with a variety of colors. Two acquaintances were walking by and stopped to ask how I was. One didn't speak a word of English, while the other one enjoyed chatting and translating into Inuktitut. My skills with Inuktitut were not such that I could carry on much of a conversation, so I was especially happy that this person was here. Inevitably, they asked what I was going to do over the weekend. I replied that I was flying up to Qikiqtarjuaq and walking to Pangnirtung, a town 180 kilometers south. Notice that I did not say "on the land." I figured that I could ask about that phrase, but hadn't gotten around to it yet. I knew that my acquaintance who was translating was from Qikiqtarjuaq and had made that same journey a number of times in her youth. She seemed pleased and asked, "Do you have a husky dog?" This was not a question I expected. I half expected her to ask if I had a gun, but certainly not a dog. I told her that I did not have a dog (or a gun for that matter). She shrugged and said, "I have my brother . . . he's up there . . . you want . . . you can take a husky dog . . . he has some."

What do you think was going on? I asked myself this question repeatedly. While I knew that these were a friendly and hospitable people, their offers just seemed to be too generous. I found out that one reason for the offer of both guns and dogs was to protect against *nanuq*. Otherwise known as ursa maritimus or the polar bear. Going out "on the land" without a gun for protection or a dog for warning was, quite simply, crazy in the minds of my friends. A more profound explanation, however, lies in the worldviews, values, and norms that shape Inuit life. To illustrate, I will briefly contrast my cultural orientation with that of many Inuit.

I grew up in Santa Fe, New Mexico. My family lived in a small house on the south side of town. We had two cars, a grocery store down the street, and when I was about 10, a new shopping mall was built about a mile down the road. While in town, I lived like everyone else. I wouldn't think twice about getting in my car to drive a couple blocks to buy a candy bar. I never thought twice about the effort it took to keep lights on or to provide heat in the winter. In short, my life was one that had all the modern conveniences associated with life in a developed nation. Growing up, my father would take me fishing or camping on weekends to the mountains around Santa Fe. It was here that I learned to love wilderness. I cherished my time in the mountains and worked to acquire camping and backpacking gear so I could spend more time in the mountains. For me, the mountains were a place to escape from the pace of everyday life in town. They were a place of awe-inspiring tranquility and a place to recharge. I knew that the mountains could be a harsh environment, but that only added to their beauty and reinforced their separation from life in an urban environment. This was how I learned to *dwell in*, or inhabit, the land around me. The urban environment was the place to engage in "important" activities like working and school while the non-urban environment was the place to go for recreation. This patterning of place represents a cultural worldview premise. It is also one that is fairly widespread throughout some of the world.

In the Arctic, spending time with nature in the way described above does occur, but there is also a different way to dwell. There is, in short, a different cultural premise surrounding dwelling. The Arctic environment is brutally harsh, especially in the winter. Depending on how far north one is, one will experience 24 hours of sunlight in the summer and 24 hours of darkness in the winter. Because the land, when it isn't covered in snow and ice remains frozen (tundra), no agricultural crops can be cultivated on a wide scale. This means that the indigenous people, the Inuit, have had to adapt to life in this environment. They have done so successfully for over 4,000 years. Traditionally, the Inuit were (and many still are) a nomadic people. They would move from hunting camp to hunting camp depending on the changing conditions of the environment around them. They would hunt seal, caribou, walrus, whale, and the occasional polar bear. They would fish for Arctic Char. In the brief late summer, they would gather berries before the snows came again. Today, in Nunavut (which means "our land" in Inuktitut), more and more Inuit are moving into permanent communities like Iqaluit ("place of many fish"), Qikiqtarjuaq ("Big Island"), or Pangnirtung ("place of Bull Caribou").

Given this brief description of the Inuit in the Arctic, it is possible to figure out why I kept speaking in ways that didn't make cultural sense. First, when someone says "on the land," she or he is using a symbolic resource that means that someone is going to live off the land, including hunting and fishing. There is a sense that this life is closer to the traditional Inuit way of living. When I kept saying it, my friends and acquaintances were surprised that I would do such a thing. First off, I'm not Inuit, which meant to them that I would need to live with a group of Inuit on the land in order to learn the appropriate behaviors. Secondly, I believe they doubted my capabilities in being able to live off the land in a traditional sense. It was well known there that I was a newcomer interested in learning about Inuit ways of life. However, I hadn't been there long enough to gain the appropriate skills necessary to be self-sufficient. I wasn't even taking a gun, which meant that either I was going to scrounge for my food or I wasn't really going "out on the land." In short, when I used this symbolic resource, I was invoking a cultural worldview about dwelling and its associated value of self-sufficiency, which my friends knew was highly unlikely. Thus, the confusion. Eventually, I made it through my backpacking trip with my close friend and had to come home to the U.S. While there though, I learned many powerful lessons about what it means to live in an environment radically different from one I'm used to and was able to begin the process of cultural adaptation.

LEARNING DIFFERENT CULTURAL SYSTEMS

We've covered a lot of ground in this brief chapter on culture up to this point. Now, we should consider what might happen if you decide to travel to a different culture. In order to begin, I'll introduce two new terms, enculturation and acculturation. Enculturation is the process of learning one's dominant cultural system. As a U.S. American, I learned a cultural system that many other U.S. Americans learned. My Inuit friends, likewise, learned a cultural system that other Inuit have learned. It's important to realize that we learn culture and are not born into it. One could take a child, for example, an Inuit child, born in Iqaluit and raise that child in the Outback of Australia and the child will be enculturated into the dominant cultural system in Australia. Acculturation, on the other hand, is the process of learning another cultural system. If we were to travel abroad or immigrate to a different country, we would have to go through this process.

One scholar of acculturation, Kalvero Oberg (1960), found that people sometimes had difficulty when they traveled to different cultures. He called this phenomenon "culture shock." Culture shock occurs when people feel discouraged and disoriented when in a new culture (Hall, 2005). This discouragement and disappointment arises when our expectations are not met. Recall that culture provides us with a framework for making sense of the world. Whenever we encounter a different culture, we are in fact encountering a different framework, and things just don't make sense. Over time, these feelings can build up and lead to frustration. Part of being able to cope with culture shock is understanding that cross-cultural adjustment takes time. Oberg sought to explain culture shock and acculturation by providing a relatively simple model. This model is known as the U-curve model and it traces cross-cultural adaptation through four distinct stages.

The first stage of the U-curve model is the Honeymoon Stage. This is the time when the traveler first arrives and finds everything new and exciting. The sights, the smells, the sounds are all exotic, creating a sense of adventure.

During this stage, the traveler may make mistakes, but because everything is so new, these mistakes are quickly forgotten as the traveler moves to the next exciting interaction or event. If a person stays long enough, however, she or he will likely move to the second stage called the Crisis Stage. Over time, the foreignness of the different cultural framework becomes difficult to cope with on a continual basis. This is the stage where culture shock is most profoundly felt. One thing that often happens to people when they travel in different places is that they get sick. Prolonged exposure to different foods, different microbes in the water, and the fatigue associated with trying to get along in a different culture can all add up to a weakened immune system and lead to illness. As you might imagine, this physical condition can compound culture shock. It is at this point that many travelers unfortunately leave. Sometimes the frustration is so great that the traveler has a hard time seeing how anything could get better, so he or she catches the next plane, train, bus, or car out of town. When people leave during this stage, they are often left with profoundly negative associations concerning the host cultural environment. This is truly unfortunate, because almost inevitably if a person stays long enough, she or he will start to enter the Recovery Stage. The Recovery Stage is characterized by a slow realization on the part of the traveler that the host culture isn't so bad after all. It's at this point that the person may begin to be able to use the language with more ease. The traveler may also begin to develop relationships with host cultural members. One interesting thing that tends to happen during this stage is that people start to develop negative attitudes toward their own cultural system. After a bit of time, however, this stage evolves into the next stage known as the Adaptation or Acculturation Stage. At this stage the traveler has fully adapted to the new cultural system. The person is likely fluent in the local language and is able to get through daily life with relative ease. Attitudes during this stage are more realistic concerning both the host culture and the traveler's own culture with the person recognizing both good and bad aspects. True adaptation is hard to achieve, and some would even argue almost impossible. I believe that with time and effort, people can and do adapt to different cultures.

While the U-curve model is useful for sketching various stages of cross-cultural adjustment in broad terms, it also has some drawbacks. For instance, it is possible that people who travel can move back and forth between stages. For this reason, other models have been developed that can help shed light on the acculturation process. One particularly useful model is that of communication researcher Y.Y. Kim. Her Stress-Adaptation-Growth model takes into account the variability of people's experiences as well as the role of communication (Kim & Ruben, 1988). In short, her argument is that traveling cross-culturally will create stress. With stress comes a need to change. Sometimes we change in ways that move us closer to cultural adaptation and sometimes we change in ways that hinder our growth. Because of this, our acculturation process more closely resembles a series of circles that move back and forth between stress and adaptation until eventually we find ourselves more in the adaptation range than the stress range. Her model is quite complex, but generally speaking the factors that influence either growth or what she calls "hibernation" are the traveler's background, the host cultural environment and the communication practices involved in the adaptation process. The traveler's background is composed of six variables that may influence one's ability to adapt. These include 1) familiarity with the host culture, 2) a person's reason or motivation for going to a different culture, 3) one's self-image, 4) one's personality in terms of extroversion or introversion or tolerance for ambiguity, 5) one's age, and 6) one's education level. The factors associated with the host cultural environment include such things as the similarity of the culture to one's own culture, the potential to interact with host cultural members, the attitudes toward outsiders and cultural others that members of the host culture share, and the amount of demand for conformity on the traveler by the host culture. Finally, the role of communication is important in terms of the number of contacts the traveler has in a host culture, exposure and ability to understand media, and an ability to engage in supportive communication with a host cultural member.

In my own travels, I have seen the relevance of both the U-curve model and Kim's adaptation model in describing my acculturation. For instance, my first trip to Iqaluit, Nunavut in the Canadian Arctic was a perfect example of Oberg's U-curve model. I remember being enormously excited when I first got off the plane and noticed the signs written in syllabics (the form of writing Inuktitut) and heard the language being spoken. I was so excited that the fact that the airline accidentally sent my bag to Edmonton didn't even bother me. As it turns out, I had packed my jacket in my bag and ended up walking through a cold Arctic squall with nothing but a t-shirt. I was able to quickly acquire appropriate clothing and set off on my adventure. This was the Honeymoon Stage. It wasn't too long, however, when things began to get frustrating. I was cold all the time, I couldn't understand the language very well, I had twisted my ankle and had a hard time walking, and the person I was supposed to meet had gone out of town for a month. Ah, culture shock. I was discouraged and frustrated and I really wanted to go home. However, despite my frustrations, I stayed there. I'm really glad I did, because it wasn't long until I began to make some friends. These friends were enormously helpful in teaching me the language and instructing me in all manner of cultural activities, including what it meant to live "on the land." I don't believe I ever fully achieved the adaptation stage. I still have a ways to go to become fluent in the language, and I believe I would need to live there for many years before I reached full adaptation. My time there, though, was perhaps the most rewarding and enriching experience of my life.

CONCLUSION

This chapter has introduced the concept of culture and intercultural communication. While we cover a number of important issues here, the study of culture and intercultural communication is much more complex and fascinating than can be adequately described in the course of a few pages. For that reason, I would encourage you to continue your study of culture in your educational choices and in your daily life. More than that, though, I would strongly encourage you to travel to different cultures. Cross-cultural experiences can be difficult, but they can also be some of the most rewarding and enriching experiences of your life.

REFERENCES

Baldwin, J. R., Faulkner, S. L., Hecht, M. L., & Lindsley, S. L. (Eds.) (2006). *Redefining culture: Perspectives across the discipline*. Mahwah, NJ: Lawrence Erlbaum Associates, Inc. Publishers.

Carbaugh, D. (Ed.) (1990). *Cultural communication and intercultural contact*. Mahwah, NJ: Lawrence Erlbaum Associates, Inc. Publishers.

Carbaugh, D. (1996). *Situating selves: The communication of social identities in American scenes*. Albany, NY: State University of New York Press.

Colapietro, V. M. (1993). *Glossary of semiotics*. New York: Paragon House.

Fitch, K. (1998). *Speaking relationally: Culture, communication, and interpersonal connection*. New York: Guilford Press.

Frake, C. O. (1990). How to ask for a drink in Subanun. In P. P. Giglioli (Ed.). *Language and social context*. New York: Penguin Books.

Geertz, C. (1973). *The interpretation of cultures*. New York: Basic Books, Inc.

Hall, B. J. (2005). *Among cultures: The challenge of communication*. Belmont, CA: Thomson Wadsworth.

Hymes, D. (1972). Models of the interaction of language and social life. In J. Gumperz & D. Hymes (Eds.) *Directions in sociolinguistics: The ethnography of communication*. New York: Holt, Rinehart, and Winston.

Katriel, T. (1990). 'Griping' as a verbal ritual in some Israeli discourse. In D. Carbaugh (Ed.). *Cultural communication and intercultural contact*. Mahwah, NJ: Lawrence Erlbaum Associates, Inc. Publishers.

Kim, Y. Y., & Ruben, B. D. (1988). Intercultural transformation: A systems theory. In Y. Y. Kim and W.B. Gudykunst (Eds). *Theories in intercultural communication*. Thousand Oaks, CA: Sage Publications.

Kroeber, A. & Kluckhohn, C. (1952). *Culture: A critical review of concepts and definitions*. Cambridge, MA: Harvard University Press.

Littlejohn, S. W. & Foss, K. A. (2005). *Theories of human communication*. Belmont, CA: Thomson Wadsworth.

Martin, J. N. & Nakayama, T. K. (2004). *Intercultural communication in contexts*. Boston, MA: McGraw-Hill.

Merriam-Webster (2006, September). Definition of table. *Merriam-Webster Online*. Retrieved September 4, 2006. http://www.m-w.com/dictionary/table

Morgan, E. (2002). Communicating environment: Cultural discourses of place in the Pioneer Valley of Western Massachusetts. Doctoral Dissertation. (University of Massachusetts, Amherst). Dissertation Abstracts International, 63, 1A.

Morgan, M. & Shanahan, J. (1996). Two decades of cultivation research: An appraisal and a meta-analysis. In B. Burleson (Ed.). *Communication Yearbook, 20*. Thousand Oaks, CA: Sage Publication.

Petzinger, T. (1995). *Hard Landing: The epic contest for power and profits that plunged the airlines into chaos*. New York: Times Business.

Oberg, K. (1960). Culture shock: Adjustment to new cultural environments. *Practical Anthropology, 7*, 177–182.

Philipsen, G. (1992). *Speaking culturally: Explorations in social communication*. Albany, NY: State University of New York Press.

Signorelli, N. (1990). Television's mean and dangerous world: A continuation of the cultural indicators perspective. In N. Signorielli & M. Morgan (Eds.). *Cultivation analysis: New directions in media effects research*. Newbury Park: Sage Publications.

U.S. Census Bureau. (2006, September). *Diversity*. Retrieved September 9, 2006 from the United States Census Bureau Website. http://www.census.gov/population/cen2000/atlas/censr01-104.pdf

PUBLIC SPEAKING

Last, but certainly not least, is the study of public speaking. This is the most A.U.-centric chapter. The Department of Communication wrote this section to reflect our collective experience in teaching public speaking to Ashland University students. Even in an age where global communication can reach millions of people, there is still a role for public speaking in our daily lives.

Teachers, scientists, businesspeople, and citizens must be able to express their ideas to key audiences. Scientists must argue for funding or explain their complicated ideas to government officials to secure implementation. Teachers must translate lessons to students. Citizens in a democratic society must argue for issues and ideas that affect their children and communities. Many people fear public speaking because they have never been trained in the art. This course is a great place to start.

THE ART OF PUBLIC SPEAKING

Two thousand years ago philosophers and sophists (teachers of public speaking) debated the nature of public address. Plato asserted that it was a "knack" akin to "cookery."[i] In other words, if one knew the recipe, anyone could put together a good speech. Two millennia later, as anyone who has struggled to master an old family recipe (and settled for take-out) knows: Cooking is not easy and can rise to the level of an art form. Public speaking like the culinary arts, or any other type of art, is a form of individual expression. Your grandmother's recipe might call for "a dash" of this or "a smidgen" of that. She knew from years of experience exactly how much of each ingredient to add. However, subsequent generations must try, taste, and try again until they get the recipe right.

Hunger is a great motivator for learning to cook. Public speaking also requires a rationale. Why do you want to do this? A speech is more than just standing up and talking. It is more than just winging it. It requires thought, preparation, organization, and practice. The first lesson for a public speaker is: *You must have something to say.* A good cook wants to prepare a special dish for a reason. In most cases, you will be asked to speak because of an expertise you possess. An audience wants to learn more about an issue, or a company wants to explain a new policy to its employees, so a speaker is invited. There will also be instances when you will want to address an audience. You want to question a new policy at work or you want to challenge a public official about a vote he made. To be properly prepared you must research and organize your message, and then find a way to make that message meaningful to an audience. Public speaking is not easy to do well. However, it can be taught, and everyone should know something about it. Few of us will ever become great chefs but we all like to eat, and, as college students soon learn, we could all benefit from a few cooking lessons. Most of us will have to deliver a presentation at some time in our lives. Teachers do so daily. Business professionals make presentations about new corporate policies. Non-profit leaders argue for funding. Scientists offer research findings to colleagues to test their ideas. Engineers testify about technical information before government officials. Citizens in a democracy advocate for candidates or address a school board about an important issue in the lives of their children. Even if you are one of the few who will never deliver an oration in your personal life or professional career, you will have to listen to thousands of speeches in your lifetime. Training in public speaking will make you a better audience member and teach you how to differentiate substance from style. Every educated person needs to know something about public speaking.

Counterargument: Okay, I'm back. I was just checking my Facebook to see if that cute girl in my Bio class changed her relationship status. Then I texted my buddy to see if he wants to go to lunch later. Oh, yeah, you were saying something about the *ancient* art of public speaking. I can Skype people around the world, my blog has thousands of followers, and my Tweets are blowin' up. (Don't you love it when old people try to sound technologically savvy?) Do you really believe that *I* need to worry about talking to a class full of students?

Rebuttal: Yes! The fact is that even in the Technological 21st Century, face-to-face communication is still vital to our daily lives. Presidential candidates spend millions of dollars on television advertisements, email messages, and cyber campaigns, but they still hold debates and town hall meetings to "sell" themselves to important audiences in key states. A Harris Interactive survey of 3,169 hiring managers for CareerBuider.com found that 44 percent of the managers said they were looking for oral and written communication skills in future employees.[ii] Humans like talking to other humans. They like to see their faces, read their nonverbal communication, and meet them personally. Think about it: Would you rather Skype a friend or be with her or him in a room? It is likely that in the age of cyber communication and avatars, human communication will only become more important in our most significant personal and professional relationships. In other words, if you are valued as a customer, voter, or possible source of funding, we will show you respect by sending a *real live human being* to speak with you. This will place more, not less, importance on your ability to deliver a speech. Your employer or the campaign will get you a meeting with the important client, but the question is: Will you be able to deliver the message? Training in public speaking will significantly improve your chances.

Question: If training in public speaking is so important, why do we wait until college to require a course in it?

Answer: We think that's a really good question. Elementary education begins training in writing and grammar as soon as a student can spell. Unfortunately, some people still think that if you can talk, you can deliver an effective speech. Sadly, one of the reasons people fear public speaking is that we are forced to do it without training. A second grader is asked to speak about his summer vacation. The proud student walks to the front of the room to share his experiences in Disneyland. Something happens. A wrong word or an unzipped zipper; the audience laughs. The student is embarrassed. His natural instinct is to think, "I will never do that again!" Who could blame him? Do people laugh at you if you fail a test? Do fans mock you if you lose a race? Of course not. It's not easy to leave the comfort of the crowd and stand alone to address an audience. You should have taken a public speaking class long ago, but fear not, it is not too late.

Important Public Speaking Lesson #1: This is a great place to begin the study of public speaking.

Yes, that's right: A college communication class is a great place to begin your study of the art of public speaking. Brilliant instruction, a fabulous text, state-of-the-art technology (or not); this is *the place* to study public speaking. (Perhaps we exaggerate a bit.) Consider for a moment why a college communication class is a great place to begin the study of public speaking. In the business world, if you are delivering a budget proposal, you are competing against everyone else who submits a proposal for a limited amount of money. Your chances of success are measured against the number of good proposals in the room. In the classroom *there is no limit to the amount of possible success!* Everyone can earn a good grade if they choose a good topic, research it, organize it, and practice their delivery. Believe us, your instructors would be thrilled if all of you succeeded. A college communication class is great place to begin your study of public speaking because everyone has the potential to succeed. Please realize that success may be defined differently for different people in the room. To those who are genuinely frightened of public speaking, merely standing up and completing a presentation would make them a success. Everyone can benefit from lessons in public speaking, whether you are honing a skill you already possess or overcoming a fear to make yourself more employable. If you learn practices that will improve your public speaking this semester, you have gained a measure of success that will help you in your personal and professional lives.

Important Public Speaking Lesson #2: There is no better audience than a public speaking class.

You are all in the same boat. You will deliver a speech, then the person two rows over will stand and move to the front of the room. When she is finished, the person behind you will speak. There is no more sympathetic or empathetic audience in the world. Everyone in the room wants you to do well. Does that mean everyone will be paying attention when you speak? Probably not. The person speaking after you will probably be trying to remember her speech while you are informing the audience. Someone in the class will have a chemistry exam or a philosophy lecture next period and their mind will be a million miles away. Still, this is the best audience in the world because everyone knows what you are going through and shares your nervousness. You will see students nodding their heads in agreement, smiling to support you, and giving all kinds of positive feedback. Rarely will you find an audience as supportive as this one. Over the course of the semester you have worked with some of the people in this audience. You may have completed a group project together or participated in an interpersonal exercise. These people may have become your friends or, at the very least, they are sharing this experience with you. College students are generally among the most polite, nice, and supportive people you would ever want to meet. When you become an audience together, you will support your fellow classmates even more. This is the *best* audience in the world.

Important Public Speaking Lesson #3: There is no *perfect* in the art of public speaking.

Would a rational artist claim to have painted the perfect sunrise? Do you think a rational composer believes she has written the perfect sonata or lyrics? (Please note we did say *rational*.) Art is not a game of *perfect*. Therefore when we write about the art of public speaking or critique it, we invoke words such as *good*, *poor*, or *excellent*. To study public speaking as an art form, one should always believe that there was something that could have been improved. A speaker may win the applause or acceptance of an audience, but there will be a phrase or thought that could have been made clearer. This isn't a bad thing.

Speakers should be liberated by this concept and try to improve, not perfect, their presentations. Humans are fallible. We create art to express ourselves and mirror the beauty we find in our world. Speakers-in-training must realize that they will make mistakes. The question to be answered is: Did the audience understand my message? The purpose of an introductory communication class is to teach the students ways to improve their public speaking skills. Students who want to excel at public speaking will continue to hone their abilities over many opportunities before a wide variety of audiences.

Every child is born an artist. We are all creative, colorful, and full of wonder when we are young. Somehow, we lose some of that magic as we grow older. The study of art in college restores some of that wonder by improving our appreciation of the art form and teaching us something about ourselves as artists. Similarly, all children speak with passion. They know what they have to say is important and they are dying to tell anyone who will listen. College students must learn to have confidence in their ideas. Research will help verify and support your arguments or suggest that you rethink them. It is important then that we test our ideas before other smart people. If we do not publish or express our ideas before an audience, our ideas will die with us. Feedback from intelligent people will only make us smarter and improve our ideas.

WHERE DO WE BEGIN? A LITTLE HISTORY

Aristotle
©2013 by Shutterstock, Inc.

In Western civilization, the study of public speaking begins with the Greeks. Philosophers and our friends the sophists debated whether instruction in the art of public speaking was worthwhile or necessary. It seems that philosophers believed that discovering "The Truth" should be the goal of academic inquiry. They asserted that instruction in logic and reasoning was the path to understanding and knowledge. Unfortunately, Greek philosophers did not respect the sophists. Philosophers stated that if one learned to make arguments, a speaker would simply tell the audience what they wanted to hear in order to win the approval of the majority. Thus, philosophers labeled teachers of public speaking "sophists," or "teachers of wisdom," as an insult to their ethics and integrity. To this day, echoes of this criticism can be found in the academic study of public relations in communication. Some academics charge public relations professionals with simply "spinning" the truth to advance a corporate or political message. Fortunately, a very smart man by the name of Aristotle addressed similar concerns a long time ago.

If one studies the liberal arts, it is difficult to overestimate the intellect or academic impact of Aristotle. An accomplished scientist, Aristotle also authored significant studies of poetry, politics, and communication. He was such a brilliant thinker and teacher that his lecture notes became one of the primary texts on the subject of ethics. *The Nicomachean Ethics* are literally Aristotle's classroom notes edited by his son, Nicomachus. We hope that the students of this class will not fear the pressure of taking such good lecture notes. Just remember, the Department of Communication will want a small percentage of any royalties from future books, t-shirts, or movie rights. (We can dream …)

Returning to semi-serious academic discussions, Aristotle was one of the first scholars to see intellectual value in the study of communication. His text, *The Rhetoric*, was the first full-length book on the subject of persuasion and remains a seminal study to this day. Aristotle recognized that the advance of communication in politics, the courts, and the ceremonial speech of citizens was building the society of his day. "The Cradle of Democracy," as Athens came to be known, enabled citizens to represent themselves in the Senate, the courts, and in public ceremonies. Politicians were not elected; a property-owning citizen advocated his own cause in the political forum. If a legal dispute arose, no lawyers were hired. Each defendant would present his case before a jury of his fellow citizens. Soon, a few clever citizens realized that lessons in public speaking might be beneficial in winning votes or cases. It was then that the job title of *sophist* was created.

In *The Rhetoric*, Aristotle defined *rhetoric* as "the observation of all available means of persuasion."[iii] It was clear that in the Athenian democracy, the chief purpose of public speaking was to influence citizen opinion. To reconcile charges of unethical behavior by the sophists, he asserted that rhetoric, or persuasive speaking, was "a tool." If a tool, such as a knife, fell into the hands of a criminal, it became a weapon that could harm innocent victims. However, if that same tool were handed to a doctor, it became a scalpel that could save lives. In other words, the art of persuasion is neither moral nor immoral; it depends on the speaker's values. One can persuade unethically by lying, manipulating, or deceiving an audience. A moral speaker presents the truth (as she knows it) to assert her message and improve the condition of the audience. Aristotle also wrote extensively about how to use evidence effectively and how to make an ethical argument in *The Rhetoric*. The common misconception in the 21st century that *rhetoric* means "empty words, not action," is an incorrect definition that denies the significant study of persuasion begun by Aristotle centuries ago.

There is much more that could be written about the contributions of Cicero, Quintilian, Kenneth Burke and others to the study of rhetoric.[iv] However, this is not a course on the history of rhetoric. One of the other important lessons that Aristotle provided for our introduction to public speaking was how to prepare for a public speech. As it was in the beginning, it is now, and ever shall be: there are three areas that every prospective speaker should analyze are: 1) the speaker, 2) the audience, and 3) the occasion.

THE SPEAKER

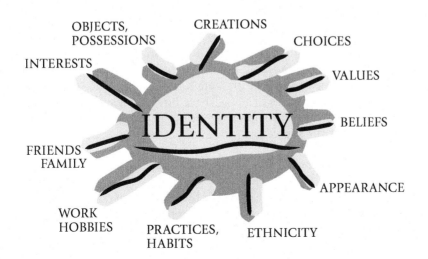

Who am I? What do I know? What could I talk about in a speech?

Who am I? What do I know? What could I talk about in a speech? In most public speaking situations, someone will be asked to address a group because of some expertise he or she possesses. Professors teach classes in their areas of study and research. Mechanics offer seminars in auto maintenance. You have probably spoken to a club, fraternity, or group of young people about a topic that you are well versed in. These are examples of experts addressing audiences about a subject they know well. However, there are also circumstances where someone is asked to speak just because of who they are. A personality or alumni might be asked to speak at a sports banquet as a form of entertainment or as a fundraiser. In this class, you are not a celebrity (sorry), but you are asked to choose your own topic. This is the initial challenge for the novice speaker.

THE PRIMARY DIRECTIVE: *NEVER* GOOGLE 'SPEECH TOPIC'

It is a sad commentary when bright, interesting people think they have nothing to say. For 17+ years you have lived on this planet. You have tasted foods, traveled, played sports or games, watched TV and videos, collected things, taken 12 years of classes, met interesting people, read books, etc., etc. All these experiences are potential speech topics; you just lack the confidence to talk about them with your classmates. Students always complain when teachers assign topics for an essay or speech. However, when you are given the opportunity to choose, suddenly you cannot think of a single idea. For most students, more than half the time you spend preparing your speech will be used in the selection of a topic. Students often reject several perfectly good ideas before they settle on "the right topic." If you can choose a topic quickly, chances are this is something you like talking about with people. If it is an *appropriate* topic for a college classroom (ask your instructor if you are unsure), then you have taken a major step to putting together a successful presentation.

Suggestion Number #1: Look around your room. See the music, pictures, and videos on your phone/ipod/computer.

If you are interested enough in a topic to decorate your room with it, download it, or view it repeatedly, this is a subject you know something about, care about, and could write a speech on. In fact, if you are interested enough in the topic, there are probably sources for the speech in the room or on your computer. Perhaps you read an article about a favorite movie or you may have downloaded an interview or video featuring a favorite musical artist; these are all sources for a presentation. We all do research. Learning more about a subject is research. So, if we buy a magazine, download an interview, or read about a subject online, we are guilty of conducting research. (If we cite the source.)

Suggestion Number #2: If you are still stuck, consider a brainstorming activity.

Sometimes we are too critical for our own good. We think, "Hey, I could do a speech on … Nah, that's no good." We repeat this exercise over and over until we are confused and frustrated. Our ideas are never given a chance to see the light of day. To correct this, try a brainstorming activity. The idea of brainstorming comes from small-group communication. One of the advantages of groups is that a team can generate a lot of ideas and sometimes create options that no single individual might have offered. One person can learn from this experience if they allow themselves to think freely and without judgment.

The exercise works like this:

1. Take out a sheet of paper and draw a line down the middle.
2. To the left of the line, write *Likes*. On the right side, write *Dislikes*.
3. For two minutes, write down as many things as you can think of that you like. Do not judge the ideas or evaluate them. Just write.
4. Take two minutes and write down things you dislike. Your chart should look something like this:

LIKES	DISLIKES*
COM 101, chocolate, golf, naps, summer, tennis shoes, beaches, Coffee, Coke, Macs, movies, Me	broccoli, homework, shopping, tests, rain, speeches, opera, corn dogs, running, loud people, old drivers, the color orange, my ex, Twilight movies

* Sadly, most people come up with more dislikes than likes.

Now, look at these ideas. Could any of these be a topic for a speech? Absolutely! You could write an informative presentation on the history of chocolate or a persuasive speech on why you should reject "Team Edward *and* Team Jacob" to avoid the Twilight movie series. Evidence could be found on the Hershey website (www.hersheys.com) or you could probably find a few movie critics who did not like the cinematic adaptation of the Vampire love saga. This exercise is a way to analyze the speaker or, in other words, get your ideas down on paper. Once you have developed a list of potential topics, your next task is to commit to one topic and research it.

The Occasion: Where Are You?

Different situations call for different kinds of talk. Think about it. During the holidays, do you talk with your grandmother the same way you would address your friends when you are out on Friday night? (We doubt it. Or you have a really hip grandmother!) Have you ever been to the banquet for a really bad sports team? We do not want to bring up painful memories, but imagine that the team was winless. What kind of speech would you expect from the coach? Would he berate the players, call them names, or review all their mistakes throughout the season? Not if he wants to coach next year. This is a banquet. The players are with their families. No one wants to be reminded of failures or look bad in front of their parents. A smart coach will find some good in the season. "We gained a lot of experience." "We grew together as a team." "We kept our jerseys really clean." (Okay, maybe the last one was a bit much.) Why does a coach talk this way? Because a banquet is a celebration, the trick is to find a reason to celebrate and move on to next year. The next season begins at that banquet, *if* the coach's speech can inspire the players to return and work hard for next year. Banquet speeches are ceremonial; they are supposed to be upbeat.

Have you ever heard (or made) a bad wedding toast? One of the authors of this text attended a wedding where the best man had dated the bride. After a few cool beverages, he thought it would be really funny if he talked about what a "wild woman" she was when they dated. Neither the bride nor her family was amused. Sorry guys, but a wedding is about the woman in the long white dress—it is *her* day. Jokes about her are not the way to impress her family and friends. What about a graduation? Do you remember your high school graduation? What did the speaker say about you? You were probably "the best class ever at your high school." "The future was yours and if you did not pay your library fees, you were not getting your diploma. (They had to do a little business.)

All ceremonies, these special occasions call for a certain kind of talk. In a bar, in class, at a football game, at a job interview, we dress differently and talk differently. We are still the same person; we are just presenting a different aspect of our personality. In our study of interpersonal communication, we called this *role-playing*. In a public address, the speaker also plays a role. She must analyze the occasion: Why are these people coming together? Then, she must choose a tone and style of language appropriate to the degree of formality or informality of the situation. You would be surprised at the number of people who do not find out about the circumstances of a presentation. The size of the room could affect your address. Will you need a microphone? Is it an intimate gathering? Know where you are and why you are there. A speaker cannot do too much preliminary research about the occasion.

Audience

Review: You have a few ideas for a topic. You have studied the occasion. Is there a theme? How large of a room? Audio/video capabilities? Now, the final question: Who is in the audience?

To whom are you talking? How old are they? What are they interested in? A few years ago, a student gave a COM 101 presentation on "How to Prepare Your Own Funeral." It seems that his family was in the mortuary business. The presentation was practical, well researched, and well organized. The 50-year-old-instructor found it interesting but most of the students were bored to tears. Why? Old teachers have one foot in the grave, whereas students are not thinking of dying anytime soon. Think back to all of the antidrinking and -driving campaigns that appeared around prom time in high school. Speeches against teenage drunk driving that threaten the consequences of death are largely ignored. Why? Because 16-year-olds believe they are immortal. Curiously, do you know what scares a new driver? Injury? Jail time? No, it is the loss of the license. What is a driver's license to a 16-year-old? It is freedom, independence, a social life. What could be more important to a high school student? This is what they value; this is how you threaten to punish them. Are there some topics you do not care to listen to? Of course there are: "Why you should listen to your elders," "the very best in minivans," "senior citizen discounts at local restaurants." A business major once offered a persuasive speech on "How to Save for Retirement." The premise was that if students could begin saving "$100 a month," they could build a comfortable retirement in 45 years. The facts were clear; the numbers all added up. The only problem was: How many of you have $100 extra at the end of the month? Most college students are scrounging for change for a Taco Bell run. For a fortunate few, the speech made perfect sense. For most mere mortals, it was out of reach.

©2013 by Shutterstock, Inc.

©2013 by Shutterstock, Inc.

TO WHOM ARE YOU TALKING?

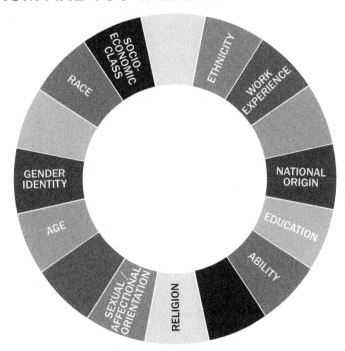

Each person is made up of many parts.

We live in the most diverse time in history. Transportation, technology, immigration, race, language, economics, religion, and a host of other factors are changing our world. Universities are global institutions. We have students from all over the world on our campus and have placed alumni in countries on every continent. Colleges have a global presence on the World Wide Web that allows them to recruit students and faculty from across the country and world. It may be hard to believe but even small liberal arts universities buried in the Midwest are more than a blip on the digital landscape. Take a look around you: We have soccer players, swimmers, faculty, business majors, and religious studies majors from all over the planet. Alumni in the military are able to stream college football games on any military base using wifi connections. Faculty are publishing research in online journals and presenting papers at international conferences. The audience that you will address in this class has traveled more, seen more, and is more culturally diverse than any previous generation of college students. When you rise to speak to your COM 101 class, you must take this modern fact into account.

In this way, a speaker must choose a topic appropriate for the audience. You might not want to discuss a great new hip-hop artist before the Rotary, a group of mostly middle-aged businesspeople. Lyrics from some of the songs could be offensive to some audience members. Similarly, the speaker must present the topic in a manner the audience will understand and appreciate. A good elementary teacher realizes how in depth he can make a math lesson for young students. Calculus would be a bit much for second graders. In a classroom of your peers, the language and style of your presentation might be more informal. If this were a job presentation, the dress, language, and tone of the speech would certainly become more formal. A speaker must know as much as possible about the audience she is about to face. In some ways, a speech is like a date. The more you know about your partner, the easier it is to make conversation.

In today's society it is far too easy to offend an audience. Border states Ohio and Michigan have produced a great rivalry in college athletics. If a Michigan football fan told Ohio State jokes at a gathering of OSU alumni, there is little doubt that the humor would wear thin pretty quickly. Ridiculous, huh? Do you know how many corporate and civic leaders have said stupid things or designed failed marketing campaigns because they did not know their audience? One famously bad campaign sought to introduce Irish Mist, a maker of whiskey and liqueurs, to the German market. Had they conducted some preliminary research, they would have discovered that *mist* in German is a colloquial term for manure.[v] (Would you like a nice glass of … you get the idea.) A former president of Purdue University once referred to the Hispanic student association as "my wetback friends." The term *wetback* may have little resonance for Caucasians or international students, but Hispanic students know it derives from a historic Texas–Mexico border slur for illegal aliens. Mexicans who swam across the Rio Grande to find a better life in America were derisively said to have wet backs. The term quickly became a negative stereotype that depicted anyone of Hispanic descent as someone who entered the United States illegally and did not belong in this country. First, few college students are illegal aliens. Second, not all Hispanic students are from Mexico. Guatemala, Puerto Rico, Panama, and a host of other distinct Central and South American cultures can be lumped into the generic category "Hispanic." Third, someone told the university President that the highly derogatory term was one of "endearment" between friends. The Purdue president was soon issuing an apology to the Hispanic student organization. Did you hear about the TV show *All-American Muslims* presented by the Learning Channel about Muslim Americans living in Michigan? A group of non-Muslim protestors complained that the characters were too "normal" and did not display their "radical" tendencies. In reaction, Lowes Corporation, advertisers who sold hardware and home supplies, pulled its commercials. Now, counter-protestors are boycotting Lowes because of its failure to support average Muslim American citizens. Again, you would be amazed at the mistakes speakers and corporations can make by failing to analyze their audiences.

©2013 by Shutterstock, Inc.

Issue for Discussion: Should audience members be on their phones during presentations and lectures?

Pro: Of course, students are on their phones all the time. This generation of students thinks faster and multitasks better than any prior generation. Smartphones would allow students to check facts and challenge an argument. Phones are present in most of our daily conversations. We have learned how to listen and comprehend the messages while playing music, checking Facebook, and texting. More young business professionals use their phones during meetings and corporate lunches. This is the communication of the present and future.

Con: Studies at Stanford University show that humans are not as effective at multitasking as we believe. The brain functions better and is more productive when it can focus on a single task. Older people (i.e., faculty) find it disrespectful when students do not offer their full attention to a lesson. Perhaps the answer is generational, but many authority figures believe an audience member is not fully "present" when she is interrupted by a text. Most messages are meaningless anyway ("What's up?" "What are you doing?" "Nothing, U?") and could be delayed until later. It is shocking but true: We don't have to be connected all the time.

PHASE 2: RESEARCH

You have chosen a topic that interests you. Your enjoyment of the topic should show in your presentation and convince the audience this speech is worth listening to. You know the occasion, because it is a class that you have been attending all semester. Some classes are more formal; the tone of your speech should reflect the tone of the class. If you are presenting in a small room, do not yell at the audience. If there is music playing in the next room, you may have to speak up. Do you know how to use the media equipment to load your PowerPoint presentation? Now, the time has come to do some research. Research should accomplish two goals: 1) The speaker should learn something new about a topic that interests her and 2) The speaker should become more believable because of the sources in her presentation.

Resources

Not all resources are created equal. The speaker may present himself as a credible source based on years of experience or training. If you are a Red Cross–certified lifeguard, you are an expert resource on the topic of CPR. If you have been playing baseball for years and have earned awards and a scholarship for your achievements, you are an expert resource on the game of baseball. These experiences make you believable. The next step is to enhance your believability with some information that will inform or persuade your audience. If you are a student of the game you play, you probably have many resources available to you. A rulebook, the Red Cross training manual, or—heaven forbid— a textbook from a class you have taken on the subject. (Yes, business majors, you can use that marketing book again.) But what if the books are at home? You may have to turn to that big building on campus called the *library*.

Believe it or not, Google is *not* the beginning and end of research. Did you know that when the American Dialect Society chose the most influential word for the first decade of this century, *9/11*, the number/term etched into American history, was not their choice? *Google*, a company name that has become a verb, was chosen as the most significant word of the first decade of the 21st century.[vi] Students think that typing a word or question into a little box on the computer screen is research. Perhaps for everyday conversation that is enough. However, if you are going present a speech or write a paper, you have to dig deeper. If anyone can access the same information with a few keystrokes, that is totally unimpressive. If grade school children are producing the same quality of research as college students, our education system is in big trouble. The worst part of this scenario is that you have a world of information only a few more clicks away. Every student has access to all the archives of the university library online. You probably have access to every college library in the state through an interlibrary loan program, every issue of *The New York Times*, magazines, academic journals, and on and on. In the digital age, your college library is a portal to the *information universe*. If you are interested in a topic, reading something new about it should be fun. If you want to make an argument, having the latest information from reputable sources makes your case that much stronger. As educated people, you need to ask for better information from the politicians/teachers/experts you listen to, and you must provide better information to the people you address. This is the way we will make the world a smarter place; each of us has to step up and do our share.

Question: Can Sources Be Biased?

Absolutely! Research provided (or paid for) by the National Rifle Association will likely support gun ownership. Why would the advocacy group print information that helps its opponents? In the Information Age there are thousands of sources available to a speaker. If you want to find a biased source, it exists. Do you want say that tanning is bad for your skin? Look at the American Academy of Dermatology website (www.aad.org). Would you like to support tanning as a healthy pre-spring break activity? Try a website for a tanning service. Are these sources equally credible? We certainly hope you would say no. In political spheres, liberals will attack Fox News, Rush Limbaugh, and the *Drudge Report* as rightwing advocacy groups. Conservatives will quickly challenge MSNBC, Jon Stewart, and *Media Matters* as examples of the elite, liberal media. To avoid such challenges, select groups that are as credible as possible. Independent researchers, scientists, and nongovernmental agencies are great resources to advance an argument. If you want advice about the perception of a topic, ask a librarian. If all else fails, you could even ask your Communication instructor if a potential source is worthwhile.

Question: (Another One? Yes, it is our attempt at Reading Interaction.) Should you memorize your speech?

When was the last time you had to memorize something? A poem, a chemical formula, a piece of music? Most of us are not good at memorizing information or texts. When we try, we get frustrated and create more trouble for ourselves. In preliterate times, orators would learn (memorize) the speeches of Demosthenes or Cicero to train as public speakers. The problem is, if you forget one word in a memorized sequence, everything else that follows can be lost as well. That is to say, if you forget *one* … I mean if you forget *one* … Uh … Uh … You get the idea. A better way to present your speech is *not* to memorize it or read it word-for-word, but to outline your presentation and focus on delivering ideas, not words.

THE OUTLINE

An *outline* is the skeleton of a presentation. It is the framework on which you build your presentation.

An Outline Is Like the Skeleton of a Presentation. It Is a Framework You Can Build On.

©2013 by Shutterstock, Inc.

Ideas, Not Words

If you can plan a presentation around ideas, you have created a plan that gives you some freedom. Mark Twain once said, "A good speech does three things: It tells you what it is going to say, it says it, and then it tells you what it said." That is what a good outline does. An outline prepares the audience for what is to come (introduction: attention getter and thesis), says it (body of the speech), and restates it (conclusion: summary and final statement). The outline helps you organize your thoughts as well as prepare the audience for what you are going to say. Topic sentences are written in the outline but you must practice the presentation enough to be comfortable presenting the ideas and not worry about each word. When a mistake is made, the well-rehearsed speaker retrieves the information and places it elsewhere in the speech. In most cases, the audience is never the wiser and all the information is still presented. The outline formats for the Informative Speech and Persuasive Speech vary slightly because of their different purposes. We show you an example of each. The text for the Informative Speech is drawn from our personal love of desserts, America's Favorite Dessert: Ice Cream.

America's Favorite Dessert: Ice Cream

I. Introduction
  A. Attention-Getter: "I scream, you scream, we all scream for Ice Cream."
  B. Thesis Statement: Today, I'm going to talk you about my and America's favorite dessert: ice cream.

II. Body
  A. The origins of ice cream
    1) According to the International Dairy Foods Association (www.idfa.org), the origins of ice cream date back to the second century BCE.
    2) Alexander the Great flavored snow with honey and nectar.
    3) Marco Polo returned from the Orient to Venice with a recipe for a dessert resembling modern-day sherbet.
    4) Ice cream remained a rare and exotic treat until advances in refrigeration technology in the 1800s.
  B. Ice Cream Today
    1) Annual U.S. production of ice cream is 1.6 billion gallons annually. (www.idfa.org)
    2) The Food Channel (www.foodchannel.com) reports that in a survey of American consumers the five most popular flavors are:
      a) Vanilla   29%
      b) Chocolate   8.9%
      c) Butter Pecan   5.3%
      d) Strawberry   5.3%
      e) Neapolitan   4.2%
  C. Not all ice cream flavors have been successful. The worst experimental flavors according to Cracked.com (www.cracked.com) were:
    1) Wasabi Ginger
    2) Fish
    3) Wheat
    4) Tomato

III. Conclusion
  A. Summary: Today I've told you about the origins and types of my favorite dessert: ice cream.
  B. Final Statement: The next time you're in the mood for a smooth, delicious dessert, have a bowl of ice cream. (Just don't try the wasabi ginger.)

Sources:
Cracked.com, www.cracked.com
The Food Channel, www.foodchannel.org
International Dairy Foods Association, www.idfa.org

The foregoing outline is an example of a topical outline. The information in the body of the speech is divided into three topics (the origins of ice cream, ice cream today, and unsuccessful flavors). This allows the speaker to frame her thoughts and tell the audience what is coming next. When a new point is presented, it alerts the audience that they should pay attention. The topical outline is probably the most popular format in informative speaking, with the chronological outline (past, present, future) as its closest rival. Many speakers offer a history of a topic ("The Origin of the Liberal Arts in Ancient Athens," "The History of the National Basketball Association," or "Three Significant Moments in the History of the American Auto Industry") in a chronological format.

In a persuasive speech, a speaker makes an argument. More than providing information, the speaker makes a *call to action* to urge the audience to do something (vote, purchase a product, donate time). If we were to take the same information about the liberal arts and present it as a persuasive speech, we would present an argument for "*Why* a Student *Should* Eat Ice Cream." More evidence would be required on the potential health or psychological advantages of ice cream (it makes us feel good or it is an excellent reward for hard work in the summer). The thesis would change, but it would still be preceded by an attention-getter. In the conclusion, the outline would maintain a summary and a final statement. The key difference comes in the body of the speech.

The most common form of body format in a persuasive speech is the Problem-Cause-Solution format. To begin a presentation—the first step—a speaker must Define the Problem. Sound simple? It may not be. A student wants to make an argument for legalizing marijuana. Is it a legal issue? Or a medical issue, as in use of marijuana by chemotherapy patients? Is it a national issue or should it be decided by individual states? Countries other than the United States have different laws about marijuana—some stricter, others more lenient. One writer suggested that people think of marijuana legalization as an economic issue. (If we legalize it, we could tax it like the drugs alcohol and tobacco.) The key is that the solution must match the definition of the problem. In other words, you cannot solve a legal or moral problem with an economic solution. (This solution is what some people call "throwing money at a problem.")

The second step is to List the Causes of the Problem. Why is marijuana a problem? How much does the country spend on drug rehabilitation, law enforcement, and incarceration? Why do people take drugs? Are programs like D.A.R.E. (Drug Abuse Resistance Education) effective? These and a host of other questions must be answered to work toward a solution.

Finally, the third step, the Solution, must offer a Call to Action! This section raises the question: What can *this* audience do about the issue? What about world hunger? Now, *there* is a problem that college students can do nothing about. Right?

You can't do anything, *unless* you believe that your community is part of the world. Most American cities have food pantries or soup kitchens serving meals to the needy in their community. Churches, mosques, temples, charities; in most cities you will find multiple sources of support for hungry people. Yes, you *can* make a difference. The small actions of many people can add up to a big solution. Did you know there is a website that donates food to the hungry? Go to www.thehungersite.com. Seriously, go there now! If you click on their icon, two cups of rice will be donated to hungry people. Big deal! Two cups of rice means nothing, right? But what if everyone in this class donates? 24 × 2 = 48 cups. And if everyone did it for a week? 48 × 7 = **336 cups**. Anthropologist Margaret Mead once said: "Never doubt that a small group of thoughtful committed citizens can change the world; indeed, it's the only thing that ever has." (We might add: If the group acted, it needed to communicate with its members and persuade others.) Consider the following Persuasive outline:

A Persuasive Speech Outline

I. Introduction
   A. Attention-Getter: America is the most prosperous country in the world. (www.aneki.com/richest.html)
      1) U.S. farmers grow more food than any other farmers on the planet. (www.fao.org/es/ess/top/commodity.html)
      2) Yet, did you know that **1 in 7 Americans** goes hungry every day? (www.worldhunger.org/articles/Learn/us_hunger_facts.html)
   B. Thesis Statement: We should take action to feed the hungry in our community.
      1) If every student at this university would donate **$1** to a food bank, we could raise more than **$2,000.**
      2) A food bank could turn our **$2,000** into **8,000 meals.**

II. Body
   A. Problem
      1) The American economy has suffered in recent years.
      2) Ohio has been particularly hard hit by the downturn.
      3) Unemployment has hurt nearly 9% of the population, but even employed people are facing tough choices. (annualreport.feedingamerica.org/)
      4) Today, people are being forced to choose among food or medicine or rent. (annualreport.feedingamerica.org/)
   B. Causes
      1) Hunger is an "unseen problem."
      2) A loss of a job or a medical emergency can leave a family in desperate shape.
      3) Today, 1 in every 4 hunger victims is under the age of 18. (annualreport.feedingamerica.org/)
      4) Good, healthy food is expensive.
   C. Solution
      1) We can make a difference by each donating $1.
      2) If money is tight, volunteer 1 hour at the local food bank.
      3) 2,000 college students can make a real difference in our community.
      4) If the students act, we can engage faculty and staff to offer a real Contribution to Our Community.

III. Conclusion
   A. Summary: Hungry people need our help.
   B. Final Statement: Give $1 to feed our neighbors.

It is simple but true: The outline is your guide to the presentation. All the main ideas are here, logically organized, and ready to be presented. If a speaker practices (and practices some more), the outline becomes the map to an effective presentation. The key is to focus on ideas, not words. The ideas you want to present are more important than the specific words you use to describe them. It does not matter if you describe something as *purple* or *violet.* If the audience has a sense of the color, you have achieved your goal. Now, let's talk about Delivery.

A Trick Question for You: What is more important? *What* you say? or *How* you say it? If you were to walk across the quad and survey 100 people, it is likely that 90 of them would respond: "*How* you say it." Does that bother anyone? It should. If this were true, then your college education is a waste of time. If content is less important than style, then all your classes should be "style-based." No more history or science, let's focus on clever phrases and colorful expressions. Sound good, write cleverly; it does not matter what you say. Balderdash! (Isn't that a great word?) As educated people you must demand more.

Do you remember the story of the Emperor's new clothes? A pair of thieves convinces the Emperor that they are weaving a garment so fashionable and so unique that only the most intelligent and sophisticated people can see it. No one wants to be seen as unfashionable or stupid, so everyone (including the Emperor) pretends to see it. When the Emperor wears this new outfit in public, one innocent youngster cries out, "The Emperor has no clothes." Suddenly, the truth is apparent to everyone. You *must* be that child. As educated people, you must demand more from political leaders, scientists, and yes, even teachers. Good people must question more and seek better information from people in authority. One of the initiatives in the field of medical communication is to improve patient–doctor communication. Too often patients feel intimidated by their physicians. Patients don't ask questions. They simply accept information or a diagnosis they do not understand. This lack of understanding could be life threatening. As intelligent members of the audience we must demand *substance.* The best speeches say important things in interesting ways. Speakers must have something worth saying. Only then they can worry about how to say it.

©2013 by Shutterstock, Inc.

STANCE

Every building needs a good foundation. If you are going to stand before an audience and speak for five minutes, you need a solid stance. Picture an athlete preparing for a big moment. A basketball player assumes a ready stance before shooting a free throw. A batter plants her feet in the batter's box before taking a swing. The quarterback sets his feet before taking the snap. The physical component of public speaking also requires a "ready position": feet shoulder-width apart, comfortable, solid, but ready to move. A speaker must look composed even when he is nervous. Do not lean on a desk or podium; it makes you look sloppy and less believable. One old trick for speakers: they move in transition. Returning to the outline format: to make a transition from the introduction to the body of the speech, take a few steps. This physically shows the audience that you are moving to a new idea as you introduce a new topic.

GESTURES

We all gesture. Humans describe, explain, illustrate, and sometimes contradict verbal messages with our nonverbal gestures. Rule number one: Relax. If you are comfortable, your gestures will be too. Sometimes when a speaker gets nervous, gestures become wild or hands disappear into pockets. Practice standing and delivering your presentation, and your gestures will flow naturally.

EYE CONTACT: WHY WOULD YOU LISTEN TO THIS SPEAKER?

©2013 by Shutterstock, Inc.

Have you ever had anyone read a PowerPoint to you? Most audiences can read the PowerPoint slides on their own. Good speakers look at their audiences to establish eye contact; they do not read from the slides. Good speakers connect with their audiences when they look at them. Avoid tricks of delivery like looking over the heads of the audience. People will turn around to see what is going on behind them. You have to look at the eyes of the audience members. Will everyone be paying attention? Probably not. The next speaker is nervously scouring his notes. Someone who studied all night is struggling to stay awake. Speak to the majority of interested listeners. Remember: A college classroom is the best audience in the world. Everyone is in the same boat as you and most of the audience has great empathy for you. Everyone wants you to succeed. There is no competition here; everyone can do well. You will find friendly faces and supportive smiles in this audience. Take comfort in their support and know that you have something to share with them.

DELIVERY

Trust Your Topic

You have chosen a topic that interests you and will interest your audience. Now, all you have to do is share it. Everyone gets nervous. Nervousness shows that you care about communicating your message. Nervousness is a good thing. The trick is to control your nerves. Remember: Communication is not a perfect art. No one, not even your mean instructor, expects you to be perfect. Everyone makes mistakes; the key is being able to correct those mistakes. It is far more impressive to see people dealing with their human errors than expecting them to be perfectly robotic speakers.

Ideas, Not Words

Have we mentioned that enough yet? If you are citing an important statistic or piece of evidence, write it down and read it word-for-word. Otherwise, the audience wants to hear *you*. Reading a speech buries your eyes in a notecard and breaks eye contact with the audience. It is difficult to memorize a speech and, if you forget a word, everything that follows is lost.

The biggest mistakes of first-time speakers are rate and vocal fillers. Rate is a problem because your adrenaline reacts with your nervousness, and you speed up. Adrenaline makes athletes focus and perform better. Unfortunately, when you are a speaker, you have little physical outlet for this surging energy. So you-begin-to-speak-really-fast-and-cannot-control-the-pace-of-your-speech. Slow down. Breathe. Practice. Time your presentation. Breathe some more. Practice again. Athletes visualize a successful outcome before a game. "I'm at the free throw line. I shoot. Swish! We win the game." The crowd goes wild. Try to do the same with your speech. Imagine the room. See your classmates sitting in their chairs. See the professor looking wise and all-knowing in the back of the room. (Okay, maybe that was a bit too much again.) If you can visualize the situation all the way through to a successful presentation, you can trick your mind into thinking that you have done this speech before and been successful. All you have to do now is repeat the performance.

VOCAL FILLER

Do you ever hear people *like, umm, you know* add unnecessary words to sentences? They have no meaning, *like, you know*? But, *umm,* because we *uhh* hate silence, we tend to fill in the spaces with sounds. You know? Right? It has been estimated that the audience thinks four times faster than the average person speaks. This is one reason an outline helps direct the attention of an audience. A factor some people forget is that a speaker also thinks four times faster than he speaks. This is why silences seem so long when you pause. A speaker must remember: Pausing is not a bad thing … Pausing … is not a bad thing. A pause can give you time to recover, to think, or to catch your breath. Audience members forgive little mistakes and are more impressed by your composure than hearing you *uh, umm, like* utter meaningless words. Relax, breathe, find your place in your notes or on your outline. A few seconds is not a long time to wait and it only takes a few seconds to correct a verbal mistake.

Finally, (yes, we are about to complete this section) enjoy yourself. The audience is far more likely to enjoy your presentation if you look like you are enjoying speaking about it. Enthusiasm cures a lot of faults. You have all heard dull, dry lecturers who sound as if they would rather be anywhere else than teaching a class. Believe it or not, most communication faculty members enjoy this section of the course because we learn new things. Our only hope of being "cool" or knowing anything about popular culture lies in your hands. For the sake of our teenage children or our soon-to-be teenage children, please help us. **You are our only hope.**

Speak Well!

i Plato. *Gorgias*. Trans. W. C. Humbold. Indianapolis: Bobbs-Merrill, 1979. Print.

ii Web. 28 March 2012. <itmanagersinbox.com/390/the-9-most-desired-skills-of-hiring-managers/>.

iii Aristotle. *The Rhetoric of Aristotle*. Trans. Lane Cooper. Englewood Cliffs, NJ: Prentice Hall, 1960. Print.

iv To learn more about the history of rhetoric, you can take a course in Argumentation and Advocacy or Advanced Public Speaking. Faculty members in the Department of Communication Studies would also be more than willing to speak with you.

v Web. 29 March 2012. <www.deborahswallow.com/2009/08/20/cross-cultural-marketing-blunders/>.

vi Matyszczek, Chris. "Google Beats 'Blog' in the Word of the Decade List." Web. 29 March 2012. <news.cnet.com/8301-17852-3-10431563-71.html>.

COM 101 Speech Demographics

Gender   M   F

Age   17 or below   18

              19   20

              21   22 or older

Which do you use most often? (Rank order with 1 being most often and 6 being least often.)

____ Twitter   ____ Instagram

____ Snap Chat   ____ Facebook

____ Tumblr   ____ Other (specify) _____

Major	CAS	Physical Sciences	COE	Early
		Arts		Middle
		Humanities		High School
		Social Sciences		Intervention
	COBE	Management/Entrepreneurship	CONHS	Nursing
		Marketing/Hospitality/Fashion		Health Sciences
		Finance/Economics		Accounting/IS
		Sport Management		Fashion Merchandising
		Undecided		Postsecondary

Do you consider yourself   Athletic or Not athletic?   Artistic or Not Artistic?

Are you on an   AU/High School Athletic team?   Do you play an intramural sport?

Hometown size	under 500	500–2000	
	2000–5000	5000–10,000	
	10,000–30,000	30,000–50,000	
	50,000–100,000	over 100,000	

Graduating class	under 50	50–100	
	100–200	200–500	over 500

Outside Job?	Part-time	Full-time	None
	On campus	Off-campus	

COM 101 Peer Critique Sheet

Name _____ Topic_____

Was the *topic* clear?

Was the *organization* clear?

Was the *support* clear/adequate?

Was *audience adaptation* clear?

Was *delivery* clear?

List two things you liked   List two suggestions

_____

_____

Name _____ Topic_____

Was the *topic* clear?

Was the *organization* clear?

Was the *support* clear/adequate?

Was *audience adaptation* clear?

Was *delivery* clear?

List two things you liked   List two suggestions

_____

_____

COM 101 Peer Critique Sheet

Name _____ Topic_____

Was the *topic* clear?

Was the *organization* clear?

Was the *support* clear/adequate?

Was *audience adaptation* clear?

Was *delivery* clear?

List two things you liked   List two suggestions

_____

_____

Name _____ Topic_____

Was the *topic* clear?

Was the *organization* clear?

Was the *support* clear/adequate?

Was *audience adaptation* clear?

Was *delivery* clear?

List two things you liked   List two suggestions

_____

_____

COM 101 Peer Critique Sheet

Name _____ Topic_____

Was the *topic* clear?

Was the *organization* clear?

Was the *support* clear/adequate?

Was *audience adaptation* clear?

Was *delivery* clear?

List two things you liked   List two suggestions

_____

_____

Name _____ Topic_____

Was the *topic* clear?

Was the *organization* clear?

Was the *support* clear/adequate?

Was *audience adaptation* clear?

Was *delivery* clear?

List two things you liked   List two suggestions

_____

_____

COM 101 Speech Presentations

Requirements for the Informative Speech assignment:

TOPIC:

Time limit:

Number of sources:

You will be judged on the following criteria:

Content

Introduction/beginning

Organization

Transitions

Conclusion

Source citation during speech

Overall content (captivating or not)

Other:_____

Physical Control

Body (head, arms/gestures, feet/legs)

Eye contact

Formal attire

Vocal Control

Pauses/pace

Projection/enthusiasm

Emotion/variation in delivery

Typed outline due _____

- Include citations within text of outline in APA format
- Include complete citations in APA format at end of outline

COM 101 Exercise
Speech Research Activity

Name _____ Speech Topic _____

List three possible outside sources. Include the title, author, and type of source.

Title   Author   Source Type

_____

_____

_____

List three pieces of supporting material you could choose from the above sources. Identify which category of supporting material they fall under.

Supporting Material   Category

_____

_____

_____

COM 101 Speech Critique Sheet

Name _____ Topic _____

Introduction

    Attention

    Credibility

    Topic

    Listening Reason

    Preview

Body

    Organization

    Support

    Audience Adaptation

    Language Use

    Transitions

    Sources cited (4)

    1. _____

    2. _____

    3. _____

    4. _____

Conclusion

Review

Closure

Delivery

Eye contact

Note card use

Volume

Rate/articulation

Vocal variety/emphasis

Posture

Gestures

Extra movements

Visual Aids

Time

COM 101 Human Communication
Topic Exploration Activity

Find a partner and talk through the following areas. I will give you about 5–10 minutes for each person's topic. Talk through all the areas for one person's topic first. I will tell you when it is time to switch to the other person.

1. Tell your partner a little bit about your speech topic. Be sure to say whether you plan to do informative or persuasive. (If you haven't decided, pick something you might be speaking about.)

2. Ask your partner these three questions about your topic:

   - How much do you know about my topic?

   - How do you feel about my topic? (positive/negative)

   - How interested are you in my topic?

3. Have your partner ask you two questions about your topic.

4. Ask your partner to give you feedback about the kind of information they would find interesting/helpful in understanding your topic. If you are doing persuasion, ask them what they think would make your case most convincing.

Be prepared to share with the class two things you learned about your topic that may be useful as you plan your upcoming speech.

COM 101 Exercise
Speech Topic Activity

1. Think of one possible topic you could give a speech on for this class.

2. Find a partner and tell each other a little bit about your topics.

3. Have each person ask two questions about the other person's topic.

4. Ask your partner these three questions about your topic

    -   How much do you know about my topic?

    -   How do you feel about my topic? (positive/negative)

    -   How interested are you in my topic?

COM 101 Tips for Using Visual Aids in Your Speech

Sometimes it is easier to forget about visual aids than prepare them. It's hard enough work writing your speech, let alone having to produce a multimedia extravaganza to push home your point—right?

Maybe some speeches don't require visual aids, such as wedding speeches or toasts. However, for a lot of speeches, using visual aids will not only enhance your presentation, but will also help you to remember key points and keep you and your audience focused. Visual aids, or "props," can be as small or large as you want. They can vary in their simplicity or complexity. How much a part of your speech they are used for—it's up to you.

Here are some tips for successful use of visual aids in your presentation:

1. Props should be visually stimulating and supportive of the topic you are speaking on.
2. If using pictures on your slides, fill up the whole screen with the illustration.
3. Don't pack the slide with wordy paragraphs and information. Break your data into bullet points.
4. Ask the organizers what visual aids are available for your presentation. Ensure everything is present and working before you begin your speech.
5. Make sure every audience member can see the visual aids.
6. When you use the visual aid, ensure the audience is focused on it. After you have made each point, remove the visual and refocus the audience on you.
7. If you have trouble remembering your speech, use your visual aids as memory joggers.
8. Visual aids aren't only overheads and slides. They can be noisemakers, costumes, and tricks. Visual aids can be used to induce a laugh, stimulate the audience, or make a passionate point. Select your "alternative props" with care.
9. When you reveal your visual aid, make sure you continue speaking to the audience, not to the prop.
10. Handouts are also considered visual aids. Determine the correct time to distribute them. You want your audience to focus on your words, not to read and discuss elements of the handout during your speech.

Why should I use visual aids?

Visual aids support your argument and increase audience understanding of the main points the mind better remembers picture information rather than word information. A visual presentation will enhance your credibility, and it may even help you with your nerves. If you have a visual aid to focus on rather than your shaking hands, your fears will be forgotten as you take the audience through the points on the screen.

*** Practice using your visual aids well before the day of your presentation. ***

COM 101 Speech Exploration Activity

Name _____ Speech Topic _____

Is it informative or persuasive? _____

Possible Main Points

_____

_____

_____

Why should we listen to you? How do you know about it?

Why should we be interested? How does it connect to us?

Possible Outside Sources

COM 101 Speech Outline Format

INTRODUCTION: (Written in *paragraph* form)

Attention (Grabbing their attention should be the very first thing out of your mouth)

Credibility (Any order) This tells them what you know about the subject

Statement of topic (Any order)

Listening Reason (Any order) This tells them why they should listen what is in it for them.

Preview (The last thing you do is briefly preview each of the main points)

BODY: (NOT written in paragraph form. Each entry should be one single full sentence only.)

I.   This would have Main Point #1 in a single full sentence.

    A.   Supporting information for Main Pt. #1.
        1.   First detail of Support A
        2.   Second detail of Support A

    B.   More supporting information for Main Pt. #1
        1.   First detail of Support B
        2.   Second detail of Support B
            a.   Further detail of 2
            b.   Further detail of 2

(Transition statement connecting Main Pt. #1 and Main Pt. #2)

II.   This would have Main Point #2 in a single full sentence.

    A.   Supporting information for Main Pt. #2
        1.   First detail of Support A
        2.   Second detail of Support A

    B.   Final supporting information for Main Pt. #2
        1.   First detail of Support B
            a.   Further detail of 1
            b.   Further detail of 1
            c.   Further detail of 1

        2.   Second detail of Support B

    C.   Final supporting information for Main Pt. #2

(Transition statement connecting Main Pt. #2 and Main Pt. #3)

III.   This would have Main Point #3 in a single full sentence.

    A.   Supporting information for Main Pt. #3
    B.   More supporting information for Main Pt. #3

    C.   More supporting information for Main Pt. #3
        1.   First detail of Support C
        2.   Second detail of Support C

    D.   Final supporting information for Main Pt. #3

CONCLUSION: (Written in *paragraph* form)

    Review/Summary (Brief recap of each main point)

    Closure (This should be the last thing you say.)

WORK CITED:

Use a standard style book. (MLA and APA are the most common.) Cite all sources used during your speech. This is like a "min-bibliography" of your sources. Remember that this list doesn't replace the need to say your sources out loud during the speech.

Books:

MLA Style:

    Smith, Jane. *Outlining as a Way of Life.* New York: Smith Publishing Company, 2014.

APA Style:

    Smith, J. (2014). *Outlining as a Way of Life.* New York: Smith Publishing Company.

Webpages: (This example shows how to cite a webpage with no author and no date.)

    Web Pages Rock. (n.d.). Retrieved March 3, 2015, from http://www.webpagesrock.com/ yaddayadda/this_is_really_long/amIdoneyet?/yesyouare.

GENERNAL REMINDERS:

1. Use a single FULL SENTENCE for each entry in the Body of the outline.

2. Check indentation consistency.

3. If you have an "A" you MUST have at least a "B."

4. Three is the "magic number" when it comes to main points.

5. The more detailed and specific your outline is, the easier it will be to speak clearly and logically.

6. Use the outline as a warning sign to spot errors before I ever get a chance to see or hear them. Look for:

   • Lack of balance. (Is Main Pt. #1 on three pages while Main Pts. #2 and #3 fit on half-a-sheet?)

   • Missing parts in the introduction or conclusion

   • Unclear organization (no method to your madness)

   • Too much information (a seven page outline is probably too much for a six minute speech)

7. Practice with your outline AT FIRST. Then write your note cards using KEY WORDS only!

COM 101 Group Project Participation Form

Name _____

Topic _____

Key: 2 = Excellent; 1 = Average; 0 = Poor   Do not evaluate yourself.

	Name	Name	Name	Name	Name	Name
Participated frequently and effectively during the project development						
Encouraged others to participate						
Carried out individual assignments promptly						
Contributed to the understanding of the group project						
Avoided unnecessary conflict with group members						
Helped keep group meetings on track						
Appeared committed to group's goals by attending every meeting and being prepared every time						
Had a good attitude about the project						
Contributed to the effectiveness of the final presentation						
Overall, this member was valuable to the group						
Totals						

COM 101 Group Project Participation Evaluation

Name _____
Topic _____

Key: 3 = Excellent; 2 = Above Average; 1 = Average; 0 = Poor   Do not evaluate yourself.

	Name	Name	Name	Name	Name	Name
Participated frequently and effectively during the development of the project						
Encouraged others to participate						
Carried out individual assignments promptly						
Contributed to the understanding of the group project						
Avoided unnecessary conflict with group members						
Helped keep group meetings on track						
Appeared committed to goals of the group by being at every meeting and by being prepared every time						
Had a good attitude about the project						
Contributed to the effectiveness of the final presentation						
Overall, this member was valuable to the group						
Totals						

COM 101 Peer Evaluation Form

Project _____   YourName_____

Circle name of group member you are evaluating:

Individual Questions

1. This individual practiced active listening skills in group meetings.
   EXCELLENT   10   9   8   7   6   5   4   3   2   1   0   POOR

2. When giving feedback, this member used both constructive and positive criticism techniques.
   EXCELLENT   10   9   8   7   6   5   4   3   2   1   0   POOR

3. This member gave equal and fair opportunity for all group members to voice their opinions..
   EXCELLENT   10   9   8   7   6   5   4   3   2   1   0   POOR

4. In discussions, this member was actively engaged and open to discussion of many solutions
   EXCELLENT   10   9   8   7   6   5   4   3   2   1   0   POOR

5. This individual exhibited productive individual and group task roles.
   EXCELLENT   10   9   8   7   6   5   4   3   2   1   0   POOR

6. This individual helped develop and support productive group norms.
   EXCELLENT   10   9   8   7   6   5   4   3   2   1   0   POOR

7. This individual operated with the best interests of the group in mind and not from a hidden agenda.
   EXCELLENT   10   9   8   7   6   5   4   3   2   1   0   POOR

8. During group meetings, this member stayed on task and encouraged each member to do the same.
   EXCELLENT   10   9   8   7   6   5   4   3   2   1   0   POOR

9. This group member was helpful to others in the group, placing the group ahead of herself or himself.
   EXCELLENT   10   9   8   7   6   5   4   3   2   1   0   POOR

10. This individual contributed to the best of her or his best ability on all tasks and projects.
    EXCELLENT   10   9   8   7   6   5   4   3   2   1   0   POOR

Overall Score _____ /10

COM 101 Exercise
Prestige of Occupation Worksheet

As a group, reach a consensus about the prestige of the following occupations. Use discussion to rank these occupations from 1 to 14. Focus more on your top/bottom 5 first and then fill in the middle if there is time.

_____	Firefighter	_____	Air Traffic Controller
_____	Farmer	_____	Journalist
_____	Doctor	_____	Television Star
_____	Police Officer	_____	Nurse
_____	Teacher	_____	Construction Worker
_____	Garbage Collector	_____	Truck Driver
_____	Physical Therapist	_____	Computer Consultant

COM 101 Exercise
Survival

It is around 10 a.m. in mid-July, and your plane has crash landed in the desert somewhere in Arizona. The twin-engine plane has completely burned, with only the frame remaining. You and the other four passengers are uninjured. Before the crash, the pilot was unable to notify any airport of the plane's position. However, based on what the pilot said, you are approximately 80 miles south of the interstate. The immediate area is flat and barren, and the temperature usually reaches 110–130°F. You are dressed in a short-sleeved-shirt, shorts, and tennis shoes. Before the plane caught fire, you and the other four passengers were able to salvage 15 items. These items are:

_____	2 quarts of water	_____	two pair of sunglasses
_____	plastic raincoat	_____	1 quart of water per person
_____	flashlight	_____	book entitled *Edible Animals of the Desert*
_____	cosmetic mirror	_____	bottle of 100 salt tablets
_____	magnetic compass	_____	compress kit with gauze
_____	jackknife	_____	sectional air map for the area
_____	one jacket per person	_____	loaded .45 caliber pistol
_____	red and white parachute		

Rank these items in the order of their importance for your survival, starting with 1 for the most important and 15 for the least important.

COM 101 Communication Contexts Exercise

Discuss the impact of each variable below on the following communication events.

1. Having a social drink with a friend

2. Studying in the library with classmates

3. Meeting with a professor after 5 p.m.

4. Texting your friend in California

5. Talking on the phone with your mom/dad

Contextual Variables

Time of day	Touch
Smells/scent	Time of year
Weather	Relationship history with other person
Other people present	Your mood/their mood
Distractions	Cultural differences
Location	Internal noise
Clothing/accessories	Furniture arrangement
Physical distance	Power/status influences

COM 101 First Impressions Exercise

A. Choose a partner for this assignment that you did not know prior to this class meeting. Without talking and basing your ideas solely on your observations this far, answer the following questions about your partner. You may tell your partner your first name only. Do not discuss the questions with your partner until all statements have been completed.

1. My partner's middle name is ⎯⎯⎯⎯⎯⎯⎯⎯⎯⎯⎯⎯⎯⎯⎯⎯⎯⎯⎯⎯⎯⎯⎯ .

2. My partner's major is ⎯⎯⎯⎯⎯⎯⎯⎯⎯⎯⎯⎯⎯⎯⎯⎯⎯⎯⎯⎯⎯⎯⎯⎯⎯ .

3. My partner's favorite food is ⎯⎯⎯⎯⎯⎯⎯⎯⎯⎯⎯⎯⎯⎯⎯⎯⎯⎯⎯⎯⎯ .

4. My partner's favorite movie is ⎯⎯⎯⎯⎯⎯⎯⎯⎯⎯⎯⎯⎯⎯⎯⎯⎯⎯⎯⎯ .

5. My partner's favorite car is ⎯⎯⎯⎯⎯⎯⎯⎯⎯⎯⎯⎯⎯⎯⎯⎯⎯⎯⎯⎯⎯⎯ .

B. After completing these statements, discuss your answers and find out how accurate your impressions were.

C. Working as a team, answer these questions about your professor.

Discussion questions:

How accurate were you?

What did you base your answers on?

Main-stream cultural assumptions?

Specific people you know that remind you of your partner?

Yourself?

Did you stereotype your partner? If so, in what ways?

Was your stereotype accurate?

COM 101 Who Will Get the Kidney

You have been hired as the kidney transplant coordinator for Summit County. On this day, you have eight patients who have been admitted to the Akron City Hospital for a kidney transplant. Unfortunately, there are only three kidneys available. Your task is to select the three recipients from the list of eight patients.

Patient #1: Joy Wise, age 27. Joy is married and has six children who range in age from 2 to 10 years old. Her husband, Louis, owns a small automotive repair business in downtown Stow, OH.

Patient #2: Peter Gafferty, age 31. Peter is a health care analyst for a pharmaceutical corporation. He is a former Rhodes Scholar with a Ph.D. in physics. He has never been married and serves as the primary caretaker for his mother who has Alzheimer's disease.

Patient #3: Mario Santini, age 46. Mario is an ex-convict, having been convicted of tax evasion, and served seven years in a federal penitentiary. It is rumored that Mario is a member of a prominent Mafia family based in New Jersey. He is responsible for his two nephews, ages 6 and 9, whose parents were tragically killed by a drunk driver two years ago.

Patient #4: John Lappelton, age 9. John has an IQ of 160, but is severely mentally disturbed after having witnessed an accident that killed his grandmother. He hasn't spoken in two years.

Patient #5: Christy Aune, age 27. Christy is an instructor at a local community college, working on her Master's degree in Communication Studies. She is married to Don, who refuses to work and spends his time playing guitar in local bands. Christy and Don are approximately $25,000 in debt.

Patient #6: Chance Thomas, age 35. Chance is a bachelor. He spends most of his free time hanging out at BW3's pub playing Trivia with his friends and has no long-term plans for his life. He works as a clerk for the Ohio State Police.

Patient #7: Reverend Jacoby, age 53. Reverend Jacoby spends a lot of time arranging missions to help the people of inner city Cleveland. He is an alcoholic.

Patient #8: Justin Mathias, age 22. Justin is a student at Ashland University and works 30 hours a week as a bartender to pay for his education.

COM 101 Activity

Listening and Hearing

You just listened to a message presented in class. Answer the following questions about the information in the message:

1. What was the overall meaning of the message?

2. What words do you believe helped deliver the intended message?

3. Why did these words stand out to you as projecting the meaning of the message?

4. What do each of these words mean?

_____

_____

_____

_____

_____

_____

_____

_____

_____

_____

_____

_____

_____

_____

_____

_____

Break into two groups, males and females. Answer each of these questions again as a group. Were your answers the same as above? Were there any differences in the response of your classmates based on gender? Do men and women, in general, focus on different content in messages? Do men and women, in general, hear and/or listen to messages differently?

_____

_____

_____

_____

_____

_____

_____

_____

_____

_____

_____

_____

_____

_____

_____

_____

Dr. Dariela Rodriguez

COM 101 Activity
The Lunch Time Realization

Take a trip to the Eagle's Nest or Convo and watch how individuals interact with each other. Watch how they approach friends and strangers. How do they greet their friends? How do they greet strangers? Do they approach males differently than they approach females? Do they speak differently with students versus faculty or staff? How do you know this based on what they say or do?

_____

_____

_____

_____

_____

_____

_____

Engage with at least three individuals you do not know. Is verbal communication necessary when first approaching strangers (i.e., introducing yourself, saying hello), or can you simply sit down at their table and be able to engage with the individual without an introduction? What nonverbal behaviors can you use/did you use to make the interaction less awkward?

_____

_____

_____

_____

_____

_____

_____

Dr. Dariela Rodriguez

COM 101
Nonverbal Video Examples

What meanings did you see expressed through:

Kinesics (body movement/gestures)

Facial expressions

Eye contact (or avoidance)

Haptics (touch)

Physical Appearance (gender, skin color, size)

Artifacts (clothing and accessories)

Proxemics (space)

Territory

Chronemics (time)

Paralanguage (rate, volume, pitch)

Silence

Discussion questions:

How does nonverbal express cultural and sub-cultural differences?

How do contradictions between verbal and nonverbal come out?

What does nonverbal tell you about people's relationships?

What do reactions tell you about expectations and rules?

CPSIA information can be obtained at www.ICGtesting.com
Printed in the USA
LVOW02s0839060715

444635LV00003BA/5/P